AWS Certified
Data Analytics
Study Guide
Specialty (DAS-C01)

AWS Certified
Data Analytics
Study Guide
Specialty (DAS-C01) Exam

Asif Abbasi

SYBEX®
A Wiley Brand

To all my teachers, family members, and great friends who are constant sources of learning, joy, and a boost to happiness!

Acknowledgments

Writing acknowledgments is the hardest part of book writing, and the reason is that there are a number of people and organizations who have directly and indirectly influenced the writing process. The last thing you ever want to do is to miss giving the credit to folks where it is due. Here is my feeble attempt to ensure I recognize everyone who inspired and helped during the writing of this book. I apologize sincerely to anyone that I have missed.

I would like to first of all acknowledge the great folks at AWS, who work super hard to not only produce great technology but also to create such great content in the form of blogs, AWS re:Invent videos, and supporting guides that are a great source of inspiration and learning, and this book would not have been possible without tapping into some great resources produced by my extended AWS team. You guys rock! I owe it to every single employee within AWS; you are all continually raising the bar. I would have loved to name all the people here, but I have been told acknowledgments cannot be in the form of a book.

I would also like to thank John Streit, who was super supportive throughout the writing of the book. I would like to thank my specialist team across EMEA who offered support whenever required. You are some of the most gifted people I have worked with during my entire career.

I would also like to thank Wiley's great team, who were patient with me during the entire process, including Kenyon Brown, David Clark, Todd Montgomery, Saravanan Dakshinamurthy, Christine O' Connor, and Judy Flynn in addition to the great content editing and production team.

About the Author

Asif Abbasi is currently working as a specialist solutions architect for AWS, focusing on data and analytics, and is currently working with customers across Europe, the Middle East, and Africa. Asif joined AWS in 2008 and has since been helping customers with building, migration, and optimizing their analytics pipelines on AWS.

Asif has been working in the IT industry for over 20 years, with a core focus on data, and has worked with industry leaders in this space like Teradata, Cisco, and SAS prior to joining AWS. Asif authored a book on Apache Spark in 2017 and has been a regular reviewer of AWS data and analytics blogs.

Asif has a master's degree in computer science (Software Engineering) and business administration. Asif is currently living in Dubai, United Arab Emirates, with his wife, Hifza, and his children Fatima, Hassan, Hussain, and Aisha. When not working with customers, Asif spends most of his time with family and mentoring students in the area of data and analytics.

About the Technical Editor

Todd Montgomery (Austin, Texas) is a senior data center networking engineer for a large international consulting company where he is involved in network design, security, and implementation of emerging data center and cloud-based technologies. He holds six AWS certifications, including the Data Analytics specialty certification. Todd holds a degree in Electronics Engineering and multiple certifications from Cisco Systems, Juniper Networks, and CompTIA. Todd also leads the Austin AWS certification meetup group. In his spare time, Todd likes motorsports, live music, and traveling.

Contents at a Glance

Contents

Chapter   6   Data Security   279

Introduction

Studying for any certification exam can seem daunting. *AWS Certified Data Analytics Study Guide: Specialty (DAS-C01) Exam* was designed and developed with relevant topics, questions, and exercises to enable a cloud practitioner to focus their precious study time and effort on the germane set of topics targeted at the right level of abstraction they can confidently take the AWS Certified Data Analytics – Specialty (DAS-C01) exam.

This study guide presents a set of topics around the data and analytics pipeline and discusses various topics including data collection, data transformation, data storage and processing, data analytics, data visualization, and the encompassing security elements for the pipeline. The study guide also includes reference material and additional materials and hands-on workshops that are highly recommended and will aid in your overall learning experience.

What Does This Book Cover?

This book covers topics you need to know to prepare for the AWS Certified Data Analytics – Specialty (DAS-C01) exam:

Chapter 1: History of Analytics and Big Data This chapter begins with a history of big data and its evolution over the years before discussing the analytics pipeline and the big data reference architecture. It also talks about some key architectural principles for an analytics pipeline and introduces the concept of data lakes before introducing AWS Lake Formation to build the data lakes.

Chapter 2: Data Collection Data collection is typically the first step in an analytics pipeline. This chapter discusses the various services involved in data collection, ranging from services related to streaming data ingestion like Amazon Kinesis and Amazon SQS to mini-batch and large-scale batch transfers like AWS Glue, AWS Data Pipeline, and the AWS Snow family.

Chapter 3: Data Storage Chapter 3 discusses various storage options available on Amazon Web Services, including Amazon S3, Amazon S3 Glacier, Amazon DynamoDB, Amazon DocumentDB, Amazon Neptune, AWS Storage Gateway, Amazon EFS, Amazon FSx for Lustre, and AWS Transfer for SFTP. I not only discuss the different options but the use cases around which each one of these are suitable and when to choose one over the other.

Chapter 4: Data Processing and Analysis In Chapter 4, we will cover data processing and analysis technologies on the AWS stack, including Amazon Athena, Amazon EMR, Amazon Elasticsearch Service, Amazon Redshift, and Amazon

Kinesis Data Analytics, before wrapping up the chapter with a discussion around orchestration tools like AWS Step Functions, Apache Airflow, and AWS Glue workflow management. I'll also compare some of the processing technologies around the use cases and when to use which technology.

Chapter 5: Data Visualization   Chapter 5 will discuss the visualization options like Amazon QuickSight and other visualization options available on AWS Marketplace. I'll briefly touch on the AWS ML stack as that is also a natural consumer of analytics on the AWS stack.

Chapter 6: Data Security   A major section of the exam is security considerations for the analytics pipeline, and hence I have dedicated a complete chapter to security, discussing IAM and security for each service available on the Analytics stack.

Preparing for the Exam

AWS offers multiple levels of certification for the AWS platform. The basic level for the certification is the foundation level, which covers the AWS Certified Cloud Practitioner exam.
We then have the associate-level exams, which require at least one year of hands-on knowledge on the AWS platform. At the time of this writing, AWS offers three associate-level exams:

- AWS Certified Solutions Architect Associate
- AWS Certified SysOps Administrator Associate
- AWS Certified Developer Associate

AWS then offers professional-level exams, which require the candidates to have at least two years of experience with designing, operating, and troubleshooting the solutions using the AWS cloud. At the time of this writing, AWS offers two professional exams:

- AWS Certified Solutions Architect Professional
- AWS Certified DevOps Engineer Professional

AWS also offers specialty exams, which are considered to be professional-level exams and require deep technical expertise in the area being tested. At the time of this writing, AWS offers six specialty exams:

- AWS Certified Advanced Networking Specialty
- AWS Certified Security Specialty
- AWS Certified Alexa Skill Builder Specialty
- AWS Certified Database Specialty
- AWS Certified Data Analytics Specialty
- AWS Certified Machine Learning Specialty

You are preparing for the AWS Certified Data Analytics Specialty exam, which covers the services that are discussed in the book. However, this book is not the "bible" on the exam; this is a professional-level exam, which means you will have to bring your A game to the table if you are looking to pass the exam. You will need to have hands-on experience with data analytics in general and AWS analytics services in particular. In this introduction, we will look at what you need to do to prepare for the exam and how to sit for the actual exam and then provide you with a sample exam that you can attempt before you attend the actual exam.

Let's get started.

Registering for the Exam

You can schedule any AWS exam by following this link `bit.ly/PrepareAWSExam`. If you don't have an AWS certification account, you can sign up for the account during the exam registration process.

You can choose an appropriate test delivery vendor like Pearson VUE or PSI or proctor it online. Search for the exam code DSA-C01 to register for the exam.

At the time of this writing, the exam costs $300, with the practice exam costing $40. The cost of the exam is subject to change.

Studying for the Exam

While this book covers information around the data analytics landscape and the technologies covered in the exam, it alone is not enough for you to pass the exam; you need to have the required practical knowledge to go with it. As a recommended practice, you should complement the material from each chapter with practical exercises provided at the end of the chapter and tutorials on AWS documentation. Professional-level exams require hands-on knowledge with the concepts and tools that you are being tested on.

The following workshops are essential for you to go through before you can attempt the AWS Data Analytics Specialty exam. At the time of this writing, the following workshops were available to the general public, and each provides really good technical depth around the technologies:

- AWS DynamoDB Labs – `amazon-dynamodb-labs.com`
- Amazon Elasticsearch workshops – `deh4m73phis7u.cloudfront.net/log-analytics/mainlab`
- Amazon Redshift Modernization Workshop – `github.com/aws-samples/amazon-redshift-modernize-dw`
- Amazon Database Migration Workshop – `github.com/aws-samples/amazon-aurora-database-migration-workshop-reinvent2019`

- AWS DMS Workshop – `dms-immersionday.workshop.aws`
- AWS Glue Workshop – `aws-glue.analytics.workshops.aws.dev/en`
- Amazon Redshift Immersion Day – `redshift-immersion.workshop.aws`
- Amazon EMR with Service Catalog – `s3.amazonaws.com/kenwalshtestad/cfn/public/sc/bootcamp/emrloft.html`
- Amazon QuickSight Workshop – `d3akduqkn9yexq.cloudfront.net`
- Amazon Athena Workshop – `athena-in-action.workshop.aws`
- AWS Lakeformation Workshop – `lakeformation.aworkshop.io`
- Data Engineering 2.0 Workshop – `aws-dataengineering-day.workshop.aws/en`
- Data Ingestion and Processing Workshop – `dataprocessing.wildrydes.com`
- Incremental data processing on Amazon EMR – `incremental-data-processing-on-amazonemr.workshop.aws/en`
- Realtime Analytics and serverless datalake demos – `demostore.cloud`
- Serverless datalake workshop – `github.com/aws-samples/amazon-serverless-datalake-workshop`
- Voice-powered analytics – `github.com/awslabs/voice-powered-analytics`
- Amazon Managed Streaming for Kafka Workshop – `github.com/awslabs/voice-powered-analytics`
- AWS IOT Analytics Workshop – `s3.amazonaws.com/iotareinvent18/Workshop.html`
- Opendistro for Elasticsearch Workshop – `reinvent.aesworkshops.com/opn302`
- Data Migration (AWS Storage Gateway, AWS snowball, AWS DataSync) – `reinvent2019-data-workshop.s3-website-us-east-1.amazonaws.com`
- AWS Identity – Using Amazon Cognito for serverless consumer apps – `serverless-idm.awssecworkshops.com`
- Serverless data prep with AWS Glue – `s3.amazonaws.com/ant313/ANT313.html`
- AWS Step Functions – `step-functions-workshop.go-aws.com`
- S3 Security Settings and Controls – `github.com/aws-samples/amazon-s3-security-settings-and-controls`
- Data Sync and File gateway – `github.com/aws-samples/aws-datasync-migration-workshop`
- AWS Hybrid Storage Workshop – `github.com/aws-samples/aws-hybrid-storage-workshop`

AWS also offers a free digital exam readiness training for the Data and Analytics exam that can be attended for free online. The training is available at www.aws.training/Details/eLearning?id=46612. This is a 3.5-hour digital training course that will help you with the following aspects of the exam:

- Navigating the logistics of the examination process
- Understanding the exam structure and question types
- Identifying how questions relate to AWS data analytics concepts
- Interpreting the concepts being tested by exam questions
- Developing a personalized study plan to prepare for the exam

This is a good way to not only ensure that you have covered all important material for the exam, but also to develop a personalized plan to prepare for the exam.

Once you have studied for the exam, it's time to run through some mock questions. While AWS exam readiness training will help you prepare for the exam, there is nothing better than sitting for a mock exam and testing yourself in conditions similar to exam conditions. AWS offers a practice exam, which I would recommend you take at least a week before the actual exam, to judge your ability to sit for the actual exam. Based on the discussions with other test takers, if you have scored around 80 percent in the practice exam, you should be pretty confident to take the actual exam. However, before the practice exam, make sure you do other tests available. We have included a couple of practice tests with this book, which should give you some indication of your readiness for the exam. Make sure you take the tests in one complete sitting rather than over multiple days. Once you have done that, you need to look at all the questions you answered correctly and why the answers were correct. It could be a case in which, while you answered the question correctly, you didn't understand the concept the question was testing or have missed out on certain details that could potentially change the answer.

You need to read through the reference material for each test to ensure that you've covered the necessary aspects required to pass the exam.

The Night before the Exam

An AWS professional-level exam requires you to be on top of your game, and just like any professional player, you need to be well rested before the exam. I recommend getting eight hours of sleep the night before the exam. Regarding scheduling the exam, I am often asked what the best time is to take a certification exam. I personally like doing it early in the morning; however, you need to identify the time in the day when you feel most energetic. Some people are full of energy early in the morning, while others ease into the day and are at full throttle by midafternoon.

During the Exam

You should be well hydrated before you take the exam.

You have 170 minutes (2 hours, 50 minutes) to answer 68±3 questions depending on how many test questions you get during the exam. The test questions are questions that are actually used for the purpose of improving the exam, as new questions are introduced on a regular basis, and the passing rate indicates if a question is valid for the exam. You have roughly two and a half minutes per question on average, with the majority of the questions being two to three paragraphs (almost one page) with at least four plausible choices. The plausible choice means that for a less-experienced candidate, all four choices will seem correct; however, there would be guidance in the question that makes one choice more correct than the other. This also means that you will spend most of the exam reading the question, occasionally twice, and if your reading speed is not good, you will find it hard to complete the entire exam.

Remember that while the exam does test your knowledge, I believe that it is also an examination of your patience and your focus.

You need to make sure that you go through not only the core material but also the reference material discussed in the book and that you run through the examples and workshops.

All the best with the exam!

Interactive Online Learning Environment and Test Bank

I've worked hard to provide some really great tools to help you with your certification process. The interactive online learning environment that accompanies the *AWS Certified Data Analytics Study Guide: Specialty (DAS-C01) Exam* provides a test bank with study tools to help you prepare for the certification exam—and increase your chances of passing it the first time! The test bank includes the following:

Sample Tests   All the questions in this book are provided, including the assessment test at the end of this introduction and the review questions at the end of each chapter. In addition, there are two practice exams with 65 questions each. Use these questions to test your knowledge of the study guide material. The online test bank runs on multiple devices.

Flashcards   The online text banks include more than 150 flashcards specifically written to hit you hard, so don't get discouraged if you don't ace your way through them at first. They're there to ensure that you're really ready for the exam. And no worries—armed with the reading material, reference material, review questions, practice exams, and flashcards, you'll be more than prepared when exam day comes. Questions are provided in digital flashcard format (a question followed by a single correct answer). You can use the flashcards to reinforce your learning and provide last-minute test prep before the exam.

Glossary   A glossary of key terms from this book is available as a fully searchable PDF.

Go to www.wiley.com/go/sybextestprep to register and gain access to this interactive online learning environment and test bank with study tools.

Exam Objectives

The AWS Certified Data Analytics—Specialty (DAS-C01) exam is intended for people who are performing a data analytics–focused role. This exam validates an examinee's comprehensive understanding of using AWS services to design, build, secure, and maintain analytics solutions that provide insight from data.

It validates an examinee's ability in the following areas:

- Designing, developing, and deploying cloud-based solutions using AWS

- Designing and developing analytical projects on AWS using the AWS technology stack

- Designing and developing data pipelines

- Designing and developing data collection architectures

- An understanding of the operational characteristics of the collection systems

- Selection of collection systems that handle frequency, volume, and the source of the data

- Understanding the different types of approaches of data collection and how the approaches differentiate from each other on the data formats, ordering, and compression

- Designing optimal storage and data management systems to cater for the volume, variety, and velocity

- Understanding the operational characteristics of analytics storage solutions

- Understanding of the access and retrieval patterns of data

- Understanding of appropriate data layout, schema, structure, and format

- Understanding of the data lifecycle based on the usage patterns and business requirements

- Determining the appropriate system for the cataloging of data and metadata
- Identifying the most appropriate data processing solution based on business SLAs, data volumes, and cost
- Designing a solution for transformation of data and preparing for further analysis
- Automating appropriate data visualization solutions for a given scenario
- Identifying appropriate authentication and authorization mechanisms
- Applying data protection and encryption techniques
- Applying data governance and compliance controls

Recommended AWS Knowledge

- A minimum of 5 years of experience with common data analytics technologies
- At least 2 years of hands-on experience working on AWS
- Experience and expertise working with AWS services to design, build, secure, and maintain analytics solutions

Objective Map

The following table lists each domain and its weighting in the exam, along with the chapters in the book where that domain's objectives and subobjectives are covered.

Domain	Percentage of Exam	Chapter
Domain 1.0: Data Collection	18%	1, 2, 3
1.1 – Determine the operational characteristics of the collection system.		
1.2 – Select a collection system that handles the frequency, volume and source of data.		
1.3 – Select a collection system that addresses the key properties of the data, such as order, format and compression.		
Domain 2.0: Storage and Data Management	22%	3, 4
2.1 – Determine the operational characteristics of the analytics storage solution.		
2.2 – Determine data access and retrieval patterns.		
2.3 – Select appropriate data layout, schema, structure and format.		
2.4 – Define data lifecycle based on usage patterns and business requirements.		
2.5 – Determine the appropriate system for cataloguing data and managing metadata.		

Domain	Percentage of Exam	Chapter
Domain 3.0: Processing	24%	3, 4

3.1 – Determine appropriate data processing solution requirements.

3.2 – Design a solution for transforming and preparing data for analysis.

3.3 – Automate and operationalize data processing solution.

Domain 4.0: Analysis and Visualization	18%	3, 4, 5

4.1 – Determine the operational characteristics of the analysis and visualization layer.

4.2 – Select the appropriate data analysis solution for a given scenario.

4.3 – Select the appropriate data visualization solution for a given scenario.

Domain 5.0: Security	18%	2, 3, 4, 5, 6

5.1 – Select appropriate authentication and authorization mechanisms.

5.2 – Apply data protection and encryption techniques.

5.3 – Apply data governance and compliance controls.

Assessment Test

1. You have been hired as a solution architect for a large media conglomerate that wants a cost-effective way to store a large collection of recorded interviews with the guests collected as MP4 files and a data warehouse system to capture the data across the enterprise and provide access via BI tools. Which of the following is the most cost-effective solution for this requirement?

    A. Store large media files in Amazon Redshift and metadata in Amazon DynamoDB. Use Amazon DynamoDB and Redshift to provide decision-making with BI tools.

    B. Store large media files in Amazon S3 and metadata in Amazon Redshift. Use Amazon Redshift to provide decision-making with BI tools.

    C. Store large media files in Amazon S3, and store media metadata in Amazon EMR. Use Spark on EMR to provide decision-making with BI tools.

    D. Store media files in Amazon S3, and store media metadata in Amazon DynamoDB. Use DynamoDB to provide decision-making with BI tools.

2. Which of the following is a distributed data processing option on Apache Hadoop and was the main processing engine until Hadoop 2.0?

    A. MapReduce

    B. YARN

    C. Hive

    D. ZooKeeper

3. You are working as an enterprise architect for a large fashion retailer based out of Madrid, Spain. The team is looking to build ETL and has large datasets that need to be transformed. Data is arriving from a number of sources and hence deduplication is also an important factor. Which of the following is the simplest way to process data on AWS?

    A. Load data into Amazon Redshift, and build transformations using SQL. Build custom deduplication script.

    B. Using AWS Glue to transform the data using built-in FindMatches ML Transform.

    C. Load data into Amazon EMR, build Spark SQL scripts, and use custom deduplication script.

    D. Use Amazon Athena for transformation and deduplication.

4. Which of these statements are true about AWS Glue crawlers? (Choose three.)

    A. AWS Glue crawlers provide built-in classifiers that can be used to classify any type of data.

    B. AWS Glue crawlers can connect to Amazon S3, Amazon RDS, Amazon Redshift, Amazon DynamoDB, and any JDBC sources.

    C. AWS Glue crawlers provide custom classifiers, which provide the option to classify data that cannot be classified by built-in classifiers.

    D. AWS Glue crawlers write metadata to AWS Glue Data Catalog.

5. You are working as an enterprise architect for a large player within the entertainment industry that has grown organically and by acquisition of other media players. The team is looking to build a central catalog of information that is spread across multiple databases (all of which have a JDBC interface), Amazon S3, Amazon Redshift, Amazon RDS, and Amazon DynamoDB tables. Which of the following is the most cost-effective way to achieve this on AWS?

A. Build scripts to extract the metadata from the different databases using native APIs and load them into Amazon Redshift. Build appropriate indexes and UI to support searching.

B. Build scripts to extract the metadata from the different databases using native APIs and load them into Amazon DynamoDB. Build appropriate indexes and UI to support searching.

C. Build scripts to extract the metadata from the different databases using native APIs and load them into an RDS database. Build appropriate indexes and UI to support searching.

D. Use AWS crawlers to crawl the data sources to build a central catalog. Use AWS Glue UI to support metadata searching.

6. You are working as a data architect for a large financial institution that has built its data platform on AWS. It is looking to implement fraud detection by identifying duplicate customer accounts and looking at when a newly created account matches one for a previously fraudulent user. The company wants to achieve this quickly and is looking to reduce the amount of custom code that might be needed to build this. Which of the following is the most cost-effective way to achieve this on AWS?

A. Build a custom deduplication script using Spark on Amazon EMR. Use PySpark to compare dataframes representing the new customers and fraudulent customers to identify matches.

B. Load the data to Amazon Redshift and use SQL to build deduplication.

C. Load the data to Amazon S3, which forms the basis of your data lake. Use Amazon Athena to build a deduplication script.

D. Load data to Amazon S3. Use AWS Glue FindMatches Transform to implement this.

7. Where is the metadata definition store in the AWS Glue service?

A. Table

B. Configuration files

C. Schema

D. Items

8. AWS Glue provides an interface to Amazon SageMaker notebooks and Apache Zeppelin notebook servers. You can also open a SageMaker notebook from the AWS Glue console directly.

A. True

B. False

9. AWS Glue provides support for which of the following languages? (Choose two.)

    A. SQL

    B. Java

    C. Scala

    D. Python

10. You work for a large ad-tech company that has a set of predefined ads displayed routinely. Due to the popularity of your products, your website is getting popular, garnering attention of a diverse set of visitors. You are currently placing dynamic ads based on user click data, but you have discovered the process time is not keeping up to display the new ads since a users' stay on the website is short lived (a few seconds) compared to your turnaround time for delivering a new ad (less than a minute). You have been asked to evaluate AWS platform services for a possible solution to analyze the problem and reduce overall ad serving time. What is your recommendation?

    A. Push the clickstream data to an Amazon SQS queue. Have your application subscribe to the SQS queue and write data to an Amazon RDS instance. Perform analysis using SQL.

    B. Move the website to be hosted in AWS and use AWS Kinesis to dynamically process the user clickstream in real time.

    C. Push web clicks to Amazon Kinesis Firehose and analyze with Kinesis Analytics or Kinesis Client Library.

    D. Push web clicks to Amazon Kinesis Stream and analyze with Kinesis Analytics or Kinesis Client Library (KCL).

11. You work for a new startup that is building satellite navigation systems competing with the likes of Garmin, TomTom, Google Maps, and Waze. The company's key selling point is its ability to personalize the travel experience based on your profile and use your data to get you discounted rates at various merchants. Its application is having huge success and the company now needs to load some of the streaming data from other applications onto AWS in addition to providing a secure and private connection from its on-premises data centers to AWS. Which of the following options will satisfy the requirement? (Choose two.)

    A. AWS IOT Core

    B. AWS IOT Device Management

    C. Amazon Kinesis

    D. Direct Connect

12. You work for a toy manufacturer whose assembly line contains GPS devices that track the movement of the toys on the conveyer belt and identify the real-time production status. Which of the following tools will you use on the AWS platform to ingest this data?

    A. Amazon Redshift

    B. Amazon Pinpoint

    C. Amazon Kinesis

    D. Amazon SQS

13. Which of the following refers to performing a single action on multiple items instead of repeatedly performing the action on each individual item in a Kinesis stream?

    A. Batching

    B. Collection

    C. Aggregation

    D. Compression

14. What is the term given to a sequence of data records in a stream in AWS Kinesis?

    A. Batch

    B. Group Stream

    C. Consumer

    D. Shard

15. You are working for a large telecom provider who has chosen the AWS platform for its data and analytics needs. It has agreed to using a data lake and S3 as the platform of choice for the data lake. The company is getting data generated from DPI (deep packet inspection) probes in near real time and looking to ingest it into S3 in batches of 100 MB or 2 minutes, whichever comes first. Which of the following is an ideal choice for the use case without any additional custom implementation?

    A. Amazon Kinesis Data Analytics

    B. Amazon Kinesis Data Firehose

    C. Amazon Kinesis Data Streams

    D. Amazon Redshift

16. You are working for a car manufacturer that is using Apache Kafka for its streaming needs. Its core challenges are scalability and manageability a current of Kafka infrastructure–hosted premise along with the escalating cost of human resources required to manage the application. The company is looking to migrate its analytics platform to AWS. Which of the following is an ideal choice on the AWS platform for this migration?

    A. Amazon Kinesis Data Streams

    B. Apache Kafka on EC2 instances

    C. Amazon Managed Streaming for Kafka

    D. Apache Flink on EC2 instances

17. You are working for a large semiconductor manufacturer based out of Taiwan that is using Apache Kafka for its streaming needs. It is looking to migrate its analytics platform to AWS and Amazon Managed Streaming for Kafka and needs your help to right-size the cluster. Which of the following will be the best way to size your Kafka cluster? (Choose two.)

    A. Lift and shift your on-premises cluster.

    B. Use your on-premises cluster as a guideline.

    C. Perform a deep analysis of usage, patterns, and workloads before coming up with a recommendation.

    D. Use the MSK calculator for pricing and sizing.

18. You are running an MSK cluster that is running out of disk space. What can you do to mitigate the issue and avoid running out of space in the future? (Choose four.)

    A. Create a CloudWatch alarm that watches the KafkaDataLogsDiskUsed metric.

    B. Create a CloudWatch alarm that watches the KafkaDiskUsed metric.

    C. Reduce message retention period.

    D. Delete unused shards.

    E. Delete unused topics.

    F. Increase broker storage.

19. Which of the following services can act as sources for Amazon Kinesis Data Firehose?

    A. Amazon Managed Streaming for Kafka

    B. Amazon Kinesis Data Streams

    C. AWS Lambda

    D. AWS IOT

20. How does a Kinesis Data Streams distribute data to different shards?

    A. ShardId

    B. Row hash key

    C. Record sequence number

    D. Partition key

21. How can you write data to a Kinesis Data Stream? (Choose three.)

    A. Kinesis Producer Library

    B. Kinesis Agent

    C. Kinesis SDK

    D. Kinesis Consumer Library

22. You are working for an upcoming e-commerce retailer that has seen its sales quadruple during the pandemic. It is looking to understand more about the customer purchase behavior on its website and believes that analyzing clickstream data might provide insight into the customers' time spent on the website. The clickstream data is being ingested in a streaming fashion with Kinesis Data Streams. The analysts are looking to rely on their advance SQL skills, while the management is looking for a serverless model to reduce their TCO rather than upfront investment. What is the best solution?

    A. Spark streaming on Amazon EMR

    B. Amazon Redshift

    C. AWS Lambda with Kinesis Data Streams

    D. Kinesis Data Analytics

23. Which of the following writes data to a Kinesis stream?

    A. Consumers

    B. Producers

C. Amazon MSK

D. Shards

24. Which of the following statements are true about KPL (Kinesis Producer Library)? (Choose three.)

A. Writes to one or more Kinesis Data Streams with an automatic and configurable retry mechanism.

B. Aggregates user records to increase payload size.

C. Submits CloudWatch metrics on your behalf to provide visibility into producer performance.

D. Forces the caller application to block and wait for a confirmation.

E. KPL does not incur any processing delay and hence is useful for all applications writing data to a Kinesis stream.

F. RecordMaxBufferedTime within the library is set to 1 millisecond and not changeable.

25. Which of the following is true about Kinesis Client Library? (Choose three.)

A. KCL is a Java library and does not support other languages.

B. KCL connects to the data stream and enumerates the shards within the data stream.

C. KCL pulls data records from the data stream.

D. KCL does not provide a checkpointing mechanism.

E. KCL instantiates a record processor for each stream.

F. KCL pushes the records to the corresponding record processor.

26. Which of the following metrics are sent by the Amazon Kinesis Data Streams agent to Amazon CloudWatch? (Choose three.)

A. MBs Sent

B. RecordSendAttempts

C. RecordSendErrors

D. RecordSendFailures

E. ServiceErrors

F. ServiceFailures

27. You are working as a data engineer for a gaming startup, and the operations team notified you that they are receiving a ReadProvisionedThroughputExceeded error. They are asking you to help out and identify the reason for the issue and help in the resolution. Which of the following statements will help? (Choose two.)

A. The GetRecords calls are being throttled by KinesisDataStreams over a duration of time.

B. The GetShardIterator is unable to get a new shard over a duration of time.

C. Reshard your stream to increase the number of shards.

D. Redesign your stream to increase the time between checks for the provision throughput to avoid the errors.

28. You are working as a data engineer for a microblogging website that is using Kinesis for streaming weblogs data. The operations team notified that they are experiencing an increase in latency when fetching records from the stream. They are asking you to help out and identify the reason for the issue and help in the resolution. Which of the following statements will help? (Choose three.)

A. There is an increase in record count resulting in an increase in latency.

B. There is an increase in the size of the record for each GET request.

C. There is an increase in the shard iterator's latency resulting in an increase in record fetch latency.

D. Increase the number of shards in your stream.

E. Decrease the stream retention period to catch up with the data backlog.

F. Move the processing to MSK to reduce latency.

29. Which of the following is true about rate limiting features on Amazon Kinesis? (Choose two.)

A. Rate limiting is not possible within Amazon Kinesis and you need MSK to implement rate limiting.

B. Rate limiting is only possible through Kinesis Producer Library.

C. Rate limiting is implemented using tokens and buckets within Amazon Kinesis.

D. Rate limiting uses standard counter implementation.

E. Rate limiting threshold is set to 50 percent and is not configurable.

30. What is the default data retention period for a Kinesis stream?

A. 12 hours

B. 168 hours

C. 30 days

D. 365 days

31. Which of the following options help improve efficiency with Kinesis Producer Library? (Choose two.)

A. Aggregation

B. Collection

C. Increasing number of shards

D. Reducing overall encryption

32. Which of the following services are valid destinations for Amazon Kinesis Firehose? (Choose three.)

A. Amazon S3

B. Amazon SageMaker

C. Amazon Elasticsearch

D. Amazon Redshift

E. Amazon QuickSight

F. AWS Glue

33. Which of the following is a valid mechanism to do data transformations from Amazon Kinesis Firehose?

A. AWS Glue

B. Amazon SageMaker

C. Amazon Elasticsearch

D. AWS Lambda

34. Which of the following is a valid mechanism to perform record conversions from Amazon Kinesis Firehose AWS Console? (Choose two.)

A. Apache Parquet

B. Apache ORC

C. Apache Avro

D. Apache Pig

35. You are working as a data engineer for a mid-sized boating company that is capturing data in real time for all of its boats connected via a 3G/4G connection. The boats typically sail in areas with good connectivity, and data loss from the IoT devices on the boat to a Kinesis stream is not possible. You are monitoring the data arriving from the stream and have realized that some of the records are being missed. What can be the underlying issue for records being skipped?

A. The connectivity from the boat to AWS is the reason for missed records.

B. processRecords() is throwing exceptions that are not being handled and hence the missed records.

C. The shard is already full and hence the data is being missed.

D. The record length is more than expected.

E. Apache Pig

36. How does Kinesis Data Firehose handle server-side encryption? (Choose three.)

A. Kinesis Data Firehose does not support server-side encryption.

B. Kinesis Data Firehose server-side encryption depends on the data source.

C. Kinesis Data Firehose does not store the unencrypted data at rest when the data source is a Kinesis Data stream encrypted by AWS KMS.

D. Kinesis Data Firehose stores the unencrypted data to S3 when the data source is a Kinesis Data stream encrypted by AWS KMS.

E. When data is delivered using Direct PUT, you can start encryption by using StartDeliveryStreamEncryption.

F. When data is delivered using Direct PUT, you can start encryption by using StartKinesisFirhoseEncryption.

37. How can you start an AWS Glue job automatically after the completion of a crawler? (Choose two.)

    A. Use AWS Glue triggers to start a job when the crawler run completes.

    B. Create an AWS Lambda function using Amazon CloudWatch events rule.

    C. Use AWS Glue workflows.

    D. This is not possible. You have to run it manually.

38. You are working as a consultant for an advertising agency that has hired a number of data scientists who are working to improve the online and offline campaigns for the company and using AWS Glue for most of their data engineering workloads. The data scientists have broad experience with adtech workloads and before joining the team have developed Python libraries that they would like to use in AWS Glue. How can they use the external Python libraries in an AWS Glue job? (Choose two.)

    A. Package the libraries in a `.tar` file, and upload to Amazon S3.

    B. Package the libraries in a `.zip` file, and upload to Amazon S3.

    C. Use the library in a job or job run.

    D. Unzip the compressed file programmatically before using the library in the job or job run.

39. You are working as a consultant for a large conglomerate that has recently acquired another company. It is looking to integrate the applications using a messaging system and it would like the applications to remain decoupled but still be able to send messages. Which of the following is the most cost-effective and scalable service to achieve the objective?

    A. Apache Flink on Amazon EMR

    B. Amazon Kinesis

    C. Amazon SQS

    D. AWS Glue streaming.

40. What types of queues does Amazon SQS support? (Choose two.)

    A. Standard queue

    B. FIFO queue

    C. LIFO queue

    D. Advanced queue

41. You are working as a data engineer for a telecommunications operator that is using DynamoDB for its operational data store. The company is looking to use AWS Data Pipeline for workflow orchestration and needs to send some SNS notifications as soon as an order is placed and a record is available in the DynamoDB table. What is the best way to handle this?

    A. Configure a lambda function to keep scanning the DynamoDB table. Send an SNS notification once you see a new record.

    B. Configure Amazon DynamoDB streams to orchestrate AWS Data Pipeline kickoff.

C. Configure an AWS Glue job that reads the DynamoDB table to trigger an AWS Data Pipeline job.

D. Use the preconditions available in AWS Data Pipeline.

42. You have been consulting on the AWS analytics platform for some years now. One of your top customers has reached out to you to understand the best way to export data from its DynamoDB table to its data lake on S3. The customer is looking to keep the cost to a minimum and ideally not involve a consulting expertise at this moment. What is the easiest way to handle this?

A. Export the data from Amazon DynamoDB to Amazon S3 using EMR custom scripts.

B. Build a custom lambda function that scans the data from DynamoDB and writes it to S3.

C. Use AWS Glue to read the DynamoDB table and use AWS Glue script generation to generate the script for you.

D. Use AWS Data Pipeline to copy data from DynamoDB to Amazon S3.

43. You have built your organization's data lake on Amazon S3. You are looking to capture and track all requests made to an Amazon S3 bucket. What is the simplest way to enable this?

A. Use Amazon Macie.

B. Use Amazon CloudWatch.

C. Use AWS CloudTrail.

D. Use Amazon S3 server access logging.

44. Your customer has recently received multiple 503 Slow Down errors during the Black Friday sale while ingesting data to Amazon S3. What could be the reason for this error?

A. Amazon S3 is unable scale to the needs of your data ingestion patterns.

B. This is an application-specific error originating from your web application and has nothing to do with Amazon S3.

C. You are writing lots of objects per prefix. Amazon S3 is scaling in the background to handle the spike in traffic.

D. You are writing large objects resulting in this error from Amazon S3.

45. Which of the following is a fully managed NoSQL service?

A. Amazon Redshift

B. Amazon Elasticsearch

C. Amazon DynamoDB

D. Amazon DocumentDB

46. Your customer is using Amazon DynamoDB for the operational use cases. One of its engineers has accidently deleted 10 records. Which of the following is a valid statement when it comes to recovering Amazon DynamoDB data?

A. Use backups from Amazon S3 to re-create the tables.

B. Use backups from Amazon Redshift to re-create the tables.

    C.   Use data from a different region.

    D.   Use Amazon DynamoDB PITR to recover the deleted data.

47. Which of the following scenarios suit a provisioned scaling mode for DynamoDB? (Choose two.)

    A.   You have predictable application traffic.

    B.   You are running applications whose traffic is consistent or ramps up gradually.

    C.   You are unable to forecast your capacity requirements.

    D.   You prefer a pay-as-you-go pricing model.

48. Which of the following statements are true about primary keys in DynamoDB? (Choose two.)

    A.   A table's primary key can be defined after the table creation.

    B.   DynamoDB supports two types of primary keys only.

    C.   A composite primary key is the same as a combination of partition key and sort key.

    D.   DynamoDB uses a sort key as an input to internal hash function, the output of which determines the partition where the item is stored.

49. You are working as a data engineer for a large corporation that is using DynamoDB to power its low-latency application requests. The application is based on a customer orders table that is used to provide information about customer orders based on a specific customer ID. A new requirement had recently arisen to identify customers based on a specific product ID. You decided to implement it as a secondary index. The application engineering team members have recently complained about the performance they are getting from the secondary index. Which of the following is a the most common reason for the performance degradation of a secondary index in DynamoDB?

    A.   The application engineering team is querying data for project attributes.

    B.   The application engineering team is querying data not projected in the secondary index.

    C.   The application engineering team is querying a partition key that is not part of the local secondary index.

    D.   The application engineering team is querying data for a different sort key value.

50. Your customer is looking to reduce the spend of its on-premises storage ensuring the low latency of the application, which depends on a subset of the entire dataset. The customer is happy with the characteristics of Amazon S3. Which of the following would you recommend?

    A.   Cached volumes

    B.   Stored volumes

    C.   File gateway

    D.   Tape gateway

51. Your customer is looking to reduce the spend of its on-premises storage ensuring the low latency of the application, which depends on the entire dataset. The customer is happy with the characteristics of Amazon S3. Which of the following would you recommend?

   A. Cached volumes

   B. Stored volumes

   C. File gateway

   D. Tape gateway

52. You are working as a consultant for a telecommunications company. The data scientists have requested direct access to the data to dive deep into the structure of the data and build models. They have good knowledge of SQL. Which of the following tools will you choose to provide them with direct access to the data and reduce the infrastructure and maintenance overhead while ensuring that access to data on Amazon S3 can be provided?

   A. Amazon S3 Select

   B. Amazon Athena

   C. Amazon Redshift

   D. Apache Presto on Amazon EMR

53. Which of the following file formats are supported by Amazon Athena? (Choose three.)

   A. Apache Parquet

   B. CSV

   C. DAT

   D. Apache ORC

   E. Apache AVRO

   F. TIFF

54. Your EMR cluster is facing performance issues. You are looking to investigate the errors and understand the potential performance problems on the nodes. Which of the following nodes can you skip during your test?

   A. Master node

   B. Core node

   C. Task node

   D. Leader node

55. Which of the following statements are true about Redshift leader nodes? (Choose three.)

   A. Redshift clusters can have a single leader node.

   B. Redshift clusters can have more than one leader node.

   C. Redshift Leader nodes should have more memory than the compute nodes.

   D. Redshift Leader nodes have the exact same specifications as the compute nodes.

   E. You can choose your own Leader node sizing, and it is priced separately.

   F. Redshift leader node is chosen automatically and is free to the users.

Answers to the Assessment Test

1. B. Option A is incorrect as storing large media files in Redshift is a bad choice due to potential cost. Option C is incorrect as EMR is not a cost-effective choice to store image metadata. Option D is incorrect as DynamoDB is not cost-effective for large scan operations. Option B is correct as Amazon S3 is the right choice for large media files. Amazon Redshift is a good option for a managed data warehousing service.

2. A. Option A is correct because MapReduce was the default processing engine on Hadoop until Hadoop 2.0 arrived. Option B is incorrect because YARN is a resource manager for applications on Hadoop. Option C is incorrect as Hive is a SQL layer that makes use of processing engines like MapReduce, Spark, Tez, and so on. Option D is incorrect as Zoo-Keeper is a distributed configuration and synchronization service that acts as a naming registry for large distributed systems.

3. B. AWS Glue is the simplest way to achieve data transformation using mostly a point-and-click interface and making use of built-in deduplication using FindMatches ML Transform.

4. B, C, D. Option A is incorrect because AWS Glue built-in classifiers cannot be used for any data type. B, C, and D are correct; refer to `docs.aws.amazon.com/glue/latest/dg/populate-data-catalog.html`.

5. D. AWS Glue is the most cost-effective way to achieve this since it provides a native catalog curation using crawlers and visibility across different AWS users.

6. D. AWS Glue is the most cost-effective way to achieve this since it provides native built-in FindMatches capability using `docs.aws.amazon.com/glue/latest/dg/machine-learning.html`.

7. A. AWS Glue stores metadata for your data that can be an S3 file, Amazon RDS table, a Redshift table, or any other supported source. A table in the AWS Glue Data Catalog consists of the names of columns, data type definitions, and other metadata about a base dataset.

8. A. More information is available at `docs.aws.amazon.com/glue/latest/dg/notebooks-with-glue.html`.

9. C, D. AWS Glue supports the Scala and Python languages.

10. D. Option A does not provide any support for analyzing data in real time. Option B is incorrect and vague. Option C involves Kinesis Firehose, which helps in aggregating the data rather than real-time data analysis. Option D is correct as it involves Kinesis Analytics and KCL.

11. C, D. Options A and B are incorrect because the question is asking about connecting your on-premises applications and loading streaming data rather than IoT connectivity. Option C is correct as Amazon Kinesis is the streaming option available on AWS. Option D is correct as Direct Connect allows connectivity from your on-premises data center to AWS.

12. C. Amazon Kinesis makes it easy to collect, process, and analyze real-time, streaming data so you can get timely insights and react quickly to new information. Amazon Kinesis offers key capabilities to cost-effectively process streaming data at any scale, along with the flexibility to choose the tools that best suit the requirements of your application. With Amazon Kinesis, you can ingest real-time data such as video, audio, application logs, website clickstreams, and IoT telemetry data for machine learning, analytics, and other applications. Amazon Kinesis enables you to process and analyze data as it arrives and respond instantly instead of having to wait until all your data is collected before the processing can begin.

13. A. Batching refers to performing a single action on multiple items instead of repeatedly performing the action on each individual item.

14. D. A *Kinesis data stream* is a set of shards. Each shard has a sequence of data records. Each data record has a sequence number that is assigned by Kinesis Data Streams.

15. B. Amazon Kinesis Firehose can deliver streaming data to S3 and hence is an ideal choice for this. While you can achieve the same with other technologies, it does involve additional work and custom implementations.

16. C. Amazon Managed Streaming for Kafka is an ideal solution for migrating from on-premises Kafka installations to the AWS platform, which ensures that the code base remains the same. You spend lot less time managing the infrastructure, and being a managed service ensures that resources are allocated to other applications rather than leaving you with the cumbersome task of managing Kafka.

17. B, D. As a best practice, use an on-premises cluster as a guideline for your cluster configuration and the MSK calculator for pricing and sizing.

18. A, C, D, E. Please refer to the following documentation link: docs.aws.amazon.com/msk/latest/developerguide/bestpractices.html#bestpractices-monitor-disk-space.

19. B. Amazon Kinesis Data Streams is the only service that can put data directly to Amazon Kinesis Firehose.

20. D. A partition key is used to group data by shard within a stream. Kinesis Data Streams segregates the data records belonging to a stream into multiple shards. It uses the partition key that is associated with each data record to determine which shard a given data record belongs to.

21. A, B, C. A *producer* is an application that writes data to Amazon Kinesis Data Streams. You can build producers for Kinesis Data Streams using the AWS SDK for Java and the Kinesis Producer Library.

22. D. The requirements in the question are streaming data, SQL skills, and pay-as-you-go pricing. All of these requirements are met with KDA.

23. B. Producers write data to a Kinesis stream.

24. A, B, C. Please refer to KPL documentation. Option D is incorrect because of its asynchronous architecture. Because the KPL may buffer records before sending them to Kinesis Data Streams, it does not force the caller application to block and wait for a confirmation that the record has arrived. Option E is incorrect as the KPL can incur an additional processing delay of up to RecordMaxBufferedTime within the library (user-configurable). Larger values of RecordMaxBufferedTime result in higher packing efficiencies and better performance. Option F is incorrect because RecordMaxBufferedTime is user configurable in the library.

25. B, C, F. Option A is incorrect because while KCL is a Java library, support for languages other than Java is provided using a multi-language interface called the MultiLangDaemon. Option D is incorrect because KCL does provide a checkpoint mechanism. Option E is incorrect because KCL instantiates a record processor for each shard.

26. B, C, E. Option A is incorrect as the metric is BytesSent rather than MBs Sent. Option D is incorrect as the metric is RecordSendErrors rather than RecordSendFailures. Option F is incorrect as the metric is ServiceErrors rather than ServiceFailures.

27. A, C. The ReadProvisionedThroughputExceeded error occurs when GetRecords calls are throttled by Kinesis Data Streams over a duration of time. Your Amazon Kinesis data stream can throttle if the following limits are breached:

Each shard can support up to five read transactions per second (or five GetRecords calls/second for each shard).

Each shard can support up to a maximum read rate of 2 MiB/second.

GetRecords can retrieve up to 10 MiB of data per call from a single shard and up to 10,000 records per call. If a call to GetRecords returns 10 MiB of data, subsequent calls made within the next 5 seconds result in an error.

28. A, B, D. GetRecords.Latency can increase if there is an increase in record count or record size for each GET request. If you tried to restart your application while the producer was ingesting data into the stream, records can accumulate without being consumed. This increase in the record count or amount of data to be fetched increases the value for GetRecords.Latency. Additionally, if an application is unable to catch up with the ingestion rate, the IteratorAge gets increased. Note: Enabling server-side encryption on your Kinesis data stream can also increase your latency.

29. B, C. Option A is incorrect as rate limiting is possible with Kinesis. Option D is incorrect as rate limiting is implemented using a token bucket algorithm with separate buckets for both Kinesis Data Streams records and bytes. Option E is incorrect as this threshold is configurable but by default is set 50 percent higher than the actual shard limit, to allow shard saturation from a single producer.

30. B. Amazon Kinesis Data Streams supports changes to the data record retention period of your stream. A Kinesis data stream is an ordered sequence of data records meant to be written to and read from in real time. Data records are therefore stored in shards in your stream temporarily. The time period from when a record is added to when it is no longer accessible is called the *retention period*. A Kinesis data stream stores records from 24 hours by default, configurable up to 168 hours.

31. A, B. The KPL supports two types of batching:

Aggregation – Storing multiple records within a single Kinesis Data Streams record

Collection – Using the API operation PutRecords to send multiple Kinesis Data Streams records to one or more shards in your Kinesis data stream

32. A, C, D. Kinesis Data Firehose can send records to Amazon Simple Storage Service (Amazon S3), Amazon Redshift, Amazon Elasticsearch Service (Amazon ES), and any HTTP endpoint owned by you or any of your third-party service providers, including Datadog, New Relic, and Splunk.

33. D. Kinesis Data Firehose can invoke your lambda function to transform incoming source data and deliver the transformed data to destinations. You can enable Kinesis Data Firehose data transformation when you create your delivery stream.

34. A, B. Kinesis Firehose can convert data to Parquet and ORC. Option C is incorrect as it is unsupported. Option D is incorrect as it is not a file format.

35. B. The most common cause of skipped records is an unhandled exception thrown from processRecords. The Kinesis Client Library (KCL) relies on your processRecords code to handle any exceptions that arise from processing the data records. Any exception thrown from processRecords is absorbed by the KCL.

36. B, C, E. If you have sensitive data, you can enable server-side data encryption when you use Amazon Kinesis Data Firehose. How you do this depends on the source of your data.

37. B, D. It's not possible to use AWS Glue triggers to start a job when a crawler run completes. Use one of the following methods instead:

Create an AWS Lambda function and an Amazon CloudWatch Events rule. When you choose this option, the lambda function is always on. It monitors the crawler regardless of where or when you start it. You can also modify this method to automate other AWS Glue functions.

For more information, see "How can I use a Lambda function to automatically start an AWS Glue job when a crawler run completes? https://aws.amazon.com/premiumsupport/knowledge-center/start-glue-job-crawler-completes-lambda"

Use AWS Glue workflows. This method requires you to start the crawler from the Work-flows page on the AWS Glue console. For more information, see "How can I use AWS Glue workflows to automatically start a job when a crawler run completes?" https://aws.amazon.com/premiumsupport/knowledge-center/start-glue-job-after-crawler-workflow

38. B,C. To use an external library in an Apache Spark ETL job:

1. Package the library files in a .zip file (unless the library is contained in a single .py file).

2. Upload the package to Amazon Simple Storage Service (Amazon S3).

3. Use the library in a job or job run.

39. C. Amazon Simple Queue Service (Amazon SQS) offers a secure, durable, and available hosted queue that lets you integrate and decouple distributed software systems and components.

40. A, B. Amazon SQS uses queues to integrate producers and consumers of a message. Producers write messages to a queue, and consumers pull messages from the queue. A queue is simply a buffer between producers and consumers. We have two types of queues:

Standard queue – Highly scalable with maximum throughput, best-effort ordering and at-least-once delivery semantics

FIFO Queue – Exactly-once semantics with guaranteed ordering with lesser scalability than standard queue

41. D. You can use a combination of the following preconditions: DynamoDBDataExists checks whether data exists in a specific DynamoDB table. DynamoDBTableExists checks whether a DynamoDB table exists.

42. D. DynamoDBDataNode defines a data node using DynamoDB, which is specified as an input to a HiveActivity or EMRActivity object. S3DataNode defines a data node using Amazon S3. By default, the S3DataNode uses server-side encryption. If you would like to disable this, set s3EncryptionType to NONE.

43. D. Server access logging provides detailed records for the requests that are made to a bucket. Server access logs are useful for many applications. For example, access log information can be useful in security and access audits.

44. C. You can send 3,500 PUT/COPY/POST/DELETE and 5,500 GET/HEAD requests per second per partitioned prefix in an S3 bucket. When you have an increased request rate to your bucket, Amazon S3 might return 503 Slow Down errors while it scales to support the request rate. This scaling process is called partitioning.
https://aws.amazon.com/premiumsupport/knowledge-center/
s3-resolve-503-slowdown-throttling

45. C. Option A is incorrect as Amazon Redshift is a relational database service. Option B is incorrect as Elasticsearch is not a NoSQL service. Option C is correct as Amazon DynamoDB is a NoSQL service. Option D is incorrect as Amazon DocumentDB is a document database, but not fully managed.

46. D. You can create on-demand backups and enable point-in-time recovery (PITR) for your Amazon DynamoDB tables. Point-in-time recovery helps protect your tables from accidental write or delete operations. With point-in-time recovery, you can restore that table to any point in time during the last 35 days. For more information, see "Point-in-Time Recovery: How It Works."
https://docs.aws.amazon.com/amazondynamodb/latest/developerguide/
PointInTimeRecovery.html

47. A, B. Provisioned mode is a good option if any of the following are true:

You have predictable application traffic.

You run applications whose traffic is consistent or ramps gradually.

You can forecast capacity requirements to control costs.

48. B, C. When you create a table, in addition to the table name, you must specify the primary key of the table. The primary key uniquely identifies each item in the table, so that no two items can have the same key.

DynamoDB supports two different kinds of primary keys:

Partition key – A simple primary key, composed of one attribute known as the partition key

Composite primary key – This type of key is composed of two attributes. The first attribute is the partition key, and the second attribute is the sort key.

DynamoDB uses the partition key value as input to an internal hash function.

49. B. Non-projected attributes in DynamoDB will result in DynamoDB fetching the attributes from base table, resulting in poor performance.

50. A. You store your data in Amazon Simple Storage Service (Amazon S3) and retain a copy of frequently accessed data subsets locally. Cached volumes offer a substantial cost savings on primary storage and minimize the need to scale your storage on-premises. You also retain low-latency access to your frequently accessed data.

51. B. If you need low-latency access to your entire dataset, first configure your on-premises gateway to store all your data locally. Then asynchronously back up point-in-time snapshots of this data to Amazon S3. This configuration provides durable and inexpensive off-site backups that you can recover to your local data center or Amazon Elastic Compute Cloud (Amazon EC2). For example, if you need replacement capacity for disaster recovery, you can recover the backups to Amazon EC2.

52. B. Amazon Athena is an interactive query service that makes it easy to analyze data in Amazon S3 using standard SQL. Athena is serverless, so there is no infrastructure to manage, and you pay only for the queries that you run.

53. A, B, D. Amazon Athena supports a wide variety of data formats, such as CSV, TSV, JSON, and textfiles and also supports open-source columnar formats such as Apache ORC and Apache Parquet. Athena also supports compressed data in Snappy, Zlib, LZO, and GZIP formats. By compressing, partitioning, and using columnar formats, you can improve performance and reduce your costs.

54. D. *Leader node* is an Amazon Redshift terminology. *Master node* is the current term for an EMR cluster.

55. A, D, F. Please read section "Redshift Architecture" in Chapter 4, "Data Processing and Analytics."

Chapter
1

History of Analytics and Big Data

There are various definitions of analytics, but in my personal opinion *analytics* is a science and an art at the same time, where the science part is the ability to convert raw data into refined ready-to-use actionable information using the right tools for the right job, while the art part is interpreting the information and the KPIs created to manage and grow your business effectively. Analytics is thus the bridge between data and effective decision making that enables organizations and business leaders to move from making decisions based on gut feel to making decisions based on supporting data.

The question arises as to whether analytics is a new phenomenon or has been around for a long time. While we started to hear about big data and analytics around a decade ago, data has always exceeded computation capacity in one way or the other, and by definition the moment the data exceeds the computational capacity of a system, it can be considered big data. From the earliest records, in 1663 John Graunt recorded the mortality rates in London in order to build an early warning system for the bubonic plague, which led to better accounting systems and systems of record.

In 1865, the term *business intelligence* was first used by Richard Millar Devens in his *Cyclopædia of Commercial and Business Anecdotes* (D. Appleton and company, 1865). Devens coined the term to explain how Sir Henry Furnese gained superior edge over his competitors by collecting information about the environment in which he operated.

In 1880, the US Census Bureau came across as the first known big data problem, where according to the estimates it would have taken them 8 years to process the data calculated in the 1890 census, and the census would take an additional 10 years, meaning that the data growth was outpacing the computational capacity at hand. In 1881, Herman Hollerith, who was working for the bureau as an engineer, invented a tabulating machine that would reduce the work from 10 years to 3 months and came to be known as the father of automated computation. The company he founded came to be known as IBM.

While many other important inventions and discoveries happened throughout the twentieth century, it was in 1989 when the term *big data* was first used by Erik Larkson, who penned an article in *Harper's Magazine* discussing the origin of junk email he received. He famously wrote, "The keepers of big data say they are doing it for the consumer's benefit. But data have a way of being used for purposes other than originally intended."

The scale of data available in the world was first theorized in a paper by Michel Lesk ("How much information there is in the world?"), estimating it to be around 12,000 petabytes in late 1990s (www.lesk.com/mlesk/ksg97/ksg.html). Google search debuted in the same year. While there was noise about growing amounts of information, overall the landscape was relatively simple, with the primary mechanism of storing information to be an online transaction process (OLTP) database, and online analytical processing (OLAP) was restricted to fewer large-scale companies.

The key takeaway is that big data and analytics have been around for a long time. Even today companies face challenges when dealing with big data if they are using incorrect tools for solving the problems at hand. While the key metrics to define big data include volume, variety, and velocity, the fact is that big data can be any data that limits your ability to analyze it with the tools at your disposal. Hence, for a few organizations, an exabyte scale data would be a big data problem, whereas for others, it can be challenging to extract information from a few terabytes.

Evolution of Analytics Architecture Over the Years

I have been working in the data domain for over 20 years now, and I have seen various stages of evolution of the analytics pipeline.

Around 20 years ago, when you talked about analytics, the audience would consider this some sort of wizardry. In fact, *statistics* was a more common term than *data science*, *machine learning*, *artificial intelligence*, or *advanced analytics*. Having a data warehouse was considered a luxury, and most systems had a standard three-tiered stack, which consisted of multiple sources of data that were typically accessed using either an extraction, transformation, and Loading (ETL) tool (which was considered a luxury) or handwritten ETL scripts using a scripting language of choice, which was, more often than not, traditional shell scripts. Figure 1.1 shows a traditional data warehousing setup that was quite common during early 2000s.

FIGURE 1.1   Traditional data warehousing setup in early to mid-2000s

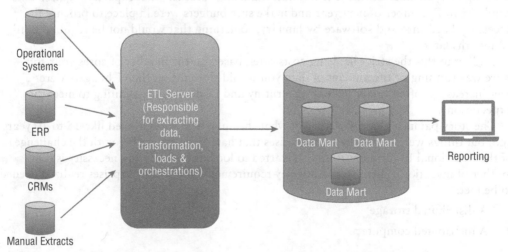

Data extraction transformation was done on the landing server running ETL scripts and in some cases an ETL tool like Informatica. If you ask me what caused the most pains in this environment, it was this ETL server, which would often be the cause of concern for enterprises due to a variety of reasons, including limited disk space, memory, compute capacity, and the overall orchestration. As you can see, this piece was the "glue" between the sources of data and the potential information and insights that were expected to be extracted from these sources.

The key challenges in such a setup included the rigid process where everything operated in a waterfall model and businesses were asked to provide the requirements really early on in the cycle. It was these requirements which were the basis of creation of an information model which normally took anywhere between 6 to 12 months for large projects. Without any prototyping capabilities, limited scalability, and available tools, it was quite common for business requirements and the eventual delivered product to be vastly different, and quite often by the time the IT delivered the requirements, the business had moved on from the requirements, leading to discontent between the two teams.

The data world was expanding with the dot-com bubble, and ever-increasing system logs were being generated, only to be shoved away in some archival system as the storage was just too expensive, and computation on such large amounts of data was becoming impossible. The world was more content with getting CSVs and TSVs and just not ready for multi-structured data like XML and unstructured data like text. While the CIOs knew there was value in these datasets, the fact that you had to provide a business case for any investment of this scale meant such datasets were often archived or discarded.

The business intelligence (BI) tools were often very rigid, where instead of the users having access to data and self-service analytics, they would have to rely on BI developers who would have to build universes based around an information schema, which would eventually service the user requirements. If you add to this the inability to elastically scale your hardware based on the business needs, you would often come across solution architects working in September of this year to understand and forecast what capacity requirements would be in December of next year and make sure budgets were in place to procure the necessary hardware and software by January, something that would not be required until 12 months later.

Adding to this the strict licensing costs often based on the number of cores your software was running or the amount of data you would store meant the IT budgets were ever increasing, often under increasing scrutiny and IT departments failing to meet the expectations.

The story paints a gloomy picture of what the analytics world looked like 15 to 20 years ago, but things weren't that bad. Enterprises that have been struggling with the challenges of the traditional BI infrastructure had started to look at options, and necessity is the mother of invention. There were a few key requirements that the enterprises realized needed to be met:

1. A distributed storage
2. A distributed compute

3. Scalability of hardware

4. Pay-as-you-go pricing model

Remember, that it was not the fact that distributed storage and compute were unavailable, it was more the realization that the price point at which these technologies were available would make them unsuitable for a number of use cases coming out from the dot-com world. The scalability of hardware was virtually nonexistent, and the strict pricing models meant failure was costly.

The New World Order

The analytics world was undergoing some massive transformation. Google had released its Google FileSystem[3] and MapReduce[4] papers in 2003 and 2004, thus paving the way for open-source projects like Apache Hadoop (discussed in more detail in our data processing chapter), whereas Amazon launched Amazon Web Services[5] in 2006, initially launching just three services—Amazon S3 cloud storage, Amazon SQS, and Amazon EC2—paving the way for a world where the pay-as-you-go model for software and services was now becoming a reality. Hadoop was becoming popular in the world, with enterprises realizing the benefits that some of the larger Internet companies had achieved using their large and highly focused engineering teams. The challenge had been to replicate those successes when the focus of the enterprise was to serve their customers better and now actually build the technology.

Because Hadoop was becoming a popular open-source project, more and more projects started to crop up in the open-source space, like Hive, Pig, Mahout, Zookeeper, and Sqoop. The objective was to enable Hadoop to be used by a larger user base, by not limiting it to the hands of the engineers who could write MapReduce code, but also to enable the business users who are more comfortable with SQL and other well-known languages. Enterprises wanted to get on the Hadoop bandwagon but realized that they not only needed a core distributed storage and compute but also other ecosystem projects with the software, which led to creation of a number of Hadoop distributions, with the most popular ones from Cloudera, Hortonworks, and MapR.

Of course, existing data warehouse vendors wanted to be a part of this change, and some created their own distributions, while others preferred a hardware-based approach by hosting a popular distribution within their appliance and making Hadoop part of the analytics stack, where Hadoop would now start to be a *data lake* for the analytics platform and the existing data warehouse systems would still host the cleanest data. The Hadoop distribution companies were not entirely happy with the relegation of Hadoop to a mere landing zone, which resulted in more innovation up the stack in terms of ease of use of analytics.

While the continuing and high speed of innovation was very beneficial to the end users and they had moved from a point where they had limited choice to a point where they were now spoiled for choice with almost half a dozen Hadoop distributions, some suggested that Hadoop was a magic bullet, whereas others suggested that Hadoop had its own place in analytics but was not yet ready to replace the "real stuff." Mind you, the open-source world was still coming up with some really cool and important projects aimed at replacing the shortcomings from existing projects. For example, Map Reduce was originally built to solve a search problem, but due to its success it was now being used as an analytics engine, fronted by the likes of Hive and Pig, which resulted in Hadoop (originally a batch processing engine) being used for iterative analytics and thus failing to meet the high expectations of users who were used to getting high-speed access to the data from the enterprise data warehouse systems.

This led to the creation of Apache Spark, a project that would find a new way to solve the data engineering and iterative analytics problem, and then other engines were added to it in the form of Spark SQL (originally called Shark), Spark Streaming, Spark ML, and GraphX. The idea was that this was a one-stop shop for all things analytics.

Since cloud computing was getting popular, more and more customers wanted to use the elastic nature of the cloud to run data engineering workloads (elastic in nature) and asked Amazon Web Services to provide support for such workloads. Customers were running Hadoop workloads on Amazon EC2 instances already; for example, the *New York Times*[6] used 100 EC2 instances to run a Hadoop application to process 4 TB of raw TIFF data (in S3) into 11 million finished PDFs in the space of 24 hours at the computation cost of $240. With the popularity of such workloads and the great demand, Amazon started working on a new project called Amazon Elastic MapReduce (EMR), released in April 2009. The initial objective of EMR was a managed Hadoop environment, but the service later became a catalog of other open-source projects in the big data domain like HBase, Spark, Presto, and Livy.

As the environment looked quite impressive on the data engineering side, the business intelligence (BI) side was also undergoing massive change with business managers increasingly requesting direct access to the data to be able to respond to business challenges more effectively, thus paving the way for tools that allowed fast and ad hoc access to data and demand for more self-service BI tools. This led to popular tools like Tableau, Spotfire, and Qlik, despite being around for a long time, becoming more popular in the market and widely accepted.

The world of BI and analytics looks very different to what we had 20 years ago, where ETL tools are much more intelligent and BI tools allow you to create a deep learning model with a few clicks. This book talks about the world of BI and analytics that you see today and beyond, and it specifically talks about the AWS platform, which offers the most depth and breadth of solutions around big data and analytics.

Analytics Pipeline

Since this is an advanced-level book, we'll jump directly to the analytics pipeline, which is a critical component that needs to be understood before you undertake any big data project. Figure 1.2 shows a typical big data pipeline that includes various phases of data management. While there would be cases and situations where you would need to alter the pipeline based on your need, in most cases this is the sort of pipeline the customers would typically build to solve their analytical problems. The technologies might change, but they key idea remains the same.

FIGURE 1.2   Overview of an analytics pipeline

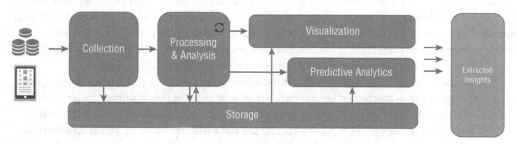

The general flow of a big data pipeline is as follows:

1. Data is collected by a collection tool.

2. Data is stored in a persistent way.

3. Data is processed and analyzed. Often this processing involves multiple steps, and there is typically movement of data between the processing system and the storage system. The result of an analysis can warrant another analysis and processing.

4. Once the processing is done, the data is made available to the business users who can then use the BI tools to visualize and generate further insights from the data.

5. The data is also often used for predictive analytics. Examples are churn prediction, customer segmentation, and product recommendation.

Let's look at each one of these phases in more detail.

Data Sources

In any analytics pipeline, you will start your work with data being produced from producer systems. The system producing data may be an OLTP system like your customer relationship management (CRM) system or your retail point of sale system running on MySQL, Postgres, Aurora, or another commercial database, or it may be your existing data warehouse, like Teradata, Oracle, or Netezza. The producers are typically not limited to relational data sources as they can often include sensors and devices on shops and factory floors producing event data like temperature, humidity, noise, and heat levels or even social media feeds that can be captured from Twitter and Facebook. The data may therefore be in various formats and need to be captured at a varying velocity, variety, and volume. These data sources are what produce the data, and quite often the analytics pipeline's key objective is to transform this raw data into information that can be consumed by business users.

This leads us to the collection part of the big data pipeline.

Collection

Data collection is a first major step in the big data pipeline, and data can originate from a number of sources in a variety of formats and at varying velocity. Having the right tool for the right job is pretty important to building a highly efficient data architecture that includes data collection, and hence the AWS platform provides a number of tools that can be used to collect the data from those sources. One of the major sources of big data include the billions of devices in homes, factories, oil wells, cars, and so on. There is an increasing demand to connect to the devices and collect, store, and analyze that data. This increases the demands on the collection technologies to not only collect the data often in near real time but also to have the ability to analyze at such huge volumes.

High velocity data capture is quite common however Analytics pipelines also encounter data arriving in mini-batches or micro-batches at relatively higher volumes, often needing an entirely different way to capture this data. There are technologies available with the AWS ecosystem that allow you to capture the data in mini-batches and micro-batches thus allowing you to do processing in a serverless fashion, on a pay-as-you-go model. We'll look at these technologies later in this chapter and in more detail during the remainder of the book.

Storage

Once the collection technologies are able to collect the data from the source systems, there is a need to retain this data for downstream processing to ensure it is consumable from other tools that can use this to produce actionable information for the business.

Typically, the need to store the data is as follows:

1. To retain within the collection services
2. To retain in a storage technology of choice

Data collection services like Kinesis (and/or other streaming technologies like Kafka) allow you to store the data in the stream for some period for in-stream analytics. However, you would often need to store data into permanent storage, and that is where permanent storage systems come into play. Often the data is initially landed onto a landing zone, with the core characteristics of the landing zone being the ability to store enormous amounts of data in a variety of file formats, including popular open-source formats like Parquet and ORC, stored at various price points depending on the importance, use, and access of the data.

While the data is stored in a landing zone or a data lake for further processing and analytics, often this is complemented by other storage technologies that are at the extreme end of the spectrum, from sub-second access to long-term archival storage. Since the objective of storage technologies is to store the data for downstream processing and analytics, there are often purpose-built file systems that allow the applications to achieve higher I/O throughput (100+ Mb/second/core), thus allowing complex applications such as machine learning, deep learning, and high-performance computing (HPC) to consume same datasets. We'll look at the storage technologies in Chapter 3, "Data Storage."

Processing and Analysis

Processing and analysis are often done hand in hand, as the processing or preprocessing of datasets is often required to do meaningful analysis, which may often lead to additional processing needs. The processing can involve converting data from one format to another (e.g., CSV to Parquet), or it can be more complicated processing that involves application of certain business rules to data coming from a variety of sources. This could often involve deduplication processes, data cleansing like replacement of missing values, and so on.

There are a variety of tools available in the market that can be used for data processing, including the most common ones like Hadoop, Spark, and SQL environments like Amazon Redshift. The choice of tool depends on the particular use case, which could be one of the use cases discussed earlier or perhaps building a data mart. We will look into this in more detail in Chapter 4, "Data Processing and Analysis."

Analysis is often an iterative process and ranges from ad hoc analysis to more recurrent query patterns based on standard access paths. Given the variety of choices available at our disposal, like Apache Presto, Amazon Redshift, Apache Hive, Apache Pig, and Apache Spark SQL, we will discuss the selection criteria for the tool based on the specific requirement and use cases at hand in Chapter 4, "Data Processing and Analysis."

Visualization, Predictive and Prescriptive Analytics

Visualization, often referred to as the BI, comprises tools, technologies, and processes that are being used by enterprises to analyze their data and provide information to key stakeholders. Analytics is often categorized by going from hindsight to foresight, and visualization typically looks at the descriptive and diagnostic analytics side of things.

The objective of visualization technologies is to understand what happened, and this is often achieved by a variety of visualization techniques. Enterprises rely on a variety of tools to understand the information available in the data and then move toward drilling down to understand the root cause of the positive or negative impacts. Gartner framed the analytic progression from information to optimization in their analytics ascendancy model published in 2012. Figure 1.3 shows the spectrum of business analytics from analyzing historical data to predicting the future state of affairs for a business and the questions you can expect during each phase of business ascendancy.

As you are aware, past is generally (not always) a good predictive of the future; however, machine learning and AI can be used to predict the future and help businesses plan for future potential outcomes. For example, if a business based on the predictive analytics realizes that a particular customer is going to churn (`https://tinyurl.com/y9ho4kbu`), they may devise policies to retain the customer using various marketing campaigns. We'll cover descriptive, diagnostic, and predictive analytics later in this book.

FIGURE 1.3   Business analytics spectrum

Source: Gartner Analytics Maturity Model, https://www.zdnet.com/article/a-guide-for-prescriptive-analytics-the-art-and-science-of-choosing-and-applying-the-right-techniques/

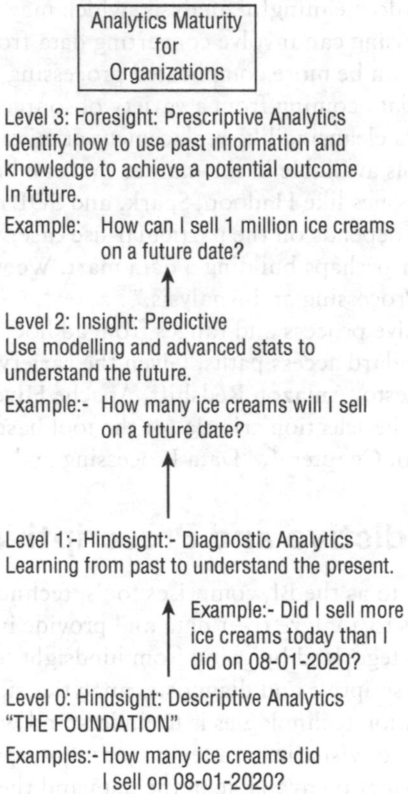

Analytics Maturity
for
Organizations

Level 3: Foresight: Prescriptive Analytics
Identify how to use past information and
knowledge to achieve a potential outcome
In future.
Example: How can I sell 1 million ice creams
on a future date?

Level 2: Insight: Predictive
Use modelling and advanced stats to
understand the future.
Example:- How many ice creams will I sell
on a future date?

Level 1:- Hindsight:- Diagnostic Analytics
Learning from past to understand the present.
Example:- Did I sell more
ice creams today than I
did on 08-01-2020?

Level 0: Hindsight: Descriptive Analytics
"THE FOUNDATION"
Examples:- How many ice creams did
I sell on 08-01-2020?

While prescriptive analytics provides recommendations on what needs to be done, the details are out of scope for this book.

The Big Data Reference Architecture

We had a look at the big data pipeline in an earlier section. It is time to now start looking at the Big Data Reference architecture and the AWS and partner components that fit the analytics ecosystem. AWS re:Invent is often a source of some of the most amazing content you will come across on Analytics in general and AWS Analytics ecosystem in particular. Figure 1.4 has been adapted from Siva Raghupathy's talk at re:Invent 2017 showing the various stages of the analytics pipeline and also maps the AWS services to the various stages of the pipeline.

FIGURE 1.4   AWS analytics architecture

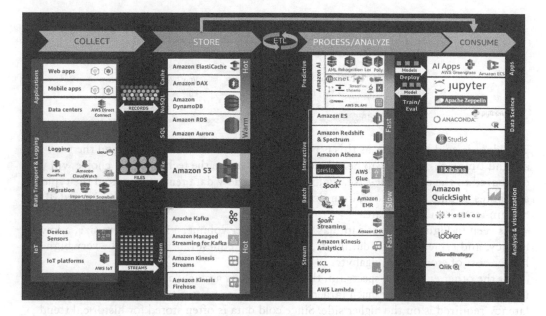

Data Characteristics: Hot, Warm, and Cold

Choosing the right technology for processing depends on the characteristics of data, which can vary from cold to hot. You may have heard of the term *multitemperature data management*, where the temperature of the data is determined by the frequency with which the data is accessed, the frequency at which the data is updated and maintained, the levels of durability needed, and the depths of history you would like to maintain.

Let us look at an example of a financial institution that has data for all its customers: their online profile, the transactions that they have done over the years, and so forth. Consider the following set of transactions: The customer is going on Amazon.com to purchase some essential items for its daily use. Any financial institution would carry fraud detection on individual transactions; hence, your use case here not only requires you to capture the data in real time, but also to identify if the transaction is fraudulent or not, based on the customer and the transaction profile. The fact that you need to not only capture the transaction in real time but also perform an analytics operation on it indicates that your data collection technology will be defined by the use case, which in this case requires you to do stream processing, and your processing technology will also be defined by the use case, which defines what temperature of data you are dealing with.

As your time to action is relatively lower, this is the case for hot data, and hence the technological choice will be defined where the selected technologies meet your demands of low latency and high-speed access.

Let us consider another transaction or sets of transactions that happened over fourteen years ago. The customer has made a complaint to a regulatory authority about overcharging (such as payment protection insurance, or PPI claims in the UK), and you have been given six weeks to respond to the complaint or reimburse the customer based on this claim.

FIGURE 1.5   Data characteristics for hot, warm, and cold data

	Hot	Warm	Cold
Volume	MB–GB	GB–TB	PB–EB
Item size	B–KB	KB–MB	KB–TB
Latency	ms	ms, sec	min, hrs
Durability	Low–high	High	Very high
Request rate	Very high	High	Low
Cost/GB	$$–$	$–¢¢	¢
	Hot data	Warm data	Cold data

This data is cold by nature, as this is not frequently accessed or updated, and the turn-around time does not have to be sub-seconds, and hence the technological choice will vary compared to the earlier use-case. Figure 1.5 shows how data temperature and the typical attributes of data like volume, item size, latency, durability, request rates, and cost/GB at certain temperature compare.

As seen in Figure 1.5, hot data has typically lower volume, a smaller item size, a lower latency, and typically lower durability, whereas the request rate can often be very high at a higher cost of storage per gigabyte.

At the other end of the spectrum, the cold data has a much larger volume, but the individual items can be of much larger size (sometimes up to a few terabytes), and the latency required is on the higher side. Since cold data is often stored for historical trend analysis or regulatory compliance purposes, the durability needs to be very high but the request rate is on the lower side. You can therefore expect to query your hot data more often than your warm or cold data. You'll see in later chapters that typically the cost per gigabyte is on the lower side, and in fact there are tools available that can use machine learning to move the data from the hot to cold and vice versa based on the request rate, or defined periods of time.

Collection/Ingest

A number of different technologies can be used to collect/ingest data. The type of technology you choose can depend on a variety of factors, including the volume of data being captured, the variety of the data, and the velocity in which it needs to be captured. Generally speaking, there are three major types of data that need to be collected from sources, including but not limited to the following types:

Transactions   Transactions include data arriving in various data structures, such as from POS systems, web apps, mobile applications, and so on. Transactions can be captured by various technologies like AWS Glue, AWS Data Pipeline, AWS Data Migration Service, and other partner ETL technologies available on AWS marketplace. An example of this would be your existing data relational database that is perhaps running MySQL and you would like to capture the transactions to perform analytics inside your analytics platform. The data can be captured with the technologies mentioned above. You might also need to capture changes happening to the main data store, and these are also captured using a variety of technologies that we will discuss later in the book.

Files   Files include data that is being captured from logging files, media files, and website logs, which often arrive in the form of data files. There are various technologies that allow you to capture the data from files including Flume, AWS CloudTrail, and Amazon CloudWatch. Typically, this is the case when data is generated from media streams or application log files.

Events   Events include data that is being generated by your IoT platforms and devices such as noise sensors and temperature sensors and often arrives in the form of streams. However, these events can be any data that is arriving in high velocity that needs to be captured for on-stream or down-stream processing. A number of technologies can be used to capture such data from AWS, including but not limited to Amazon Kinesis, Amazon Managed Streaming for Kafka, Apache Kafka, and some partner solutions.

Storage

AWS offers a variety of storage options. One of the best practices for building a future-proof, scalable, secure, and high-performance analytics platform is to choose the right tool for the right job. Today there is a large choice of tools that you can use, depending on the requirements of your use case. The storage choices include in-memory storage for high-speed process, NoSQL for well-defined access paths, SQL for ad hoc access, file/object storage for data files without any defined structure and for huge volumes at a relatively cheaper price point, and stream storage for low-latency access and analytics.
The AWS platform offers stream storage for hot data, which can either be Kafka-based or Amazon Kinesis-based. Stream storage allows you to decouple your producers and consumers and provide a persistent buffer for your data and ensures client ordering.

Stream storage options:

- Kafka
  - Apache Kafka
  - Managed Streaming for Kafka

- Kinesis
  - Amazon Kinesis Data Streams
  - Amazon Kinesis Firehose

For warm and cold data, Amazon supports Amazon S3 (Simple Storage Service), which is natively supported by major ETL tools and also most popular big data frameworks like Spark, Hive, and Presto. Amazon S3 allows you the option to scale your compute independently of storage. We will look at the data lake architecture later in this chapter and explain how S3 forms the key pillar of an analytics ecosystem built on the cloud. You must have heard a lot about S3 and possibly used it as well. The key reasons customers decide to use S3 are as follows:

- Support for infinite volumes of data (the ability to easily scale your storage to exabytes)

- Support for big data frameworks (Spark, Hive, Presto, and so on)

- High durability
- Intelligent tiering (moving the data from high-durability/high-cost to low-durability/low-cost automatically)
- Secure
- Low cost per gigabyte

Some customers tend to look at Apache Hadoop Distributed File System (HDFS) on a Hadoop cluster as a persistent store; however, there are certain cases where HDFS can be used for the hottest datasets (e.g., when working iteratively on a certain dataset), and Amazon S3 can be used for frequently accessed data. We'll discuss this in more detail in Chapter 4, "Data Processing and Analysis."

For the warm and hot data, Amazon supports various options that fall into three major categories:

SQL-Based Systems Amazon offers Amazon RDS, which is a managed relational database service for SQL-based operations to store the data.

NoSQL-Based Systems Amazon offers Amazon DynamoDB and Amazon DocumentDB, which are managed NoSQL services. We will learn more about them in Chapter 3, "Data Storage."

Cache Repositories Amazon also offers Amazon ElastiCache, which is a managed Memcached and Redis service, and Amazon DynamoDB Accelerator (DAX), which is an in-memory cache for DynamoDB to offer low latency and high throughput.

As discussed earlier in this chapter, it is important to pick the right tool for the right job. The decade-old tradition of trying to retrofit every use case in a relational engine, a NoSQL engine, or any other technology that you have had previous success with on a different use case makes things complicated not only from initial implementation but for long-term management as well. The abundance of managed solutions and partner products from the marketplace on the AWS platform allows you to pick the right tool for the job. Your application architecture can now benefit from a variety of in-memory, graph, NoSQL, SQL, and search technologies, thus allowing you to focus on the correct long-term architecture rather than working around the technological limits to ensure that you can focus on the true essence of your business problem. The amount of integration effort that organizations have spent in retrofitting their use cases to a technological limitation has been huge. and the breadth and depth of the AWS ecosystem allows us to shun these anti-patterns.

Process/Analyze

Once the data has been ingested and stored based on the optimum storage option, you can either process the data for downstream analytics or run analytics as is if the data is in a suitable format. The types of processing and analytics depends on a number of factors but can be categorized into the following categories:

Batch Processing and Analytics   Batch processing includes workloads that take minutes to hours to run and often include things like daily, weekly, or monthly reports. For batch processing, the technologies that generally work well include Amazon EMR. Customers often use AWS Glue, which is a fully managed (serverless) ETL service that makes it simple and cost effective to categorize your data.

Interactive Analytics   Interactive analytics includes workloads that take seconds, and examples include self-service dashboards built using technologies like Amazon QuickSight or technologies like Tableau and ad hoc access with Amazon Athena and Amazon EMR with Presto and Spark.

Stream Processing and Analytics   Stream processing analytics includes workloads like fraud detection where the latency is seconds to milliseconds and includes technologies like Spark Streaming (within Amazon EMR), Amazon Kinesis Analytics, KCL, AWS Lambda, Apache Flink, and Kafka.

Predictive Analytics   Predictive analytics includes workloads like churn prediction, fraud detection, anomaly detection, demand forecasting, and speech recognition with response time from milliseconds (real-time predictive analytics) to minutes (batch) using technologies like Lex, Polly, Amazon Rekognition, and Amazon machine learning (ML) and deep learning AMIs with frameworks like MxNet, TensorFlow, Theano, Torch, CNTK, and Caffe.

Consumption

Once an entire data pipeline is established to capture, store, and process the data, you then have a number of options to consume the data in various forms. There are various personas who consume the data and insights generated on AWS, and it is important to understand what those personas are and how they consume the information and insights generated on your analytical platform.

Developers and Operations   Developers and operations teams often develop, manage, and run apps on EC2 or ECS containers consuming the data assets generated via the data pipeline.

Data Scientists   Data scientists work with the data to understand patterns within it, build models, and deploy models in production. They like to work with interactive interfaces like Notebooks (Jupyter, Zepplin), SageMaker, and other data science platforms and IDEs.

Data scientists also like to work directly with APIs (e.g., Spark DataFrame API, Glue DynamicFrame API) to work natively with them and have more control over how the data engineering and data modeling happens.

Business Users   Business users consume the data to build reports and dashboards using a variety of tools available on AWS, such as first-class services like Kibana or QuickSight or tools available on the AWS marketplace like Tableau, Qlik, MicroStrategy, and Looker.

Data Lakes and Their Relevance in Analytics

Data is growing at enormous rates, and all industry reports point toward exponential growth of data. The variety of data types include structured and semi-structured data and multiple open-source formats. Based on what we have seen at various customer sites, data grows tenfold every 5 years, and with the average life of a platform around 15 years, a platform built for 1 terabyte today would need to host around 1 petabyte (a thousandfold increase) in 15 years' time. The growth of data with the rise of open-source formats, along with the growth in the number of people accessing the data in a variety of ways, places greater demand on the flexibility in the ways in which the data is accessed, the service-level agreements (SLAs) in which the data is made available, and the massive scale of operation required to achieve optimal results. All of this needs to be done within the security parameters defined for an organization. Customers are demanding an architecture that solves these problems, and one of the answers the industry has to offer for these requirements is a data lake architecture. This is an advanced-level book, and I expect more people to be aware of what a data lake is, but I would still like to recap some of the major concepts.

What Is a Data Lake?

Wikipedia's definition of *data lake*, which can be found at en.wikipedia.org/wiki/ Data_lake, is quite a comprehensive definition. I often talk to customers about data lakes, and I often emphasize the fact that data lake is a not a technology but rather an architectural concept. The objective of a data lake is to create a central repository where you can store data in a variety of formats, and the repository itself is built on a technology that is scalable in nature and provides ways and means to load and access the data from a variety of tools.

In summary any data lake platform needs to have the following properties:

- All data in a single place
- Handles structured/semi-structured/unstructured/raw data
- Supports fast ingestion and consumption
- Schema on read vs. Schema on write
- Designed for low-cost, multi-tiered storage
- Decouples storage and compute—the key objective is to scale the storage tier independently of the compute tier. This is required in cases where your storage would grow exponentially but your compute grows linearly.
- Supports protection and security rules

Now that you have a brief idea of what a data lake is, you might be interested in the key steps involved in building one data lake. The next section, "Building a Data Lake on AWS," explains on a high level the key steps required to build a data lake. Whatever technological choice that you make for a data lake, the steps would remain the same. Figure 1.6 is a pictorial representation of various important steps in building a data lake and has been referenced from AWS's public-facing material on Data Lakes.

There are various steps involved in building a data lake; the major ones are as follows:

1. **Set up storage:** Data lakes hold a massive amount of data. Before doing anything else, customers need to set up storage to hold all of that data in raw formats. If they are using AWS, they would need to configure S3 buckets and partitions. If they are doing this on-premises, they would need to acquire hardware and set up large disk arrays to hold all of the data for their data lake.

2. **Move data:** Customers need to connect to different data sources on-premises, in the cloud, and on IoT devices. Then they need to collect and organize the relevant datasets from those sources, crawl the data to extract the schemas, and add metadata tags to the catalog. Customers do this today with a collection of file transfer mechanisms and ETL tools, like AWS Glue, Informatica, and Talend.

3. **Clean and prepare data:** Next, the data must be carefully partitioned, indexed, and transformed to columnar formats to optimize for performance and cost. Customers need to clean, deduplicate, and match related records. Storing data in columnar formats benefits the analytical workloads, which often operate on a subset of the columns rather than the entire list. Today this is done using rigid and complex SQL statements that only work so well and are difficult to maintain. This process of collecting, cleaning, and transforming the incoming data is complex and must be manually monitored in order to avoid errors.

4. **Configure and enforce policies:** Sensitive data must be secured according to compliance requirements. This means creating and applying data access, protection, and compliance policies to make sure you are meeting required standards: for example, restricting access to personally identifiable information (PII) at the table, column, or row level; encrypting all data; and keeping audit logs of who is accessing the data. Today customers use access control lists on S3 buckets, or they use third-party encryption and access control software to secure the data. And for every analytics service that needs to access the data, customers need to create and maintain data access, protection. and compliance policies for each one. For example, if you are running analysis against your data lake using Redshift and Athena, you need to set up access control rules for each of these services.

5. **Make data available to analysts:** Different people in your organizations, like analysts and data scientists, may have trouble finding and trusting datasets in the data lake. You need to make it easy for those end users to find relevant and trusted data. To do this you must clearly label the data in a catalog of the data lake and provide users with the ability to access and analyze this data without making requests to IT.

FIGURE 1.6   Typical steps in building a data lake

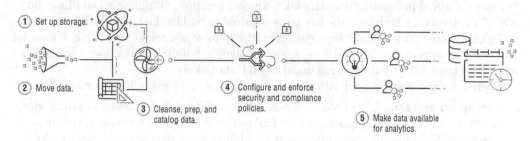

The steps in the data lake are defined clearly. The following list presents a set of best practices that are important while building a data lake project. The key architectural principles for your data lake and analytics project are as follows:

Decouple your data bus: data > store > process > analyze > answers.   For solution architects, this is the key to building a scalable architecture. Each individual piece of the data bus needs to be decoupled, thus allowing each of the pieces to be replaced by different components if and when needed or scaled independently of the other. If your storage is growing faster than your compute, it is important to separate both of them to ensure that you can scale one of them independently of the other.

Don't retrofit use cases into the tool: data structure, latency, throughput, access patterns.   There is an old saying that if all you own is hammer, everything looks like a nail. This architectural principle is the key to building an architecture that meets the needs of your business rather than limiting your implementation because of a choice of a tool that was made based on certain other requirements in the past. Companies were traditionally limiting themselves to a single tool because of the huge costs involved in acquiring new software. It is always important to remember that with the AWS cloud, you have a number of different tools available, each meeting a particular business need, and hence using the appropriate tool is not only cost effective but also provides better performance. It goes without saying that this helps the organization to focus on the actual business problem and innovation rather than spending time building the data pipelines. The benefit of the AWS platform is that you will only be paying for the amount of usage rather than the number of tools you are using, and hence the cost of failure is minimal, thus allowing you to experiment and innovate.

Use managed services whenever and wherever possible: scalable/elastic, available, reliable, secure, no/low admin.   The most successful organizations I have worked with are the ones that are focusing on solving their business problems rather than spending resources on the technical plumbing, which is not their core business. For example, if your core business is running a financial services organization, you would gain little value by running your own fleet of clusters of a particular technology. Most successful customers would opt for managed services rather than opting to build complex technology stacks that are hard to build but even harder to maintain and extend.

Use log-centric design patterns: immutable logs (data lake), materialized views.   It is important to ensure that the original data loaded to the data lake or arriving at the analytics platform remains immutable and does not change. I often see a few customers who change the data from one format to another using any given transformation tool but then discarding the original source data. This is a non-recommended approach for most use cases as it leads to an inability to trace any reporting inaccuracies back to the original source. The value of keeping the original data in its original state cannot be emphasized more, other than stating that it is quintessential to keep the raw data in the raw format for data lineage and compliance reasons.

Be cost conscious: big data should not be big cost.   Big data does not imply that the cost of building an analytics pipeline should be big too. Decoupling storage and compute and using multi-tiered storage would allow you to reduce your storage and compute costs. Furthermore, using managed services would allow you to reduce your operational and management costs.

AI/ML enable your applications.   As an end user developing products, you need to understand that having AI/ML in your applications and products is no more a nice-to-have, and in fact you need to rely on the data that you produce to build more effective models and use them to improve your products.

Now that we have looked at the concepts of a data lake, the steps behind building a data lake, and some of the key architectural patterns, let us look at how you can build a data lake on AWS.

Building a Data Lake on AWS

AWS offers a depth and breadth of different services that are useful in building the data lake on the platform. While Figure 1.7 looks at the AWS platform, a number of these technologies can be replaced by other products from the partner ecosystem that offer the same features and functions. We'll look at the different steps required to build a data lake on AWS.

Step 1: Choosing the Right Storage – Amazon S3 Is the Base

Amazon S3 is the central pillar of the AWS data lake story. Amazon S3 is secure and highly scalable and offers durable object storage with millisecond latency for data access. It allows you to store any type of data, from unstructured (logs, dump files) and semi-structured (XML, JSON) to structured data (CSV, Parquet), including data from websites, mobile apps, corporate applications, and IOT sensors at any scale.

Amazon S3 integrates storage lifecycle management and uses machine learning to move data from S3-Standard Access to S3-Infrequent Access, thus optimizing the cost for your analytics platform. S3 also allows you to create lifecycle policies for deep archive, ensuring that all data can be stored at an optimum price point.

Amazon S3 includes inbuilt disaster recovery by having the data replicated across multiple AZs and provides very high aggregated bandwidth.

In addition, Amazon S3 natively supports big data frameworks like Spark, Hive, Presto, and many others, which makes the partner ecosystem very strong. A lot of companies have moved

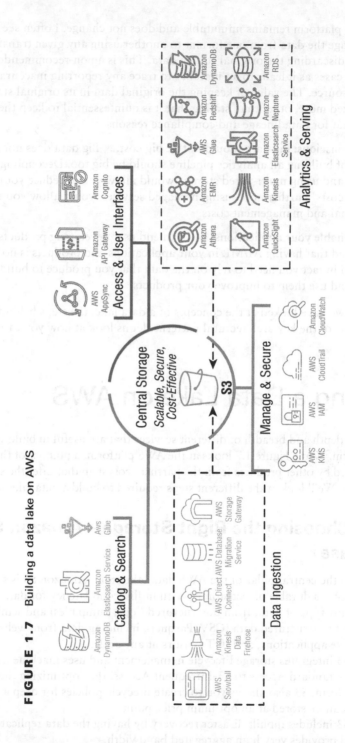

FIGURE 1.7 Building a data lake on AWS

to S3 from Hadoop Distributed File System (HDFS), with one of the major reasons being S3's ability to apply various computation techniques on the same dataset, thus effectively separating compute and storage. Amazon S3 supports 99.999999999% (eleven nines) of durability and provides huge volumes of storage at a fraction of the cost of traditional data storage options.

Step 2: Data Ingestion – Moving the Data into the Data Lake

Once you have identified S3 as your core storage engine, you need to find ways to move the data into S3. Data movement depends on a variety of factors, including the volume, variety, and velocity at which it is appearing. If you look at the left-hand side of Figure 1.8, you can see that AWS provides a number of data ingestion options, with each technology working best in certain situations.

If you need to move data from on-premises data centers to S3 and you require high throughput and bandwidth, you might need to provide a dedicated connection between the source data center and your data lake in S3. AWS Direct Connect would be the right choice in such a case. We would look at Direct Connect in more detail during in Chapter 2, "Data Collection" later in the book.

Moving large amounts of data is always tricky in data migrations. If you would like to move multiple terabytes of data into S3, the S3 CLI, which operates over an Internet connection, might not be the fastest option, and hence options like AWS Snowball make more sense. If your data exceeds a few terabytes and is in the petabyte or exabyte zone, AWS provides options like AWS Snowmobile. We'll look at each of these options in Chapter 2, "Data Collection" later in the book.

FIGURE 1.8   Moving data into S3

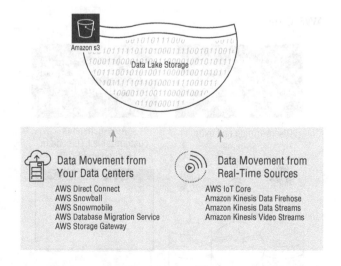

Data from IOT devices like sensors arrives in high velocity and needs to be captured for further processing. Amazon offers engines like Kinesis Firehose, which can be used to capture the data and store it in Amazon S3 for other analytical processing.

When moving data from databases onto Amazon S3, there are a couple of options when it comes to AWS native services. AWS Glue and AWS Database Migration Service can be used to move data from existing SQL database engines into an S3 data lake.

We'll look into each of these services in more detail in Chapter 2, "Data Collection" and Chapter 4, "Data Processing and Analysis."

Step 3: Cleanse, Prep, and Catalog the Data

Once the data has been acquired from the source systems and brought into Amazon S3, it is a common practice to cleanse, prep, and catalog the data. Amazon provides AWS Glue, which is a serverless ETL engine that allows you to automatically discover the data and identify its schema, making the metadata searchable to author other ETL jobs. Glue will allow you to generate code that can be customized, and schedule your ETL jobs, allowing you to bookmark your progress. Figure 1.9 shows the Data Catalog and ETL Job authoring aspects of AWS Glue. As Glue is a managed service, Glue users benefit from the serverless nature of the platform, where they develop their ETL on the console, and Glue runs the jobs in Spark clusters at the backend, managing the spin up of clusters, execution of the jobs, and shutdown of the clusters without manual user intervention. We'll look at AWS Glue in Chapter 2, "Data Collection" later in this book.

Building a catalog of your data is essential and invaluable as it allows other AWS services like Athena, EMR, and Redshift to reuse the catalog. We'll look into the details of the catalog and another service called AWS Lake Formation, which simplifies the process of building a data lake, later in this book.

FIGURE 1.9 AWS Glue

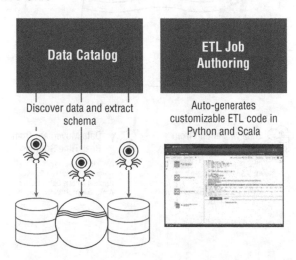

Step 4: Secure the Data and Metadata

Since your data is in a central place, and you have already extracted the metadata for your data lake in the form of a catalog, it becomes critical to secure not only the data but also the associated metadata. By default, all Amazon S3 buckets are private, and you have the ability to use resource-based policies (S3 bucket policies and IAM user policies) and KMS to enable client and server-side encryption for your data. S3 also allows you to use object tagging in conjunction with IAM. We'll look at all of these in Chapter 3, "Data Storage" and Chapter 6, "Data Security" where we will be discussing S3 in more detail.

As discussed earlier, you can use AWS Glue to furnish metadata for the data available without your data lake, and the metadata can be secured using various policies.

1. Use of identity-based policies to secure metadata:
   a. AWS IAM policies that are managed by IAM
   b. AWS IAM policies, which are attached to IAM principals such as IAM users and IAM roles
2. Use of resource-based policies to secure metadata:
   a. Resource-based policies are managed by AWS Glue.
   b. One policy per account/catalog
   c. Allows cross-account access

We'll look into these in much more detail in Chapter 6, "Data Security."

Step 5: Make Data Available for Analytics

Once the data has been acquired, stored, and preprocessed, the next step is to make data available for analytics. There are various analytics services available, like Redshift, Amazon ElasticSearch Service, EMR, and QuickSight, to name a few within AWS, with each one of them serving a variety of use cases. We've looked on a higher level at the types of services available in the Process/Analyze section earlier in this chapter, and will look to go into more detail during the Chapter 4, "Data Processing and Analysis" and Chapter 5, "Data Visualization" later in this book.

Using Lake Formation to Build a Data Lake on AWS

As you can see from the process just discussed, the building of a data lake is often a very involved process, and once the lake is built, setting up the security to ensure that different downstream services can access the data in the lake can be quite laborious, and it can often take months to set up the lake internally. Amazon announced AWS Lake Formation during re:Invent 2018 to automate the process of building a data lake in a few clicks from a single unified dashboard. The objective of the service is to reduce the time to set up a data lake from months to days.

AWS simplifies the process of setting up a data lake by bringing the various stages involved to a single console. AWS Lake Formation allows you to crawl your data sources, move the data into an Amazon S3 data lake, and then uses machine learning to automatically lay out the data into Amazon S3 partitions and change it into a columnar format like Parquet and ORC for faster analytics.

Deduplication of data is one of the most critical data processing tasks that is required since the data is coming from a number of different sources. AWS Lake Formation allows you to deduplicate and find matching records to increase the data quality.

Setting up access and permissions at the user, table, and column level is also a challenge in a traditional data lake build and usually consumes lots of time during the data lake build phase.

AWS Lake Formation allows you to set up all the permissions for the data lake from a single screen, which will then be implemented across all services consuming the data from the data lake, including but not limited to Amazon Redshift, Amazon Athena, and Amazon EMR.

Now that we have looked on a higher level at the services, let's look at the exam objectives. This book is essentially written to help you learn more about AWS Analytics stack but also to pass the AWS Certified Data Analytics - Specialty certification.

Exam Objectives

The *AWS Certified Data Analytics – Specialty certification exam* is intended for people who have experience designing and building analytical projects on AWS. You should understand the following exam concepts:

- Designing, developing, and deploying cloud-based solutions using AWS
- Designing and developing analytical projects on AWS using the AWS technology stack
- Designing and developing data pipelines
- Designing and developing data collection architectures
- An understanding of the operational characteristics of the collection systems
- Selection of collection systems that handle frequency, volume, and the source of the data
- Understanding the different types of approaches of data collection and how the approaches differentiate from each other on the data formats, ordering, and compression
- Designing optimal storage and data management systems to cater for the volume, variety, and velocity
- Understanding the operational characteristics of analytics storage solutions

- Understanding of the access and retrieval patterns of data
- Understanding of appropriate data layout, schema, structure, and format
- Understanding of the data lifecycle based on the usage patterns and business requirements
- Determining the appropriate system for the cataloging of data and metadata
- Identifying the most appropriate data processing solution based on business SLAs, data volumes, and cost
- Designing a solution for transformation of data and preparing for further analysis
- Automating appropriate data visualization solutions for a given scenario
- Identifying appropriate authentication and authorization mechanisms
- Applying data protection and encryption techniques
- Applying data governance and compliance controls

Objective Map

The following table lists each domain and its weighting in the exam, along with the chapters in the book where that domain's objectives and subobjectives are covered.

Domain	Percentage of Exam	Chapter
Domain 1.0: Data Collection	18%	1, 2,3
1.1– Determine the operational characteristics of the collection system.		
1.2– Select a collection system that handles the frequency, volume and source of data.		
1.3– Select a collection system that addresses the key properties of the data, such as order, format and compression.		
Domain 2.0: Storage and Data Management	22%	3,4
2.1– Determine the operational characteristics of the analytics storage solution.		
2.2– Determine data access and retrieval patterns.		
2.3– Select appropriate data layout, schema, structure and format.		
2.4– Define a data lifecycle based on usage patterns and business requirements.		
2.5– Determine the appropriate system for cataloguing data and managing metadata.		

Domain	Percentage of Exam	Chapter
Domain 3.0: Processing	20%	3, 4
3.1– Determine appropriate data processing solution requirements.		
3.2– Design a solution for transforming and preparing data for analysis.		
3.3– Automate and operationalize a data processing solution.		
Domain 4.0: Analysis and Visualization	16%	3, 4, 5
4.1– Determine the operational characteristics of an analysis and visualization layer.		
4.2– Select the appropriate data analysis solution for a given scenario.		
4.3– Select the appropriate data visualization solution for a given scenario.		
Domain 5.0: Security	24%	2, 3, 4, 5, 6
5.1– Select appropriate authentication and authorization mechanisms.		
5.2– Apply data protection and encryption techniques.		
5.3– Apply data governance and compliance controls.		

It is important to understand and note that this book will provide you with an understanding of the exam objectives: however, the exam covers such a vast area of expertise that it is impossible to cover in a single book. It is highly recommended that you ensure reading additional topics as discussed in the further reading sections at the end of each chapter. We are also providing sample labs and workshops that will help you get acquainted with the technology under discussion. Finally, it is certainly likely that you will get questions in the exam which are around topics which are not directly addressed in the book, and hence a reading of the whitepapers, FAQs, and supplemental reading material is key to acing the exam.

Assessment Test

The following assessment test will give you a general idea about your analytics skillset on AWS and can identify areas where you should apply more focus. This test touches upon some basic concepts but will give you an indication of what types of questions you can expect from the AWS Analytics Certified Data Specialty certification exam.

1. An organization looking to build a real-time operational analytics dashboard for its mobile gaming application is looking at various options to build the dashboard. Which of the following options will provide the right performance characteristics for such an application?

   A. Use Amazon S3 to power the dashboard.

   B. Use Amazon Redshift to power the dashboard.

   C. Use Amazon Elasticsearch Service to power the dashboard.

   D. Use Amazon DynamoDB to power the dashboard.

2. An administrator has a 6 GB file in Amazon S3. The administrator runs a nightly COPY command into a 2-node (32 slices) Amazon Redshift cluster. The administrator wants to prepare the data to optimize performance of the COPY command. What is the best way for the administrator to prepare the data?

   A. Compress the file using gzip compression.

   B. Split the file into 64 files of equal size.

   C. Split the file into 500 smaller files.

   D. Split the file into 32 files of equal size.

3. A customer wants to build a log analytics solution on AWS with sub-second latency for the search facility. An additional requirement is to build a dashboard for the operations staff. Which of the following technologies would provide a more optimal solution?

   A. Store the logs in Amazon S3 and use Amazon Athena to query the logs. Use Amazon QuickSight to build the dashboard.

   B. Store the logs in Amazon Redshift and use Query Editor to access the logs. Use Amazon QuickSight to build the dashboard.

   C. Store the logs in Amazon Elasticsearch Service and use Kibana to build a dashboard.

   D. Store the logs in HDFS on an EMR cluster. Use Hive to query the logs. Use Amazon QuickSight to build the dashboard.

4. A leading telecommunications provider is moving to AWS and has around 50 TB of data in its on-premises Hadoop environment, stored in HDFS, and is using Spark SQL to analyze the data. The customer has asked for a cost-effective and efficient solution to migrate onto AWS quickly, over a 100 mbps (megabits per second) connection, to be able to build a catalog that can be used by other services and analyze the data while managing as few servers as possible. Which solution would be best for this customer?

   A. Migrate the data using S3 commands using CLI interface to Amazon S3, use AWS Glue to crawl the data and build a catalog, and analyze it using Amazon Athena.

B. Migrate the data to S3 using AWS Snowball, use AWS Glue to crawl the data and build a catalog, and analyze it using Amazon Athena.

C. Migrate the data using Amazon Snowball to Amazon S3, use Hive on EMR running Spark to build a catalog, and analyze the data using Spark SQL.

D. Migrate the data using CLI interface to AMAZON S3, use Hive on EMR running Spark to build a catalog, and analyze the data using Spark SQL.

5. A leading financial organization is looking to migrate its enterprise data warehouse to AWS. It has 30 TB of data in its data warehouse but is only using 500 GB for reporting and dashboarding while the remaining data is occasionally required for compliance purposes. Which of the following is a more cost-effective solution?

A. Migrate the data to AWS. Create an EMR cluster with attached HDFS storage hosting the 30 TB of data. Use Amazon QuickSight for dashboarding and Hive for compliance reporting requirements.

B. Migrate the data to Amazon S3. Create a Redshift cluster hosting the 30 TB of data. Use QuickSight for dashboarding and Athena for querying from S3.

C. Migrate the data to Amazon S3. Create a Redshift cluster hosting the 500 GB of data. Use Amazon QuickSight for dashboarding and Redshift Spectrum for querying the remaining data when required.

D. Migrate the data to AWS in an Amazon Elasticsearch Service cluster. Use Kibana for dashboarding and Logstash for querying the data from the ES cluster.

6. An upcoming gaming startup is collecting gaming logs from its recently launched and hugely popular game. The logs are arriving in JSON format with 500 different attributes for each record. The CMO has requested a dashboard based on six attributes that indicate the revenue generated based on the in-game purchase recommendations as generated by the marketing departments ML team. The data is on S3 in raw JSON format, and a report is being generated using QuickSight on the data available. Currently the report creation takes an hour, whereas publishing the report is very quick. Furthermore, the IT department has complained about the cost of data scans on S3.

They have asked you as a solutions architect to provide a solution that improves performance and optimizes the cost. Which of the following options is most suitable to meet the requirements?

A. Use AWS Glue to convert the JSON data into CSV format. Crawl the converted CSV format data with Glue Crawler and build a report using Amazon Athena. Build the front end on Amazon QuickSight.

B. Load the JSON data to Amazon Redshift in a VARCHAR column. Build the report using SQL and front end on QuickSight.

C. Load the JSON data to Amazon Redshift. Extract the reportable attributes from the JSON column in the tables. Build the report using SQL and front end on QuickSight.

D. Use AWS Glue to convert the JSON data into Parquet format. Crawl the converted Parquet format with Glue Crawler, and build a report using Athena. Build the front end on Amazon QuickSight.

7. A leading manufacturing organization is running a large Redshift cluster and has complained about slow query response times. What configuration options would you check to identify the root cause of the problem?

    A. The number and type of columns in the table

    B. Primary and secondary key constraints

    C. Alignment of the table's sort key with predicates in the SELECT statement

    D. The number of rows in the table

    E. The partition schema for the database

8. Your customer has asked you to help build a data lake on S3. The source system is MySQL, Oracle, and standard CSV files. The data does not have any incremental key. The customer expects you to capture the initial data dump and changes during the data lake build phase. What tools/technologies would you recommend to reduce the overall cost of migration?

    A. Load the initial dump and changes using AWS Glue.

    B. Load the initial dump and changes using DMS (Database Migration Service).

    C. Load the initial dump with AWS Glue and capture changes with AWS Glue and DMS (Database Migration Service).

    D. Load the initial dump using DMS (Database Migration Service) and changes in the data with AWS Glue.

9. A QuickSight dashboard allows you to view the source data but not make any changes to it.

    A. True

    B. False

10. Amazon QuickSight can interpret your charts and tables for you and suggest insights in plain English.

    A. True

    B. False

References

1. www.weforum.org/agenda/2015/02/a-brief-history-of-big-data-everyone-should-read/

2. www.kdnuggets.com/2017/07/4-types-data-analytics.html

3. research.google.com/archive/gfs-sosp2003.pdf

4. research.google.com/archive/mapreduce-osdi04.pdf

5. en.wikipedia.org/wiki/Amazon_Web_Services

6. open.blogs.nytimes.com/2007/11/01/self-service-prorated-super-computing-fun/

7. AWS Re-Invent Presentation by Siva Raghupathy in 2017 www.youtube.com/watch?v=a3713oGB6Zk

Chapter

2

Data Collection

As discussed in the first chapter, data collection is the first step in building a big data pipeline. The objective of data collection is to store the data on the AWS platform to extract insights and predict possible events happening in the future. In this chapter, we will discuss the different types of ingestion and the appropriate technologies that are suitable for each type. In summary, there are three types of data sources that we will have to work with to collect the data:

- Existing transactional systems (such as CRM systems or POS systems), which are typically based on databases like Aurora, MySQL, Oracle, Microsoft SQL Server
- Streaming data coming from IoT devices, sensors, social media
- Files coming from web servers (such as logs)

Each of these sources can provide data with different volume and velocity, depending on the type of the source. For example, existing transactional systems would typically provide structured data, which is pretty consistent in terms of its structure, whereas data coming from sensors and IoT devices can often change its structure based on the latest OS versions, application types, and so on.

Exam Objectives

This chapter maps to Domain 1: Collection which represents 18% of the exam questions. The key objectives of the exam include the following:

1.1 Determine the operational characteristics of the collection system.

1.2 Select a collection system that handles the frequency, volume, and source of data.

1.3 Select a collection system that addresses the key properties of data, such as order, format, and compression.

This section covers almost 1/5th of your exam. You will have to read the text given in this chapter, including the additional reading material and ensure that you run the workshops provided at the end of this chapter. A majority of the questions will provide a scenario, and give you multiple possible solutions, where one of the solutions fits the given requirement. It is important to understand that during these professional level exams, most if not all solutions are generally practical and possible; however, only one of them is the best fit for the given scenario on a cost, scalability, reliability, and security requirement.

AWS IoT

The *Internet of Things (IoT)* has emerged as a critical driver for our technological future, both at work and at home. With around 20 billion data generating devices in use today, the influence of the IoT is everywhere, touching nearly every facet of our daily lives. The proliferation of devices across our daily lives means that there is a need to connect the devices and collect, store, and analyze the data being generated from them. The AWS platform provides AWS IoT as a means to provide broad and deep functionality, spanning the edge to the cloud, so that customers have the right tools to build IoT solutions for virtually any use case across a wide range of devices. The software kit includes device software, *Amazon FreeRTOS* (IoT operating system for microcontrollers), and *AWS IoT Greengrass*, which provides the ability for local data collection and analysis.

Since AWS IoT integrates with AI services, you can make devices smarter even without Internet connectivity. AWS IoT provides the ability to create models in the cloud and then deploy them on the devices, thus providing superior performance while sending data back to the cloud to retrain the models for continuous improvement.

AWS IoT is built on the AWS cloud and is used by millions of customers across the globe. It can easily scale as your device fleet grows and your business requirements evolve. With integration to services like AWS Lambda, Amazon S3, and Amazon SageMaker, you can create end-to-end solutions with services that natively integrate with each other and reduce the time spent on technical plumbing.

AWS IoT also offers comprehensive security features so you can create preventative security policies and respond immediately to potential security issues. Security offerings including encryption, access controls, and continuous monitoring and auditing and alerting for potential issues, thus allowing you the ability to react faster to any potential issues and push security fixes back to the devices.

AWS IoT is not a single service but rather provides the complete ecosystem to build, monitor, and analyze an IoT platform. These are the three biggest challenges in the IoT world:

- Connectivity to devices, data collection, and performing actions on the devices
- Controlling, managing, and securing large fleets of devices
- Extracting the insights from the data being generated by the devices

AWS IoT provides three categories of services to help resolve these challenges:

Device Software   AWS IoT provides software to securely connect devices, gather data, and take intelligent actions locally on the device in the absence of Internet connectivity, as shown in Figure 2.1. The device software includes Amazon FreeRTOS (an IoT operating system for microcontrollers) and AWS IoT Greengrass, which extends AWS to the edge devices so that they can act locally on the data they generate while still using the cloud for management, analytics, and storage.

FIGURE 2.1   AWS IoT device software services

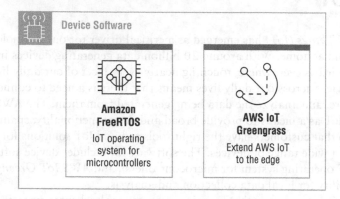

Control Services   AWS IoT also provides control services to control, manage, and secure large and diverse fleets of devices, as shown in Figure 2.2. The control services include AWS IoT Core, which is responsible for securing the device connectivity and messaging; AWS IoT Device Management to onboard fleets of devices and provides management and software updates to the fleet; AWS IoT Device Defender, which is responsible for fleet audit protection; and AWS IoT Things Graph, which is responsible to connect devices and web services.

FIGURE 2.2   AWS IoT control services

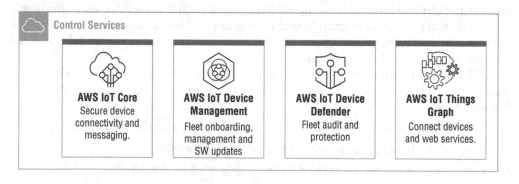

Data Services   Data generated from the IoT devices can help improve business processes and implement various use cases like predictive maintenance, improving business productivity, and providing overall connectivity within the building and throughout the supply chain (see Figure 2.3). AWS IoT therefore provides the following data services:

> **AWS IoT Analytics**   A fully managed service designed to run and operationalize sophisticated analytics on massive volumes of IoT data without worrying about associated complexity and expenses required to build such a massive

system. AWS IoT Analytics is not directly covered in the exam and hence we are not covering it in more detail during this book. If you would like to learn more on AWS IoT Analytics, please follow the link `https://aws.amazon.com/iot-analytics`

AWS IoT SiteWise   A fully managed service designed to make it easy to collect and organize data from industrial equipment at scale. You can monitor equipment across your industrial facilities to identify waste, such as breakdown of equipment and process, production inefficiencies, and defects in the products. AWS IoT SiteWise is not directly covered in the exam and hence we are not covering it in more detail during this book. If you would like to learn more on AWS IoT SiteWise, please follow the link `https://aws.amazon.com/iot-sitewise`.

AWS IoT Events   A fully managed service that makes it easier to detect and respond to events from IoT sensors and applications. Events are basically patterns of data identifying more complicated circumstances than normally expected. An example could be changes in equipment when a conveyer belt in an assembling plant is stuck or motion detectors using movement signals to activate lights and security cameras.

FIGURE 2.3   AWS IoT data services

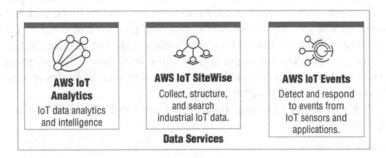

Common Use Cases for AWS IoT

Customers are using AWS IoT for many interesting use cases, but the top ones among them are as follows:

- Predictive maintenance
- Smart inventory management
- Wellness and health solutions
- Optimal asset utilization
- Productivity and process optimization

- Connected buildings, factories, and cities
- Facility management
- Logistics and supply chain optimization
- Geofencing
- Device fleet management
- Energy efficiency monitoring
- Payment and connected commerce
- Safeguarding manufacturing facilities
- Automated checkouts
- Smart shelves
- In-store layout optimization

How AWS IoT Works

AWS IoT is a managed platform that enables you to connect IoT devices to various AWS services and other devices in a secure manner. The AWS IoT platform allows you to process and act upon the device data and enable applications to interact with devices even when they are offline. The scale of the service allows it to support billions of devices and messages and process and route the messages to other devices. One of the major producers of big data are IoT devices, and hence the ability to have IoT devices work with big data services you can use to analyze the data on the stream and process and store it in a seamless fashion irrespective of the scale makes it easy to architect the big data applications.

From the exam perspective, it is important to know how these IoT devices interact with AWS IoT services and how each AWS IoT service interacts with analytics services on AWS to analyze the data and extract insights.

When an IoT device sends a message to the AWS IoT service, the IoT service triggers a "rule action" to write data to:

- An Elasticsearch domain
- A Kinesis Firehose stream
- A Kinesis Data Stream
- DynamoDB table
- Amazon ML

IoT services rule actions allow you to do the following:

- Change cloud watch alarm or capture metric.
- Write to S3 bucket.
- Write to SQS queue.
- Write to SNS as a push notification.
- Invoke a lambda function.

It is important for you as a candidate to know that you can create rule actions for various services, include Amazon Kinesis Data Streams and Amazon Kinesis Data Firehose, AWS Lambda service, Amazon DynamoDB, and Amazon ML service.

If you look at the Figure 2.4, on the left side is the AWS IoT Device SDK, which allows you to connect your devices to the AWS IoT service using HTTP, WebSockets, MQTT protocol, and other protocols.

FIGURE 2.4   AWS IoT - How it Works

Source: www.amazonaws.cn/en/iot-core/features

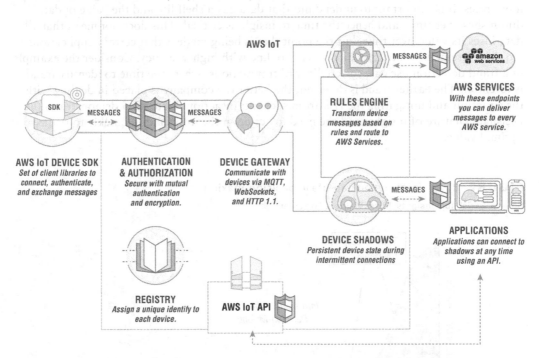

Security is essential from an IoT perspective when your devices have to connect to the AWS IoT service; authentication and authorization becomes critical. AWS IoT Core provides identity service for authentication and end-to-end encryption throughout all points of connection so that data is never exchanged between devices and AWS IoT without proven identity. You can secure access to your devices and applications by applying policies with granular permissions.

While AWS IoT was a critical part of the AWS Big Data Specialty exam, it is not a core service that you will be tested on in the new AWS Data Analytics Specialty certification exam, and hence we are not going to spend more time on it during this book. If you would like to learn more about AWS IoT and related services please visit https://docs.aws .amazon.com/iot/index.html.

Amazon Kinesis

Amazon Kinesis is part of the analytics portfolio within the AWS Analytics portfolio of services. Amazon Kinesis was launched after a huge demand from the customer to provide native AWS services to capture, process, and analyze streaming data. Most of the data generated today, as much as 95 percent of it, is unstructured data. With the growth of data, a majority of it is arriving in high velocity and needs to be captured, processed, analyzed, and acted upon while providing tremendous value in mining this data for insight. Streaming systems need to produce continual results at low latency on data with high and variable input rates. It is important to understand that data has a shelf life and the value of data diminishes over time, and hence the time to insight is critical. This does not mean that all data loses its value over time, but the point that is being made is that certain applications require extreme low latency while others are fine with higher latency. Consider the example of a fraud detection use case for credit card transactions, where the time to identify fraud is essential. The earlier fraud is detected, the better the company is placed in dealing with the situation and mitigating the risk from such a transaction. Figure 2.5 demonstrates the perishable nature of insights and the need to act upon the information quickly to realize optimal value.

FIGURE 2.5   Information half-life in decision-making

Source: Perishable insights, Mike Gualtieri, Forrester

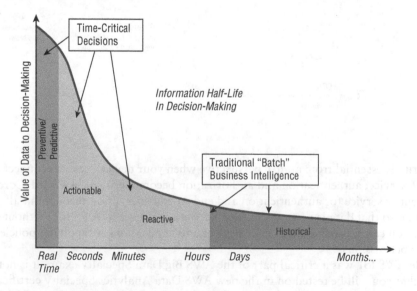

There are two major types of data processing:

- **Batch processing** – Supports a finite amount of data. An example is jobs scheduled on an hourly or a nightly basis.
- **Stream processing** – Supports a continuous stream of data being produced from the systems. Examples are real-time data integration, data analysis, and data operations.

There are certain scenarios where stream processing is the ideal choice of data processing:

Decouple collection and processing.   Stream processing decouples the data from your collection system (producers) and the processing system (consumers). It provides a persistent buffer for your incoming data. The data can be processed, and you can pump the data at your own rate depending on your needs.

Collect multiple streams together.   Different data producers can write the data to the same endpoint. For example, in an IoT solution, a million devices can write their data into the same endpoint easily.

Preserve client ordering.   There are often times when it is important to process the data in the way it is generated. This is often true for transactions such as a debit followed by a credit.

Client ordering preserves the data and guarantees that it is received by the consumer in the same order that the producer sent it. For example, the producer sends data in a certain order (1, 2, 3, 4), and the consumer receives the data in the same sequence (1, 2, 3, 4).

Parallel Consumption   Parallel consumption lets multiple users work simultaneously on the same data to build parallel applications on top of the data and have their own time to market.

These are the key features of the stream processing application:

- Data is processed in very low latency.
- Stream processing applications guarantee delivery of messages.
- Stream processing applications support lambda architecture implementation.
- State management of stream data is possible.
- Streaming processing applications provide support for operating in a time window or a count window based on the number of records. The windows can be a fixed size or sliding windows.
- Streaming processing applications are fault tolerant and resilient to failures.

While data streaming is critical for many use cases, many companies find it very hard to build streaming capabilities to benefit from in the business. We see the following key challenges with customers:

- Streaming platforms are hard to set up.
- Streaming platforms are tricky to scale. Generally speaking, a streaming platform will need to horizontally scale as the organization goes from processing thousands of events daily to millions and billions of events daily.
- Distributed streaming platforms are often hard to configure in a highly available application.
- Integrating streaming platforms with core systems becomes a challenge.
- Streaming platforms are often error prone, complex to manage, and expensive to maintain.

Because of these challenges, customers had asked AWS to simplify streaming data ingestion and processing. AWS has therefore added the following services to its platform:

- Amazon Kinesis Data Streams
- Amazon Kinesis Video Streams
- Amazon Kinesis Firehose
- Amazon Kinesis Analytics (SQL and Managed Apache Flink)
- Amazon Managed Streaming for Kafka

Amazon Kinesis Introduction

Amazon Kinesis as a service was built to provide a managed streaming platform to customers to make it easy to ingest, process, and analyze data at low latency in a new real-time and cost-effective manner. You can ingest a wide variety of data like video, audio, application and web logs, and website clickstreams as well as IoT telemetry data for machine learning, analytics and other applications. Kinesis provides four different ways to ingest, process, and analyze data. Let's look at each one.

Amazon Kinesis Data Streams

Amazon Kinesis Data Streams is a massively scalable, near real-time data streaming service that allows you to scale GBs of data per second from thousands of sources. Processing latencies of data fall in the range of seconds rather than hours as in traditional batch processing systems. Amazon Kinesis provides client libraries that allow you to build near real-time applications and seamlessly scale to match the data throughput rate and volume. Amazon Kinesis Data Streams is a very cost-effective solution and provides a pay-as-you-go model, where you don't pay any upfront costs or minimum fees but pay based on the shard hour and PUT payload unit.

As Figure 2.6 indicates, you can ingest and store data and then pass it onto a different application for processing, including Kinesis Data Analytics, Spark on EMR, and processing with AWS Lambda. You can even visualize the processed data in your favorite BI tool.

FIGURE 2.6   Kinesis Data Streams overview

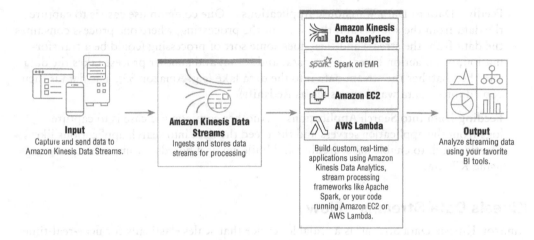

What Is Kinesis Data Streams Used For?

While from a technical perspective Kinesis Data Stream can be used for any high-velocity data capture and aggregation, there are some key scenarios where Kinesis Data Streams really shines:

Accelerated Log and Data Feed Intake and Processing   Quite often web servers, application servers and IoT devices produce logs that need to be captured as soon as they are created. Kinesis Data Streams allows you to capture this data in low latency and process it in real-time fashion, thus protecting you from server, disk failures, and data loss.

Real-Time Metrics Collection and Reporting   Quite often enterprises need a real-time view of the business—for example, to see how many devices are active at any single time on a factory floor and what the current level of production is. These metrics are important to be viewed in real-time fashion, as any delay in capturing a failure can result in losses of millions of dollars.

Real-Time Data Analytics   Kinesis Data Streams is used to capture data for real-time analytics. For example, anomaly and fraud detection are common use cases that need real-time understanding and intervention.

Complex Stream Processing   Quite often you need data from multiple producers to be aggregated and then eventually processed differently based on the data elements. Kinesis Data Streams supports complex event processing.

Feeding Data to Data Warehouse Applications   One common use case is to capture the data from the sources and then fan out the processing, where one process consumes the data from the stream and then does some sort of processing (could be a transformation, or an action based on the data, and so on) and another process takes the data and then batches the stream data into the data lake (e.g. Amazon S3). The data is then copied into a data warehouse such as Redshift.

Feeding Data into Search Applications   Another common use case is to capture logs from the application servers and then feed the data into search applications like Elasticsearch to enable log searching and building dashboards for important events using Kibana.

Kinesis Data Streams – Flow

Amazon Kinesis Data Streams is a scalable service that scales elastically for near-real-time processing of streaming big data. The service stores large streams of data (gigabytes of data per second) in durable, consistent storage, reliably, for near-real-time (few seconds) processing of data by an elastically scalable fleet of data processing servers.

Streaming data processing has two layers: a storage layer and a processing layer (see Figure 2.7). The storage layer must support specialized ordering and consistency semantics that enable fast, inexpensive, and repayable reads and writes of large streams of data.

The processing layer is responsible for reading data from the storage layer, processing that data, and notifying the storage layer to delete data that is no longer needed.

Customers can compile the Amazon Kinesis library into their data processing application. Amazon Kinesis notifies the application (the worker) when there is new data to process. The control plane works with workers to solve scalability and fault tolerance problems in the processing layer.

FIGURE 2.7 Kinesis Data Streams data flow

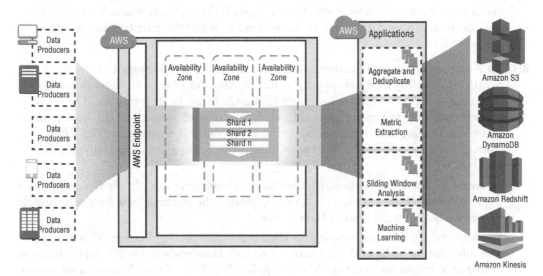

1. Before you create a Kinesis data stream, determine the initial size of the stream. A Kinesis Data Stream is composed of multiple shards. A *shard* is a uniquely identified sequence of streams and provides fixed capacity. You can consider shards as partitioning of your data inside a stream. Each shard can support up to five read transactions per second, up to a maximum total of 2 MB of data read per second. Each shard can support up to 1000 write transactions per second, up to a maximum total of 1 MB of data written per second. Multiple Amazon Kinesis applications can read from a shard. You can dynamically resize your Kinesis Data Stream or add and remove shards after the stream has been created and while a Kinesis application is consuming data from the stream. For more information about sizing a stream, see docs.aws.amazon.com/ streams/latest/dev/amazon-kinesis-streams.html.

2. Producers submit data records to the Kinesis Data Stream. You can configure the producers to put data into the stream. To put data into the stream, you can call the PutRecord() operation for the Amazon Kinesis service on your Kinesis Data Stream. Each invocation of the PutRecord() call requires the name of the Kinesis Data Stream, a partition key, and the data blob to be added to the Kinesis Data Stream.

   The *partition key* is an important concept as it is used to determine which shard in the stream the data record is added to. All the data in the shard is sent to the same

Kinesis worker that is processing the shard. The ideal choice for the partition key depends on your application logic. For example, if the application is calculating a bill for a customer using data on the customer's usage, a suitable partition key would be customer ID.

3.   An Amazon Kinesis application can use the Kinesis Client Library to simplify parallel processing of the stream by a fleet of Amazon Kinesis workers running on a fleet of Amazon Elastic Compute Cloud (Amazon EC2) instances. The client library simplifies the code required to read data from the shards in the stream and ensures that there is a worker allocated to every shard in the stream. The Kinesis Client Library also provides help with fault tolerance by providing checkpointing capabilities.

To create a Kinesis application, you will have to implement the Kinesis Client Library's IRecordProcessor Java class. This class implements the business logic for processing the data retrieved from the Kinesis Data Stream.

You also specify the configuration for the Amazon Kinesis application. This configuration information includes the name of the Kinesis Data Stream that the data is retrieved from and a unique name for the Kinesis application. Each of your Kinesis applications must have a unique name that is scoped to the AWS account and region used by the application. This name is used as a name for the control table in DynamoDB and the namespace for Amazon CloudWatch metrics. From an implementation perspective, when your Kinesis application starts, it automatically creates a DynamoDB table to store the application state, connects to the specified Kinesis Data Stream, and then starts consuming data from the stream. You can view the Amazon Kinesis application metrics in the CloudWatch console.

4.   You can follow your own best practices for deploying code to an Amazon EC2 instance when you deploy a Kinesis application. For example, you can add your Kinesis application to one of your Amazon EC2 AMIs. You can elastically scale the entire Kinesis application by running it on multiple Amazon EC2 instances under an *Auto Scaling* group. Using an Auto Scaling group can help automatically start new instances if an Amazon EC2 instance fails and can also elastically scale the number of instances as the load on the Kinesis application changes over time. Auto Scaling groups ensure that a certain number of Amazon EC2 instances are always running for the Kinesis application. To trigger scaling events in the Auto Scaling group, you can specify metrics such as CPU to scale up or down the number of Amazon EC2 instances that are processing data from the Kinesis Data Stream.

Writing Data to Streams

Once you have created a stream, you can use various ways to write data to the data stream, including KPL, AWS SDK, and Kinesis agents. KPL stands for Kinesis Producer Library, which is a library designed to enable applications (aka producers) to write data to Kinesis streams in order to simplify the entire process of writing data to a stream and achieve better throughput.

Kinesis Producer Library

Writing data to a stream can be quite challenging for many reasons, some of which are highlighted below:

- Writing the same event to multiple data streams
- Retrying logic for data being written to the streams in case of failure
- Multi-threading and aggregation in case of events being small in volume but overall velocity being very high
- De-aggregation at the consumer side
- Providing insights and metrics into the overall performance of the ingestion and consumption of data over a stream

Managing the preceding tasks can be challenging, and that is where Kinesis Producer Library comes to the rescue. KPL can be used for synchronous or asynchronous use cases; however, an asynchronous use case is often recommended due to its superior performance benefits. The key benefits of KPL are as follows:

Performance Benefits   Let's assume you have millions of devices on a factory floor, each producing 100-byte events. You are using an EC2 instance as a proxy to collect the data from those devices and then writing it to a Kinesis data stream. The EC2 instance would need to write millions of events per second to the data stream. To achieve your required throughput and SLA, you would need to implement complex logic such as *batching* the events and using multi-threading in addition to implementing retry logic to detect and handle failures. Since you are batching the events on the producer side, you would need to de-aggregate them on the consumer side as well. This can be quite tricky, and this is where Kinesis Producer Library can be used to simplify this process by letting it handle all the complexities. Batching improves the overall performance as you use a single HTTP request to put multiple records on the Kinesis stream. Aggregation also helps increase throughput of the producers as you can increase the number of records that you write per call. Kinesis Data Streams supports a put capacity of 1,000 Kinesis data stream records per second or a 1 MB throughput, whichever comes first. Let us consider the example of a single shard running at a PUT rate of 1000 records per second with 512 bytes each. With KPL aggregation, you can pack 1,000 records into 10 Kinesis Data Streams records, reducing the PUT records per second to 10 (at 50 KB each).

Figure 2.8 indicates how the KPL aggregates user records to improve overall Kinesis performance.

FIGURE 2.8 Aggregation and collection with KPL

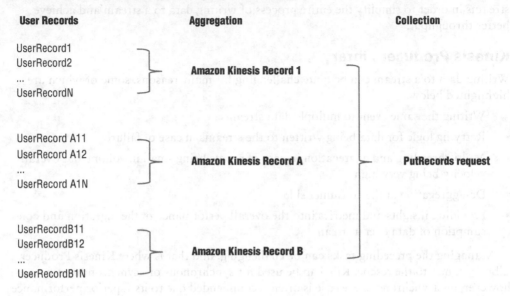

Ease of Use at the Consumer Side   Consumer-side developers can opt to use Kinesis Consumer Library (KCL) or simply use API methods like GetRecords() to retrieve the data from the stream.

If you are using KCL, it automatically works with KPL to retrieve individual records before returning them to the user. However, if you are not using KCL, you can use the KPL java library to extract individual records before returning them to the user.

KCL will make life easier on the consumer side, just as KPL does on the production side.

Monitoring of Producers   KPL works closely with CloudWatch and emits throughput, error, and other metrics to CloudWatch. You can configure the level at which the events are published, ranging from a stream level to a shard and to a producer level.

Asynchronous Architecture   KPL has an asynchronous architecture. Any call to put the data to KPL will return immediately without waiting for either the record to be sent or a response to be received from the server. A "Future" object is created that receives the result of sending the record to KPL at a later time.

Kinesis Producer Library is a library that acts as an intermediary between your application code that produces the events and the actions that need to be called for Kinesis Data Streams API.

For more details on KPL please visit AWS Documentation (amzn.to/2ztbMeZ).

Writing to a Kinesis Data Streams Using KPL

The basic Kinesis producer code is as follows:

```
KinesisProducer kinesis = new KinesisProducer();
For (int i=0; i< 100; i++) {
    Bytebuffer data = ByteBuffer.wrap("myData".getBytes("UTF-8"));
    kinesis.addUserRecord("mystream","mypartitionkey", data);
}
```

Writing Data to a Stream Using Kinesis Agent

Kinesis Agent is a standalone Java software application that offers an easy way to collect and send data to Kinesis streams. The agent handles the following:

- Monitoring files and sending data to Kinesis streams
- Rotation of the files
- Checkpointing last processed data
- Monitoring data writing failures and retrying after failures
- Emitting CloudWatch metrics.

By default, Kinesis Agent uses the new line \n character to identify individual records; however, the agent can be configured to handle multiline records.

Steps in writing data to a Kinesis stream using Kinesis Agent:

1. Install Kinesis Agent:

   Installing using Amazon Linux AMI:
   ```
   sudo yum install -y aws-kinesis-agent
   ```

   Installing using Red Hat Enterprise Linux:

   sudo yum install -y https://s3.amazonaws.com/streaming-data-agent/
   aws-kinesis-agent-latest.amzn1.noarch.rpm

   Set up using GitHub:

   a. Download agent from awslabs/amazon-kinesis-agent.
   b. Install agent:
   ```
   sudo ./setup --install
   ```

3. Configure and start the agent:

   a. Configure the agent: Edit the configuration file: /etc/aws-kinesis/agent
      .json. The configuration file has two major parts: filepattern (the agent will
      pick up the files that match this pattern and collect data from those files) and
      kinesisstream (Kinesis stream is the stream to which the agent writes the data).

      Kinesis Agent recognizes file rotations. Files can be rotated, or new files can be cre-
      ated, no more than once per second.

      Kinesis Agent uses the file creation timestamp to identify which files need to be
      streamed to the system. Since Kinesis Agent measures the new file creation every
      second, any files created within the same second cannot be tracked by the agent.

   b. Start the agent: You can start the agent manually or configure it to be started on a
      system startup. To start the agent manually:

      ```
      sudo service aws-kinesis-agent start
      ```

      To configure the agent to start on system startup:

      ```
      sudo chkconfig aws-kinesis-agent on
      ```

      Once you start the agent, it will run as a background service on that system and
      monitor the files specified by the file pattern and send it to the Kinesis stream.

Writing Data to a Kinesis Stream Using AWS SDK for Java

You can use AWS SDK for Java to write data to an Amazon Kinesis Stream. There are two
different operations in the Kinesis Data Stream API that add data to the stream:

PutRecords   This operation is used to send multiple records to your stream in a single
HTTP request. PutRecords allows you to achieve a higher throughput when sending
data to a Kinesis data stream. Each PutRecords can support up to 500 records, with
each record being as big as 1 MB in size, and the total size of the request can be up to
5 MB, including partition keys. The following code example shows the PutRecords()
API in Java, where we are creating a record entry and then using PutRecordsRequest
to write multiple records to a Kinesis stream.

```
AmazonKinesisClientBuilder clientBuilder = AmazonKinesisClientBuilder
.standard();
clientBuilder.regionName(regionName);
clientBuilder.setCredentials(credentialsBuilder);
clientBuilder.setClientConfiguration(config);

AmazonKinesis kinesisClient = clientBuilder.build();
```

```
PutRecordsRequest putRecordsRequest = new PutRecordsRequest();
putRecordsRequest.setStreamName(streamName);
List <PutRecordsRequestEntry> putRecordsEntryList = new ArrayList();

for (int i=0; i<100;i++){
  PutRecordsRequestEntry putRecordsRequestEntry= new
PutRecordsRequestEntry();
  putRecordsRequestEntry.setData(ByteBuffer.wrap(String.valueOf(i)
.getBytes()));
  putRecordsRequestEntry.setPartitionKey(String.format
("partitionKey-%d"),i));
  putRecordsRequestEntryList.add(putRecordsRequestEntry);
}

putRecordsRequest.setRecords(putRecordsRequestEntryList);
PutRecordsResult putRecordsResult = kinesisClient.putRecords
(putRecordsRequest);
System.out.println("Put Result: "+ putRecordsResult);
```

PutRecord   This operation is used to send a single record to your stream per HTTP request. Each record has a unique sequence number that is assigned by Kinesis Data Streams when you call putRecord() to add data to the stream. It is generally recommended to use PutRecords() instead of a single PutRecord() call. A partition key is used to group the data within the stream, and the data record is assigned to the shard within the stream based on the partition key.

Reading Data from a Kinesis Streams

We've seen a variety of ways by which you can write data to a Kinesis Data Stream. Kinesis also offers a number of ways to consume data from the stream as well. Multiple consumers can read the data from the data stream in parallel. By default, shards in a stream provide 2 MB/second of read throughput or 5 transactions per second for reads per shard. This throughput capacity is shared across all consumers reading from the shard. However, when a consumer uses Enhanced Fan-out, it gets its own 2 MB/second capacity of read throughput, thus allowing multiple consumers to read the data in parallel at high capacity.

You can use one of the following ways to consume data from a Kinesis data stream.

Kinesis Data Analytics   You can use an Amazon Kinesis Data Analytics application to process and analyze data in a Kinesis stream using SQL or Java. Kinesis Data Analytics can enrich data using data from other reference sources, perform data aggregation, or use machine learning to find data abnormalities.

Kinesis Data Firehose   You can use Kinesis Data Firehose to process data from an Amazon Kinesis data stream. Amazon Kinesis Data Firehose is a fully managed service for delivering real-time streaming data to destinations such as Amazon S3, Amazon Redshift, Amazon Elasticsearch Service, and Splunk. Amazon Kinesis Data Firehose allows you to transform the data and convert data record formats before delivering to the destination.

AWS Lambda   AWS Lambda can be used to be transform and process data coming from the data streams. AWS Lambda is a fully managed, scalable service where customers pay for the computation time with zero administration.

Custom Consumers Using Kinesis Client Library   You can use Amazon Kinesis Client Library to consume and process data from a Kinesis data stream. Consuming records from streams with multiple shards can be quite complex as you need to balance the load across multiple instances, respond to instance failures, checkpoint processed records and often react to re-sharding of the data. KCL abstracts you from the complexity by letting you focus on business logic while handling the nitty-gritty details of distributed record consumption.

You can develop a consumer using KCL in Java or Python.

Amazon Kinesis Firehose

Processing data in a stream is achieved using Amazon Kinesis Data Streams and AWS Lambda in combination; however, often there is a need to persist the data for either long-term storage or further analysis. While Amazon Kinesis Data Streams was the first service that was built, the team soon realized that one of the most popular use cases for a streaming application was to capture data being emitted from these devices in real time and buffer it before storing it for longer-term analysis. Amazon, with its usual customer obsession, decided to build Amazon Kinesis Firehose, a fully managed service, to allow users to deliver streaming data to destinations like Amazon S3, Amazon Redshift, Amazon Elasticsearch Service, and Splunk. Amazon Kinesis Firehose allows you to create a delivery stream, which can have the data written to it by various producers (max record length of 1000 KB), and buffer the data (configurable parameter in MBs or seconds) before delivering it to a target destination.

One of the most popular use cases is customers transforming the data arriving to a Kinesis Firehose stream by fanning the transformed and raw data to different destinations (see Figure 2.9).

Streaming data to different destinations is handled differently. For example, when your destination is an Elasticsearch cluster, the data is streamed directly to the cluster, but when the destination is Redshift, it is delivered to an S3 bucket and then a Copy command is issued to copy the data from the S3 bucket to Amazon Redshift (see Figure 2.10 and Figure 2.11).

FIGURE 2.9   Data flow - S3 destination

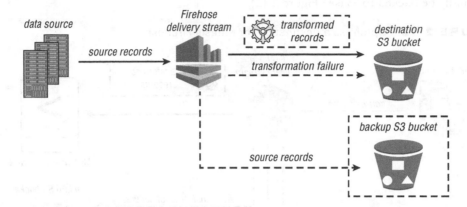

FIGURE 2.10   Amazon Redshift as a destination for Kinesis Firehose

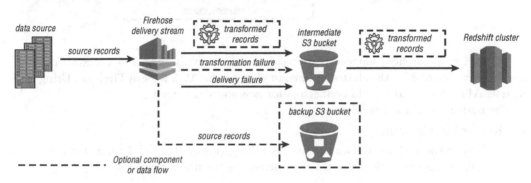

FIGURE 2.11   Amazon Elasticsearch Service as a destination for Kinesis Firehose

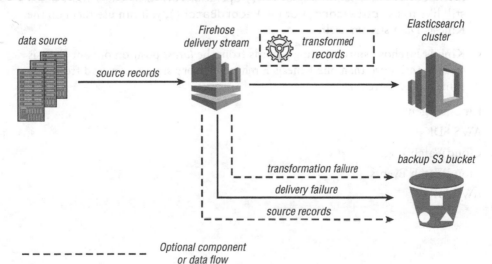

When the destination is Splunk, streaming data is delivered to Splunk but can also optionally be backed to S3 (see Figure 2.12).

FIGURE 2.12   Splunk as a destination for Kinesis Firehose

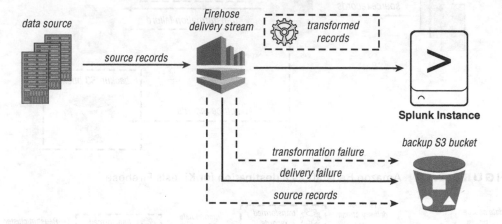

While Kinesis Firehose supports multiple destinations, it also provides a number of different native sources on the platform that can write to the AWS Kinesis Firehose. Using the Kinesis API, you can also build connectors for new sources as well.

The native sources are as follows:

- Kinesis Data Streams:
  - If your source Kinesis data stream has aggregation configured, Kinesis Firehose will de-aggregate the records before delivering them to a destination.
  - When Kinesis Data Streams is used as a source for Kinesis Firehose, the `putRecord()` and `putRecordBatch()` operations are disabled. If you would still like to use `putRecord()` or `putRecordBatch()`, you can use them on the Kinesis Data stream itself.
  - Kinesis Firehose starts reading records from the *latest* position of your Kinesis stream and more than one Kinesis Firehose delivery stream can read from the same Kinesis stream.
- Kinesis Agent
- AWS SDK
- CloudWatch Logs
- CloudWatch Events
- AWS IoT

Data Transformation with Amazon Kinesis Firehose

While capturing data is critical, you will often need to perform data transformations for data streaming at high velocity. You can enable data transformation with Amazon Kinesis Firehose, which will buffer incoming data to 3 MB by default. Kinesis Firehose will invoke the specified lambda function asynchronously, with each buffered batch using the AWS Lambda synchronous invocation mode. Any Lambda invocation has a maximum payload size limit of 6 MB for both the request and the response, and hence you have to ensure that the buffering size for the function is less than or equal to 6 MB.

You can also use pre-built Lambda blueprints with Kinesis Data Firehose. The following Lambda blueprints can be used for the most common transformations:

- General Firehose processing: Use this for any custom transformation logic.
- Apache Log to JSON
- Apache Log to CSV
- Syslog to JSON
- Syslog to CSV
- Kinesis Data Firehose processes record streams as a source: a basic lambda function that provides access to the Kinesis Data Stream records in the input and returns them with a processing status.
- Kinesis Data Firehose CloudWatch Logs processor: Parses and extracts each individual log event from your records sent by CloudWatch Logs subscription filters.

Each lambda function invocation from Kinesis Firehose can be a maximum of 5 minutes.

Converting Input Record Formats in Amazon Kinesis

One of the most common analytical needs is to convert your row format into columnar to optimize your analytical queries. The most common columnar formats used by customers are either Parquet or ORC because they not only compress the data but also provide optimal performance for analytical queries. Amazon Kinesis Firehose allows you to convert JSON data into Parquet or ORC. Amazon Kinesis Firehose requires three elements to convert the record format of your data:

1. A deserializer to read the JSON of your input data: You can choose one of the two deserializers:
   - Apache Hive JSON SerDe
   - OpenX JSON SerDe
2. A schema to determine how to interpret your data: You can use AWS Glue to infer a schema from the data and store it in the Glue Data Catalog. Kinesis Firehose then references the schema and uses it to interpret your data.

3. A serializer to convert the data to Parquet or ORC: You can use ORC SerDe or Parquet SerDe to convert the data into columnar storage.

 If record conversion is enabled, the destination of the data can only be S3. You cannot use Amazon Redshift, Amazon Elasticsearch Service, or Splunk as a destination for your converted data.

Amazon Kinesis Data Analytics

Kinesis Data Streams and Amazon Kinesis Firehose allow you to capture the streaming data from a variety of sources and process it using AWS Lambda. However, as discussed earlier, there are certain insights that are time critical and need to be derived as soon as possible for optimal results. An example of such a use case is fraud detection where an early detection of fraud is directly proportional to dollar savings. An early detection of customer churn can potentially provide an opportunity to retain the customer via a focused marketing campaign. While collection of the data is key, running analytics on streaming data has been a challenge.

Amazon Web Services provides Amazon Kinesis Data Analytics (see Figure 2.13), which allows you to query and analyze streaming data using SQL or Java.

FIGURE 2.13   Amazon Kinesis Data Analytics

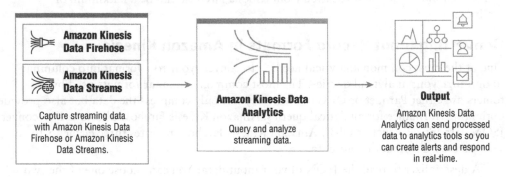

Amazon Kinesis Data Analytics makes it simple to connect to a streaming source to start consuming data and write SQL or Java code to process the data before delivering results to analytical tools to raise alerts/notifications in real time. Amazon Kinesis Data Analytics provides sub-second processing latencies, in addition to allowing you to chain various steps together in serial or parallel fashion. It provides various pre-built functions, from machine learning algorithms to application development, and provides aggregations for long-running application processes over a defined time window.

Use Cases for Amazon Kinesis Data Analytics

You should use Amazon Kinesis Data Analytics for the following use cases:

Time-Series Data Analytics   Amazon Kinesis Data Analytics allows you to operate over various time windows. You can calculate metrics that are relevant to your business applications and use cases and stream the results to Amazon S3 or an Amazon Redshift database using a Kinesis data delivery stream. For example, a telecommunications provider needs to understand account activations and deactivations over a 30-minute period. This can be achieved using Kinesis Data Analytics.

Feed real-time dashboards.   Amazon Kinesis Data Analytics provides the ability to aggregate results and feed real-time dashboards. An example could be a loans department for a financial institution calculating real-time loan disbursements. You can also have law enforcement trying to understand real-time crime reporting and dashboards indicating patterns of crime across the city.

Create real-time metrics.   Businesses of the twenty-first century often need to create real-time metrics that can be monitored in real time to understand the health of the business. Examples of metrics can be the average production of cars per hour across a factory floor to understand the production performance across the factory, or the number of faulty products produced per hour to indicate an issue with the manufacturing process.

Amazon Kinesis Data Analytics provides two interfaces to write your application, and those can be chosen from the console or via the API (see Figure 2.14 and Figure 2.15). When you create an application (here we are using AWS Management Console), you get the two options to choose from, the SQL interface and the Apache Flink interface.

FIGURE 2.14   Kinesis application creation via Console

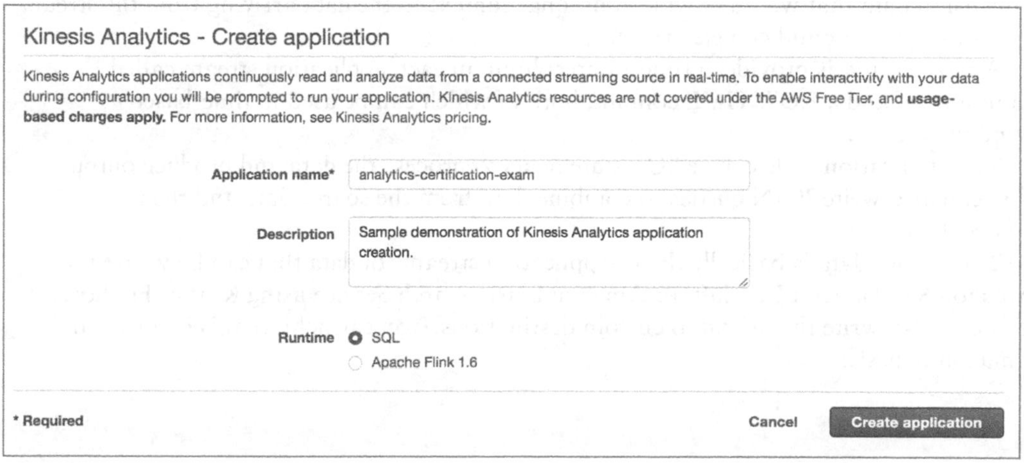

FIGURE 2.15   Kinesis Data Analytics application

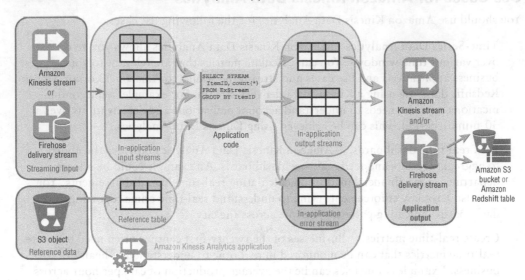

SQL Interface

An application using the SQL runtime will read and process the data in real time, with the code for the processing logic being written in SQL language.

The source for a Kinesis application can be a Kinesis data stream or a Kinesis Firehose delivery stream. The data from these streams is provided to the application developer in the form of an in-application input stream that can be considered a continuously updating table. You can use standard SQL SELECT/INSERT in your application code to process this data. You can also configure an S3 object to be made available to you as a reference table, which Kinesis reads from S3 when the application starts. This reference data is often dimension data that would provide additional context to the data arriving from the stream and allow you to build complex rules.

Amazon Kinesis provides a timestamp column in each application stream called Timestamps and a ROWTIME column, both of which can be used in time-based window queries.

The application code can be SQL statements to process the data and produce output. You can also write JOIN queries to combine data from the source data and the reference data.

The output data is basically the in-application streams of data that can be written to Amazon S3, Amazon Redshift, or Amazon Elasticsearch Service using Kinesis Firehose. You can also write the output to custom destinations. You can achieve this by using an Amazon Kinesis.

The process of creating a Kinesis SQL application is as follows:

1. Create an application (choose a runtime).

2. Select the source. You can connect to an existing streaming source (Kinesis stream/ Firehose delivery stream) or create a new streaming source from the console as well. In the example in Figure 2.16, I created an "analytics-cert" Firehose delivery stream, which is now pumping in demo data.

FIGURE 2.16   Connecting to a streaming source

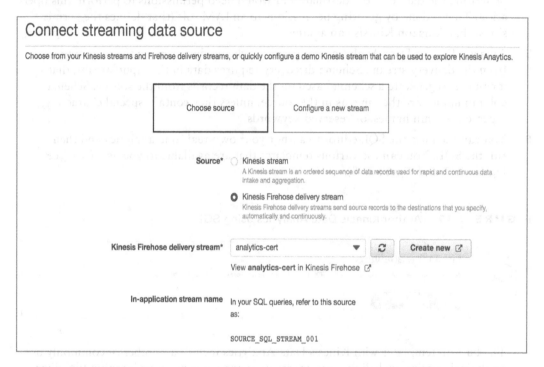

3. Kinesis Data Analytics can call your lambda function to pre-process records before they are used in your kinesis analytics application. To preprocess records. Your lambda function must be compliant with the required record transformation output model. Using a lambda function in your Kinesis application can be useful in the following scenarios:

    a. Transforming records from other formats (such as KPL or GZIP) into formats that Kinesis Data Analytics can analyze. Kinesis Data Analytics currently supports JSON or CSV data formats.

    b. Expanding data into a format that is more accessible for operations such as aggregation or anomaly detection. For instance, if several data values are stored together in a string, you can expand the data into separate columns.

    c. Data enrichment with other AWS services, such as extrapolation or error correction

    d. Applying complex string transformation to record fields

    e. Data filtering for cleaning up the data

4. Amazon Kinesis Data Analytics needs permissions to read records from the streaming source that you have just chosen in the configuration above. In my example, I need permissions to read from the delivery-cert Firehose stream. Since Kinesis Analytics would be writing the data out to a destination, I would need permissions to perform this operation. This is done by granting permissions to an IAM role (that defines the permissions) that Amazon Kinesis can assume.

5. Amazon Kinesis Data Analytics can perform schema discovery on the incoming data from the delivery stream. Schema discovery requires data in the input stream, that it can use to generate a schema based on the data records from the source. Schema column names are the same as in the source, unless they contain special characters, repeated column names, or reserved keywords.

6. You can then use the SQL editor to author your own real-time analytics and then run the SQL. You can use various templates that are available to you as a user (see Figure 2.17 and Figure 2.18).

FIGURE 2.17   Author Kinesis Data Analytics using SQL

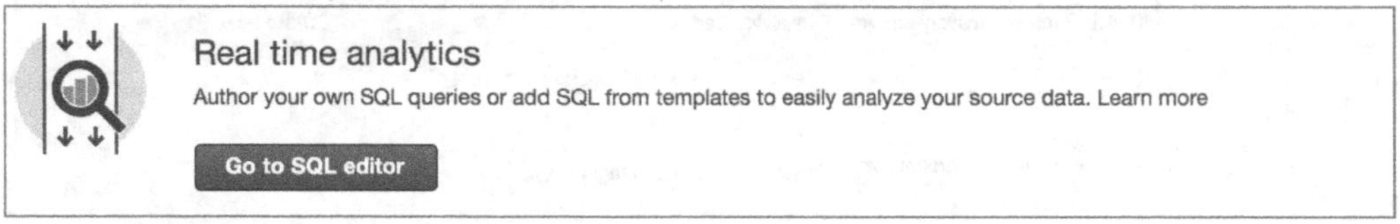

Real time analytics

Author your own SQL queries or add SQL from templates to easily analyze your source data. Learn more

Go to SQL editor

The built-in templates with Kinesis Data Analytics include a number of commonly used analytical queries, including basic aggregation and some machine learning functions (see Table 2.1).

7. You can then choose to connect your Kinesis Data Analytics stream to a destination that can be a Kinesis stream, a Kinesis Firehose delivery stream, or an AWS lambda function.

TABLE 2.1   ML algorithms with Amazon Kinesis

ML/Approximation	Aggregation	Filtering/Enrichment
Anomaly detection	Aggregate function in a tumbling time window	Continuous filter
Approximate top-K items	Aggregate function in a sliding time window	Multistep application
Approximate distinct count	Aggregate function in a sliding row window	Data enrichment
	Aggregate using two time windows	Simple Alert
	Parse and Aggregate Apache Logs	

FIGURE 2.18   Kinesis Data Analytics authoring screen

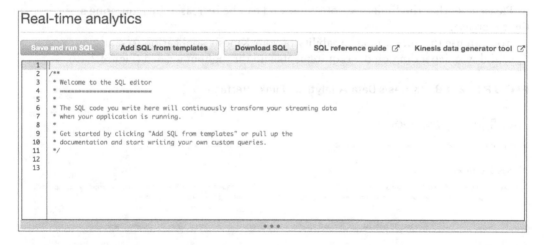

Apache Flink Interface

Apache Flink is a top-level Apache project that has a simple programming model and makes it easier to build streaming applications using the flexible APIs. It provides low latency and high throughput with its in-memory computing and provides stateful processing and exactly-once semantics.

Apache Flink has a rich ecosystem and hence is considered to be one of the most popular platforms to build streaming applications.

You can also use an Apache Flink interface for your Kinesis Data Analytics application. Essentially you would create your Flink application in your favorite integrated development environment (IDE) and then upload the application code to Kinesis Data Analytics. This would allow you to run your application in a fully managed elastic service. You can then use the AWS ecosystem to manage your application. For example, you can configure various metrics with Amazon CloudWatch—such as Applications, Tasks, Operator, and Parallelism—and also display the Job graph in the AWS Management Console.

Kinesis provides a Kinesis process unit (KPU) as a resource to run the code. Each KPU is 1 vCPU, 4 GB of RAM, and 50 GB of storage at the time of this writing. The number of KPUs needed for your application is calculated using the Parallelism and ParallelismPerKPU properties:

- **Parallelism** – This is the property that is used to set the default Apache Flink application parallelism. All operators, sinks, and sources will use this level of parallelism unless they are explicitly overridden in the application. The default value is 1 and the maximum value is 64.

- **ParallelismPerKPU** – This property is used to set the number of parallel tasks that can be scheduled per KPU of your application. The default is 1 and the maximum is 8.

Please note that the limits are soft limits and can be increased by requesting a limit increase.

You can use the autoscaling capability of your Kinesis application to scale your resource up and down depending on the requirements and throughput needed (Figure 2.19).

FIGURE 2.19 Kinesis Data Analytics - Flink Interface

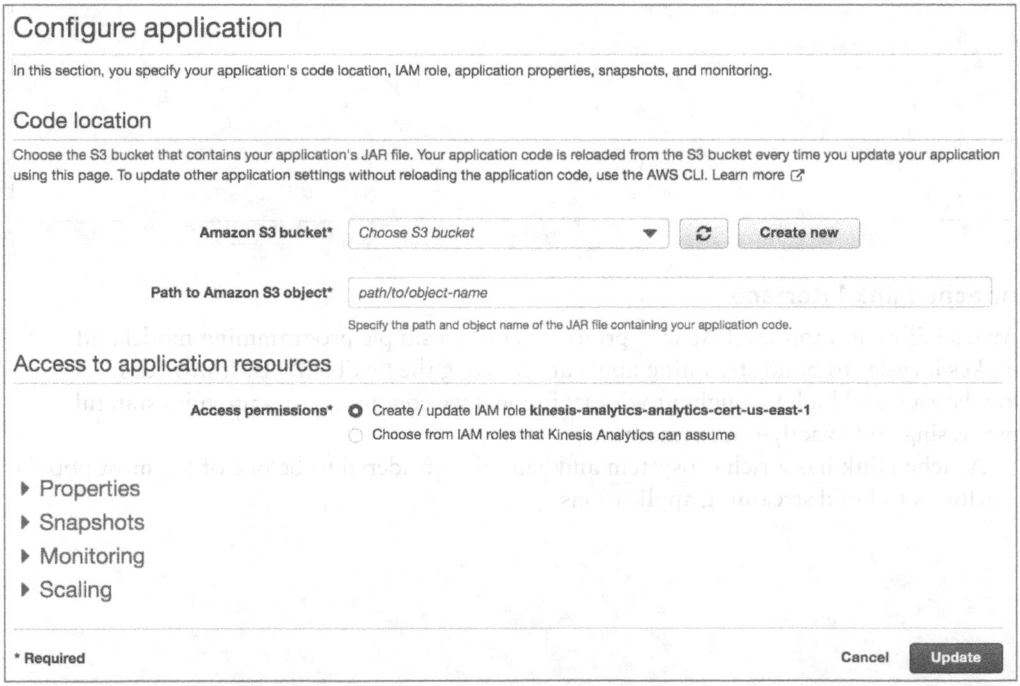

You can configure parallelism and parallelism per KPU in addition to enabling autoscaling on the AWS console while configuring your Kinesis Data Analytics application (Figure 2.20).

FIGURE 2.20   Scaling your Flink applications with Kinesis

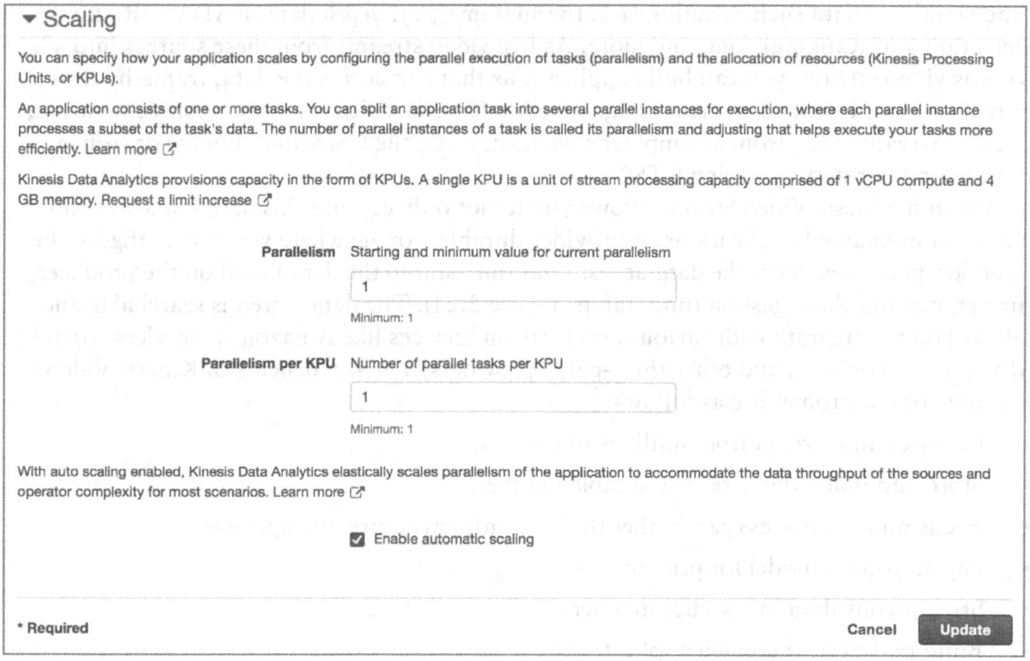

▼ Scaling

You can specify how your application scales by configuring the parallel execution of tasks (parallelism) and the allocation of resources (Kinesis Processing Units, or KPUs).

An application consists of one or more tasks. You can split an application task into several parallel instances for execution, where each parallel instance processes a subset of the task's data. The number of parallel instances of a task is called its parallelism and adjusting that helps execute your tasks more efficiently. Learn more ☐

Kinesis Data Analytics provisions capacity in the form of KPUs. A single KPU is a unit of stream processing capacity comprised of 1 vCPU compute and 4 GB memory. Request a limit increase ☐

Parallelism   Starting and minimum value for current parallelism

| 1 |

Minimum: 1

Parallelism per KPU   Number of parallel tasks per KPU

| 1 |

Minimum: 1

With auto scaling enabled, Kinesis Data Analytics elastically scales parallelism of the application to accommodate the data throughput of the sources and operator complexity for most scenarios. Learn more ☐

☑ Enable automatic scaling

* Required   Cancel   Update

Amazon Kinesis Video Streams

With the advent of IoT and integrated devices that capture other measurements you can now capture video data, which needs to be stored, analyzed, and reacted to in a real-time fashion. Video is critical to many applications like smart home, smart city, video surveillance security monitoring, industrial automation, and computer vision. While the requirements to stream, process, and analyze video in real time has grown, building such a video ingestion system is quite complex to say the least. As it turns out, there are many different devices and different operating systems you need to integrate with, and writing code for various devices and development environments is very complex. Furthermore, as the number of devices grows, there is a need to scale your streaming and analysis applications while supporting the latency, cadence, and jitter on the streams. APIs need to be made available to retrieve the videos, process them, and replay them.

Video streams analysis was one of the most common requests from media customers, and Amazon responded by releasing Amazon Kinesis Video Streams at the re:Invent event in 2017, with the key objective to stream video and time-encoded data for analytics. Amazon Kinesis Video Streams is a fully managed service that is scalable and allows you to stream videos from millions of sources, including smart phones, security cameras, webcams, drones, cameras embedded in cars, and other sources. You can also send non-video time-serialized data such as audio data, thermal imagery, depth data, RADAR (Radio Detection and Ranging) data, and more. As live video streams from these sources into a Kinesis video stream, you can build applications that can access the data, frame-by-frame, in real time for low-latency processing. Amazon Kinesis Video Streams is source-agnostic; you can stream video from a computer's webcam using the GStreamer library or from a camera on your network using RTSP.

Amazon Kinesis Video Steams allows you to not only capture this data but also easily build vision-enabled applications. It provides durable storage where you can configure the retention period, encrypt the data at rest, and time-stamp the data based on the producer time stamp and the ingestion time stamp (Figure 2.21). The data stored is searchable and allows you to integrate with various downstream services like Amazon AI services, *Apache MXNet*, *TensorFlow*, and other third-party providers. The key benefits of Kinesis Video Streams for a customer are as follows:

- Connect and stream from millions of devices.

- Store and index the data in a durable manner.

- Focus on the business case rather than the infrastructure management.

- Pay-as-you-go model for pricing

- Stream your data in a secure manner.

- Build real-time and batch applications.

The key concepts are as follows:

Producer   Producer is any application, device, or source that feeds the data into Kinesis Video Streams. A producer can be a video-generating device or even send non-video data like audio streams, images, or RADAR data.

Kinesis Video Producer Library   These libraries are supposed to be installed on your device and allow you to connect to the Kinesis stream and stream video to the stream in real time or with some buffering.

Kinesis Video Streams   The producers put the videos in a Kinesis video stream, which is basically a resource that enables you to transport live video data, optionally store it, and make the data available for consumption both in real time and on a batch or ad hoc basis. You can create a Kinesis video stream from the AWS Console or using the AWS SDK (see Figure 2.22).

FIGURE 2.21 Working with Kinesis Video Analytics

Reference: (amzn.to/2oZOif6)

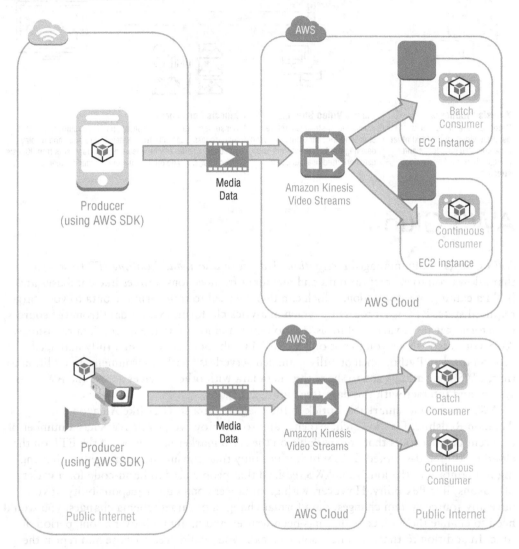

Consumer A consumer is someone who reads the data from a Kinesis video stream to view, process, and analyze it. The data is consumed by Amazon Kinesis video stream applications in real-time fashion for low-latency queries or after it has been stored and time-indexed for processing that is not low latency. You can also use the Kinesis Video Streams parser library to get the media from the Kinesis video streams in a low-latency manner and let the applications focus on processing and analyzing the frames rather than the underlying complexity of detecting frame boundaries.

FIGURE 2.22 Kinesis Video Streams

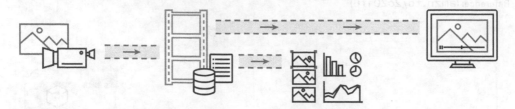

Kinesis Producers

Producers are devices that generate video, audio, and other time-encoded data feeds and publish them to Kinesis video streams.

Kinesis Video Streams

Kinesis video streams capture, store, and index the time-encoded data fragments for real-time and batch-oriented use cases.

Kinesis Consumers

Consumers are custom applications that process fragments from Kinesis video streams for machine learning, video analytics, and other workflows.

Consumers can also request and display fragments from Kinesis video streams.

AWS Glue

AWS Glue is a fully managed *Extraction, Transformation, and Loading (ETL)* service that allows you to extract the data and metadata from various sources like databases and build a catalog of information, which can then be used to transform the data to your target required state. ETL is a process by which analytics platforms extract data from the sources, transform it using a variety of tools/technologies, and load it to the target data repository. AWS Glue also allows you to not only build ETL jobs but run them in a fully managed fashion inside a Python shell or fully managed serverless Spark environment. In addition to that, AWS Glue allows you to share this metadata with other services across the AWS ecosystem and interact with this data (see Figure 2.23).

AWS has seen a remarkable uptick in the usage of data services like Amazon S3, Amazon Redshift, Elasticsearch, Athena, and so on. However, while AWS has a number of different partner tools that are available on the AWS marketplace, most of the ETL on the cloud is still hand-scripted ETL, which is not only time consuming to create but challenging to maintain in the long run. AWS realized that people used to hand-code for a variety of reasons, like flexibility. However, with great power comes great responsibility. If you have any source system changes, data format changes, or target schema changes, you would need to change the ETL code that has been written and maintain it over a long period of time. In addition to that, each new source means you would need to rinse and repeat the exact same process.

AWS Glue was built to automate this cumbersome and error-prone process of manual ETL scripting by providing a user interface that allows customers to focus on writing their core transformations rather than maintaining the infrastructure to run this code.

AWS Glue also offers built-in and custom classifiers. A classifier is a piece of code that classifies the source data into numbers, strings, phone numbers, Social Security numbers, and addresses using a number of rules.

FIGURE 2.23 Glue flow

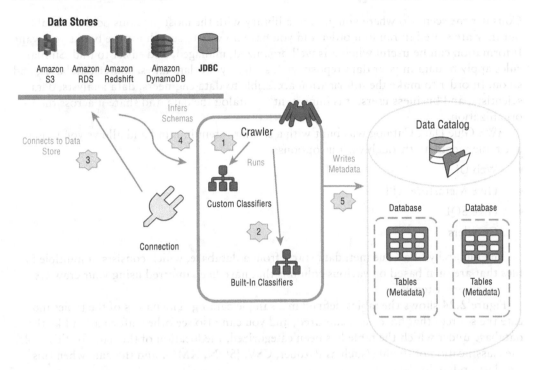

A *crawler* is a program that connects to a data store (source or target), progresses through a prioritized list of classifiers to determine the schema for your data, and then creates metadata in the AWS Glue Data Catalog. AWS Glue crawlers can scan, classify, and extract schema information and then store the metadata automatically in the AWS Glue Data Catalog. The metadata is stored in the form of tables. Crawlers can also detect schema changes and version the tables for previously crawled data stores and detect hive-style partitions on Amazon S3. For previously crawled Amazon S3 partitioned data, the crawler will add new partitions or update the changed partitions by default. Crawlers run on demand or on a schedule to suit your needs.

The glue process starts with a crawler using a custom classifier or a built-in classifier using a connection to one of the data sources (S3, RDS, Redshift, DynamoDB, or JDBC), inferring a schema, and writing the metadata to the data catalog.

There are three major components of AWS Glue:

- Data Catalog
- Authoring ETL Jobs
- Executing ETL Jobs

Glue Data Catalog

Consider the scenario where you go into a library with the most precious books available but they are stored in random order and you have no way to search for the books you want. Information can be useful when it is well organized, managed, and easier to find. Similar rules apply to data in your data repositories, such as your data lakes, source databases, and so on. In order to make the information accessible to data engineers, data analysts, data scientists, and business users, it is important to catalog the data and share it across the organization.

AWS Glue Data Catalog was built with a similar intent in mind and allows you to manage table metadata through various options:

- Web UI
- Hive Metastore API
- Hive SQL
- Crawlers

The hierarchy of a Glue metadata starts from a database, which consists of multiple tables that are then based on various columns that have been inferred using your crawlers (standard or custom).

Figure 2.24 shows the tables defined in a sample catalog. The names of the tables indicate the sources that have been captured, and you can also see other information like the database under which the table has been categorized, the location of the data for this table, the classification of the file (such as Parquet, CSV, JSON, XML), and the date when this was last updated.

FIGURE 2.24 Tables defined in a sample catalog

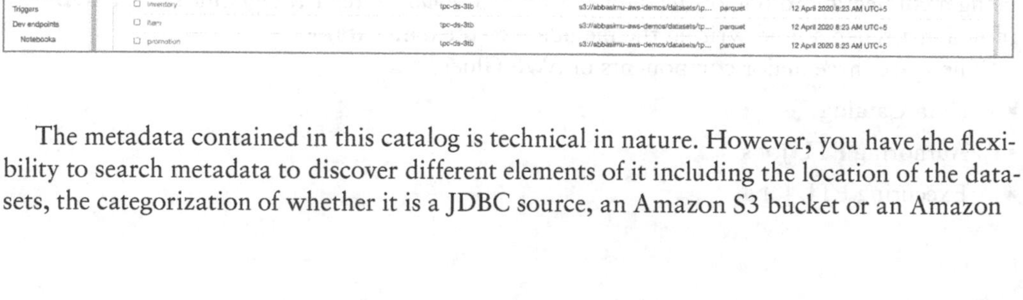

The metadata contained in this catalog is technical in nature. However, you have the flexibility to search metadata to discover different elements of it including the location of the datasets, the categorization of whether it is a JDBC source, an Amazon S3 bucket or an Amazon

DynamoDB table, and even the versioning of a particular metadata element. If you click a particular table in the GUI, you can see the details of the table and properties. Figure 2.25 indicates the type of details that you can see when you click a particular table in the catalog.

FIGURE 2.25   Table details

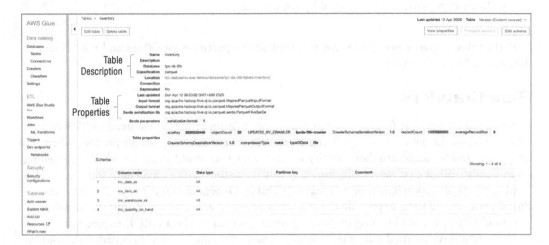

- Name
- Database
- Classification
- Location
- Connection (if table is from JDBC source)
- Last Updated timestamp
- Input format
- Output format
- Serialization SERDE
- SERDE parameters
- Table properties:
  - Crawler used to crawl/update the table
  - Number of records
  - Average record size
  - Whether columns are ordered

- Whether columns are quoted
- Delimiter
- Schema of the table:
  - Column names
  - Data type which, was inferred by the crawler
  - Comments

If the table is partitioned, you can also look at the partitioning values and the objects that are linked to it on S3.

Glue Crawlers

A crawler in its simplest form is a piece of Java code running inside a managed Docker container to crawl the data sources. Defining a new crawler is a relatively simple process, where you define the crawler name and then identify which source you would like to crawl. You can either crawl data stores or existing catalog tables. A new data store can be an S3 data source, an RDS database, a JDBC connection, or a DynamoDB table. Depending on the type of source you choose, you would need to provide the connectivity parameters. You can limit the files that you would like to crawl by using exclusion patterns, which can be a GROK expression.

Once you have defined a crawler, you can create schedules to run it on demand, hourly, daily, weekly, monthly, or on specific days of the week, and optionally, you can use a cron expression to define a schedule. When you rerun the crawler, it can detect schema changes in the data store and update the table definition in the catalog or add new columns only. You can optionally configure to ignore any changes in the source and update the catalog. Figure 2.26 shows how GlueCrawlers can crawl JDBC and object data sources.

FIGURE 2.26   Glue crawlers

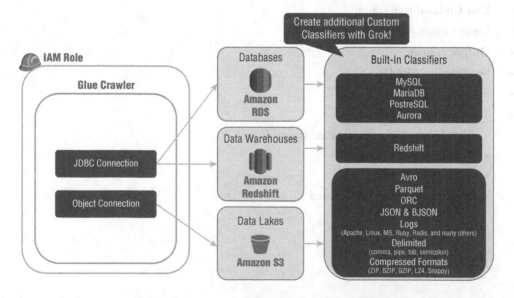

Authoring ETL Jobs

A job is actually the business logic that performs ETL in AWS Glue. When you start a job, AWS Glue runs a script that extracts data from sources, transforms the data, and loads it into the target repository. Amazon Glue allows you to author jobs in a seamless way and makes it possible for you to do the following:

- Author a script from scratch.
- Extend a templated script generated by AWS Glue.
- Use an existing script bought into AWS Glue.

To author an ETL job, you select a source table and a target table and then customize the job parameters (see Figure 2.27).

FIGURE 2.27   Authoring jobs in AWS Glue

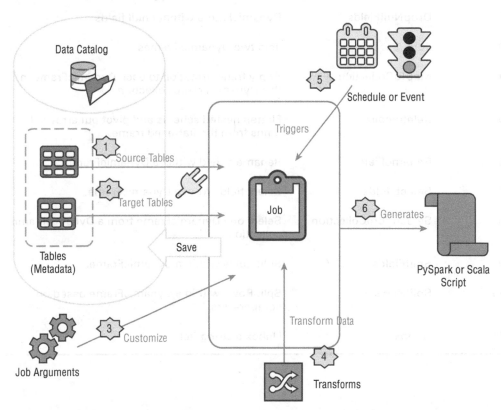

You can then choose transforms that you would require and then choose the schedule or the event that triggers the job. Glue would use the job generator to author a Python or Scala script, based on your choosing.

During Glue job authoring, Glue offers the concept of a DynamicFrame, which is basically an extension of Apache Spark SQL Data Frame. Your data passes from transform to transform in this data structure, and you can move between the DataFrame and the DynamicFrame concept pretty easily. For more information about DynamicFrames, please visit Glue documentation. The AWS Data Analytics Specialty certification, however, does not expect you to know the API details of a DynamicFrame.

Glue has a number of pre-built transformations that you can use during your job authoring process. The transformations are listed in Table 2.2.

TABLE 2.2 Transformations available within AWS Glue

Serial No.	Transformation Name	Transformation Details
1	DropFields	Drop fields from a dynamic frame.
2	DropNullFields	DynamicFrame without null fields
3	Join	Join two Dynamic Frames.
4	MapToCollection	Apply transformation to each DynamicFrame in this DynamicFrame collection.
5	Relationalize	Flatten nested schema and pivot out array columns from the flattened frame.
6	RenameField	Rename a field within a DynamicFrame.
7	SelectFields	Select fields from a DynamicFrame.
8	SelectFromCollection	Select one DynamicFrame from a DynamicFrame collection.
9	SplitFields	Split fields within a DynamicFrame.
10	SplitRows	Split Rows within a DynamicFrame based on comparators.
11	Unbox	Unbox a string field.

Executing ETL Jobs

Once you have created ETL (extract, transform and load) jobs, you can orchestrate and automate them via AWS Glue. AWS Glue would provide metrics to monitor the crawlers and jobs running on the platform and provide additional statistics about the health of your environment. You can automate the invocation of crawlers and jobs with a time-based scheduled based on cron. You can also use event-based triggers to start an AWS Glue job.

The main objective of AWS Glue is to provide an easier way to extract and transform your data from source to target. The ETL job flow with AWS Glue is as follows:

1. A job is fired with a trigger. You can set up schedules to run the job or run the job when a particular dependency is satisfied.

2. Once the job starts, it extracts the data from the configured source based on the connection properties.

3. The job would use the script that has been authored by Glue, which can be either a PySpark or a Scala code, to transform the data.

4. The transformed data is loaded to your data targets. If required, connection properties are used to access the target.

5. Statistics are collected about the job run and are written to your data catalog.

Change Data Capture with Glue Bookmarks

Quite often we need to capture data from sources in a variety of ways, such as full data extracts from the source or identifying delta records. Identifying detail is often complicated because you need to ensure that only the updated data in the source is captured. This can be done for simplicity and performance reasons. AWS Glue uses Glue bookmarks to track the processed data from pervious runs of an ETL job by persisting the state information from the job run.

This persisted state information is called a job bookmark. Job bookmarks help AWS Glue maintain state information and prevent the reprocessing of old data. Job bookmarks allow you to process new data when rerunning on a scheduled interval. A job bookmark is composed of the states for various elements of jobs, such as sources, transformations, and targets. For example, your ETL job might read new partitions in an Amazon S3 file. AWS Glue tracks which partitions the job has processed successfully to prevent duplicate processing and duplicate data in the job's target data store.

Job bookmarks are implemented for some of the most common file formats on Amazon S3, like JSON, CSV, Apache Avro, XML, Parquet, and ORC.

For relational data sources like a JDBC connection, job bookmarks have certain limitations when it comes to capturing the delta of the sources. For this input source, job bookmarks are supported only if the table's primary keys are in sequential order. Also, job bookmarks search for new rows but not updated rows. This is because bookmarks look for the primary keys, which already exist in the target, and hence AWS Glue cannot identify the changes in the source. At the time of this writing, this limitation was actively being worked on.

Use Cases for AWS Glue

From an exam perspective, the following are the key use cases for AWS Glue:

- Large-scale data processing
- ETL processing
- Building a catalog of information

Amazon SQS

Customers are moving rapidly from the monolithic applications toward serverless architectures to support the pace of innovation needed to sustain their business during this day and age. Customers are adopting event-driven architectures where the objective is to move away from direct integration between systems and have different systems interact with each other via events. Amazon provides a number of services that offer the capability to decouple the state of your application from the code by using messaging technologies. These are the three major technologies in use today:

- Amazon Simple Queue Service (SQS)
- Amazon Simple Notification Service
- Amazon CloudWatch events

As the name indicates, *Amazon SQS* uses queues to integrate producers and consumers of a message. Producers write messages to a queue, and consumers pull messages from the queue. A queue is simply a buffer between producers and consumers (see Figure 2.28).

We have two types of queues:

Standard Queue   Highly scalable with maximum throughput, best-effort ordering, and at-least-once delivery semantics. A Standard queue decouples applications allowing for individual scalability.

FIFO Queue   Exactly-once semantics with guaranteed ordering with lesser scalability than Standard queue

Amazon SQS is a massively scalable technology with native integration to the rest of AWS and Lambda in particular. Amazon SQS allows you to build simple and cost-effective solutions and transmit data of any volume between various services.

FIGURE 2.28   Amazon Simple Queue Service

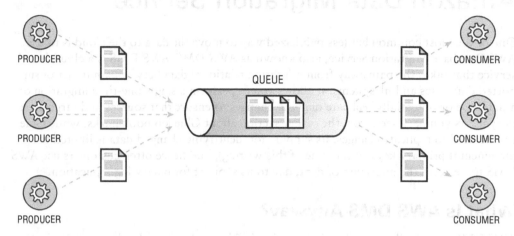

The key benefits of Amazon SQS are as follows:

- **Reduce administrative and maintenance overhead:** As SQS is a managed service, AWS manages the underlying infrastructure and complexity needs to provide you with a highly available, fault-tolerant, and scalable messaging service. With pay-as-you-go pricing, queues can be dynamically created and automatically scaled to help you build highly decoupled applications, thus letting you focus on the business needs of the application rather than worrying about underlying infrastructure for communication between key components.

- **Reliable:** Amazon SQS delivers large volumes of data in a reliable, fault-tolerant manner. Behind the scenes, multiple copies of the data are stored in a redundant manner to minimize data loss in the event of a failure.

- **Security:** Amazon SQS can be used to securely and reliably exchange data using server-side encryption to encrypt the message and using KMS to manage the keys that protect SQS messages.

- **Scalability:** Amazon SQS allows you to dynamically scale your queue based on the demand patterns without having to pre-provision any resources. Queues are not limited to the number of messages.

- **Cost-effective:** Amazon SQS provides a flexible pricing model, with zero upfront fees and a pay-as-you-go model.

Exam Tip

The AWS Data Analytics Specialty certification exam will not test you on the service limits and the specific pricing details for various services. You do, however, need to understand which services will be more cost-effective in certain scenarios.

Amazon Data Migration Service

One of the most common but less publicized way to move the data to the cloud is to use AWS Database Migration Service, also known as *AWS DMS*. AWS DMS is a cloud-based service that takes the pain away from migrating relational data between a number of supported databases and filesystems. It allows you to perform a single one-time migration of a database or potentially replicate ongoing changes to ensure that sources and targets are in sync. As you have seen from the earlier section about Glue job bookmarks, while Glue can be used to replicate changes, its support for identifying changed data is limited to incremental primary keys (at the time of this writing), and hence often customers use AWS DMS to perform the migration of data, due to its support for binary log replication.

What Is AWS DMS Anyway?

AWS DMS is basically an application running inside the Amazon cloud on an EC2 instance running software that replicates data from one endpoint (source) to another endpoint (target). This replication can be a one-time activity or a recurring activity that captures only data that has changed since the last run. The EC2 instance can be a T2, C4, or R4 instance type. Figure 2.29 shows a high-level view of AWS Database Migration Service.

FIGURE 2.29 AWS Database Migration Service

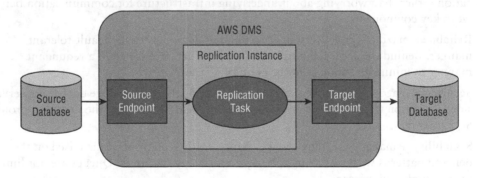

A replication task can be defined by providing a name for the task, a definition of the endpoints to connect to, a migration type, a definition of how to prepare the target for the load, and finally, a choice between various Large Binary Object (LOB) modes. Tasks are the workhorse of the migration and run on a replication instance. Multiple tasks can be run in parallel, and the settings can be defined in JSON format, which give you control over performance and debugging of the task.

There are three types of migrations, each having its own nuances.

- Existing data:
  - Creates files or tables in the target database
  - Populates the tables with data from the source
  - Migrates Existing Data option in the AWS console and Full Load in the API
- Existing data and replicate changes:
  - Captures changes on the source during migration
  - Once initial migration completes, changes are applied to the target as units of completed transactions.
  - Migrate Existing Data And Replicate Ongoing Changes option in the AWS console and full-load-and-cdc in the API
- Replicate changes only:
  - Reads the recovery file on the source database
  - Groups together transactions and applies them to the target. Buffering as needed.
  - Replicate Data Changes Only option in the AWS console

For target preparation, you can choose between the following three options:

- **Do Nothing:** In Do Nothing mode, AWS DMS assumes target tables are pre-created. In full load or full load plus CDC, ensure that the target tables are empty before starting the migration
- **Drop Tables On Target:** In Drop Tables On Target mode, AWS DMS drops the target tables and re-creates them before starting the migration. This ensures that the target tables are empty when the migration starts
- **Truncate:** In Truncate mode, AWS DMS truncates all target tables before the migration starts.

What Does AWS DMS Support?

AWS DMS supports managed hardware, software, patching, upgrades, and error reporting seamlessly while you focus on migrating the data. It provides a scalable solution for migration activity. Resources can be scaled up or down based on resource requirements. It has cost-effective pricing, where you pay based on the usage of the resources. It supports automatic failover in case your primary replication server fails.

In addition, AWS DMS provides seamless migration to either new software or new hardware. For example, you may want to migrate from old databases to new databases like

Amazon Aurora with cutting-edge features, or you may even want to upgrade underlying infrastructure while keeping the same database engine. It supports a number of different databases as source databases:

- Oracle
- Microsoft SQL Server
- MySQL
- MariaDB
- PostgreSQL
- Db2 LUW
- SAP
- MongoDB
- Amazon Aurora

And a number of databases as targets:

- Oracle
- Microsoft SQL Server
- PostgreSQL
- MySQL
- Amazon Redshift
- SAP ASE
- Amazon S3
- DynamoDB

AWS DMS supports secure migrations using the following:

- KMS for encryption of data at rest
- SSL for data in motion

To learn more about AWS DMS, please visit amzn.to/2Vvfj6i.

> From an exam perspective, it is important to know that DMS can actually be used to load data to Amazon S3 and Amazon Redshift. In addition to that, it gives better flexibility when it comes to capturing delta records.

AWS Data Pipeline

There are a number of technologies in the AWS Analytics and partner ecosystem that work together to meet the needs of various customer use cases. *AWS Data Pipeline* allows you to orchestrate workflows and automate the movement and transformation of the data. An example of a data pipeline can be extraction of data from a source system, landing it on to S3, transforming the data into a Parquet file, and running various data cleansing transformations before copying it into Amazon Redshift.

AWS Data Pipeline has three major components that work together:

- Pipeline definitions
- Pipeline schedules
- Task Runner

Pipeline Definition

A pipeline definition defines the structure of your pipeline in terms of the sources, the actual transformation, and the data targets. A pipeline definition is how you communicate your business logic to the AWS Data Pipeline. It contains the following information:

- Names, locations, and formats of your data sources
- Activities that transform the data
- The schedule for those activities
- Resources that run your activities and preconditions
- Preconditions that must be satisfied before the activities can be scheduled
- Ways to alert you with status updates as pipeline execution proceeds

The pipeline definition is the main asset that is referenced by AWS Data Pipeline to determine the tasks that need to be scheduled. AWS Data Pipeline uses this definition to create tasks and then schedule them on appropriate task runners. Depending on the success, AWS Data Pipeline might have to retry the task as per the instructions or reassign it to a different task runner. Notifications can be configured in case of repeated failures of the tasks.

A pipeline can be defined in one of the following manners:

- AWS Data Pipeline GUI on the AWS Console
- A JSON file created by any text editor
- Programmatically using one of the following:

  - AWS SDK
  - AWS Data Pipeline API

Pipeline Schedules

A pipeline would schedule your work by creating Amazon EC2 instances to perform the defined work. You can create a pipeline definition and then activate the pipeline. These other activities can also be performed:

- Edit pipeline definition of a running pipeline. You need to activate the pipeline again for this to take effect.
- Deactivate the pipeline.
- Modify a data source.
- Delete the pipeline.

There are three types of components associated with a scheduled pipeline.

- **Pipeline components:** Pipeline components represent the business logic of the pipeline and are represented by the different sections of a pipeline definition. They specify the data sources, activities, schedule, and preconditions of the workflow. They can inherit properties from parent components. Relationships among components are defined by reference. Pipeline components define the rules of data management.

- **Instances:** When AWS Data Pipeline runs a pipeline, it compiles the pipeline components to create a set of actionable instances. Each instance contains all the information for performing a specific task. The complete set of instances is the to-do list of the pipeline. AWS Data Pipeline hands the instances out to task runners to process

- **Attempts:** To provide robust data management, AWS Data Pipeline retries a failed operation. It continues to do so until the task reaches the maximum number of allowed retry attempts. Attempt objects track the various attempts, results, and failure reasons if applicable. Essentially, it is the instance with a counter. AWS Data Pipeline (see Figure 2.30) performs retries using the same resources from the previous attempts, such as Amazon EMR clusters and EC2 instances

FIGURE 2.30   AWS Data Pipeline

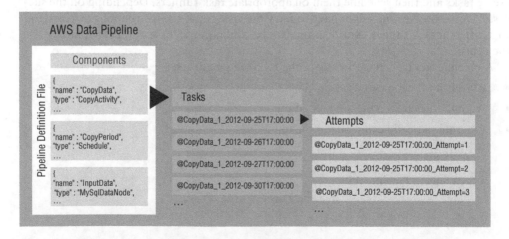

Task Runner

Task running is a process that continuously polls for new tasks and then performs them. *Task Runner* is installed and automatically run on resources created by your pipeline definitions. When Task Runner is installed and configured, it would poll the activated AWS pipelines for tasks. Once a task is assigned, Task Runner performs the task and reports the status back to AWS Data Pipeline. It is important to remember that while a pipeline may be evaluated into multiple tasks, a single task is a discrete unit of work. The general flow of a Task Runner is explained next.

AWS Data Pipeline can work with the following services to perform data transformation:

- Amazon EC2
- Amazon EMR

AWS Data Pipeline works with the following services to store the data:

- Amazon DynamoDB
- Amazon RDS
- Amazon Redshift
- Amazon S3

AWS Data Pipeline can be accessed using the following interfaces:

- AWS Management Console
- AWS CLI
- AWS SDK
- Query API: Provides low-level APIs that you call using HTTPS requests. This is one of the most direct ways to access AWS Data Pipeline, but it requires your application to handle low-level details. This can be cumbersome, but AWS Data Pipeline provides good documentation around this.

AWS Data Pipeline has certain other concepts as well, which are covered in the User Guide:

- **Data nodes:** A data node defines the location and the type of data that the pipeline uses as input or output. The following data nodes are supported:
  - DynamoDBDataNode
  - SqlDataNode
  - RedshiftDataNode
  - S3DataNode

- **Databases:** AWS Data pipeline supports the following databases:
  - JdbcDatabase – Any JDBC-compliant database
  - RdsDatabase – Any RDS database
  - RedshiftDatabase
- **Activities:** In AWS Data Pipeline, an activity is actually the work performed. AWS Data Pipeline provides several prepackaged activities that accommodate common scenarios found at customer sites:
  - CopyActivity – Copies data from one location to another
  - EmrActivity – Runs an Amazon EMR cluster
  - HiveActivity – Runs a hive query on an Amazon EMR cluster
  - HiveCopyActivity – Runs a Hive query on an Amazon EMR cluster with support for advanced filtering and support for S3 data node
  - PigActivity – Runs a Pig script on an Amazon EMR cluster
  - RedshiftCopyActivity – Copies data to and from Amazon Redshift tables
  - ShellCommandActivity – Runs a custom Unix/Linux shell command activity
  - SqlActivity – Runs an SQL query on a database
- **Preconditions:** Quite often it is important to check certain conditions before starting an activity. For example, you might want to check if a particular DynamoDB table exists, or you might want to check if a particular S3 Key for a particular date exists before you can run the downstream processing. AWS Data Pipeline supports two major types of preconditions:
  - System managed preconditions are run by AWS Data Pipeline on your behalf and do not require a computation resource. Here are some examples of system managed preconditions:
    - DynamoDBDataExists
    - DynamoDBTableExists
    - S3KeyExists
    - S3PrefixNotEmpty
  - User-managed preconditions:
    - Exists – checks to see if a data node exists
    - ShellCommandPrecondition – Runs a custom Unix/Linux command as a precondition

- **Resources:** An activity needs resources to be performed. For example, an activity like PigActivity or EMRActivity requires computational resources like EMR to be available. AWS Data Pipeline supports the following types of resources:

  - Ec2Resource

  - EMRCluster

- **Actions:** During a pipeline execution, steps can succeed, fail, or get delayed. You would need to take appropriate actions when such an event happens. AWS Data Pipeline caters to this need of pipeline building and supports the following actions:

  - SnsAlaram – This action sends an SNS notification to a topic based on onSuccess, onFail, and onLateAction events.

  - Terminate – This action triggers the cancellation of pending or unfinished activities, resources, or data nodes.

Large-Scale Data Transfer Solutions

We have seen a number of different technologies that allow you to collect data from different data sources when the volumes are low to moderate. However, when you would come across situations when you need to migrate large data volumes, such as when data sizes are over multiple terabytes or petabytes, transferring the data over an Internet connection could take enormously large amounts of time. There are also scenarios where you need portable data transfers but having the ability to transfer multiple Terabytes of data. Those are the scenarios in which you either need a portable solution like AWS Snowcone or large-scale data transfer options like AWS Snowball and AWS Snowmobile and connectivity options like AWS Direct Connect. Let's look in a bit more detail about what these options are.

AWS Snowcone

AWS Snowcone is the smallest member of the AWS Snow family which weighs as little as 2.1 kg and provides you with 8 terabytes of usable storage. Its small size makes it ideal for tight spaces or where portability is the key. It is useful in a number of scenarios including cases where organizations want to move multiple Terabytes of data to the cloud but lack adequate network bandwidth, or in some cases little to no connectivity in places where the data resides.

Furthermore, AWS Snowcone might be useful in Healthcare IoT where it can be used for data collection and data processing in healthcare facilities or remote medical areas. It can be used to transfer crucial data from emergency vehicles in real-time.

Some key characteristics of AWS Snowcone are as follows:

1. Military-grade security
2. 4.5 pounds (2.1 kg) weight
3. Portable computing, anywhere
4. Ability to withstand harshest of environments
5. Offline & online data transfer
6. 8 TB of storage
7. 2 CPU and 4 GB of Compute memory

AWS Snowball

AWS Snowball is a data transport solution that accelerates moving terabytes to petabytes of data into and out of AWS using storage devices designed to be secure for physical transport (see Figure 2.31). Using Snowball helps to eliminate challenges that can be encountered with large-scale data transfers, including high network costs, long transfer times, and security concerns.

FIGURE 2.31 AWS Snowball

AWS Snowball uses devices designed to be secure and the Snowball Client to accelerate petabyte-scale data transfers into and out of AWS. You start by using the AWS Management Console to create one or more jobs to request one or multiple Snowball devices (depending on how much data you need to transfer) and download and install the Snowball Client Once the device arrives, connect it to your local network, set the IP address either manually or with DHCP, and use the Client to identify the directories you want to copy. The Client will automatically encrypt and copy the data to the device and notify you when the transfer job is complete. When the transfer is complete and the device is ready to be returned, the E Ink shipping label will automatically update to indicate the correct AWS facility to ship to, and you can track the job status by using Amazon Simple Notification Service (SNS), text messages, or directly in the console.

Snowball is the right data transfer choice if you need to more securely and quickly transfer terabytes to many petabytes of data to AWS. Snowball can also be the right choice if you don't want to make expensive upgrades to your network infrastructure, if you frequently experience large backlogs of data, if you're located in a physically isolated environment, or if you're in an area where high-bandwidth Internet connections are not available or are cost prohibitive.

You can transfer virtually any amount of data with Snowball using multiple devices in parallel or serially one after another. For example, move 150 TB at one time with two 80 TB devices, or order a single device to move 80 TB and then order a second device for the remaining 70 TB.

The AWS Snowball Client is software that you install on a local host computer and that helps you to efficiently identify, compress, encrypt, and transfer data from the directories you specify to a Snowball.

You can use the AWS Snowball Client to estimate the time it takes to transfer your data (AWS Snowball transfer details). Data transfer speed is affected by a number of factors, including local network speed, file size, and the speed at which data can be read from your local servers.

The Snowball Client will copy data to Snowball as fast as conditions allow (for example, less than a day to copy 48 TB of data, depending on your local environment). End-to-end time to transfer the data into AWS is approximately a week, including the usual shipping and handling time in AWS data centers. You can copy twice that much data in the same amount of time by using two Snowball devices in parallel, or copy up to 80 TB of data in two and a half days on a larger Snowball device, which would increase your end-to-end time to about a week and a half.

For security purposes, data transfers must be completed within 90 days of a Snowball's preparation. This should be enough time to transfer up to 80 TBs of data using one Snowball device.

Snowball has 10 Gbps network interfaces with RJ45, SFP+ copper, and SFP+ optical network ports. You can check the AWS Snowball specifications page (amzn.to/2RDCn1H) for more details.

Snowball is a strong choice for data transfer if you need to more securely and quickly transfer terabytes to many petabytes of data to AWS.

As a rule of thumb, if it takes more than one week to upload your data to AWS using the spare capacity of your existing Internet connection, then you should consider using Snowball. For example, following the guidelines in Table 2.3, if you have a 100 Mb connection that you can solely dedicate to transferring your data and need to transfer 100 TB of data, it takes more than 100 days to complete data transfer over that connection. You can make the same transfer by using multiple Snowballs in about a week.

TABLE 2.3   Transferring 100 TB of data over an Internet connection

Available Internet Connection	Theoretical Min. Number of Days to Transfer 100TB at 80% Network Utilization	When to Consider AWS Snowball?
T3 (44.736 Mbps)	269 days	2 TB or more
100 Mbps	120 days	5 TB or more
1000 Mbps	12 days	60 TB or more

AWS Direct Connect provides you with dedicated, fast connections from your premises to the AWS network. If you need to transfer large quantities of data to AWS on an ongoing basis, AWS Direct Connect might be the right choice.

Snowball encrypts all data with 256-bit encryption. You manage your encryption keys by using the AWS Key Management Service (KMS). Your keys are never sent to or stored on the device.

In addition to using a tamper-resistant enclosure, Snowball uses an industry-standard Trusted Platform Module (TPM) with a dedicated processor designed to detect any unauthorized modifications to the hardware, firmware, or software. AWS inspects every device for any signs of tampering and to verify that no changes were detected by the TPM.

Export is a feature of Snowball that enables customers to export terabytes to petabytes of data from Amazon Simple Storage Service (S3) to on-premises storage.

The Snowball Job Management API provides programmatic access to the job creation and management features of a Snowball. It is a simple, standards-based REST web service interface, designed to work with any Internet development environment.

The AWS Snowball Job Management API allows partners and customers to build custom integrations to manage the process of requesting Snowballs and communicating job status. The API provides a simple web service interface that you can use to create, list, update, and cancel jobs from anywhere on the web. Using this web service, developers can easily build applications that manage Snowball jobs. To learn more, please refer to the following link amzn.to/2FCfxV4.

The S3 SDK Adapter for Snowball provides a S3-compatible interface to the Snowball Client for reading and writing data on a Snowball.

The S3 Adapter provides functions to communicate with Snowball, allowing customers to build tools to copy data from file and non-file sources. It includes interfaces to copy data to Snowball with the same encryption that is available through the Snowball command-line tool. To learn more, please refer to the AWS Snowball documentation at https://amzn .to/2DZZvEh. Key use cases for Snowball include cloud migration, disaster recovery, data center decommission, and content distribution.

AWS Snowmobile

AWS Snowmobile is the first exabyte-scale data migration service that allows you to move very large datasets from on-premises to AWS. Each Snowmobile is a secured data truck with up to 100 PB storage capacity that can be dispatched to your site and connected directly to your network backbone to perform high-speed data migration. You can quickly migrate an exabyte of data with 10 Snowmobiles in parallel from a single location or multiple data centers. Snowmobile is offered by AWS as a managed service.

After an initial assessment, a Snowmobile will be transported to your data center and AWS personnel will configure it for you so it can be accessed as a network storage target. When your Snowmobile is on-site, AWS personnel will work with your team to connect a removable, high-speed network switch from Snowmobile to your local network and you can begin your high-speed data transfer from any number of sources within your data center to the Snowmobile. After your data is loaded, Snowmobile is driven back to AWS where your data is imported into Amazon S3.

Snowmobile uses multiple layers of security to help protect your data, including dedicated security personnel, GPS tracking, alarm monitoring, 24/7 video surveillance, and an optional escort security vehicle while in transit. All data is encrypted with 256-bit encryption keys you manage through the AWS Key Management Service (KMS) and designed for security and full chain of custody of your data.

After you have placed your inquiry for a Snowmobile, AWS personnel will contact you to determine requirements for deploying a Snowmobile and schedule the job and will drive the required Snowmobile equipment to your site. Once on-site, they will connect it to your local network so that you can use your high-speed local connection to quickly transfer data from your local storage appliances or servers to the Snowmobile. After the data transfer is complete, the Snowmobile will be returned to your designated AWS Region where your data will be uploaded into the AWS storage services you have selected, such as S3 or Glacier. Finally, AWS will work with you to validate that your data has been successfully uploaded.

Snowmobile enables customers to quickly migrate exabyte-scale datasets from on-premises to AWS in a more secure, fast, and low-cost manner. Use cases include migrating 100s of petabytes of data (such as video libraries, genomic sequences, seismic data, satellite images) and financial records to run big data analytics on AWS, or shutting down legacy data centers and moving all local data in exabytes to AWS. Before Snowmobile, migrating data at such a scale would typically take years, which was too slow for many customers. With Snowmobile, you can now request multiple data trucks each with up to 100 PB capacity to be dispatched on-site and connected to your local high-speed network backbone, and you can then transfer your exabyte-scale datasets to AWS in as quickly as a few weeks, plus transport time.

Each Snowmobile comes with up to 100 PB of storage capacity housed in a 45-foot long High Cube shipping container that measures 8 feet wide, 9.6 feet tall, and has a curb weight of approximately 68,000 pounds. The ruggedized shipping container is tamper-resistant, water-resistant, temperature controlled, and GPS-tracked.

To migrate large datasets of 10 PB or more in a single location, you should use Snowmobile. For datasets less than 10 PB or distributed in multiple locations, you should use Snowball. In addition, you should evaluate the amount of available bandwidth in your network backbone. If you have a high-speed backbone with hundreds of gigabits per second of spare throughput, then you can use Snowmobile to migrate the large datasets all at once. If you have limited bandwidth on your backbone, you should consider using multiple Snowballs to migrate the data incrementally.

The Snowmobile needs physical access to your data center to allow for network connectivity. It comes with a removable connector rack with up to two kilometers of networking cable that can directly connect to the network backbone in your data center. The Snowmobile can be parked in a covered area at your data center, or in an uncovered area that is adjacent to your data center, and close enough to run the networking cable. The parking area needs to hold a standard 45-foot High Cube trailer with a minimum of 6'0" (1.83 m) of peripheral clearance. Snowmobile can operate at ambient temperatures up to 85°F (29.4°C) before an auxiliary chiller unit is required. AWS can provide the auxiliary chiller if needed based on the site survey findings.

A fully powered Snowmobile requires approximately 350 kW. Snowmobile can be connected to available utility power sources at your location if sufficient capacity is available. Otherwise, AWS can dispatch a separate generator set along with the Snowmobile if your site permits such generator use. This generator set takes a similar amount of space as the Snowmobile, which is parking for a vehicle approximately the same size as a 45-foot container trailer.

AWS Direct Connect

AWS Direct Connect (Figure 2.32) is a cloud service solution that makes it easy to establish a dedicated network connection from your premises to AWS. Using AWS Direct Connect, you can establish private connectivity between AWS and your data center, office, or colocation environment, which in many cases can reduce your network costs, increase bandwidth throughput, and provide a more consistent network experience than Internet-based connections.

FIGURE 2.32   AWS Direct Connect

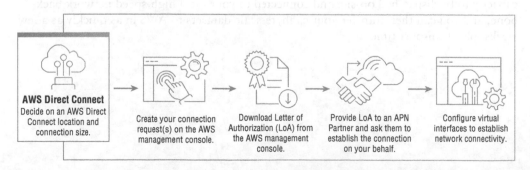

AWS Direct Connect
Decide on an AWS Direct Connect location and connection size.

Create your connection request(s) on the AWS management console.

Download Letter of Authorization (LoA) from the AWS management console.

Provide LoA to an APN Partner and ask them to establish the connection on your behalf.

Configure virtual interfaces to establish network connectivity.

AWS Direct Connect lets you establish a dedicated network connection between your network and one of the AWS Direct Connect locations. Using industry standard 802.1q VLANs, this dedicated connection can be partitioned into multiple virtual interfaces. This allows you to use the same connection to access public resources such as objects stored in Amazon S3 using public IP address space, and private resources such as Amazon EC2 instances running within an Amazon Virtual Private Cloud (VPC) using private IP space while maintaining network separation between the public and private environments. Virtual interfaces can be reconfigured at any time to meet your changing needs.

The key benefits of AWS Direct Connect are as follows:

- Reducing your bandwidth costs
- Consistent network performance
- Compatibility with all AWS services
- Private connectivity to your Amazon VPC
- Elastic scaling between 1 Gbps to 10 Gbps

Exam Tip

AWS Direct Connect is an important topic from the exam perspective and hence your understanding for AWS Direct Connect will aid in the exam preparation.

Summary

During this chapter we discussed the various components of the data pipeline when it comes to ingesting data onto the AWS cloud. We looked at ingesting data from IoT devices using AWS IoT, streaming data using Amazon Kinesis, transferring data from databases and other data sources using AWS Glue, and using Amazon Data Migration Service for migrating large-scale data from databases and capturing delta changes. We also looked at Amazon SQS for events, Amazon Snowball and Snowmobile for data transfers that are too huge to be transmitted over a standard Internet connection, and AWS Direct Connect for direct connectivity between your data center and AWS.

Now that the data has been made available to AWS, the next chapter will cover processing of the data using the various tools available to us.

Review Questions

The following review questions will help your understanding of the contents in this chapter. Please do read all the content mentioned in the references to be better prepared for the actual exam.

1. You work for a large ad-tech company which has a set of predefined ads displayed routinely. Due to the popularity of your products, your website is getting popular garnering attention of a diverse set of visitors. You are currently placing dynamic ads based on user click data; however, you have discovered the process time is not keeping up to display the new ads since a user's stay on the website is short-lived (few seconds) compared to your turnaround time for delivering a new ad (> 1 minute). You have been asked to evaluate AWS platform services for possible solution to analyze the problem and reduce overall add serving time. Which of the below is your recommendation?

   A. Push the click stream data to an Amazon SQS queue. Have your application subscribe to the SQS queue, and write data to an Amazon RDS instance. Perform analysis using SQL.

   B. Move the website to be hosted in AWS and use AWS Kinesis to dynamically process user click stream in real-time.

   C. Push web clicks to Amazon Kinesis Fire hose and analyze with kinesis analytics or Kinesis Client Library.

   D. Push web clicks to Amazon Kinesis Stream and analyze with Kinesis Analytics or Kinesis Client Library (KCL).

2. An upcoming startup with self-driving delivery trucks fitted with embedded sensors has requested that you capture data arriving in near real time and track the vehicles' movement within the city. You will be capturing information from multiple sensors with data that includes the vehicle identification number, make, model, color and its GPS coordinates. Data is sent every 2 seconds and needs to be processed in near real time. Which of the following tools can you use to ingest the data and process it in near real time?

   A. Amazon Kinesis

   B. AWS Data Pipeline

   C. Amazon SQS

   D. Amazon EMR

3. Which of the statements are true about AWS Glue crawlers? (Choose three.)

   A. AWS Glue crawlers provide built in classifiers that can be used to classify any type of data.

   B. AWS Glue crawlers can connect to Amazon S3, Amazon RDS, Amazon Redshift, Amazon DynamoDB, and any JDBC sources.

   C. AWS Glue crawlers provide the option of custom classifiers which provide options to classify data that cannot be classified by built-in classifiers.

   D. AWS Glue crawlers write metadata to AWS Glue Data Catalog.

4. You have been tasked to work on a new and exciting project where data is coming from smart sensors in the kitchen and is sent to the AWS platform. You have to ensure that you can filter and transform the data being received from the sensors before storing them in DynamoDB. Which of the following AWS service is ideally suited for this scenario?

    A. IoT Rules Engine

    B. IoT Device Shadow service

    C. IoT Message Broker

    D. IoT Device Shadow

5. You are working for a fortune-500 financial institution which is running its databases on Microsoft Azure. They have decided to move to AWS and are looking to migrate their SQL databases to Amazon RDS. Which of the following services can simplify the migration activity?

    A. Amazon Kinesis

    B. Managed Streaming for Kafka

    C. AWS Glue

    D. AWS Data Migration Service

6. Your customer has an on-premises Cloudera cluster and is looking to migrate the workloads to the AWS platform. The customer does not want to pay the licensing and any fixed cost. His objective is to build a serverless pipeline in a pay-as-you-go model, ensuring that there is limited impact of migration on existing PySpark code. What would be your recommendation from the following options?

    A. Migrate the on-premises Cloudera cluster to the AWS platform by running it on EC2 instances.

    B. Migrate the on-premises Cloudera cluster to a long-running Amazon EMR cluster.

    C. Migrate the on-premises PySpark code to a transient Amazon EMR cluster.

    D. Migrate the code to AWS Glue.

7. You are working for a ride-hailing company that has recently ventured into food delivery and order processing. The order processing system is built on AWS. The order processing runs into scaling issues particularly during lunch and dinner times when there is an excessive amount of orders received. In the current infrastructure, you have EC2 instances that pick up the orders from the application and EC2 instances in an Auto Scaling group to process the orders. What architecture would you recommended to ensure that the EC2 processing instances are scaled correctly based on the demand?

    A. Use SQS queues to decouple the order receiving and order processing components of the architecture. Scale the processing servers based on the queue length.

    B. Use SQS queues to decouple the order receiving and order processing components of the architecture. Scale the processing servers based on notifications sent from the SQS queues.

    C. Use CloudWatch metrics to understand the load capacity on the processing servers. Ensure that SNS is used to scale up the servers based on notifications.

    D. Use CloudWatch metrics to understand the load capacity on the processing servers and then scale the capacity accordingly.

8. Your CIO has recently announced that you will be migrating to AWS to reduce your costs and improve overall agility by benefitting from the breadth and depth of the platform. You have a number of on-premises Oracle databases, which are not only expensive from a licensing perspective but also difficult to scale. You have realized that you can get the same performance from Amazon Aurora at 1/10 of the cost and hence would like to proceed with the migration. You want to create the schema beforehand on the AWS My SQL instance. Which of the following is the easiest approach in getting this done?

   A. Use the AWS Database Generation Tool to generate the schema in the target database.

   B. Use the AWS Schema Conversion Tool to generate the schema in the target database.

   C. Create scripts to generate the schema in the target database.

   D. Use the AWS Config Tool to generate the schema in the target database.

9. Which of the following can be used to move extremely large amounts of data to AWS with up to 100 PB per device?

   A. AWS Snowmobile

   B. AWS Snowball

   C. AWS S3 Export

   D. AWS S3 Transfer Acceleration

   E. AWS Direct Connect

10. You have recently moved to AWS but still maintain an on-premises data center. You have already migrated your BI/analytics and DWH workloads to Amazon Redshift and now need to migrate large volumes of data to Redshift to ensure that the weekly reports have fresh data. Which AWS-managed service can be used for this data transfer in a simple, fast, and secure way? (Choose two.)

    A. Direct Connect

    B. Import/Export to AWS

    C. Data Pipeline

    D. Snowball

References

1. aws.amazon.com/iot/

2. https://docs.aws.amazon.com/streams/latest/dev/introduction.html

3. https://docs.aws.amazon.com/glue/latest/dg/what-is-glue.html

4. https://docs.aws.amazon.com/datapipeline/latest/DeveloperGuide/what-is-datapipeline.html

5. https://docs.aws.amazon.com/snowball/latest/snowcone-guide/index.html

6. https://docs.aws.amazon.com/snowball/latest/developer-guide/index.html

7. `https://docs.aws.amazon.com/snowball/latest/ug/index.html`
8. `https://docs.aws.amazon.com/directconnect/latest/UserGuide/Welcome.html`
9. `aws.amazon.com/iot-core/features/`
10. `docs.aws.amazon.com/cognito/latest/developerguide/authentication-flow.html`

Exercises & Workshops

We would highly recommend that the reader goes through the following list of exercises and workshops to make themselves comfortable with the products and services. AWS Data Analytics Specialty certification exam expects users to have practical knowledge of the services being tested, and hence a theoretical knowledge will not be enough to pass the exam.

1. Building Streaming Analytics applications on AWS
   `https://real-time-streaming-with-kinesis.workshop.aws`

2. Database Migration Immersion Day – Database Migration Service and Schema Conversion tool
   `https://www.immersionday.com/dms`

3. Data Engineering Immersion Day – AWS Glue, Data Lakes, Amazon Athena and Amazon Quicksight
   `https://www.immersionday.com/data-engineering`

4. Serverless Data Lake Day
   `https://www.immersionday.com/serverless-data-lake`

5. Copy CSV data between Amazon S3 buckets using AWS Data Pipeline
   `https://docs.aws.amazon.com/datapipeline/latest/DeveloperGuide/dp-copydata-s3.html`

6. Export MySQL Data to Amazon S3 using AWS Data Pipeline
   `https://docs.aws.amazon.com/datapipeline/latest/DeveloperGuide/dp-copydata-mysql.html`

7. Process real-time stock data using KPL and KCL 2.x
   `https://docs.aws.amazon.com/streams/latest/dev/tutorial-stock-data-kplkcl2.html`

8. Analyze Real-Time stock data using Kinesis Data Analytics for Java Applications
   `https://docs.aws.amazon.com/streams/latest/dev/tutorial-stock-data.html`

9. Using AWS Lambda with Amazon Kinesis Data Streams
   `https://docs.aws.amazon.com/streams/latest/dev/tutorial-stock-data-lambda.html`

Chapter

3

Data Storage

THE AWS DATA ANALYTICS SPECIALTY CERTIFICATION EXAM OBJECTIVES COVERED IN THIS CHAPTER MAY INCLUDE, BUT ARE NOT LIMITED TO, THE FOLLOWING:

✓ **Domain 2.0: Storage and Data Management**

- 2.1 Determine the operational characteristics of a storage solution for analytics

- 2.2 Determine data access and retrieval patterns

- 2.3 Select an appropriate data layout, schema, structure, and format

- 2.4 Define a data lifecycle based on usage patterns and business requirements

- 2.5 Determine an appropriate system for cataloging data and managing metadata

Introduction

In this chapter, you will learn about how to store data which is arriving from different ingestion sources, on the AWS platform based on the requirements of the use cases and make the data available for downstream consumption. We'll talk about various services, such as Amazon S3, Amazon DynamoDB, Amazon DocumentDB, Amazon Neptune, Amazon Timestream, Amazon FSx for Windows, Amazon FSx for Lustre, and Amazon Storage Gateway. As you have seen in earlier chapters, each of these services fits certain use-case profiles. The key theme of the exam is to gauge your understanding of how these services fit use cases rather than individual configuration parameters. This chapter covers almost 22% of the exam questions, and hence a better understanding of these objectives will help you in improving your overall exam score. Figure 3.1 shows the importance of data storage during an analytics pipeline.

FIGURE 3.1   Importance of data storage in an analytics pipeline

In the old days, customers would pick up a single database for all their storage needs, often complicating the pipeline, and try to retrofit their use cases into a technology that they had chosen due to a particular use case. The days of limited choice are over, and customers now can pick the right tool for the job. It is for this specific need and customer demand that AWS offers a variety of storage choices for your analytical applications.

Figure 3.2 shows the number of different services available on the AWS platform to support a wide variety of use cases ranging from general storage like Amazon S3, Amazon EBS, and Amazon EFS to specific use-case-specific storage like Amazon ElasticCache, Amazon DynamoDB, Amazon RDS, Amazon DocumentDB, Amazon Neptune, Amazon

EMR, Amazon CloudSearch, and Amazon ES. Some of these services are database services and are not covered under the AWS Data Analytics Specialty certification exam. I'll cover all the necessary services that are required to pass this exam.

FIGURE 3.2   Types of storage solutions provided by AWS

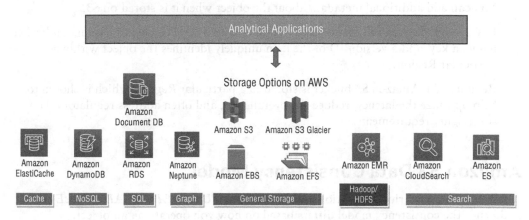

Let's look at different AWS storage services and architectural patterns and when to use them.

Amazon S3

Amazon Simple Storage Service (S3) forms the backbone of most data and analytics applications built on the AWS platform. Amazon S3 is a web service that allows you to store and retrieve any amount of data from anywhere in the world. It provides a number of different interfaces for interaction, including console- and API-based access. Amazon S3 is an object store and hence provides specific APIs to interact with it to store and retrieve data and metadata about objects. To be able to use Amazon S3 effectively, you need to be aware of the following concepts, which are important to build an understanding of the service:

Bucket   A *bucket* is just a container of objects. No object can exist in S3 without a bucket, and hence the bucket is the fundamental concept in S3. Buckets are helpful as they provide certain key abilities:

You use them to organize the Amazon S3 namespace at the highest level.

As each bucket has an associated storage and retrieval cost, it helps identify the account responsible for data storage and transfer charges.

Buckets help you define appropriate access controls to different data within your organization.

Buckets can be created in specific AWS Regions and can be configured to generate a unique version ID and can be attached to the object, upon addition of a new object.

Object   While a bucket is just a container, the items that you store inside of S3 are referred to as *objects*. Amazon S3 has no idea about the data contained inside your S3 object, but it does understand where an item is stored based on the name-value pairs. You can add additional metadata about the object when it is stored on S3.

Key   Each object in S3 is uniquely identified with a *key*. The combination of a bucket name, a key, and a version ID of the item uniquely identifies the object within a particular Region.

Region   An Amazon S3 bucket is stored in a particular *Region*, which is chosen to help optimize the latency, reduce the overall cost, and often address regulatory data sovereignty requirements.

Amazon S3 Data Consistency Model

Amazon S3 offers various operations for objects, like *PUTs, GETs, HEADs, DELETEs*, and hence the consistency model differs based on how you operate on an object. Amazon S3 provides read-after-write consistency for PUTs of new objects. However, if you make a HEAD or GET request to the key name (generally used to see if an object exists), Amazon S3 provides eventual consistency for read-after-write.

Similarly, for overwrite PUTs and DELETEs, Amazon S3 offers an eventual consistency model. Updates to a single key are atomic in nature, and hence when you update an existing key, you might get either the old object or the new object, but you will never get corrupt or partial data.

When you store an object on Amazon S3, it replicates the data behind the scenes for high availability and fault tolerance, which does come with its own gotchas. The main challenge is that if you replace or delete an object and immediately try to read the object, Amazon S3 might return stale data depending on the status of the propagation of the change:

Impact on List-after-Writes   For example, when you write an object to Amazon S3 and then list the keys within the bucket, where the object was written, you might occasionally not see the object in the list. This obviously depends on whether Amazon S3 has been able to propagate the changes and how soon you make a call to list the objects after the write.

Impact for Reads-after-Write   If a process replaces an existing object and immediately tries to read the object, Amazon S3 might return the older object until the propagation of the object has happened fully.

Impact for Reads-after-Deletes   If a process deletes an existing object and immediately tries to read it, Amazon S3 might return the deleted object if the propagation has not gone through fully.

Impact of List-after-Deletes   If a process deletes an object and immediately lists an object within the bucket, Amazon S3 might list the deleted object until the propagation has gone through fully.

Data Lake and S3

Before we talk further about S3, it is important to talk about the data lake, which is an important architectural concept when it comes to setting up analytical platforms. The data lake is not a technology but a popular pattern to store and analyze large volumes of structured, semi-structured, and multi-structured data in a centralized repository. One of the key benefits of a data lake is that it allows an organization to store all of its data as is, irrespective of the structure and without a predefined schema and without the requirement of having to know the questions that the data will answer before the data actually arrives at the platform. This is totally opposite from how traditional data platforms like enterprise data warehouses were set up and used to operate. The key benefits of the data lake architectural concept are as follows:

- The ability to store the data in a central location and to use a variety of services to analyze it, depending on the use case

- The ingesting of data to a central repository without a predefined schema

- Separate storage and computation, allowing each layer to scale independently of the other

- The ability to perform ad hoc analysis of the data and to move the computation of the data for optimal processing

Customers who have built data warehouses might believe that bringing the data from multiple sources into a centralized storage is quite similar to the data warehouse's story of a single source of truth. While some of the data warehouse vendors do pitch their existing software for building data lakes, in most cases, the data warehouses are actually relational databases, which mandate defining a schema before ingesting the data (schema-on-write), unlike a data lake, where the schema should not be predefined and in fact the applications consuming the data will define the schema based on the use case. Furthermore, a data lake, due to its schema-less nature, allows you to ingest data of any structure, including structured, semi-structured, and unstructured data (whereas a data warehouse typically operates on structured datasets only). This leads to data lakes providing a flexibility of tools rather than just being compatible with SQL as in the case of relational databases.

Typically, the technologies supporting the data lake architecture provide cheaper storage options, hence you can store data at a more granular level of detail rather than at an aggregated level. This allows data scientists to work with the detailed data and do feature engineering at scale on the raw data.

S3 is perfectly suited to act as a storage layer for data lakes due to various factors like these:

- *Cost:* Data storage on S3 is relatively cheap compared to other options. For example, at the time of writing of this book, you could store 100 TB data on S3 for as low as $2,150 per month on a standard tier. If the data is accessed infrequently, you can in fact store it at a much cheaper price point.

- *Durability:* S3 provides 11 nines (99.999999999) of durability. Just to put things into perspective, 11 nines of durability implies, statistically, you would lose one file every 659,000 years. You are about 411 times more likely to get hit by a meteor.

- *Availability:* S3 is designed to provide 99.99 percent availability. A 100 percent service availability means that system would experience zero downtime; however, most services fall between 99 and 100 percent availability.

- *High Performance:* S3 provides high performance data ingest and retrieval, and applications can achieve thousands of transactions per second in request performance. For example, your application can achieve at least 3,500 PUT/COPY/PASTE/DELETE and 5,500 GET/HEAD requests per second per prefix in the bucket. There are, however, no limits to the number of prefixes in the bucket. For example, if your application needs half a million read requests per second, you can create 100 prefixes in your S3 bucket to parallelize reads. S3 also supports multipart uploads and Range GETs to optimize ingest and read performance. S3 also provides a multipart upload option, which basically enables you to upload large objects in parts.

- *Easy to Use:* You can interact with S3 using a variety of ways. You can use the AWS console to work with S3 or use the REST API or AWS SDK. You can also configure event notifications so that you can receive notifications when certain events happen in your bucket. Event notifications typically are delivered within a few seconds but can occasionally take longer, and in rare circumstances they can be lost.

- *Lifecycle Management:* Lifecycle management is an important part of data management, and S3 provides the feature out of the box, whereby you can transition objects to different storage classes, archive them, or delete them after a specified period of time. S3 provides a number of different classes of storage for the objects you store, and the classes are generally use-case dependent.
  - Frequently accessed objects/performance-sensitive use cases: S3 provides two types of storage for performance-sensitive use cases. Performance-sensitive use cases are typically use cases where access to objects is required at a millisecond level.
    - Standard – Default storage class used by S3
    - Reduced Redundancy – Storage class used for noncritical and reproducible data. This is not recommended for production use cases.

- Cost-effective intelligent storage: S3 provides INTELLIGENT_TIERING storage, which moves the data to the appropriate storage tier, thus optimizing costs and reducing an operational redesign of systems required to move the data between hot and cold tiers. This is entirely based on the user's access patterns and thus is ideal when you want to optimize your costs for use cases where access patterns are unknown or unpredictable.

> The INTELLIGENT_TIERING (S3 INT) storage class is only suitable for objects that are larger than 128 KB and the minimum storage time is 128 days. If you store smaller objects, you will be paying the frequent access tier costs, and if the objects are deleted before the 30-day period, you'll be charged for the entire 30-day period of storage.

- Infrequently accessed objects: S3 provides *STANDARD_IA (S3 S-IA)* (redundancy across multiple Availability Zones) and *ONEZONE_IA (S3 Z-IA)* (stored in one Availability Zone only—susceptible to physical loss in case of AZ failure) for objects that are accessed less frequently. While these objects can be accessed at a millisecond latency, a retrieval fee for accessing objects on this tier means that the tiers are not suitable for frequently accessed data. The ideal use cases for these are as follows:

- Backups
- Old data accessed infrequently but still requiring millisecond latency while accessing
- *Long Term Archiving:* S3 also provides *GLACIER* and *DEEP_ARCHIVE* storage classes for low-cost data archiving. While the durability of these storage classes is similar to STANDARD storage class, the access times vary from minutes for GLACIER to 12 hours for DEEP ARCHIVE. As the name indicates, these are suitable for only cold data, or data that has to be archived for regulatory reasons with longer SLAs. Figure 3.3 shows different types of AWS S3 storage classes provided by AWS.
- *Scalable:* S3 is scalable as it allows you to store as much data as you need, with no minimum usage commitments. You can store a few KBs of data to multiple petabytes, and storage can scale independently of the computation required on this data.
- *Integrated:* S3 is fully integrated to the AWS Analytics stack so that you can seamlessly process the data using Amazon EMR, Amazon Redshift, DynamoDB, and Amazon Athena. S3 also has native integration with technologies like AWS Glue and Amazon Kinesis Firehose, which allow you to rapidly ingest the data onto the platform. This native integration makes S3 an ideal choice for building data lakes on AWS.

FIGURE 3.3   Types of AWS S3 storage classes provided by AWS

Source: re:Invent 2018 Optimizing cost (bit.ly/2QQ3IhM)

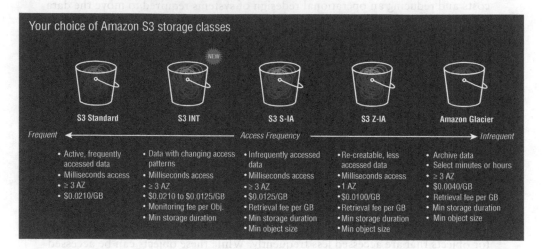

Data Replication in Amazon S3

Amazon S3 can automatically replicate your data inside an S3 bucket to a bucket in the same account or a different account. You can also copy objects within the same AWS Region using *same-region replication (SRR)* or between different AWS Regions using *cross regional replication (CRR)*. See Table 3.1 for more information. You can use replication to do the following:

- Replicate objects including metadata like creation time, version IDs, etc.

- Replicate objects to a different storage class.

- Change ownership of the replicated objects.

- Replicate objects using Replication Time Control (RTC) in a predictable time frame (99.99 percent of the objects can be replicated within a 15-minute interval).

TABLE 3.1   Same-region replication (SRR) vs. cross-region replication (CRR)

Same-Region Replication	Cross-Region Replication
Aggregate logs into a single bucket for simpler processing.	▪ Meet compliance requirements.
Replicate data between production and test accounts.	▪ Minimize latency for customers in different geographical locations.
Honor data sovereignty laws and compliance requirements.	▪ Optimize performance for computation needed in multiple AWS Regions.

SRR and CRR are important concepts from an exam point of view. It is highly recommended to look into more details of this topic in AWS documentation (amzn.to/34cWDf3).

Server Access Logging in Amazon S3

Security, audit, and compliance requirements often mandate you to provide details of all access made to the data. S3 server access logging is used to track requests made to an S3 bucket. By default, server access logging is disabled, so you'll need to enable it. Once the logging is enabled, logs of access are saved to buckets within the same Region, and each log provides detailed information about the access, such as the requester, name of the bucket, action requested (GET/HEAD), resultant response, and optionally an error code. While server access logging is free, you do incur charges for the logs being stored on S3.

To enable access logging, you must do the following:

1. On the bucket where access logging needs to be enabled, add logging configuration to turn on the log delivery. S3 will deliver logs of all access made to this bucket.

2. The logs need to be stored in a target bucket, and hence write permissions to the S3 Log Delivery group must be provided. The permissions need to be made via a bucket access control list (ACL) rather than a bucket policy.

Logs are delivered, collected, and consolidated before being delivered to a target bucket on a best-effort basis. Logs are delivered within a few hours but can be delivered more frequently. The core objective of access logging is to give you an idea of the type of traffic that your bucket is receiving, and while it is rare to lose a record, the server access logs are not a complete accounting of all requests.

Partitioning, Compression, and File Formats on S3

S3 is an object store and forms the core storage for data lakes built on AWS. S3 can be optimized for performance and cost using partitioning and compression and choosing optimal file formats. The optimal file formats can use compression, thus reducing the capacity needed for storage and substantially increasing query performance for analytical services like Athena and others using S3 as a data lake. One of the most common file formats is Apache Parquet (parquet.apache.org), which is a compressed columnar storage format designed for querying large amounts of data. Apache Parquet supports a variety of data processing frameworks, such as Apache Spark and Apache Hadoop. While S3 allows you to store any type of data, Apache Parquet can perform significantly better than raw file formats like CSV, JSON, and TSVs by reducing the storage needed and improving overall querying cost. The cost of S3 is based on two major factors:

- Size of the data scanned
- Amount of data scanned

A columnar compressed format allows analytical queries to scan smaller amounts of data compared to data stored in raw format, thus improving performance and reducing overall cost.

Partitioning data has a similar impact on performance and cost, since by partitioning your data, you can restrict the amount of data that you scan for each query and hence improve performance and reduce cost. While you can use any column to partition your data, it is often a good practice to partition based on data and time, which results in a multilevel partition. For example, you might have credit card transactions stored on a data lake and you can partition based on year, month, day, and hour. This partitioning schema would improve queries that are filtering data on a particular time variable, thus reducing the data scanned and improving performance. Tests have shown that this can result in up to 70 percent faster queries and 90 percent cheaper scans. The blog at amzn.to/33dF11f shows some good tips to optimize performance and cost on Amazon S3.

Compression provides similar performance gains as the data to be scanned is lesser and hence the resultant network traffic between S3 and the analytic tool is also lesser, thus reducing overall cost as well. It is, however, important to choose a compression format that is splittable because splitting a file allows the execution engine to split the reading of the file by using multiple readers and thus increase the overall parallelism for the query. A non-splittable file negatively impacts query performance because only a single reader can read the data while other readers are sitting idle. This is one of the most common problems in distributed computing where the workload among the workers is uneven and heavily skewed, thus impacting the overall performance of the system. Table 3.2 lists the most common compression algorithms, their supported compression ratio, the speed of the algorithm during compression, and their optimum use. For example, Gzip, a very commonly used algorithm, is most optimal for raw storage as it has a high compression ratio; however, due to its non-splittable nature, it is not suitable for parallel processing.

TABLE 3.2 Compression algorithms and relevant use cases

Algorithm	Splittable	Compression Ratio	Algorithm Speed	Good For
Gzip (DEFLATE)	No	High	Medium	Raw storage
bzip2	Yes	Very high	Slow	Very large files
LZO	Yes	Low	Fast	Slow analytics
Snappy	Yes and no*	Low	Very fast	Slow & fast analytics

*Snappy and GZip blocks are not splittable, but files with Snappy blocks inside a container file format such as SequenceFile or Avro can be split.

Amazon S3 Glacier

Amazon S3 Glacier is a low-cost object storage service which you can use to store data in a secure and durable manner. The typical use cases for Amazon S3 Glacier are data archiving and data backups. You should use Amazon S3 Glacier for cold data that is not frequently accessed, and where you can wait for a few hours for data retrieval. You can use data life-cycle policies to move the data between Amazon S3 and Amazon S3 Glacier.

The Amazon S3 Glacier data model has two core concepts: vaults and archives.

Vault

In Amazon S3 Glacier, a *vault* is a container for storing archives. Creating a vault requires a name and a Region. A vault name is unique on an account-per-region basis. You can store multiple archives within a vault. Amazon Glacier supports various vault operations, all of which are Region-specific. Each vault resource in Amazon S3 Glacier has a unique address:

```
https://<region-specific endpoint>/<account-id>/vaults/<vaultname>
```

For example, if you are creating an `analyticscert` vault in the US East (North Virginia) Region, for the account number 1234567890, the vault will be addressed in the following URI:

```
https://glacier.us-east-1a.amazonaws.com/1234567890/vaults/analyticscert
```

Figure 3.4 shows you the `analyticscert` vault, created in the North Virginia Region.

FIGURE 3.4   Amazon S3 Glacier – vault creation

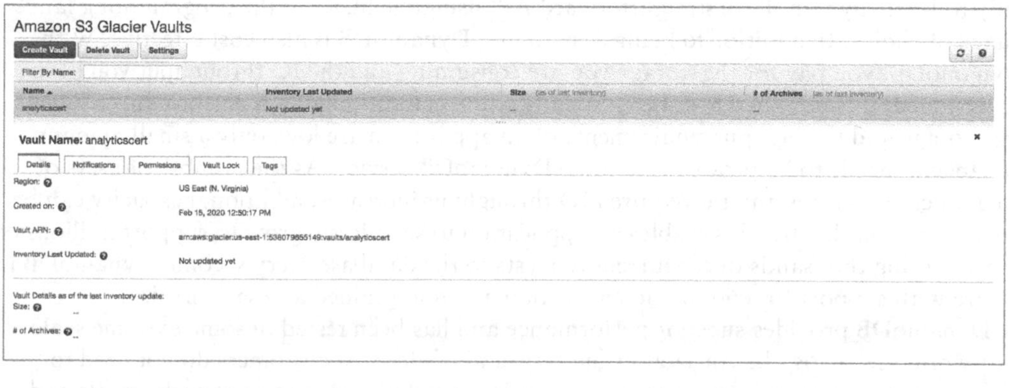

Archive

An *archive* is the actual data you store in a vault. It can be of any data type (an image, a video clip, or PDF/Word/JSON document) and is a base unit of storage in Glacier. Each archive needs to have a unique ID and an optional description. The rules governing the optional description include the limitation to add it only during the upload of the archive. Glacier assigns a unique identifier for the archive, which is unique across the AWS Region where the archive is stored.

Similar to a vault, an archive also has a unique resource identifier in the following form:

```
https://<region-specific endpoint>/<account-id>/vaults/<vault-name>/
archives/<archive-id>
```

If you stored an object in the `analyticscert` vault created earlier, it will look something like this:

```
https://glacier.us-east-1a.amazonaws.com/1234567890/vaults/
analyticscert/archives/gwbOONqON5wZwsFiz6HIEVKgnniD0eE45ZBC0P
```

Amazon DynamoDB

Amazon DynamoDB is a fully managed NoSQL database service running in the AWS cloud. The complexity of running a massively scalable, distributed NoSQL database is managed by the service itself, allowing software developers to focus on building applications and the core business of the enterprise rather than managing infrastructure. NoSQL databases are designed for scale, but their architectures are sophisticated, and there can be significant operational overhead in running a large NoSQL cluster. Instead of having to become experts in advanced distributed computing concepts, the developers need only to learn DynamoDB's straightforward API using the SDK for the programming language of choice. In addition to being easy to use, DynamoDB is also cost effective. With DynamoDB, you pay for the storage you are consuming and the IO throughput you have provisioned. It is designed to scale elastically while maintaining high performance. When the storage and throughput requirements of an application are low, only a small amount of capacity needs to be provisioned in the DynamoDB service. As the number of users of an application grows and the required IO throughput increases, additional capacity can be provisioned on the fly. This enables an application to seamlessly grow to support millions of users making thousands of concurrent requests to the database every second. DynamoDB is secure with support for end-to-end encryption and fine-grained access control.

DynamoDB provides superior performance and has been tested in some extreme scale real-world scenarios like Amazon Prime Day, and while most customers do not need to operate at this scale, it is useful to know that DynamoDB can operate at such a scale and still provide low single-digit millisecond read and write performance. Ad-Tech applications are a specific type of application where the system needs to decide on an advert and furnish it within the page load times without adding extra latency, and they are suitable for DynamoDB's low single-digit millisecond read and write performance. Mobile applications that require scalability in the case of sudden growth and voting applications that require handling the peak read-write performance in the case of a surge in read/write activity are also suitable for DynamoDB's horizontal scalability. Applications that require a schema-less model like application monitoring solutions that ingest hundreds of thousands of data points per minute are also suitable for DynamoDB's schema-less model with native JSON support.

It is important from the exam perspective that you understand the use cases where DynamoDB can be used compared to other services. You will come across a number of questions in which the scenario fits ideally to a DynamoDB use case, and hence knowing DynamoDB's latency and throughput can aid you in making the right choice.

DynamoDB delivers seamless throughput and storage scaling via an API and an easy-to-use management console, so you can easily scale up or down to meet your needs.

DynamoDB tables do not have fixed schemas, and each item may have a different number of attributes. Multiple data types add richness to the data model. Secondary indexes add flexibility to the queries you can perform without affecting performance. Performance, reliability, and security are built in, with solid-state drive (SSD) storage and automatic three-way replication. DynamoDB uses proven cryptographic methods to securely authenticate users and prevent unauthorized data access.

DynamoDB is a regional service that provides fault tolerance using Multi-AZ replication. Regional service means that if you have a customer's data stored in DynamoDB, it can be processed with Amazon EMR (Elastic Map Reduce), a service that I will discuss more in Chapter 4, "Data Processing and Analysis." On a high level, Amazon EMR is a managed Hadoop framework on a pay-as-you-go service model and can process data stored in Amazon DynamoDB and other data stores such as Amazon RDS and Amazon S3. Data processing is done inside Amazon EMR, and the results can be stored in Amazon S3. You can also work with data in DynamoDB from Apache Hive, a project within Amazon EMR, and join it with other data in the ecosystem that Hive can access directly (e.g., data from Amazon S3).

Amazon DynamoDB Data Types

Amazon DynamoDB supports many different data types for attributes within a table, which can be categorized in three major categories: scalar, document, and set.

Scalar Data Types

A scalar type can represent exactly one value. The scalar types are number, string, binary, Boolean, and null. See Table 3.3.

TABLE 3.3   Scalar data types in DynamoDB

Data Type	Description	Range
Number	Numbers can be positive, negative, or zero. Numbers are represented as variable length. You can also use the number data type to represent a date or a time stamp using epoch time or any other representation of time. All numbers are sent across the network to DynamoDB as strings, to maximize compatibility across languages and libraries.	Numbers can have up to 38 digits of precision.
String	Strings are Unicode with UTF-8 encoding.	Length of a string must be greater than zero up to a maximum of 400 KB (DynamoDB item size limit). For a simple primary key, the maximum length of the first attribute value (the partition key) is 2048 bytes. For a composite primary key, the maximum length of the second attribute value (the sort key) is 1024 bytes.
Binary	Binary type attributes can store any binary data such as compressed text, encrypted data, or images. During the comparison of binary values in DynamoDB, each byte is treated as unsigned. Your applications must encode binary values in base64-encoded format before sending them to DynamoDB. Upon receipt of these values, DynamoDB decodes the data into an unsigned byte array and uses that as the length of the binary attribute.	Length should be greater than 0 up to 400 KB (DynamoDB item size limit).
Boolean	Boolean data type is a data type that has one of two possible values (usually denoted true and false), which is intended to represent the two truth values of logic and Boolean algebra.	A Boolean type attribute can be stored as either "true" or "false."
Null	In databases, a Null value represents absence of a value. A Null value is different from the number zero.	Null represents an unknown or undefined state.

Document Data Types

A document type can represent a complex structure with nested attributes—such as you would find in a JSON document. The document types are list and map. It is important to note that DynamoDB has an item size limit of 400 KB, and hence while there is no limit on the number of values in a list or a map, the value must fit within the DynamoDB item size limit (400 KB). An attribute value cannot be an empty set (string set, number set, or binary set). However, empty lists and maps are allowed. See Table 3.4.

TABLE 3.4   Document data types in DynamoDB

Data Type	Description	Range
List	List type can store an *ordered* collection of values. Lists are enclosed in square brackets. DynamoDB lets you work with individual elements within lists, even if those elements are deeply nested. Example: `TopActors: ["Matt Damon", "Tom Cruise","Kate Winslet"]`	Up to 400 KB (DynamoDB item size limit). Empty list is allowed.
Map	Map type can store an unordered collection of name-value pairs. Maps are enclosed in curly braces. A map is similar to a JSON object. There are no restrictions on the data types that can be stored in a map element, and the elements in a map do not have to be of the same type. If your use case involves storing raw JSON documents, maps are ideal for this data type. Similar to a list data type, DynamoDB lets you work with individual items within a map even if the items are deeply nested.	Up to 400 KB (DynamoDB item size limit). Empty map is allowed.

Set Types

A set type can represent multiple scalar values. The set types are string set, number set, and binary set. DynamoDB supports types that represent sets of Number, String, or Binary values. All of the elements within a set must be of the same type. For example, an attribute of type Number Set can only contain numbers; String Set can only contain strings; and so on. There is no limit on the number of values in a Set, as long as the item containing the values fits within the DynamoDB item size limit (400 KB). Each value within a set must be unique. The order of the values within a set are not preserved; therefore, your applications must not rely on any particular order of elements within the set. Finally, DynamoDB does not support empty sets.

Examples of sets, a string set, a number set and a binary set are as follows:

```
["Emirates", "Turkish", "British"]
[130,79, 149, 110]
["U3Vubnk=", "UmFpbnk=", "U25vd3k="]
```

Amazon DynamoDB Core Concepts

In Amazon DynamoDB, tables, items, attributes, and partition keys and sort keys are the core concepts:

Tables   The table is similar to that of other databases. Amazon DynamoDB stores data in tables. A *table* is a collection of data, and it contains multiple items.

Items   An *item* is similar to a row, a tuple, or a record in relational databases, where an item is a group of multiple attributes that are uniquely identifiable among other items in the table.

Attributes   Each item is composed of one or more attributes. An *attribute* is similar to a field or a column in a relational database, where it is not broken down any further.

Partition Keys and Sort Keys   The first attribute in an item is a partition key. A *partition key* is very important from a performance perspective as it is used as an input to an internal hash function, the output of which determines where this item is physically stored on the DynamoDB infrastructure. The second attribute within the item is the *sort key*, which is optional and is used to sort the data in sort key/value order. Items that have similar partition keys are stored together to improve performance. If two items have the same partition key/values, they need to have different sort key/values.

Read/Write Capacity Mode in DynamoDB

Amazon DynamoDB's superior performance in terms of reads and writes means it has to have ample capacity to read and write data in huge volumes to those tables. Amazon DynamoDB provides two modes for ensuring you have ample capacity to read/write to the underlying tables: *on-demand capacity mode* and *provisioned capacity mode*.

On-Demand Capacity Mode

On-Demand capacity mode is an ideal option when you have tables with unknown workloads or unpredictable application traffic or when you prefer the ease of paying based on your usage. In an on-demand mode, DynamoDB instantly accommodates your workloads as they ramp up or down to any previously reached traffic level. When your workload's traffic level hits a new peak, DynamoDB adapts rapidly to accommodate the new workload. You can achieve single-digit millisecond latency using the on-demand mode and can configure new and existing tables with on-demand mode without changing the code.

Two important components for defining capacity on a DynamoDB table in an on-demand mode are a read request unit and a write request unit. While in an on-demand capacity mode, you do not need to specify the read and write request units; DynamoDB charges you for the data reads and writes your application performs on the tables.

Read Request Unit

One read request unit represents a strongly consistent read request or two eventually consistent read requests, for an item size of up to 4 KB. A transaction read request therefore requires two read request units to perform one read for items up to 4 KB. If you need to read an item that is larger than 4 KB, DynamoDB will require an additional read request. To calculate the total number of read request units, you will need the following information:

- Item size
- Read type (eventually consistent/strongly consistent)

For example, let's say you read an item size of 8 KB. You will need the following number of read requests:

- One strongly consistent read requires two read requests.
- One eventually consistent read requires one read request.
- One transactional read requires four read requests.

Write Request Unit

One write request represents a write for an item up to 1 KB in size. If your item size is larger than 1 KB, DynamoDB will consume additional write requests.

For an item size of 1 KB, the following number of read requests are needed:

- One write request for a standard write
- Two write requests for a transactional write

Therefore, if you need to write an item size of 8 KB, DynamoDB will consume 8 write requests for a standard write and 16 write requests for a transactional write.

Handling Scaling in an On-Demand Capacity Mode

On-demand capacity mode handles lots of complexities when it comes to read and write traffic peaks and adapts to the requirements of your application. For example, if you had an application that has a traffic pattern between 10,000 strongly consistent reads per second to 20,000 strongly consistent reads per second, where your previous peak was 20,000 reads per second, on-demand capacity mode will be able to handle the sustained traffic of 40,000 reads per second. If your current application sustains 40,000 reads per second, this will become the new peak on which DynamoDB calculates your new capacity demands, and the subsequent traffic can reach up to 80,000 reads per second.

You might be wondering why one would choose a provisioned capacity mode (discussed in the next section) when DynamoDB can automatically scale based on your application traffic. The reason is that you may encounter throttling if your new peak is more than double your previous peak within 30 minutes. DynamoDB recommends spacing out your traffic growth over at least 30 minutes, which may be a limitation for some applications. In addition to that you may overrun your budgeted costs on AWS, as an application can drive up large volumes of traffic, and if you do not have appropriate monitoring in place, you can be in for a billing shock.

Provisioned Capacity Mode

While on-demand mode can be really beneficial for certain applications, you may want to turn on provisioned capacity mode when you have a predictable application traffic or your application has a consistent growth with well-defined peaks and low periods and you want to control costs for you overall platform.

In provisioned capacity mode, you can provision the capacity for your tables in terms of *read capacity units (RCUs)* or *write capacity units (WCUs)*.

Read Capacity Unit (RCU)

A read capacity unit is a mechanism-defined data access capacity with DynamoDB in a provisioned capacity mode. The exact semantics on the total number of read capacity units required for your application depends on a number of factors, including the following key factors:

- Item size
- Type of read (strongly consistent, eventually consistent, or transactional read)

One read capacity unit for an item of up to 4 KB in size represents the following:

- One strongly consistent read per second
- Two eventually consistent reads per second
- Transactional read requests require two read capacity units to perform one read per second for items up to 4 KB.

If you need to read an item that is larger than 4 KB, DynamoDB must consume additional read capacity units.

Write Capacity Unit (WCU)

A write capacity unit defines the amount of data you can write to DynamoDB. DynamoDB consumes one write capacity unit to write an item of 1 KB in size. For item sizes larger than 1 KB, DynamoDB requires additional write capacity units. Transactional write requests require two write capacity units to write an item of up to 1 KB in size.

DynamoDB has a maximum item size limit of 400 KB, and so your application will consume more capacity units if it writes item sizes larger than 400 KB. While you can theoretically scale your application infinitely with an on-demand capacity model, a provisioned capacity model means that your application will be subject to throttling if you exceed your provisioned capacity. Throttling helps your application to operate within the budgeted capacity but throws an HTTP 400 (Bad Request | ProvisionedThrougputExceededException) error code when you exceed your provisioned capacity. If you would like to retry a request that has been throttled, you can use the AWS SDK, which provides built-in support to handle such scenarios. You do not need to write this logic to handle this yourself.

You can use the capacity calculator at the table creation screen to calculate the capacity needed for your DynamoDB application.

DynamoDB Auto Scaling and Reserved Capacity

You can opt to use DynamoDB's auto scaling to manage throughput capacity for tables and global secondary indexes (gsi). You can define a range (upper–lower) for read and write capacity units, or a target utilization percentage within the range. DynamoDB auto scaling will try to maintain your target utilization as your workload increases.

Autoscaling helps you get the benefit of provisioned capacity but also the ability to scale up when there are sudden bursts in traffic to avoid throttling for your application. If you use the AWS Management Console to create a table or a global secondary index, DynamoDB auto scaling is enabled by default.

If you have a consistent workload you can reduce your overall cost for purchasing a reserved capacity in advance.

Read Consistency and Global Tables

Amazon DynamoDB is a regional service and hence a table with the same name in two different regions is considered a different table. For example, if you have two "transactions" tables, one in eu-west-1 and other in eu-west-2, both of them are considered to be separate tables. DynamoDB also provides built-in fault tolerance and durability by replicating the data between AZs in a Region. Each Region in AWS comprises multiple Availability Zones (AZs), and a successful write to a table in a single AZ with an HTTP 200 (OK) response means that DynamoDB has replicated your data to another AZ behind the scene. The data is eventually consistent across all storage locations usually within one second or less.

Due to this latency of writes between AZs, DynamoDB supports two consistency models for reads:

Eventually Consistent Reads   When you read data from a DynamoDB table after completing a recent operation, the result of the read might not reflect the latest result, and hence you might read stale data. However, eventually, after the replication has been done, if you repeat the read request after a short time, you will get the latest data. By default, DynamoDB provides eventually consistent reads unless you specify a strongly consistent read. Eventually consistent reads maximize throughput at the cost of a potentially stale date as discussed earlier.

Strongly Consistent Reads   In the case of a strongly consistent read, DynamoDB returns a response for the most up-to-date data and reflects the updates from all prior operations that were successful. The caveats to a strongly consistent read are that the read might not be available if there is a network delay or an outage and you cannot have a strongly consistent read from a global secondary index. The read operations like GetItem, Query, and Scan provide a ConsistentRead parameter, which can be set to true to ensure that DynamoDB uses strongly consistent reads during the operation.

DynamoDB *global tables* are a mechanism by which you can build a fully managed multi-region and multi-master database without having to build your own replication solution. When you build a global table, you specify the AWS Regions where you want the table to be available and Amazon DynamoDB manages the complexity of creating identical tables in the chosen Regions and then replicates data among them. A great use case for global tables is when you have a global customer base spread across multiple geographical areas (e.g., US, Europe, Middle East, and Asia Pacific). One of the options is to create three separate tables in each of the Regions and then manually replicate the data across the Regions. This is not only error-prone but also complex to set up and configure. A simpler option is to create a global table with DynamoDB, select the Regions where you want these tables to be created, and then let DynamoDB manage the complex task of replicating the data across these Regions. Figure 3.5 indicates how global tables work across AWS Regions.

FIGURE 3.5   DynamoDB global tables

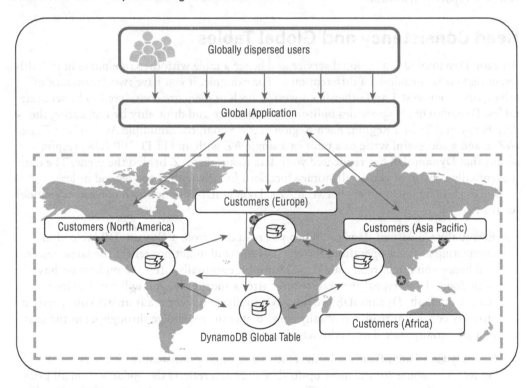

Amazon DynamoDB: Indexing and Partitioning

An ideal way to access data is through primary keys, as it provides the fastest access path. In DynamoDB, when you create a table, you must specify both the table name and the primary key of the table. The primary key uniquely identifies each item, so no two items in a table can have the same primary key.

DynamoDB supports two different kinds of primary keys:

- A partition key
- A composite (partition key and sort key).

Amazon DynamoDB provides fast access to items in a table by specifying primary key/values. However, many applications might benefit from having one or more secondary (or alternate) keys available to allow efficient access to data with attributes other than the primary key. To address this, you can create one or more secondary indexes on a table and issue Query or Scan requests against these indexes.

A secondary index is a data structure that contains a subset of attributes from a table and an alternate key to support Query operations. You can retrieve data from the index using a Query, which is similar to using a Query with a table. A table can have multiple secondary indexes, which gives your applications access to many different query patterns. Every secondary index is associated with exactly one table, from which it obtains its data. This is called the base table for the index. When you create an index, you define an alternate key for the index (partition key and sort key). You also define the attributes that you want to be projected, or copied, from the base table into the index. DynamoDB copies these attributes into the index along with the primary key attributes from the base table. You can then query or scan the index just as you would query or scan a table.

Every secondary index is automatically maintained by DynamoDB. When you add, modify, or delete items in the base table, any indexes on that table are also updated to reflect these changes.

DynamoDB supports two types of secondary indexes:

Local Secondary Index (LSI)   An LSI is an index that has the same partition key as the base table but a different sort key. A *local secondary index* is "local" in the sense that every partition of a local secondary index is scoped to a base table partition that has the same partition key/value. The total size of indexed items for any one partition key/value can't exceed 10 GB. A local secondary index shares the same throughput as provisioned for the table being indexed. It is important for you to understand the limits of LSIs per table, although the exam does not test on service limits, but it is useful to know that you can define a maximum of five local secondary indexes per table. You can look at the latest DynamoDB limits on the AWS Documentation page at amzn.to/ DDBLimits.

Global Secondary Index (GSI)   GSI is an index with a partition key and a sort key that can be different from those on the base table. A *global secondary index* is considered "global" because queries on the index can span all of the data in the base table, across all partitions. A global secondary index has no size limitations like a local secondary index, and it has its own provisioned throughput for read and write capacity, separate from the original table.

You can define up to 20 global secondary indexes and 5 local secondary indexes per table, but the limit can be increased by reaching out to the AWS support team.

Partitioning

DynamoDB stores data in partitions. A partition is an allocation of storage for a table, backed by solid-state drives (SSDs) and automatically replicated across multiple Availability Zones within an AWS Region. You can find the partition keys' and sort keys' limits at amzn.to/DDBLimits.

Partition management is handled entirely by DynamoDB; customers never need to manage partitions themselves.

Amazon DynamoDB automatically partitions the data using the hash key (also called a partition key), which distributes the data and workload across the partitions. Automatic partitioning is driven by dataset size and the amount of provisioned throughput.

 From an exam perspective, it is important for you to understand that you can provision throughput on a DynamoDB table in addition to having multiple access paths for the same dataset using global secondary indexes. It is also important to note that LSIs and GSIs treat the provisioned throughput of the base tables differently.

Amazon DynamoDB Accelerator

While low single-digit millisecond reads suffice for most applications, some applications want an even lower latency for eventually consistent reads. *Amazon DynamoDB Accelerator (DAX)* is a DynamoDB-compatible caching service that enables in-memory performance for such applications.

DAX addresses three core scenarios:

- Reducing response time to microseconds

- Simplifying application development by providing an API that is compatible with Amazon DynamoDB to minimize changes to your existing applications while trying to reduce the response times

- Reducing the cost for read-heavy workloads by reducing the need to overprovision read capacity units (RCUs)

Simply put, DAX does all the heavy lifting required to add in-memory acceleration to your DynamoDB tables, without requiring developers to handle cache invalidation, data population, or cluster management. Figure 3.6 shows how you can use DAX with your existing applications.

FIGURE 3.6 DynamoDB Accelerator

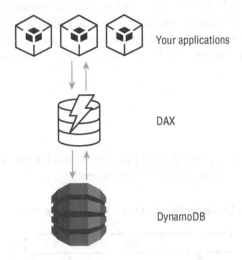

Your applications

DAX

DynamoDB

Amazon DynamoDB Streams

Let's consider a scenario where you have a popular mobile application and you would like to provide near real-time metrics about the mobile application. You need a mechanism by which you can capture the item changes to your DynamoDB table as they are happening in real-time. DynamoDB streams enables such solutions where a DynamoDB stream captures a time-ordered sequence of item-level modifications in a DynamoDB table and stores this information in a log for up to 24 hours. Applications can access this log and view the data items as they appeared before and after they were modified, in near-real time.

DynamoDB stream is an ordered flow of information about changes to items in DynamoDB tables. When you enable a stream on a table, DynamoDB captures information about every modification to the data items in the table. Whenever an application makes any change (e.g., creating an item in a table, updating an item in a table, or deleting an item in a table), DynamoDB writes a stream record with the primary key attributes of the items that were modified. You can configure the stream to capture additional information like the "before" and "after" images of the modified items. DynamoDB stream ensures the following:

- Each stream record appears exactly once in the stream.

- For each item modified in a DynamoDB table, the stream record appears in the same order as the actual modifications to the item.

You can enable a stream on a new table or an existing table. Since DynamoDB streams operate in an asynchronous manner, there is no performance impact on the original table.

Amazon DynamoDB Streams – Kinesis Adapter

It is recommended to use Amazon Kinesis Adapter to consume data from the Amazon DynamoDB streams. The API for the Amazon DynamoDB streams is intentionally similar to Amazon Kinesis Data Streams, a real time data processing service (as seen in Chapter 2, "Data collection"). In both the services, data streams are composed of shards, which are actually containers for stream records. Both services' APIs contain the following:

- ListStreams
- DescribeStream
- GetShards
- GetShardIterator

You can use Kinesis Client Library (KCL) to interact with Kinesis Adapter. Figure 3.7 illustrates how these libraries interact with each other.

FIGURE 3.7   Amazon DynamoDB Streams – Kinesis Adapter

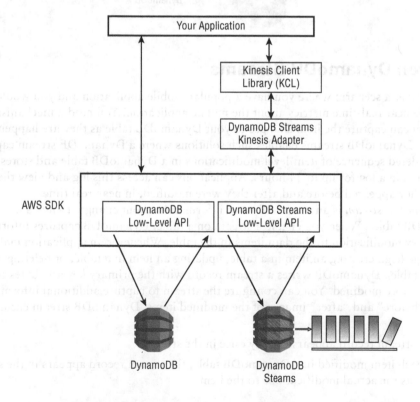

Amazon DocumentDB

During re:Invent 2018, AWS released Amazon DocumentDB with the intent of meeting customer demands around managed document databases. I will try to introduce the benefits of a Document Database, before looking at the architecture and the interfaces for the database.

Why a Document Database?

The data world today is pretty complex, and we have a variety of data types and file formats. Gone are the days when companies would retrofit their use cases into a single tool, as now you have the option to choose the tool that fits your specific use cases. The common categories of data and use cases are depicted in the following table, Table 3.5.

TABLE 3.5 Common data categories and use cases

Data Category	Key Features	Use Case
Relational	Referential integrity ACID transactions schema-on-write	Databases, data warehouses ERP Finance CRMs Lift and shift from other systems
Key/value	High-throughput Low latency (typically milliseconds) read and writes Unlimited scale	Real-time bidding Shopping cart Social Product catalog Customer preferences Recommendations Adverts
Document	Raw JSON documents Quick access Native reads	Content management Personalization Mobile Catalog Retail and marketing
In-memory	Microsecond latency	Leaderboards Real-time analytics Caching

TABLE 3.5   Common data categories and use cases *(continued)*

Data Category	Key Features	Use Case
Graph	Finding complex relationships Navigate/traverse between data elements	Fraud detection Social network analysis Recommendation engine
Time series	Collect/Store/process data sequenced by time	IoT applications Event tracking
Ledger	Complete Immutable and verifiable history of all changes to data	Systems of record Supply Chain Healthcare Registrations Financial

A document database is useful when storing raw JSON data and navigating through the JSON document. Since JSON documents are semi-structured in nature, they do not naturally fit with relational databases, which don't have native JSON handling capabilities. A JSON document model maps naturally to application data, and each document can have a different structure and is independent of other documents. You can index on any key within the document and run ad hoc aggregation and analysis across your entire dataset.

As you know, in a relational database, each row has the same number of attributes, whereas non-relational data tends to have varying attributes for each item. Let us consider a use case where a relational database doesn't scale as effectively as a document database.

You are running a leading social media company and you have decided to add a new game to the platform called *Ring-o-Ring*. You would like to track the stats of the users that play the game. You have two options, a relational database or a document database. In a relational database, you would create a user's table:

userid	username	firstname	lastname
101	fati1122	Fatima	Abbasi

And then create a Ring-o-Ring table:

UserId	HiScore	LeaderboardLevel
101	383442	99

This may work for one game, but the moment you add more games and apps on your platform, this can become really complex. You can "normalize" your way out of complexity at the cost of performance by doing joins at runtime, but the complexity moves from one side to another, making it more expensive to maintain the application.

In a document database, you can simply add the stats to the document. No table creation is needed, and no expensive joins are required at runtime, making it simple to develop and cheaper to maintain.

Amazon DocumentDB Overview

Amazon DocumentDB is a fast, scalable, highly available and fully managed MongoDB-compatible service. It has the following key features that make it an ideal fit for storing, processing, and analyzing documents:

- It can handle millions of requests at a single-digit millisecond latency.
- It is deeply integrated with the AWS platform.
- You can use the same code, drivers, and tools that you use with MongoDB.
- It is secure.
- It is fully managed.

Amazon DocumentDB supports flexible storage, where the storage volume grows as your database storage needs to grow in increments of 10 GB up to a maximum of 64 TB. You don't need to provision any excess storage for your cluster to handle growth as this is done behind the scenes. For read-heavy applications, Amazon DocumentDB can support up to 15 read replica instances. Since the replicas share the same underlying storage, you can reduce the overall cost by eliminating the need to perform writes at read-replica nodes. The replica lag time is reduced to a single-digit number of milliseconds and provides you with better response for your read heavy workloads. Amazon DocumentDB provides a cluster endpoint for read/write and a reader endpoint for reading data, which allows applications to connect without having to track replicas as they are added or removed. You can add read replicas in minutes regardless of the storage volume sizes. You can scale the compute and memory resources of your cluster up and down, and these scaling operations complete within a few minutes.

Amazon DocumentDB continuously monitors the health of your cluster, and upon detecting an instance failure, it will automatically restart the instance and associated processes. Amazon DocumentDB doesn't require a crash recovery replay of database redo logs, which greatly reduces restart times. Amazon DocumentDB also isolates the database cache from the database process, enabling the cache to survive an instance restart. Upon failure, one of the 15 read replicas provisioned can act as a failover instance, and in case a customer hasn't provisioned a read replica, a new Amazon DocumentDB instance is created automatically.

Amazon DocumentDB also allows point-in-time recovery (PITR), which allows you to restore your cluster to any second during the retention period, up to the last 5 minutes. The retention period can be configured up to 15 days, with backups being stored in Amazon S3. Backups are done in an automatic incremental fashion without impacting the cluster performance.

Amazon Document DB Architecture

Figure 3.8 displays the DocumentDB architecture. An Amazon DocumentDB cluster contains 0 (zero) to 16 instances, and a cluster storage volume manages the storage for the instance. All writes are done through the primary instance, whereas the reads are done through primary or read replicas.

Amazon DocumentDB instances can only run in a VPC, which therefore gives you full control over your virtual networking environment.

Amazon DocumentDB architecture separates storage and compute. For each storage layer, Amazon DocumentDB will replicate six copies of your data across three AWS Availability Zones, which provides additional fault tolerance and redundancy.

FIGURE 3.8   Amazon DocumentDB architecture

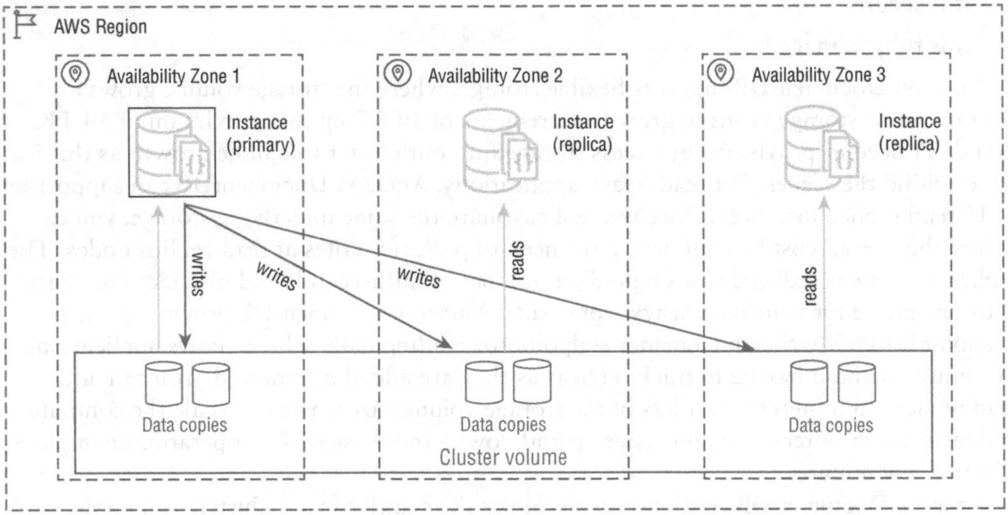

Amazon DocumentDB Interfaces

There are multiple ways in which you can interact with Amazon DocumentDB:

- **AWS Management Console**
- **AWS CLI**
- **The Mongo shell:** You can use the Mongo shell to connect to your cluster to create, read, update, and delete documents in your database.
- **MongoDB Drivers:** For developing applications against an Amazon DocumentDB cluster, you can use the MongoDB drivers with Amazon DocumentDB.

Graph Databases and Amazon Neptune

A relational database consists of *tables* with *rows* and *columns*. The key objective of a relational database is to store the data rather than the relationship between the data items itself. The relationship is therefore modeled using primary keys and foreign keys. This imposes constraints like referential integrity, which is not only complex when writing data into a relational database, it also possesses complex challenges when retrieving the data by joining the data between multiple tables. For example, consider the example where you have a table containing airline passengers (customers), and another table containing the trips that they have made.

Passengers:

Id, Name, Age, Country, PassportNo

Trips:

Id, OriginAirport,DestinationAirport,PassengerId,Timestamp

Now, if I want to understand which of the passengers had traveled from DXB (Dubai) to SFO (San Francisco), I have to join two tables to get the result. If I have to query the passengers, who went from DXB (Dubai) to SFO (San Francisco) to LHR (London Heathrow) or ISB (Islamabad), this can become a very complicated query. Why is this difficult to express in SQL language? The challenge is that relational databases are built to store data and do not contain the idea of a fixed relationship between records.

A graph database, on the other hand, gives relationships a higher priority, which means that applications don't have to infer data connections like foreign keys, thus simplifying the process of expressing relationships.

A *graph database* uses graph structures for semantic queries with nodes, edges, and properties to represent and store data. A key concept of the system is the graph, which relates the data items in the store to a collection of nodes and edges.

Nodes represent the entities and the edges represent the relationships between the entities, thus allowing data in the store to be linked together directly and, in many cases, retrieved with one operation.

Graph databases hold the relationships between data as a priority, which means that querying relationships within a graph database is fast because they are perpetually stored within the database itself. Relationships can be intuitively visualized using graph databases, making them useful for heavily interconnected data.

Graph databases have advantages over relational databases for certain use cases—including social networking, recommendation engines, and fraud detection—when you want to create relationships between data and quickly query these relationships. There key challenges to building these applications in a relational database include using multiple tables with multiple foreign keys. The SQL queries to navigate this data require nested queries and complex joins that quickly become challenging to write and interpret. Furthermore, as more joins are introduced, the queries become complex and take longer to run with the increase in the size of the data.

Graph databases uses graph structures such as nodes (data entities), edges (relationships), and properties to represent and store data. The relationships are stored as first-order citizens of the data model. This condition allows data in nodes to be directly linked, dramatically improving the performance of queries that navigate relationships in the data. The interactive performance at scale in a graph database effectively enables a broad set of graph use cases.

A graph in a graph database can be traversed along specific edge types or across the entire graph. Graph databases can represent how entities relate by using actions, ownership, parentage, and so on. Whenever connections or relationships between entities are at the core of the data that you're trying to model, a graph database is a natural choice. Therefore, graph databases are useful for modeling and querying social networks, business relationships, dependencies, shipping movements, and similar items. You can use edges to show typed relationships between entities (also called vertices or nodes). Edges can describe parent-child relationships, actions, product recommendations, purchases, and so on. A relationship, or edge, is a connection between two vertices that always has a start node, end node, type, and direction.

Amazon Neptune Overview

Amazon Neptune is a high-performance, reliable, fully managed graph database service that makes it easy to build and run applications that work with highly connected datasets. The core of Neptune is a purpose-built, high-performance graph database engine. This engine is optimized for storing billions of relationships and querying the graph with milliseconds latency. Neptune supports the popular graph query languages Apache TinkerPop, Gremlin, and W3C's SPARQL, enabling you to build queries that efficiently navigate highly connected datasets. Neptune powers graph use cases such as recommendation engines, fraud detection, knowledge graphs, drug discovery, and network security.

Neptune is highly available, with read replicas, point-in-time recovery, continuous backup to Amazon S3, and replication across Availability Zones. It provides data security features, with support for encryption at rest and in transit. Neptune is fully managed, so you no longer need to worry about database management tasks like hardware provisioning, software patching, setup, configuration, or backups.

An example of a common use case that is suited to a graph is social networking data. Amazon Neptune can quickly and easily process large sets of user profiles and interactions to build social networking applications. Neptune enables highly interactive graph queries with high throughput to bring social features into your applications. For example, suppose you want to build a social feed into your application. You can use Neptune to provide results that prioritize showing your users the latest updates from their family, from friends whose updates they "like," and from friends who live close to them.

Amazon Neptune Use Cases

Here is a list of some likely Amazon Neptune use cases:

- Fraud detection
  - Determine irregular use of credit cards or identify fraudulent accounts.

- Recommendation engines
  - Make product recommendations.
  - Make social recommendations (people you may know).

- Knowledge graphs
  - Build complex knowledge graphs to recommend other items of interest similar to current interests.

- Life sciences
  - Model diseases and gene interactions.
  - Integrate information to tackle healthcare and life sciences research.

- Network/IT operations
  - Model your network.
  - Answer questions like which hosts are running a specific application.

Storage Gateway

The storage gateway is an important concept from a hybrid architecture perspective, where some of the customers' applications need to stay on-premises for a variety of reasons but need to benefit from the agility and ease of use of the cloud. In the following sections, I will discuss why customers are looking for hybrid storage and how AWS Storage Gateway can help in such use cases. This is an important concept from an exam perspective as well.

Hybrid Storage Requirements

Customers are interested in moving their storage to the cloud due to the following potential benefits:

- Increased agility can be gained by having the ability to scale the resources up and down based on the need instantaneously.
- Faster innovation is possible by having a variety of services available to process the data natively on the platform, including machine learning and large-scale analytics.

- Customers get better security as they get a better understanding of how the data is being used in addition to having the ability to use more advanced encryption tools and certifications designed for the most security conscious organizations in the world.

- Data storage costs are reduced by using a flexible buying model, reducing the need for overprovisioning and providing the ability to move the data between various storage tiers based on the usage and the value of the data.

However, while the move to the cloud seems straightforward and the right logical choice, some applications need to stay on-premises, and this could be due to performance reasons, compliance reasons, or the complexity of the applications and their intertwining with other on-premises applications. CIOs and CTOs would still like to leverage the benefits of cloud storage for the applications that might have to stay on-premises indefinitely and hence like to explore the possibility of hybrid cloud storage.

We have already explored various options of moving data to the cloud, including S3 multipart PUTs and AWS Snowcone, AWS Snowball, and AWS Snowmobile. It is important to look at the hybrid cloud storage option for on-premises applications using the AWS Storage Gateway.

It is important from the exam perspective that you understand the use cases where Storage Gateway can fit the use cases of a hybrid storage requirement. You'll see few questions discussing the need around faster on-premises access to Amazon S3 and cases where one of File, Tape, or Volume Gateway makes sense over other options.

The major use cases for hybrid cloud storage include moving backups to the cloud, shifting on-premises storage to cloud-backed file shares, and providing low latency access for on-premises applications to the cloud data.

Working with hybrid cloud storage brings its own challenges, with the following key challenges:

- *Protocols:* You need to work with existing applications in the on-premises world that have not been developed with cloud storage in mind. In addition, you would like to integrate with the AWS storage options in the cloud.

- *Applications:* On-premises applications typically expect a lower latency to the data in the cloud, and when the data is moved to the cloud, customers would like to access the in-cloud processing of the data.

- *Management:* Customers prefer to keep the same management and monitoring environment to integrate and operate with the cloud in the enterprise environments.

- *Networking:* When the on-premises application is integrated with the cloud, it needs to have an optimized data transfer in addition to resiliency in case of network dropouts.

AWS Storage Gateway

AWS Storage Gateway is the hybrid cloud storage service that provides on-premises applications with access to the unlimited cloud storage offered by AWS, such as Amazon S3, S3 Glacier, S3 Glacier Deep Archive, Amazon EBS (Elastic Blockstore), and AWS Backup. Customers can use the AWS Storage Gateway to reduce the cost of the storage for their hybrid storage use cases.

AWS Storage Gateway brings the following core benefits to these applications:

- AWS Storage Gateway allows you to use a variety of protocols (NFS, SMB), which simplifies integration with existing applications.

- AWS Storage Gateway uses local caching, which provides low latency access to frequently used data.

- AWS Storage Gateway uses optimized data transfers to minimize network traffic between on-premises systems and AWS.

- AWS Storage Gateway reduces your overall cost and is integrated with AWS, which allows you to use AWS Management and Monitoring solutions in addition to using other services.

AWS Storage Gateway offers three types of solutions: file, volume, and tape.

File Gateway

A *file gateway* supports a file interface to Amazon S3 by combining a service and a virtual software appliance. The benefit is that you can store and retrieve objects from Amazon S3 using industry-standard protocols like Network File System (NFS) and Server Message Block (SMB). You will run the software appliance inside your on-premises environment as a virtual machine (VM), which can run on ESXi or Microsoft Hyper-V hypervisor. The gateway appliance will provide access to objects stored in Amazon S3 as files or a file share mount point. The benefit of this approach is that your application has seamless access to the S3 using standard protocols and provides a cheaper alternative to on-premises storage. You can get superior performance as the appliance will transparently cache objects locally and manage the data transfer between on-premises and AWS using parallel streaming and managing bandwidth consumption. A File Gateway integrates with the following AWS services:

- AWS IAM (Identity and Access Management) for access controls
- AWS KMS (Key Management Service) for encryption
- Amazon CloudWatch for monitoring
- AWS AuditTrail for audit purposes
- AWS Management Console and AWS CLI for operations
- AWS Billing and Cost management tools

How to Use a File Gateway

To use a file gateway, you start by downloading a VM image for the file gateway. You then activate the file gateway from the AWS Management Console or through the Storage Gateway API. You can also create a file gateway using an Amazon EC2 image. After the file gateway is activated, you create and configure your file share and associate that share with your Amazon S3 bucket. Doing this makes the share accessible by clients using either the NFS or SMB protocol. Files written to a file share become objects in Amazon S3, with the path as the key.

There is a one-to-one mapping between files and objects, and the gateway asynchronously updates the objects in Amazon S3 as you change the files. Existing objects in the bucket appear as files in the file system, and the key becomes the path.

Objects are encrypted with Amazon S3–server-side encryption keys (SSE-S3). All data transfer is done through HTTPS. The service optimizes data transfer between the gateway and AWS using multipart parallel uploads or byte-range downloads, to better use the available bandwidth. Local cache is maintained to provide low latency access to the recently accessed data and reduce data egress charges.

CloudWatch metrics are available and can provide insight into resource use on the VM and data transfer to and from AWS. CloudTrail tracks all API calls. With file gateway storage, you can do such tasks as ingesting cloud workloads to S3, performing backups and archiving, tiering, and migrating storage data to the AWS Cloud. [1]

Figure 3.9 shows the file storage deployment of a storage gateway.

FIGURE 3.9   File Storage Deployment – storage gateway

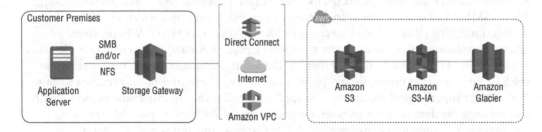

Volume Gateway

A *volume gateway* provides AWS storage-backed storage volumes that you can mount as iSCSI devices from your on-premises application services. There are two types of configurations for volume gateway, cached and stored.

Cached Volumes

As the name indicates, *cached volumes* store the data in Amazon S3, but the frequently accessed data is stored locally. While providing the cost benefits of Amazon S3, it also provides a low latency access for applications that need lower SLAs. Cached volumes range from 1 to 32 TB in size and must be rounded to the nearest GB. Each gateway configured for cached volumes can support up to 32 volumes, giving a maximum storage of 1,024 TB (1 PB).

For more details about cached volumes and the underlying architecture please visit the AWS Documentation page (amzn.to/2qPB9GN).

Stored Volumes

While cached volumes will work for a variety of applications requiring low-latency access, there are cases when you would like low-latency access to the entire dataset and the cached volumes do not fit the use case. In those cases, you can used stored volumes. The on-premises gateway will store all of your data locally and then asynchronously back up point-in-time snapshots of this data to Amazon S3. This is a great way to get durable and low-cost off-site backups that can be recovered to your local data center or Amazon EC2.

For more details about storage volumes and the underlying architecture, please visit the AWS Documentation page at amzn.to/34D5hDU.

Tape Gateway

While we have looked at various options to provide access to hot and warm data, a *tape gateway* provides you with cost-effective and durable archive data in Amazon S3 Glacier or Amazon S3 Glacier Deep Archive to minimize storage costs. A tape gateway, in essence, provides a virtual tape infrastructure that can scale as your demands grow and eliminates the need to provision, scale and maintain an on-premises tape infrastructure.

You can use the virtual tape library (VTL) interface to use your existing tape-based infrastructure and store data on virtual tape cartridges that you can create on your tape gateway. Each tape gateway is preconfigured with a media changer and tape drives.

Each gateway can contain up to 1,500 tapes or up to 1 PiB of total tape data at a time. The size of each virtual tape, which you can configure when you create the tape, is between 100 GiB and 5 TiB.

For more details about Tape Gateway and the underlying architecture, please visit the AWS Documentation page at amzn.to/2Lpwl1Z.

Amazon EFS

Amazon Elastic File System (Amazon EFS) provides a simple, scalable, fully managed elastic NFS file system for use with AWS cloud services and on-premises resources. It is built to scale on demand to petabytes without disrupting applications, growing and shrinking automatically as you add and remove files, eliminating the need to provision and manage capacity to accommodate growth.

Amazon EFS offers two storage classes: Standard storage class (EFS Standard) and Infrequent Access storage class (EFS IA).

EFS IA provides price/performance that's cost-optimized for files not accessed every day. If you simply enable EFS Lifecycle Management on your file system, files that are not accessed according to the lifecycle policy of your choosing will be automatically and transparently moved into EFS IA.

While workload patterns vary, customers typically find that 80 percent of files are infrequently accessed (and suitable for EFS IA) and 20 percent are actively used (suitable for EFS Standard), resulting in an extremely low storage cost. Amazon EFS transparently serves files from both storage classes in a common file system namespace.

Amazon EFS is designed to provide massively parallel shared access to thousands of Amazon EC2 instances, enabling your applications to achieve high levels of aggregate throughput and IOPS with consistent low latencies.

Amazon EFS is well suited to support a broad spectrum of use cases from home directories to business-critical applications. Customers can use EFS to lift-and-shift existing enterprise applications to the AWS cloud. Other use cases include big data analytics, web serving and content management, application development and testing, media and entertainment workflows, database backups, and container storage.

Amazon EFS is a regional service storing data within and across multiple Availability Zones (AZs) for high availability and durability. Amazon EC2 instances can access your file system across AZs, Regions, and VPCs, while on-premises servers can access using AWS Direct Connect or AWS VPN.[2]

The key benefits of Amazon EFS are as follows:

- *Managed Service:* Because it's a managed service, you have no hardware to configure or maintain and no file software layer to maintain, which makes it simple to use the service.

- *Standard File System Access Semantics:* With Amazon EFS you get what you'd expect from a file system: Read-after-write consistency, file locking, the ability to have a hierarchical directory structure, file operations like appends, atomic renames, and the ability to write to a particular block in the middle of a file.

- *Standard OS APIs:* EFS appears like any other file system to your operating system and hence applications that leverage standard OS APIs to work with files will work with EFS.

- *Sharable:* Amazon EFS is a common data source for applications and workloads across EC2 instances.

- *Elastically Grows to PB Scale:* Amazon EFS allows you to scale, allowing you to not specify a provisioned size upfront. You just create a file system, and it grows and shrinks automatically as you add and remove data.

- *Performance for a Wide Variety of Workloads:* Amazon EFS is based on SSD drives with consistent latencies, providing low latency vs. high throughput.

- *Available/Durable:* Amazon EFS replicates data across AZs within a Region. Means that your files are highly available, accessible from multiple AZs, and also well protected from data loss.

- *NFSv4.1 Based:* NFS is a network protocol for interacting with file systems. In the background, when you connect an instance to EFS, the data is sent over the network via NFS.

- *Open Standard, Widely Adopted:* NFS support is available on virtually all Linux distributions.

Beyond the tenets of simplicity, elasticity, and scalability, let's talk some more about some of the other features EFS provides. From a performance perspective, EFS offers two different file system performance modes:

- General Purpose mode (GP mode, default) [Recommended for the majority of the workloads]

- Max I/O [Recommended for scale-out workloads]

The trade-off between the two performance modes is essentially one of lower metadata latencies vs. an operations per second limit. GP Mode provides the lowest metadata operation latencies EFS is capable of, while Max I/O mode is not subject to any IO limits and provides the highest levels of aggregate throughput.

EFS also offers two system performance modes:

- **Bursting Throughput Mode (default):** Throughput scales linearly with the size of the file system and allows for periodic bursting above the standard amount. This is recommended for the majority of the workloads.

- **Provisioned Throughput Mode:** You can provision exactly what you need for more consistent and deterministic throughput performance. This is recommended for higher throughput to storage ratio workloads.

You can access EFS across thousands of clients simultaneously and across multiple Availability Zones, and AWS also supports accessing EFS across VPC-peered connections, over a VPN, or from a data center via AWS Direct Connect.

From a security compliance perspective, EFS of course supports encryption of data at rest and in transit, and offers compliance with the SOC, ISO, PCI-DSS, and HIPAA and Hi-TRUST CSF programs for the healthcare vertical, among others.

Amazon EFS Infrequent Access, or EFS IA, is a new storage class that can save customers up to 92 percent compared to the pre-existent EFS storage class, which is now called EFS Standard. Customers can use EFS IA to cost-effectively store larger amounts of data in their file systems and expand their use of EFS to an ever wider set of applications.

EFS IA doesn't require any changes to existing applications as EFS provides a single file system namespace that transparently serves files from both storage classes—Standard and IA. To move data to EFS IA, you can enable the Lifecycle Management capability for your file system that automatically moves files into IA, and by doing so, you can obtain huge cost savings (up to 92 percent compared to the EFS Standard storage class). You can also enable EFS A for any existing EFS file system by selecting the Lifecycle Management option in the EFS console.

Amazon EFS Use Cases

EFS supports a wide variety of use cases which range from jobs that run highly parallelized, scale-out jobs (those workloads that require the highest possible throughput, things like big data applications, and media workflows) to single-threaded, latency-sensitive workloads and everything in between (Figure 3.10).

FIGURE 3.10   Amazon EFS use cases

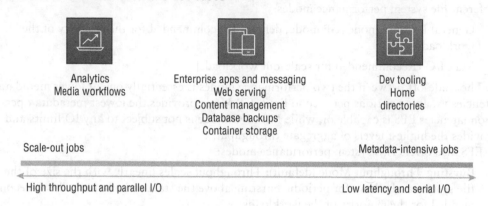

The following list is a summary of Amazon EFS use cases:

Web Serving   Web serving requires shared access to static content. EFS provides the ability to serve files to web applications quickly and in a scalable way to meet the demands of your business. As website traffic increases, you can scale the number of web servers to support your user demand and provide consistent access to the files stored in EFS with no need to modify or reconfigure the file system. With EFS being designed for 11 nines of durability, your web content is stored in highly available, highly durable storage. And since EFS uses standard file system semantics, your web developers can use naming and permissions that they are familiar with.

Analytics   For customers running analytics, EFS can be a great option. EFS is a POSIX-compliant file system, so applications that can access data over NFS can utilize EFS with no code modification required. For example, if you are running analytics against an on-premises or built-in-the-cloud NFS file store, your application is seamlessly portable to EFS. Additionally, there are many data sources feeding analytics applications that understand how to write to a file system. This may be lab equipment in the healthcare and life sciences world or machine data in manufacturing. For these applications, having a common interface where data can be written, transformed if needed, and then analyzed provides ease of use and flexibility. Additionally, since EFS provides a scalable, decoupled datastore accessible from thousands of EC2 instances simultaneously, processing analytics jobs can be done quickly and efficiently, providing businesses with faster time to insights from their data.

Container Storage   Stateful containers store data in shared storage, and you often need to scale container instances without reconfiguring the file system. Using Amazon EFS means you do not need to monitor or provision storage as your persistent storage grows. Amazon EFS supports rapid failover and event-based provisioning.

Media Workflows   Media companies are heavy users of file storage throughout the media post-production pipeline. Everything from ingesting data once it is captured on a recording device to distribution of the end product to consumers of the produced content. At ingest, EFS provides high throughput and high durability, which helps companies generating content upload it to the cloud quickly and store it durably. There are also many compute-intensive process steps where it's important to have the data in a shared file system and provide access to on-demand compute resources that can be quickly scaled to process jobs efficiently. EFS provides that familiar NFS interface and provides access to thousands of EC2 instances that can be employed as needed to reduce cycle times, reduce idle time in the creative process, and keep creative professionals occupied. EFS provides elasticity benefits that allow you to scale these jobs when needed and shut them down when not, which gives your creative organization extremely high rates of infrastructure utilization for batch-oriented activities. Common use cases on EFS include rendering, encoding, and transcoding operations.

Content Repositories   EFS provides an organized and secure repository that is easily accessible within an organization's cloud development environments. When collaboration across a distributed organization is required, having familiar access permissions that can be enforced is a key consideration. EFS provides a standards-based permissions structure to enable access control. As many customers are running CI/CD workflows in AWS, EFS provides a great way to enable a cloud-based code repository, providing shared access in a common file system hierarchical structure that is familiar to your developers. Additionally, EFS is supported by many of the top code repository platforms.

Scale-Out Applications   There are a number of scale-out applications that require the ability to run thousands of concurrent EC2 instances across a common dataset. EFS is great for these applications because you can spin up EC2 instances on demand as your application requires. EFS has Max IO mode, which provides high levels of aggregate throughput and IO to support these workloads efficiently. Additionally, Amazon EFS also supports the provision throughput mode, so if you need to maintain consistently high throughput, particularly if your dataset is not huge, you can use provisioned throughput to support the throughput requirements of your application.

Database Backup   Database backup is another use case for EFS that works particularly well. EFS provides an NFS file system, which is the preferred backup repository for many of the common database backup applications. Customers are backing up Oracle, SAP Hana, IBM DB2, and others onto EFS utilizing the management tools offered by those database vendors. The tools offer a lifecycle policy that allows for backups to remain on EFS for a defined period and then expire per the policy. With high levels of aggregate throughput, EFS allows database volumes to be quickly restored, providing low RTO for the applications using these databases. Additionally, when storing these backup images in EFS, a distributed architecture for your application provides you with highly durable HA storage without the need to configure replication or manage capacity, making using EFS really easy for database admins and backup administrators.

Interacting with Amazon EFS

You can set up and manage EFS in three ways:

- AWS Management Console
- AWS Command Line Interface (CLI)
- AWS Software Development Console (SDK)

Amazon EFS Security Model

Amazon EFS has multiple layers of security and protection to enable you to secure your data and assure compliance:

Layer 1: Amazon VPC security groups and standard network ACLs are available at the network layer to control network access to EFS.

Layer 2: You can control who has access to specific files or directories using standard POSIX permissions.

Layer 3: AWS IAM provides an additional layer of security by locking down administrative access to EFS.

Layer 4: You can create a file system and can enable encryption of data at rest so all the data in your file system is encrypted. Encryption of data at rest can only be enabled during file system creation.

Layer 5: You can also encrypt data in transit. Data encryption in transit uses industry-standard Transport Layer Security (TLS 1.2) to encrypt data sent between your clients and your EFS file systems. This is configured per client for each file system using the EFS mount helper tool.

Backing Up Amazon EFS

EFS file systems can be backed up using AWS Backup, which provides automated backup scheduling and retention per user-defined policy.

AWS Backup is controlled by a backup plan, which is a set of user-defined rules for scheduling and automating your backup process. Once a backup plan is defined, you can associate an EFS file system with it. AWS Backup will then begin backing up that file system per the backup plan. The backup plan will define the window in which the backups occur, the frequency of the backups, the retention period for the backups, and the elapsed time at which the backups will lifecycle to cold storage. AWS Backup also allows you to provide a secondary level of encryptions for your backups using KMS and stores the data in storage that is independent of the source file system for additional security.

Amazon FSx for Lustre

While Amazon provides a number of options for compute-intensive workloads, there are cases where the current file systems like EFS are unable to handle the needs to quickly scale out to millions of cores reading in excess of 100 Gb/s per core. This is typical with grid-computing architectures and some analytics applications working on big data looking to process the results instantaneously. Figure 3.11 indicates how a compute-intensive work-load looks.

FIGURE 3.11   Amazon EFS use cases

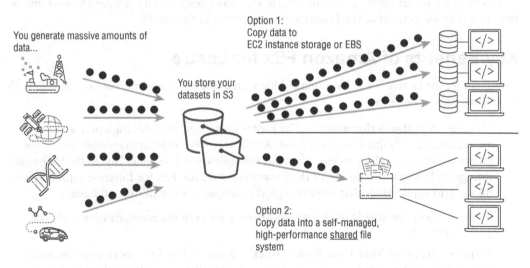

You have two options to work with such fast-paced large sets of data:

- Copy data to EC2 instance storage or EBS.
- Copy data to a self-managed, high-performance shared file system.

As you see, both options that we have require a file system. This is the case because when you are reading such high amounts of data and require low latencies, you cannot use S3 where the request costs for reading such data regularly can be quite expensive. In addition to that, you require a file interface to your data so that applications can natively handle the data.

The key requirements for such a shared file system include:

- A POSIX interface
- High levels of throughput and IOPS

The solution to this need is a parallel file system like Lustre where clients interact with the servers hosting the data in parallel and each server has multiple disks and data striped across disks and servers.

Running a file system like Lustre is hard because of the following key challenges:

- Configuring and maintaining the file system is cumbersome.
- Keeping the file system alive is hard.
- Parallel file systems typically have lots of configuration parameters that are hard to tune appropriately.

Keeping in view these challenges, Amazon provided *Amazon FSx for Lustre*, a fully managed parallel file system on AWS, which can seamlessly integrate with existing data repositories and is easy to set up and scale as per the demands of the application.

Lustre is a parallel open-source file system that has been around for over 15 years and is being used by 60 percent of the fastest supercomputers in the world.

Key Benefits of Amazon FSx for Lustre

Amazon FSx for Lustre is a fully managed file system for compute-intensive workloads with the following key benefits:

Massively Scalable Performance   The Lustre file system provides high performance up to hundreds of gigabytes per second. Amazon FSx is a fully managed version of the Lustre file system and provides consistent, sub-millisecond latencies due to the SSD-based storage and the parallel design of the file system. Amazon FSx for Lustre is especially useful for grid applications that require high throughput at sub-millisecond latency.

It also supports hundreds of thousands of cores for even the most massive-scale compute workloads.

Seamless Access to Your Data Repositories   Amazon FSx for Lustre provides your applications fast access to your repositories. Lustre linearly scales with the storage capacity whereby every 200 TB of storage provides 200 MB/second of file system throughput.

Simple and Fully Managed   Amazon FSx for Lustre is fully managed and abstracts the underlying storage to S3 by moving data between S3 and Lustre behind the scenes for faster processing and long-term retention. You can reduce the cost by deleting your file system without worrying about the data, which is natively available on S3 for long-term retention.

Native File System Interfaces   Amazon FSx for Lustre uses the POSIX-compliant nature and read-after-write consistency model of the Lustre file system to make it seamless for your applications. It also supports locking of files, which can be quite handy when working with a parallel application accessing data on a shared file system.

Cost Optimized for Compute-Intensive Workloads   Amazon FSx for Lustre is cost optimized for compute-intensive workloads due to its non-replicated nature and S3-backed long-term storage. The pay-as-you-go model with the additional ability to launch and delete file systems in minutes provides you with additional benefits from a cost perspective.

Secure and Compliant   Data encryption is automatically provided by Amazon FSx for Lustre. You also benefit from Amazon VPC security groups for network traffic control and AWS IAM for access controls. Additional AWS services like AWS CloudTrail provide the ability to monitor and log API calls.

Use Cases for Lustre

Amazon FSx for Lustre is useful in the following scenarios:

- High-performance computing
- Machine learning
- Big data analytics
- Seismic processing
- Geospatial analysis
- Financial modeling
- Media rendering and transcoding
- Electronic design automation

AWS Transfer for SFTP

SFTP(Secure File Transfer Protocol) is a widely used protocol that has been around for many years. As such, it is deeply embedded in a wide variety of workloads that span many areas of the enterprise as well as many different industries.

Many companies still rely on SFTP to share and move data. For example, you may need to receive third-party uploads, or say you're in a pharma company and you receive medical prescription data or you're an online real estate mortgage company and need to receive interest rates from banks on a regular basis. If you're an advertising tech company and need to receive files associated with an upcoming ad campaign, SFTP may very likely be your protocol of choice for its reliability and security.

Another common use case is sharing data with your customers. You might have a pay-per-subscription data service, and you want to provide SFTP as yet another channel to distribute the data stored in the cloud (in addition to the Amazon S3 API and, say, HTTPS) or maybe you use SFTP in your own internal organization for internal data sharing and it may be hard to change to other protocols as you move all your on-premises data to the cloud.

AWS Transfer for SFTP is a fully managed service enabling transfer of data and files over a Secure File Transfer Protocol into and out of Amazon S3. The service provides seamless migration of existing SFTP workflows in a cost-effective manner and provides native integration with other AWS services. SFTP is also known as Secure Shell (SSH) File Transfer Protocol.

Figure 3.12 shows how AWS Transfer for SFTP works.

FIGURE 3.12   AWS Transfer for SFTP

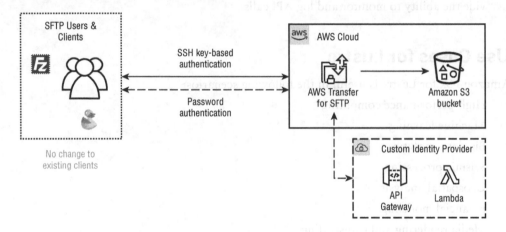

Summary

In this chapter, we went through a number of different technologies like S3, Glacier, DynamoDB, Neptune, Amazon EFS, Amazon Storage Gateway, Amazon FSx for Lustre, and AWS Transfer for SFTP.

For the AWS Data Analytics Specialty certification exam, you will be expected to understand the technologies listed in the preceding paragraph and have an understanding of the use cases for which they apply. It is highly recommended that you look at the associated documentation mentioned throughout the chapter to get a better understanding of the concepts. For each technology that has been mentioned in the book, please log on to the AWS console and get hands-on knowledge of these technologies before attempting the exam. It is highly recommended that you complete the workshops provided at the end of the chapter to get better hands on knowledge with the technologies discussed during this chapter.

The next chapter will discuss data processing and analysis which are the most critical components of an Analytics pipeline.

Exercises

The following exercises should give you a good ground of the basis of the data storage technologies. For assistance in completing the following exercises, refer to the user guides of the associated services.

EXERCISE 3.1

Working with S3

1. Creating a bucket

   docs.aws.amazon.com/AmazonS3/latest/gsg/CreatingABucket.html

2. Adding an object in a bucket

   docs.aws.amazon.com/AmazonS3/latest/gsg/
   PuttingAnObjectInABucket.html

3. Viewing an object in Amazon S3

   docs.aws.amazon.com/AmazonS3/latest/gsg/OpeningAnObject.html

4. Moving an object in Amazon S3

   docs.aws.amazon.com/AmazonS3/latest/gsg/CopyingAnObject.html

5. Deleting an object and a bucket

   docs.aws.amazon.com/AmazonS3/latest/gsg/DeletingAnObjectandBucket
   .html

EXERCISE 3.2

Working with DynamoDB

1. Creating a table

   docs.aws.amazon.com/amazondynamodb/latest/developerguide/
   getting-started-step-1.html

2. Writing data to a table

   docs.aws.amazon.com/amazondynamodb/latest/developerguide/
   getting-started-step-2.html

3. Reading data from a table

   docs.aws.amazon.com/amazondynamodb/latest/developerguide/
   getting-started-step-3.html

4. Updating data in a table

   docs.aws.amazon.com/amazondynamodb/latest/developerguide/
   getting-started-step-4.html

5. Query data in a table

   docs.aws.amazon.com/amazondynamodb/latest/developerguide/
   getting-started-step-5.html

6. Create a global secondary index

   docs.aws.amazon.com/amazondynamodb/latest/developerguide/
   getting-started-step-6.html

7. Query the global secondary index

   docs.aws.amazon.com/amazondynamodb/latest/developerguide/
   getting-started-step-7.html

EXERCISE 3.3

Working with DocumentDB

1. Create an Amazon DocumentDB cluster

   https://docs.aws.amazon.com/amazondynamodb/latest/developerguide/
   getting-started-step-7.html

2. Launch Amazon EC2 instance

   https://docs.aws.amazon.com/documentdb/latest/developerguide/
   getting-started.launch-ec2-instance.html

3. Access and use your cluster using Mongo shell

   https://docs.aws.amazon.com/documentdb/latest/developerguide/
   getting-started.connect.html

4. Delete the Amazon Document DB and Cluster

   https://docs.aws.amazon.com/documentdb/latest/developerguide/
   getting-started.delete-cluster.html

EXERCISE 3.4

Working with Amazon Neptune

1. Using Amazon Neptune workbench

   https://docs.aws.amazon.com/neptune/latest/userguide/notebooks.html

2. Creating an Amazon Neptune Cluster

   https://docs.aws.amazon.com/neptune/latest/userguide/
   get-started-create-cluster.html

3. Accessing the graph
   https://docs.aws.amazon.com/neptune/latest/userguide/
   get-started-access-graph.html

4. Using Gremlin to access the Graph

   https://docs.aws.amazon.com/neptune/latest/userguide/
   get-started-graph-gremlin.html

5. Using RDF/SPARQL to access the Graph

   https://docs.aws.amazon.com/neptune/latest/userguide/
   get-started-graph-sparql.html

EXERCISE 3.5

Working AWS Transfer for SFTP

1. Creating an SFTP server

   https://docs.aws.amazon.com/transfer/latest/userguide/
   getting-started-server.html

2. Adding a user
   https://docs.aws.amazon.com/transfer/latest/userguide/
   getting-started-add-user.html

3. Transfer files using AWS Transfer for SFTP

   https://docs.aws.amazon.com/transfer/latest/userguide/
   getting-started-use-the-service.html

Review Questions

1. You need a cost-effective solution to store a large collection of audio, video, and PDF files and provide users with the ability to track and analyze all your data efficiently using your existing business intelligence tools. Which of the following would form the solution required to fulfill the requirements?

    A. Store the data in Amazon Dynamo DB and reference its location in Amazon Redshift. Amazon Redshift will keep track of metadata about your audio, video, and PDF files, but the files themselves would be stored in Amazon S3.

    B. Store the data in Amazon S3 and reference its location in Amazon Redshift. Amazon Redshift will keep track of metadata about files. but the files themselves would be stored in Amazon 53.

    C. Store the data in Amazon S3 and reference its location in Amazon Dynamo DB. Use Amazon DynamoDB only for the metadata, but the actual files will remain stored in Amazon S3.

    D. Store the data in Amazon S3 and reference its location in HDFS on Amazon EMR. Amazon EMR will keep track of metadata about your files, but the files themselves would be stored in Amazon 53.

2. You have recently joined an online video streaming company that is looking to stream video files onto Amazon S3. Which of the following services can be used to deliver real-time streaming data to S3 with little to no coding required. Please select one option.

    A. Spark Streaming on Amazon EMR

    B. Amazon Kinesis Data Firehose

    C. Amazon Kinesis Data Streams

    D. Amazon Redshift

    E. Amazon EMR

3. You have recently joined a new gaming company as data architect. The company's latest game, Chocolate Bites, has been an overwhelming success, resulting in log files. You have been asked to ensure that the log files are made available for access at the cheapest price point. The data will be accessed once every few weeks, but it needs to be readily available when the access request is made. You have realized that S3 is a good option for such a scenario. Which of the following S3 storage option should you use?

    A. AWS S3 Standard - Infrequent Access

    B. AWS S3 Standard

    C. AWS Glacier

    D. AWS Reduced Redundancy Storage

4. You are working with a team of engineers who are using DynamoDB to build the leaderboard for their online multiplayer gaming application. In order to boost performance of reads, a caching layer is being considered. Which of the following is a caching service compatible with your DynamoDB-based application?

   A. Memcached

   B. DAX

   C. Redis

   D. ElastiCache

5. Rogers Inc, a video rental company, has set up an online site to make its rentals available to a wider community. It ships the latest videos that are not available on other streaming sites and charges a small percentage in addition to the shipping costs. The company has its website on AWS and is using DynamoDB behind its web application. The database has a main table called videos, which contains two attributes, *videoid* and the *subscriberid*, the user who has rented the video. You are required to select a primary key for this table to optimize access based on the subscriber identifier. Which of the following would you use as a primary key for this table?

   A. *videoid*, where there is a single video with lots of subscribers

   B. *subscriberid*, where there are lots of subscribers to a single video

   C. *Genre*, where there are few genres to a huge number of videos

   D. None of the above

6. Which of the following statements about Amazon DocumentDB are true? (Choose two.)

   A. Amazon DocumentDB is Cassandra compatible.

   B. Amazon DocumentDB is MongoDB compatible.

   C. Amazon DocumentDB can scale up to 10 TB per cluster.

   D. Amazon DocumentDB can scale up to 64 TB per cluster.

7. Amazon DocumentDB can only run in a VPC. Is this statement true or false?

   A. True

   B. False

8. Which of the following is an ideal use case for a graph database like Amazon Neptune?

   A. Fraud detection

   B. Recommendation engines

   C. Knowledge graph

   D. All of the above

Further Reading

I would highly recommend that at this point you review the AWS Well-Architected Analytics Lens available at `https://d1.awsstatic.com/whitepapers/architecture/wellarchitected-Analytics-Lens.pdf`.

This is a part of AWS Well-Architected Framework and helps you understand the pros and cons of decisions you make while building Analytics pipelines on AWS. We have just scratched the surface of AWS Analytics portfolio, but this will provide you with a better understanding of building Analytics systems on AWS.

References

1. `docs.aws.amazon.com/storagegateway/latest/userguide/WhatIsStorageGateway.html`
2. `aws.amazon.com/efs/`

Chapter

4

Data Processing and Analysis

THE AWS CERTIFIED ANALYTICS SPECIALTY EXAM OBJECTIVES COVERED IN THIS CHAPTER MAY INCLUDE, BUT ARE NOT LIMITED TO, THE FOLLOWING:

✓ **Domain 3.0: Processing**

- 3.1 Determine appropriate data processing solution requirements

- 3.2 Design a solution for transforming and preparing data for analysis

- 3.3 Automate and operationalize a data processing solution

✓ **Domain 4: Analysis and Visualization**

- 4.1 Determine the operational characteristics of an analysis and visualization solution

- 4.2 Select the appropriate data analysis solution for a given scenario

- 4.3 Select the appropriate data visualization solution for a given scenario

Introduction

In this chapter, you will learn about how to process and analyze the data stored on the AWS platform. Data processing is one of the most critical phases within a data and analytics pipeline and is an important exam topic. From an exam perspective, data processing, analysis and visualization make up forty two percent of the exam questions, and hence understanding the concepts and related technologies are going to be critical if you are looking to do well during the exam. The AWS platform provides multiple technologies to let you process the data, including AWS Glue, Amazon EMR, Amazon Redshift, and Amazon Athena. We'll primarily cover data processing and data analysis; however, data visualization will be covered in Chapter 5, "Data Visualization."

As has been the theme throughout the book, we would like to look at the various options provided by the AWS platform to process and analyze the data. The available options are dependent on the type of processing needed, which is directly linked to the type of use case.

The complexity of processing and analyzing the data revolves around various factors like the size of the data, the structure, the processing speed demands, the SLA requirements, and the skill level. There is more than one way to process and analyze the same dataset, but choosing the right solution depends on your understanding of why one particular set of solutions and architecture is preferable over the other. The AWS Data Analytics Specialty Certification exam expects you to not only know the various options but also the key reasons that make one choice better than the other in a given scenario.

Data processing and analysis is the process of identifying, cleaning, transforming, and structuring the data in a way to make it suitable to identify useful information, draw conclusions, and support decision-making. Let's look at the different types of analytical workloads that you may come across when working with data within your organization.

Types of Analytical Workloads

There are five different analytical workloads:

Batch Workload   Batch processing typically involves querying large amounts of "cold" data, and the turnaround time can vary from minutes to many hours. A typical batch processing report could be your daily, weekly, or monthly report. A batch query is a query that is run over different datasets repetitively. For example, your monthly reporting may run at the end of the month, with the same query running over a different set of data every time it is run. A batch workload gains certain benefits by running over the same data, primarily being able to operate on partial data or semi-structured or unstructured datasets. Examples of batch jobs include Hadoop MapReduce jobs, which run over large datasets and can process structured, semi-structured, and unstructured datasets and Amazon Redshift jobs, which can be used to transform large amounts of structured data using SQL.

Interactive Analysis   Interactive analysis is a cyclic process, which involves experimentation on data by making assumptions, validating your assumptions, and adjusting your experiments to achieve a business objective. The processing time can vary from seconds to minutes. Examples of interactive analysis includes ad hoc querying of data ranging from understanding the structure of data to meeting compliance requirements and needs using technologies like Amazon Athena and Apache Presto.

Messaging   Messaging workloads typically involve application-to-application integration, often involving processing latency between milliseconds to a few seconds. Latency is of utmost importance and typical applications include IoT message processing.

Streaming Workloads   Streaming data processing workloads include activities that ingest a sequence of data and incrementally update functions in response to each record. Typically, you ingest continuously produced streams of data records, such as metering data, monitoring data, audit logs, debugging logs, website clickstreams, and location-tracking events for devices, people, and physical goods. As the data is being generated continuously in huge volumes often at high velocity, it is important to capture it in near real time and respond to the events in as quick a time as possible. Examples of stream processing use cases include fraud alerts and real-time recommendations using technologies like Amazon Kinesis Data Streams and Amazon Kinesis Data Analytics.

Streaming workloads often require and support the following:

- Streaming workloads require near real-time response to content in semi-structured data streams.
- Streaming workloads often require relatively simple computations.
- Streaming workloads support workflows by moving data to other data stores and open-source systems.
- Streaming workloads are great for massive scale and less predictable data volumes.
- Streaming workloads require streaming (ingest) tools to convert individually produced records into fewer sets of sequential streams.
- Streaming workloads support sequential streams and are easier to process.
- Streaming workloads need simpler scalability mechanisms.

- Streaming workloads are easier to persist.

    Machine Learning   Machine learning workloads may have a varying latency, which can be from a few milliseconds to a few minutes to hours of processing. A typical use case involves predicting customer churn, recommending products, or forecasting demand for a particular product. An example of machine learning workload is Spark ML on Amazon EMR and Amazon SageMaker.

Let's look at some of the data processing and analysis tools available on the AWS platform.

Amazon Athena

Amazon Athena is an interactive querying service that makes it easy to analyze data in S3 using standard SQL. It is serverless in nature, which means that you don't have to manage and maintain any infrastructure but rather you can start analyzing data immediately. Amazon Athena supports the schema-on-read concepts, which is essential in this age of growing semi-structured and multi-structured data. It supports ANSI SQL operators and functions, which allows you to port queries from other analytical tools. Amazon Athena is massively scalable, which means that you don't have to manually scale the infrastructure when the data size grows. It also allows you to run cross-region queries and manage your costs.

Amazon Athena has the following key benefits:

- Query data directly on S3 and other sources – Amazon Athena enables data engineers, data analysts, and data scientists to execute SQL queries against data stored in relational, nonrelational, and custom data sources. Before November 2019, Athena was primarily used to query data from S3 (an object store); however, with the announcement of Athena Federated Query (`amzn.to/2YtsR3u`), Amazon Athena can now be used to query multiple data sources using built-in and custom connectors.

- Serverless – Amazon Athena is serverless, and hence you don't have to manage any infrastructure. You don't need to manage configuration, software updates, failures, or infrastructure scalability. Users can focus on the core business problems rather than the infrastructure required.

- Highly performant – Amazon Athena provides superior performance by accessing the data in a parallel fashion.

- Pay-as-you-go model – Amazon Athena has a simple pay-as-you-go model where you are charged per query, and it offers best practices to reduce the cost of the query by using optimal file formats, compression and partitioning of data.

Amazon Athena uses Apache Presto for SQL queries and Apache Hive for DDL functionality behind the scenes.

Apache Presto

Apache Presto is an open-source distributed SQL query engine optimized for low latency and ad hoc analysis of the data. It originated at Facebook due to the growing needs of their data analytics team and was later open sourced. Apache Presto can be used to query multiple terabytes to petabytes of data and provides an extensible architecture. It is optimized for low-latency interactive querying and provides cross-platform querying capability rather than just SQL on a single non-relational store.

Apache Presto has a master-slave architecture (similar to Hadoop and some MPP databases), where the coordinator acts as the master of the cluster and the workers are slaves. Figure 4.1 shows the Apache Presto architecture.

FIGURE 4.1   Apache Presto architecture

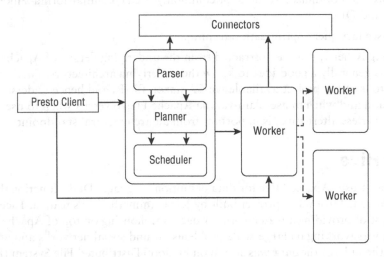

The key components in the architecture are as follows:

- *Coordinator* – The brains of a Presto cluster. Clients connect to the coordinator to submit their queries. The coordinator has three major subcomponents:
  - *Parser* – Responsible for parsing the queries coming from the client and parses the query to identify any syntax issues
  - *Planner* – Responsible for optimizing the plan for running the work across the workers. It uses rule-based and cost-based optimization techniques.
  - *Scheduler* – The component that tracks the worker nodes' activities and the actual execution of the query
- *Worker* – The component responsible for scheduling tasks on the worker nodes. Worker nodes are the actual workhorses of a Presto installation. They are able to connect to the data sources using the connectors. The coordinator is responsible to fetch results from worker nodes and return them to the client.

- *Connectors* – Being a distributed query engine, Presto provides various connectors that make it easy to connect to different data sources. It has a number of built-in connectors for common data sources like Hive, Kafka, MySQL, MongoDB, Redshift, Elasticsearch, SQL Server, Redis, and Cassandra, including many others. However, you also have the ability to develop custom connectors.

Presto provides superior performance due to the following reasons:

- Data is piped across many workers in a massively parallel processing (MPP) fashion in multiple stages and data is streamed across multiple stages.

- Multi-threaded execution makes the processing across multiple workers faster.

- Presto uses flat-memory data structures, which minimize garbage collection and optimize processing.

- Presto provides optimized readers for commonly used columnar formats like Parquet and ORC.

- Presto uses fast query optimization techniques.

While using Athena, you are abstracted from the underlying details of Apache Presto. However, it is generally a good idea to know the underlying architecture. Furthermore, Apache Presto is also a project available with Amazon EMR, and hence understanding the background and when to use plain-vanilla Apache Presto versus when to use Amazon Athena, a serverless alternative, is important from an architectural standpoint.

Apache Hive

Amazon Athena uses Apache Hive for data definition language (DDL) functionality behind the scenes. Apache Hive was a project built by Jeff Hammerbacher's team at Facebook, with the intent of providing a framework for data warehousing on top of Apache Hadoop.

Facebook was working on large-scale problems around social networks and association graphs, and the bulk of the data was stored on Hadoop Distributed File System (HDFS). Since the primary processing framework on Hadoop was MapReduce, which required extensive Java skills and thinking of problems in terms of key/value pairs, it became difficult to analyze the data for analysts who were more comfortable with the SQL skillset. Hive framework was created for the analysts to continue writing SQL but have the framework transform the SQL into a MapReduce paradigm. SQL as a language is ideal for set processing and is well known in the industry, which made Hadoop as a project become more popular and much widely used. Hive supports Hive-QL (a SQL-like language) and allows you to run the SQL in either a MapReduce or Apache Tez paradigm. Hive supports primitive types like integers, floating-point numbers, and string, data, time, and binary types in addition to complex types like structs, maps (Key/Value tuples), and arrays (indexable lists). Apache Hive supports multiple data formats like Apache Parquet and Apache ORC and partitioning of data for optimal process.

You can use Apache Hive for DDL functionality with Amazon Athena, but the complexity is abstracted from you as an end user.

Amazon Athena Use Cases and Workloads

Amazon Athena is most commonly used to analyze logs, be it from web servers or applications, discovering the data to understand and mine for patterns and then using Amazon QuickSight and other BI tools to perform ad hoc analysis.

Amazon Athena has a distinct place within the AWS ecosystem, where you have multiple other tools for data processing and analysis. If you have set up a data lake based on S3, you can use Amazon Athena to understand the key relationships and patterns within the dataset and then use this knowledge to model these in the form of data marts within Amazon Redshift for analyzing historical data and running pre-canned reports. One of the common questions is the choice between Amazon EMR and Amazon Athena for data processing and analytics. While we will look at Amazon EMR in a lot more detail, on a high level, Amazon EMR offers a lot more than just SQL processing. It offers a number of different framework choices like Hive, Pig, Presto, Spark, HBase, and Hadoop. Amazon EMR is more suitable if your workload requires you to use custom Java/Python/Scala code and you would like more control over the optimization and configuration parameters to run your workload. Amazon EMR offers you a lot more control, which comes with additional responsibility but also is usable for a wider spectrum of use cases and offers multiple price points depending on your use cases. For example, Amazon EMR also allows you to benefit from spot instances, which can make your workload processing quite cheap compared to on-demand instances. We'll look into Amazon EMR in a lot more detail later in this chapter.

The key use cases for Athena are as follows:

- Query data in your Amazon S3–based data lake.

- Analyze infrastructure, operation, and application logs.

- Interactive analytics using popular BI tools

- Self-service data exploration for data scientists

- Embed analytics capabilities into your applications.

Until November 2019, Amazon Athena was only limited to using a managed data catalog to store information about the databases and schemas for the data available in Amazon S3, and in the regions where AWS Glue was available, you could actually use the AWS Glue catalog, which is typically crafted using AWS Glue crawlers. In non–AWS Glue regions, Athena was using an internal data catalog, which was a hive-metastore–compliant store. Amazon Athena's internal data catalog stores all metadata for tables and columns, is highly available, and doesn't need user management. The catalog is compliant with hive-metastore and hence you can use hive queries for DDL.

In November 2019, before the AWS re:Invent conference, Amazon introduced support for custom metadata stores, which was welcomed by the customers as it meant that you could then use a data source connector to connect Amazon Athena to any metastore of choice. Amazon Athena can now run queries that can scan data across Hive Metastore, Glue catalog, or any other federated data sources.

Amazon Athena DDL, DML, and DCL

Amazon Athena uses Apache Hive for data definition language (DDL) statements. In order to create a table in Amazon Athena, you can choose to do the following:

- Run a DDL statement in Amazon Athena Console.

- Run a DDL statement from a JDBC or an ODBC driver.

- Using Amazon Athena, create a table wizard.

Amazon Athena will use the schema-on-read approach to project the schema when you execute a query, thus eliminating the need for the loading data or transformation. Athena will not modify your data in Amazon S3. When you are creating your schema such as databases/tables, you simply point to a location of the data from where it should be loaded at runtime.

As an example, the following code snippet shows you how to create a table in Amazon Athena.

```
CREATE [EXTERNAL] TABLE [IF NOT EXISTS]
[db_name.]table_name [(col_name data_type [COMMENT col_comment] [, ...] )]
[COMMENT table_comment]
[PARTITIONED BY (col_name data_type [COMMENT col_comment], ...)]
[ROW FORMAT row_format]
[STORED AS file_format]
[WITH SERDEPROPERTIES (...)]
[LOCATION 's3_loc']
[TBLPROPERTIES ( ['has_encrypted_data'='true | false',]
['classification'='aws_glue_classification',] property_name=property_value
[, ...] ) ]
```

Details of the key parameters can be found in AWS Documentation at amzn.to/2LFRm8n. While the exam generally does not specifically expect you to know about each of these parameters, they are good to know when you are developing applications on Amazon Athena.

Athena supports JSON, TXT, CSV, Parquet, and ORC formats via SerDes (Serializer/ Deserializer is an interface used by Apache Hive for input and output and for interpreting the different data formats). Amazon Athena uses the same SerDes to interpret the data coming from Amazon S3.

Using columnar formats like Apache Parquet and ORC can dramatically improve the performance of your queries. Typically, analytical queries access a subset of the columns from the rows rather than the entire row. Using columnar formats can dramatically reduce the size of data you query, thus improving overall IO and CPU requirements, resulting in overall better performance and reduced cost. Table 4.1 indicates the performance improvement and cost reduction on a 1 TB (terabyte) dataset stored on Amazon S3 (amzn.to/2LKT0Wt).

TABLE 4.1   Performance improvements with columnar formats

Data Format	Size on Amazon S3	Query Run Time	Data Scanned	Cost
Text files	1 TB	236 seconds	1.15 TB	$5.75
Apache Parquet	130 GB	6.78 seconds	2.51 GB	$0.013
Savings/Speedup	87% less with Parquet	34x faster	99% less data scanned	99.7% saving

Partitioning Your Data

Partitioning allows you to restrict the amount of data scanned by your Athena queries, thus providing better performance and reducing the overall cost. Partitioning can be done by any column in the table, and it is quite common to define multilevel partitions based on time. Table 4.2 compares runtimes of queries between partitioned and nonpartitioned tables. Both queries are supposed to operate on a 74 GB uncompressed dataset in text format.

Amazon Athena Workgroups

Amazon Athena is priced by the amount of data scanned on S3. You can use Amazon Athena workgroups to isolate queries between different teams, workloads, or applications and set the limits on the amount of data each query or an entire workgroup can process. Amazon Athena workgroups can also be used to isolate a workload, identify query metrics, and control the costs of your queries.

You can identify a unique query output location per workgroup, encrypt the results with a unique AWS KMS key per workgroup, collect and publish aggregated metrics per workgroup in Amazon CloudWatch, and use workgroup settings to eliminate the need to configure individual users.

Athena workgroups can also provide workgroup metrics reports like these:

- Total bytes of data scanned per workgroup
- Total successful/failed queries per workgroup
- Total query execution time per workgroup

You can also define per-query data scan thresholds, exceeding which a query can be canceled. And you can trigger alarms to notify the user of increasing usage and cost and disable a workgroup when queries exceed a certain defined threshold.

TABLE 4.4 Performance improvements with columnar formats

Data Format	Size on Amazon S3	Query Runtime	Data Scanned	Cost	Savings
Text file	1 TB	236 seconds	1.15 TB	$5.75	
Apache Parquet	130 GB	6.78 seconds	2.51 GB	$0.013	
Savings	87% less with Parquet	34x faster	99% less data scanned	$5.75/query Saving	

TABLE 4.2 Performance improvements with partitioned data

Query	Nonpartitioned Table			Partitioned Table			Savings
	Runtime	Data scanned	Cost	Runtime	Data scanned	Cost	
Select count(*) from lineitem where l_shipdate = '1996-09-01'	9.71 seconds	74.1 GB	$0.36	2.16 seconds	29.06 MB	$0.0001	99% cheaper 77% faster
Select count(*) from lineitem where l_shipdate >= '1996-09-01' and l_shipdate < '1996-10-01'	10.41 seconds	74.1 GB	$0.36	2.73 seconds	971.39 MB	$0.004	98% cheaper 73% faster

Source: (amzn.to/36m4eZm)

Amazon Athena Federated Query

Amazon Athena supports *federated query*, which means you can run queries using Athena across relational, non-relational, object, or custom-data sources (see Figure 4.2). The query can be run across on-premises or cloud data sources and can be used for ad hoc investigations and for building complex pipelines and applications.

FIGURE 4.2   Amazon Athena federated query

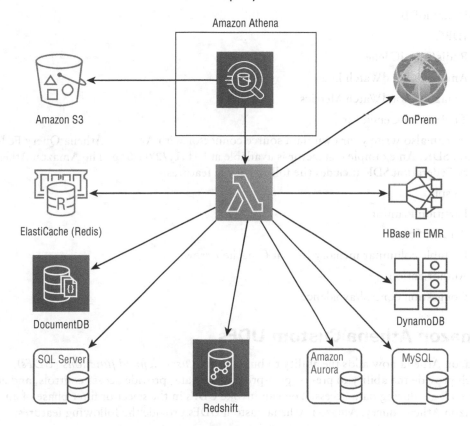

Athena federated query is relatively simple to use; you can deploy a data source connector, register a connector, specify the catalog name, and write the SQL query to access the data.

Athena uses Lambda-based data source connectors, which can be deployed in two ways:

- One-click deploy using AWS Serverless Application repository
- Deploy connector code to AWS Lambda.

You can also use registration-less federated query, which is really useful for quick prototyping. All you need to do is add the prefix `"lambda:<function_name>".` as the catalog name, and you can access the data source.

For example, `"SELECT * from "lambda:cmdb".ec2.ec2_instances".`

At the time of writing this book, the following connectors are available:

- HBase
- DocumentDB
- DynamoDB
- JDBC
- Redis/ElastiCache
- Amazon CloudWatch Logs
- Amazon CloudWatch Metrics
- TDPS Data Generator

You can also write your own data source connector with Amazon Athena Query Federation SDK. An example connector is available at `bit.ly/2YEm0og`. The Amazon Athena Query Federation SDK includes the following key features:

- S3 spill
- Partition Pruning
- Parallel Scans
- Portable columnar memory format (Apache Arrow)
- Authorization
- Congestion control/avoidance

Amazon Athena Custom UDFs

Amazon Athena now adds the ability to build custom *user-defined functions (UDFs)*, which provide the ability to pre- or post-process the data, provide access controls, and add custom logic during data access. You can invoke UDFs in the select or filter phase of an Amazon Athena query. Amazon Athena custom UDFs provide the following features:

- UDFs are powered by AWS Lambda.
- UDFs support network calls.
- UDF invocation can be used in the select and/or filter phase of the query.
- Athena optimizes performance, thus allowing you to focus on the business logic.

Using Machine Learning with Amazon Athena

Amazon Athena allows you to invoke ML models for inference directly from SQL queries. You can use ML with your SQL analysis for anomaly detection, customer cohort analysis, and sales prediction from your standard analytical queries. The models available on Sage-Maker can be used for inference, and no additional setup is needed to invoke the models.

Combining the federated query with ML makes Athena a very powerful asset in your analytical ecosystem. A typical workflow might have a data scientist using Amazon Athena federated query to select data from multiple data sources to understand the patterns and then perform data transformation using other tools or Athena UDFs before using this curated dataset to train a model on SageMaker and deploy it. Once the model is available on SageMaker, any user having access can use it for ML inference.

Please follow the blog to get some hands-on experience with using Amazon Athena in your ML pipeline (amzn.to/2YBsc02).

The following code snippet shows a sample query to invoke inference from Amazon Athena:

```
USING FUNCTION predict
   (platform int,
    genre int,
    critic_score int,
    user_score int,
    rating int)
   returns double TYPE_SAGEMAKER_INVOKE_ENDPOINT WITH
(Sagemaker_endpoint='myxgboostendpoint')

USING FUNCTION normalize_genre(value VARCHAR)
 returns int TYPE LAMBDA_INVOKE WITH (lambda_name='myLambdaFunction')

SELECT predict(platform,genre,critic_score, user_score,rating), name
FROM
      (SELECT name,
          normalize_genre(genre) as genre,
              critic_score,
              user_score
          FROM video_game_data.video_games);
```

Amazon Athena is a very powerful tool, used for ad hoc analysis, and with the new features on federated query and ML integration, it can be a very valuable tool for any data scientist.

Amazon EMR

Amazon EMR is Amazon's offering for running large-scale distributed workloads in the cloud using open-source projects like Apache Hadoop, Apache Spark, Apache Hive, Apache

Presto, Apache Pig, and a few others. We'll look into the details of some of these projects later in the chapter.

Apache Hadoop Overview

Apache Hadoop is an open-source project at www.hadoop.apache.org that allows distributed processing of large datasets across clusters of computers using simple programming models. It was designed with linear scalability, high availability, and fault tolerance in mind. Apache Hadoop is one of the most popular open-source projects and is a key part of Amazon EMR.

The cofounders of Apache Hadoop, Doug Cutting and Mike Cafarella, credit the creation of Hadoop to the two papers published by Google. "The Google File System" was published in 2003, whereas "MapReduce: Simplified data processing on large clusters" was published in 2004. Hadoop 0.1 was released in April 2006 and has since revolutionized the area of large-scale data processing.

Apache Hadoop includes the following major modules:

Hadoop Common   These are the common utilities in the Apache Hadoop project that support other Hadoop modules.

Hadoop Distributed File System (HDFS)   HDFS is a distributed file system that provides high-throughput access to the data, with inherent data replication (3x by default).

Hadoop MapReduce   MapReduce was the original default processing framework for Hadoop, later spun out into YARN (resource handling) and MapReduce (processing).

YARN   YARN stands for *Yet Another Resource Negotiator* and is a framework to schedule jobs and manage resources across a Hadoop cluster.

Apache Hadoop became a popular data processing framework with lots of promise to replace traditional large-scale data processing systems, which were not only inefficient but also expensive. While the technology promised so much in terms of scale and performance, its usability left a lot to be desired. Traditional enterprises looking to replace their traditional in-house data processing systems were running many different workloads, and retrofitting them on Hadoop via MapReduce seemed quite challenging if not impossible.

For example, among the most common users of traditional data processing systems were analysts who were more familiar with data flow languages and SQL, and writing MapReduce in Java programming language was not their cup of tea. This led to the creation of projects like Apache Hive and Apache Pig.

In addition to that, data scientists wanted to use this scalable platform for machine learning, but it became challenging to develop, train, and deploy models on this platform, which lead to projects like Apache Mahout and Spark ML.

With the abundance of so many open-source projects, the landscape became very busy and it became challenging to deploy a Hadoop platform with the necessary projects as each project team was working independently with their own release cycles. This created an opportunity for companies like Hortonworks, Cloudera, MapR, and the traditional data warehouse vendors like Teradata, IBM, and others to come up with Hadoop distributions, which would package the most common projects and add additional layers to deploy, secure, and manage the ecosystem of projects.

The original intent of Hadoop was to crunch large datasets in a scalable manner. However, deploying the platform in an on-premises environment where scalability is a challenge and adding and removing hardware can be problematic; the public cloud is the best place to deploy a Hadoop platform. In a public cloud like AWS, you can scale to any number of resources, spin up/down clusters in minutes, and pay based on the actual utilization of resources.

While you can run any of the managed distributions on Hadoop, Amazon offered Amazon EMR (Elastic MapReduce) as a managed Hadoop distribution on the cloud, with the intent to make it easier to deploy, manage, and scale Hadoop on the Amazon platform. The overarching goal of EMR was to combine the integration and testing rigor of commercial Hadoop distribution with the scale, simplicity, and cost effectiveness of the cloud.

Amazon EMR Overview

Amazon EMR is a managed Hadoop and Spark environment, which allows you to launch Hadoop and Spark clusters in minutes without the need to do node provisioning, cluster setup, Hadoop configuration, or cluster tuning.

At the time of this writing, EMR has 21 open-source projects that are tested and integrated into a single service designed to work seamlessly. One of the core requirements from customers is to work with the latest releases of Hadoop but ensure that it is tested for an enterprise-grade deployment. Each project in EMR is updated within 30 days of a version release, ensuring that you have the best and latest releases from the community and they have been tested for enterprise-grade installations.

Amazon EMR enables you to provision one, hundreds, or thousands of compute instances in minutes. You can use autoscaling to have EMR automatically scale your Hadoop and Spark clusters to process data of any size and back down when your job is complete to avoid paying for unused capacity.

With S3 being the core storage engine for your data lake, Amazon EMR processes data stored in an S3 data lake, which is designed to deliver 99.999999999 percent durability, with data automatically being distributed to three physical facilities (AZs) that are geographically separated within an AWS region. Amazon EMR monitors your cluster, will retry failed tasks, and will automatically replace poorly performing instances. You can monitor your cluster using Amazon CloudWatch to collect and track metrics, log files, set alarms, and automatically react to changes in the cluster. Amazon EMR provides multiple levels of security for your Hadoop and Spark clusters, including network isolation using Amazon VPC, encryption of data at rest in S3 using keys controlled via AWS KMS (Key Management Service) or customer-managed keys. Amazon EMR also includes security that uses ML models to discover, classify, and protect sensitive data using Amazon

Macie, with the ability to control access and permissions using IAM and authentication with Kerberos.

Amazon EMR makes deployments of a Hadoop cluster easy by providing you with the ability to launch a Hadoop or a Spark cluster within minutes. You don't have to worry about provisioning, cluster setup, Hadoop configuration, or cluster tuning. It enables you to provision hundreds or thousands of compute instances in minutes. Amazon EMR can use Autoscaling to automatically scale up your Hadoop or Spark clusters to process data of any size and can scale it back down when you job is complete. This helps you to avoid paying for any unused capacity and thus save cost.

You can also save on running your long-running Hadoop clusters by committing to reserved instances and saving up to 75 percent on the cost, or for intermittent workloads you can utilize the spare compute capacity and save up to 90 percent with spot instances. With Amazon EMR, the cost savings add up due to a variety of factors:

- Less admin overhead to manage and support a Hadoop cluster
- No up-front costs for hardware acquisition or software installation
- Reduced operating expense from saving on data center space and power and cooling expenses
- Faster business value due to reduced cost of delays and better competitive abilities by having access to the latest and greatest software, and an improved security in the cloud due to the needs of the most security conscious organizations

Apache Hadoop on Amazon EMR

I discussed Apache Hadoop briefly earlier in the chapter. Let's look into the architecture of Hadoop, the key use cases, and the projects in the ecosystem like Hive, Tez, Pig, and Mahout and the need for Apache Spark.

Hadoop works in a master-slave architecture for distributed storage and computation, with the master node called a *name node* and the slave node(s) called *data node*(s). The architecture originated from the *massively parallel processing (MPP)* world of large-scale data processing, and some of the databases like Teradata were already running on similar architectural frameworks. The objective of an MPP architecture was to split the storage and compute across multiple machines (data nodes), and have them managed through a single master node (name node).

The name node (master node) is responsible for managing the namespace such as the entire filesystem metadata, and also the location of the nodes and the block location(s) for a particular file. This information is reconstructed from the data nodes at system startup time. Due to the importance of the name node, considering it has the location map of the files and blocks, it is important to make it resilient to failures. This is typically achieved either by making a backup of the filesystem metadata or by running a secondary name node process (typically on a separate machine). A secondary name node, however, does not provide high availability in case of a failure. You will need to recover the failed name node by starting a new name node and use the metadata replicas to rebuild the name node, a process that can take between 30 minutes and one hour.

Data nodes are the actual workers in the cluster, who store and retrieve the actual data and communicate with the name node to keep the namespace updated at the name node level.

The major components that we discussed earlier are as follows:

Hadoop Distributed File System (HDFS)   This is an open-source filesystem that would manage storage across a number of machines, each containing a portion of the dataset. The objective of HDFS was to manage large datasets across sets of commodity machines, where failure was a norm rather than an exception. HDFS was optimized for high throughput of data, on commodity hard disks, which comes at cost—the latency of your queries. HDFS is not designed for queries that require low latency access to the data. Figure 4.3 shows the HDFS architecture and anatomy of a client read and client write.

FIGURE 4.3   HDFS architecture

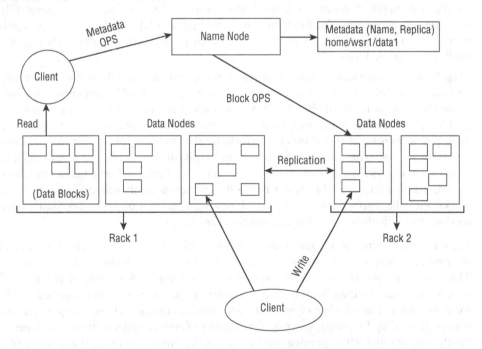

    During the exam, if you come across a scenario demanding low latency access or a large number of small files, HDFS will not be an option. You are better off working with tools like HBase when such a requirement is demanded from the situation.

Also, the filesystem metadata is kept in memory by the name node, which means that small files can be a huge problem for Hadoop. I've seen cases in practice where the name node runs out of memory, resulting in the crash of the entire cluster when storing metadata of lots of small files. When you talk about small files, a common question is about the recommended file size on HDFS. It is important to first understand how the filesystem is built before the answer can be given.

Since IO is one of the most important factors that contributes to latency, typical filesystems deal with blocks of data to optimize disk reads and writes. A block size is the minimum amount of data that can be read or written, and while the disk block sizes are 512 bytes, most filesystems will deal with block sizes of a few kilobytes. HDFS also uses a block size, but the default block size is 128 MB. The reason HDFS has large block sizes is that it was intended to operate on large volumes of data, and hence you would like to minimize the cost of seeks and fetch more data with each individual IO.

HDFS was built with the intent of being run on commodity hard disks, where failure was a norm rather than the exception, and hence it provides a default 3x replication (configurable), which means each block written to HDFS is replicated to a physically separate set of machines for fault tolerance and high availability. When a client application seeks to read data, HDFS decides which copy of the data to read depending on the availability of the block.

MapReduce   *MapReduce* was the de facto programming model for data processing on Hadoop before Hadoop 2.0, when it spun out Apache YARN (which will be discussed in a bit more detail shortly). A MapReduce job is basically a solution to a problem, such as, for example, a data transformation job or some basic analytics that an application (or a client) wants to perform on the cluster (typically on the data stored on HDFS or any other shared storage) in the MapReduce programing model. A Map Reduce job is divided into two major tasks: Map and Reduce. These tasks are scheduled across the nodes on the cluster by YARN, which not only schedules the tasks but works with the Application Master (we'll look into this in a bit more detail in a later section) to reschedule the failed tasks across the cluster.

Mapper tasks write the output to the local disk and not to HDFS, as the output is an intermediate output, and it is then picked up by the reducer phase for final output. The mapper output is thrown away once the job is completed. Generally speaking, the reduce tasks receive data from multiple mapper tasks, and the output is stored to HDFS for persistence. The number of mapper tasks depends on the number of splits (an input split is defined by Hadoop), whereas the number of reduce tasks is defined independently and not directly dependent on the size of the input. Choosing the number of reducers is considered to be an art rather than a science, as having too few reducers can impact the overall parallelism, thus slowing the job, and having too many reducers may create lots of smaller files and lots of inter mapper-reducer traffic (the shuffle/sort).

Figure 4.4 depicts the anatomy of a MapReduce job and the major steps involved like converting input data to splits, running a mapper phase, using a combiner, shuffle and sort before running a reduce phase to create an output data to be stored on HDFS.

FIGURE 4.4   Anatomy of a MapReduce job

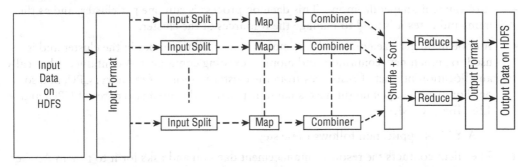

This book is more about giving you an overview of the components within different AWS services and how they relate to the exam. If you would like to learn more about the topic and details on individual phases, I highly recommend the book *Hadoop: The Definitive Guide* by Tom White (amzn.to/2ElqYwJ).

YARN (Yet Another Resource Negotiator)   *YARN*, as the name indicates, is a project that was created to manage the negotiation process between applications running on the Hadoop platform and the cluster resources. The objective was to split the resource management and computing framework from MapReduce v1.0 so that scheduling can be done independently of compute, thus paving the way for additional compute engines on the platform like Apache Tez and Apache Spark.

Figure 4.5 shows how frameworks like MapReduce, Spark, and Tez can benefit from YARN's resource negotiation capabilities. Applications like Apache Hive, Apache Pig, and Apache Crunch can make use of the lower-level frameworks rather than natively integrating with YARN.

FIGURE 4.5   YARN applications

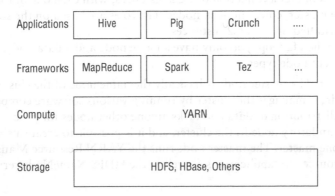

YARN has two types of long-running daemons:

- A resource manager daemon – This daemon process is run one per cluster, and as the name indicates it is used to manage the resources of the cluster.

- A node manager daemon – This daemon is run on all the nodes in the cluster and is used to launch new containers and monitor existing containers. A container is basically an allocation of a set of resources from the cluster in terms of memory, CPU, and so on. For example, you might have a container that is allocated two cores of CPU, and 128 GB of RAM.

A YARN application follows these steps:

1. The client contacts the resource management daemon and asks for it to run an Application Master.

2. The resource manager has a full view of resource availability across the cluster and finds a node manager that can launch the Application Master in a container.

3. The Application Master's next steps are dependent on the Application Master's intended purposes:

    a. Run the application inside the container it itself is running in, compute the results, and send it back to the client.

    b. Request (like a MapReduce YARN application) the resource manager for additional containers and run the application in a distributed fashion.

    YARN applications can have a short-lived lifespan, running an application for a few seconds to minutes, or it can live for the duration of the cluster.

Hadoop on EMR

Now that you have seen the different components in Apache Hadoop, let's look at what is offered by AWS within EMR. Since Amazon offers EC2 (Elastic Compute Cloud) instances, an EMR cluster is in fact a collection of EC2 instances, with each one of them having different roles, like master, core, and task nodes. The roles are based on the software components that get installed on the EC2 instances.

While on Apache Hadoop, you only have a name node and a data node, but in EMR you have three different node types:

- *Master nodes:* The master node is basically the name node of the cluster, and similar to a name node, it manages the cluster by running various software components to coordinate the distribution of data and tasks among other nodes for processing. The master node is a mandatory node in the cluster, and it is possible to create a single-node cluster with only one master. The master node runs the YARN Resource Manager service to manage resources for applications as well as the HDFS NameNode service.

- *Core nodes:* The core node performs the role of a data node in a Hadoop cluster; it acts as a workhorse to run the tasks and also stores the data in HDFS. If you have a multi-node cluster, it is mandatory to have a core node. Core nodes run the DataNode daemon to coordinate storage as a part of HDFS. They also run the Task Tracker daemons and perform other parallel computation tasks.

- *Task nodes:* The task nodes also perform the role of a workhorse but are optional in nature as they do not store any data in HDFS. They are added to the cluster to add power and perform parallel computation on the data, such as running Hadoop MapReduce tasks and Spark executors. Task nodes do not run the DataNode daemon. Task nodes are often used with spot instances, and hence Amazon EMR provides the default functionality that when a task node running on spot instance is terminated, the running jobs don't fail. It is for this specific reason that the Application Master process is only run on the core nodes.

Types of EMR Clusters

Amazon EMR decouples storage and compute, which allows you to run different workloads on differently configured clusters and make the best use of the resources available while identifying the right price point for different workloads based on SLAs.

- *Persistent cluster:* Traditionally Hadoop on-premises clusters have always been persistent clusters that are long running. If you have a workload that requires a 24x7 cluster availability, long-running persistent clusters are the way to go.

- *Transient clusters:* Transient clusters are suitable for batch jobs. An example of a batch job is a nightly job that extracts data from some source systems and integrates it into a data mart that is then made available for querying. The storage and compute separation of EMR makes this possible and reduces the overall cost of running Hadoop on AWS.

- *Workload-specific clusters:* Since there are various versions of Hadoop, you can optimize your cluster to a specific workload. Running a workload-specific Amazon EMR cluster can give you the best performance while providing optimal cost. You can tweak the settings of your container based on individual workload needs.

What Instance Types to Choose

Amazon EMR offers a variety of instances types, and it can become quite complicated to pick the right instance type for your workloads.

Typically, there are four major types of workloads that are run on EMR, as described in Table 4.3. The table is important as you might be asked to identify the best instance family for a workload type.

TABLE 4.3 Amazon EMR instance types

Workload Type	Instance Recommendation
General purpose – batch processing	M5 family M4 family
Compute intensive – machine learning	C5, C4m, z1d family
Memory intensive – interactive analysis	X1, R4, R5a, R5d family
Storage intensive – large HDFS requirements	D2, I3 family
Deep learning – GPU instances	G3, P2 family

Creating an EMR Cluster

You can create an EMR cluster in three different ways: with the AWS Management Console, AWS CLI, and the Java SDK.

AWS Management Console

Please watch the video at bit.ly/2RXBguQ for a demonstration on the creation of an EMR cluster. You should practice this by doing Exercise 4.1 for a quick setup, or follow the advanced options to have more control over how the cluster must be created.

AWS CLI

You can create the same cluster from a CLI with the following command:

```
aws emr create-cluster
    --name "demo-cluster"
    --release-label emr-5.28.0
    --applications Name=Hive Name=Spark
    --use-default-roles
    --instance-groups
InstanceGroupType=MASTER,InstanceCount=1,InstanceType=m5.xlarge
InstanceGroupType=CORE,InstanceCount=2,InstanceType=m5.xlarge
```

AWS SDK

You can create the same cluster using the Java SDK. Please follow the example in AWS Documentation to get an idea of how to create such a cluster (amzn.to/2qWJdpb).

> The exam will not test you on the exact semantics of creating an EMR cluster from the CLI or programmatically. This knowledge is, however, good from an architecture perspective, and it's good to know that you can programmatically create an EMR cluster in a data pipeline.

During the cluster creation, especially in the console, you might have seen various options like EMR MultiMaster and Glue Data Catalog. Let's take a quick look at what those mean:

- *EMR MultiMaster* – As discussed earlier during the Hadoop overview, the name node (also known as the master node) can be a single point of failure in a Hadoop cluster. EMR MultiMaster allows you to create a cluster with three master nodes, which therefore supports high availability by automatically failing over to the standby master node if the primary master node fails.

- *Glue Data Catalog settings* – Glue Data Catalog can act as a central catalog for your platform. EMR allows you to use Glue Data Catalog as an external metastore, which once configured will be supported in Hive, Spark, and Presto. This is a very useful option when you need to share the metadata between different clusters, services, applications, and AWS accounts.

- *Editing software settings* – Another option that you might have seen during the cluster creation is Edit Software Settings. You can edit the default configurations for Hadoop applications by supplying a configuration object, which helps in configuring software on your EMR cluster. Configuration objects consist of a classification, properties, and optional nested configurations. The benefit of this option is a simpler way to edit the most common Hadoop configuration files, including hive-site, hadoop-env, hadoop-log4j, and core-site.

- *Adding steps* – A *step* is a unit of work you can submit to the cluster, and it can be one of the following:
  - Streaming program
  - Hive program
  - Pig program
  - Spark application
  - Custom JAR

    You also have the option to auto-terminate the cluster upon completion. Long-running clusters have the option of enabling termination protection, which protects the cluster from accidental termination.

- *Instance group configuration:* You have the option to provision your cluster from a list of instance types, which can be acquired in an on-demand fashion or from the spot market. You can choose one of the following configurations:
  - *Uniform instance groups* – You can specify an instance type and purchasing option for each node type. This is the default selection.
  - *Instance fleets* – You have the option to specify a target capacity and Amazon EMR will fulfill it for each node type. You can specify a fleet of up to five EC2 instance types for each Amazon EMR node type (master, core, task). As a best practice you should be flexible on the kind of instances your application can work with, as that gives you the best chance to acquire and maintain spot capacity for your EMR cluster.
- *Logging* – Logging is one of the most important aspects considering anything that goes wrong in your cluster can be identified from the error logs. By default, logs are written to the mater node in /mnt/var/log for the following components:
  - Step logs
  - Hadoop and YARN component logs
  - Bootstrap action logs
  - Instance state logs

  If you have checked the logging box while configuring your cluster, the logs will also be written to S3 on a 5-minute interval.
- *Debugging* – When debugging is enabled, Amazon EMR will archive the log files to Amazon S3 and the files will be indexed. You can then use the console to browse the step, job, task, and task-attempt logs on the cluster. The debugging logs are also pushed to S3 at a 5-minute interval.

EMRFS

EMRFS is an implementation of HDFS used by Amazon EMR clusters to read and write data to Amazon S3. EMRFS provides the ability to store data onto S3 in addition to providing features like consistent view and data encryption while supporting IAM role authentication and pushdown optimization with S3 SELECT.

As discussed earlier, data in S3 is eventually consistent. Amazon EMRFS provides consistent views that provide consistency checks for lists and read-after-write for objects in Amazon S3. Furthermore, EMRFS provides data encryption, which means you can encrypt and work with encrypted objects EMRFS.

EMRFS consistent view uses DynamoDB as a file registry and provides configuration options for the following:

- Number of times EMRFS calls S3 after finding an inconsistency
- Amount of time until the first retry. Subsequent retries will use an exponential back-off.

Bootstrap Actions and Custom AMI

Bootstrap actions are scripts that can be executed on a Hadoop cluster before Hadoop daemons start up on each node. They are typically used for installing additional software, and Amazon EMR allows you to run up to 16 bootstrap actions. You can run the bootstrap actions based on certain conditions, as in the following examples:

- *RunIf* – Amazon EMR provides the RunIf predefined bootstrap action to run a command when an instance-specific value is found in any of the following files:
- `instance.json`
- `job-flow.json`

  An example of a condition statement is `isMaster=true`, which means that the action is run if the node running the action has a master role in the cluster.

- *Custom* - Run a custom script such as to copy data from S3 to each node.

  You can also use a Custom AMI, which can reduce the cluster start time by pre-installing applications and performing other customizations instead of using bootstrap actions. This also prevents unexpected bootstrap action failures.

  There are certain limitations for a custom AMI:

- Must be an Amazon Linux AMI
- Best be an HVM- or EBS-backed AMI
- Must be 64-bit AMI
- Must not have users with the same names as used by Hadoop applications (for example, hadoop, hdfs, yarn, or spark)

Security on EMR

An EC2 key pair is needed enable SSH into master node. You also have a check box, which indicates the visibility of the cluster to parties other than the creator. If the check box is unchecked (checked by default), the cluster would only be visible to the creator of the cluster in the console and CLI.

Permissions for EMR

Amazon EMR requires three different roles for operating in the platform:

- EMR role – Allows EMR to access resources such as EC2.
- EC2 instance profile – Allows EC2 instances in a cluster to access resources such as S3.
- Auto scaling role – Allows autoscaling to add and terminate instances.

  Amazon EMR can create default roles for you while creating a cluster. If the roles are already available, they will be used, and if they are unavailable, the roles would be created. You can also specify custom roles.

Security Configurations

You can also define security configurations to configure data encryption, Kerberos authentication, and Amazon S3 authorization for EMRFS. The security configuration can be used for multiple EMR clusters. Security configurations can be created via AWS Console, AWS CLI, and AWS SDK and can also be created with a cloud formation template.

For data encryption, you can specify the following:

- Encryption of data at rest
- Encryption of data in motion/transit

Amazon EMR has different places for data at rest, including local discs and S3 via EMRFS.

You can also choose in-transit encryption by choosing options for open-source encryption features that apply to in-transit data for specific applications. The available in-transit encryption options may vary by EMR release.

For authentication, you can enable Kerberos authentication for interactions between certain application components on your cluster using Kerberos principals. For the majority of the development and test workloads and some production workloads, you can choose between having EMR install a KDC server on the master node of the cluster or configuring an External KDC. For production workloads, customers often prefer using an External KDC which requires you sharing the KDC details with the EMR cluster.

You can also configure Lake Formation integration and use corporate credentials together with Lake Formation permissions to control access to the data catalog and underlying data store. You must create a data lake and configure associated permissions in Lake Formation.

Figure 4.6 and Figure 4.7 show how you can create a security configuration within EMR.

EMR Notebooks

Jupyter notebooks have become one of the most common ways for data engineers and data scientists to work with the data. While you can configure a Jupyter notebook inside an EMR cluster, AWS announced the feature of an EMR notebook, which meant you can use EMR notebooks based on Jupyter to analyze data interactively with live code, narrative text, visualizations, and more (see Figure 4.8). You can create and attach notebooks to Amazon EMR clusters running Hadoop, Spark, and Livy. Notebooks run free of charge and are saved in Amazon S3 independently of clusters.

When you create a notebook in Amazon EMR, you can choose to connect to an existing cluster or create a new cluster. Creating a new cluster from the Notebook interface is typically done in dev/test scenarios.

You can also link the notebook to a Git repository.

FIGURE 4.6   Security configurations in EMR (Encryption)

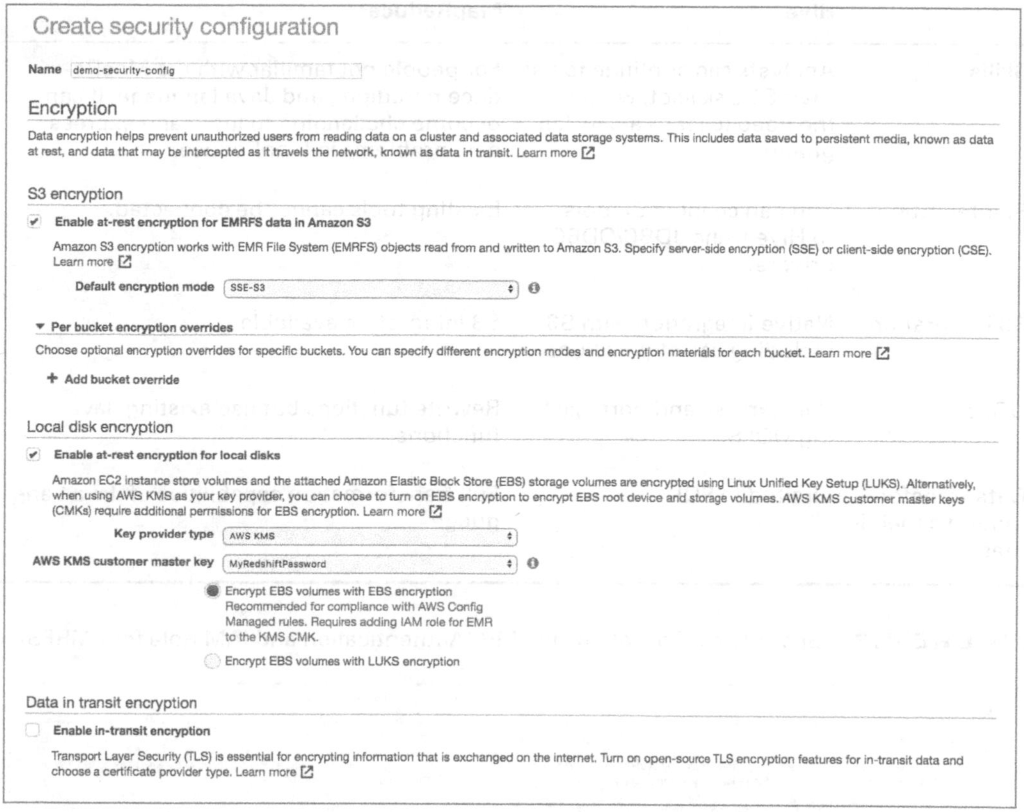

Create security configuration

Name demo-security-config

Encryption

Data encryption helps prevent unauthorized users from reading data on a cluster and associated data storage systems. This includes data saved to persistent media, known as data at rest, and data that may be intercepted as it travels the network, known as data in transit. Learn more ⧉

S3 encryption

☑ **Enable at-rest encryption for EMRFS data in Amazon S3**

Amazon S3 encryption works with EMR File System (EMRFS) objects read from and written to Amazon S3. Specify server-side encryption (SSE) or client-side encryption (CSE). Learn more ⧉

Default encryption mode   SSE-S3   ⇅ ⓘ

▼ Per bucket encryption overrides

Choose optional encryption overrides for specific buckets. You can specify different encryption modes and encryption materials for each bucket. Learn more ⧉

✚ Add bucket override

Local disk encryption

☑ **Enable at-rest encryption for local disks**

Amazon EC2 instance store volumes and the attached Amazon Elastic Block Store (EBS) storage volumes are encrypted using Linux Unified Key Setup (LUKS). Alternatively, when using AWS KMS as your key provider, you can choose to turn on EBS encryption to encrypt EBS root device and storage volumes. AWS KMS customer master keys (CMKs) require additional permissions for EBS encryption. Learn more ⧉

Key provider type   AWS KMS   ⇅

AWS KMS customer master key   MyRedshiftPassword   ⇅ ⓘ

⦿ Encrypt EBS volumes with EBS encryption
   Recommended for compliance with AWS Config
   Managed rules. Requires adding IAM role for EMR
   to the KMS CMK.

◯ Encrypt EBS volumes with LUKS encryption

Data in transit encryption

☐ Enable in-transit encryption

Transport Layer Security (TLS) is essential for encrypting information that is exchanged on the internet. Turn on open-source TLS encryption features for in-transit data and choose a certificate provider type. Learn more ⧉

Apache Hive and Apache Pig on Amazon EMR

As discussed in previous sections, Apache Hadoop has quickly started to become the de facto standard for data processing in the data center landscape; however, the complexity with MapReduce as a programming model meant that people wanted to use traditional programming languages like SQL and data flow languages, which led to the rise of projects like Apache Hive (originated at Facebook) and Apache Pig (originated at Yahoo).

Apache Hive Overview

We touched upon Apache Hive in the section "Amazon Athena" earlier in this chapter. Apache Hive is an open-source SQL-like data warehousing solution running on Hadoop and is built for SQL analysts, SQL developers, and data scientists who would like to use the Hadoop framework but want to benefit from the power and simplicity of a SQL-like language.

Apache Hive has certain pros and cons over the MapReduce programming paradigm, some of which are described in Table 4.4, which will help you answer the exam questions.

TABLE 4.4 Apache Hive Pros and Cons

	Hive	MapReduce
Skills	Analysts can continue to use their SQL skillset, without the need to learn a new language.	For people not familiar with the MapReduce paradigm, and Java language, it can become challenging to learn and express new problems in MapReduce.
BI integration	You can connect BI tools to Hive using JDBC/ODBC drivers.	Existing tools cannot be connected.
S3 integration	Native integration with S3 including use of partitions	S3 Integration available
UDFs	You can use and port existing UDFS.	Rewrite functions but use existing Java functions.
Data transformation capabilities	Limited to SQL	Full transformation capabilities of Java Language

FIGURE 4.7 Security configurations in EMR (Authentication and IAM Role for EMRFS)

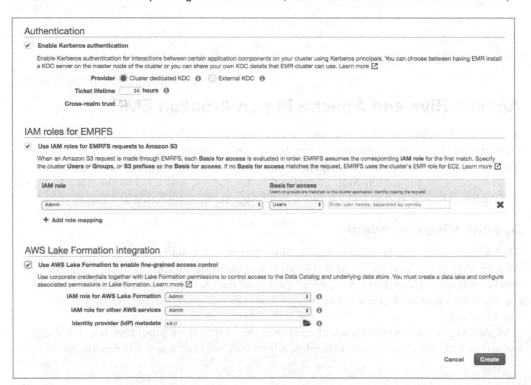

FIGURE 4.8 Creating an EMR notebook

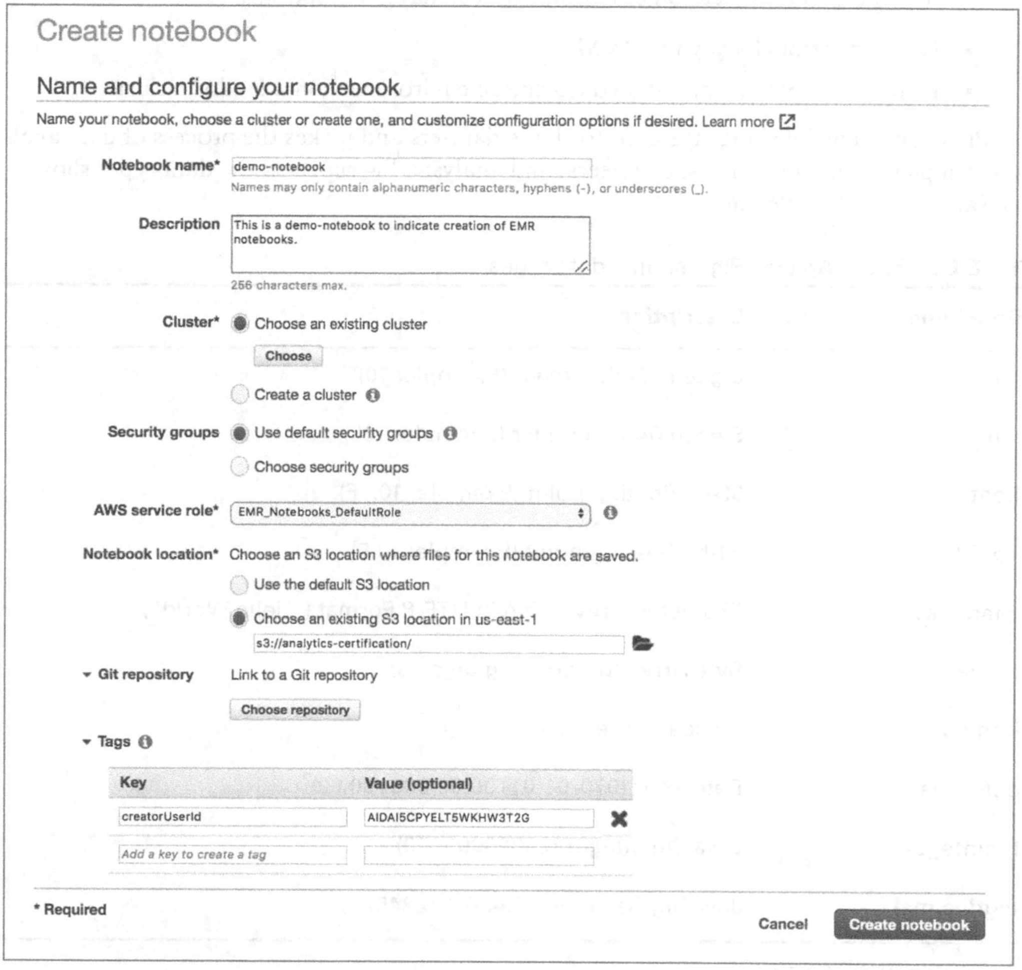

Apache Pig Overview

Apache Pig was originally developed as a higher level abstraction to MapReduce, with the added benefit of having much richer multivalued and nested data structures, including most common data transformation tasks like joins between two datasets, which can easily become quite complicated with the MapReduce model.

Apache Pig has two major components:

- Pig Latin language – Pig Latin language is used to express the data flows. A data flow is basically a series of operations that converts and inputs dataset to a transformed dataset.

- Pig execution environment – The Pig scripts developed by the analysts/programmers are executed in an execution environment. You have two options:

  - Run the scripts locally in a JVM.
  - Run the scripts in a distributed execution environment on a Hadoop cluster.

Pig is an extensible language used for large datasets and makes the process of data analysis simpler for data scientists, engineers, and analysts. Pig supports the data types shown in Table 4.5 and Table 4.6:

TABLE 4.5   Apache Pig – simple data types

Data Type	Description
int	Signed 32-bit integer (Example: 10)
long	Signed 64-bit integer (Example: 10L)
float	32-bit floating point (Example: 10.5F)
double	64-bit floating point (Example: 10.5)
chararray	Character array string in UTF-8 Format ("Hello World")
bytearray	Byte Array (Binary long objects)
boolean	Boolean (true/false)
datetime	Datetime (1970-01-01T00:00:000+00:00)
biginteger	Java Big Integer (20000000000)
bigdecimal	Java Big Decimal (33.4567812345)

Source: bit.ly/2sG6zQs

TABLE 4.6   Apache Pig – complex data types

Data Type	Description
tuple	An ordered set of fields (19,2)
bag	A collection of tuples {(19,2),(23,1)}
map	A set of key/value pairs

Source: bit.ly/2sG6zQs

The following code sample demonstrates loading "student" data and then printing their names and ages:

```
dataset = LOAD 'students' USING PigStorage() as (name:chararray, age:int,
gpa:float);
studentsage= FOREACH dataset GENERATE name,age
DUMP studentsage;
(Roger,25)
(Tom,22)
(Cristina,29)
(Steffen,26)
(Vincent,29)
```

From the exam's perspective, you need to understand the scenarios where Apache Pig and Apache Hive would be useful compared to traditional MapReduce programs.

Apache Presto on Amazon EMR Overview

We already discussed Apache Presto in the section "Amazon Athena," and as you may remember, Apache Presto is the technology behind Amazon Athena. You can also run Apache Presto as a part of EMR installation. Apache Presto is used by data scientists and data analysts who are looking for quick interactive query responses. Its pros and cons are listed in Table 4.7, which will help you answer exam questions around the technology.

TABLE 4.7   Apache Presto Pros and Cons

Pros	Cons
SQL-based and hence you can bring your own SQL skillset	Optimization needed during join planning for large tables
Low latency response	Unsuitable for batch processing
JDBC ODBC complaint	Limited fault tolerance (/rerun failed jobs)
BI integration	Memory requirements high
Support for UDF	
Federated queries (Hive/Cassandra/relational databases/object stores)	

Apache Spark on Amazon EMR

With the popularity of Hadoop, new use cases started cropping up, including data analysts who had a traditional data warehousing background and were looking to run low-latency queries on the platform. While Apache Hive and Apache Pig solved the problem of using well-known higher-level languages like SQL to do data analysis, the frameworks were still running the analysis on Hadoop using MapReduce, a framework that was never built to do interactive analysis. As is common with the open-source community, this problem resulted in many different tools to solve the problem, including Apache Tez, Apache Impala, and Apache Spark.

Apache Spark was built from the ground up to do interactive analysis (as can be inferred from the name "Spark") by using its own purpose-built distributed runtime rather than MapReduce. The key differences between Spark and MapReduce were better use of memory and the avoidance of spilling to disk for different tasks of the same job. This resulted in Apache Spark outperforming MapReduce in all major benchmarks. In addition to in-memory processing, Apache Spark used lazy evaluation to optimize the job before it was physically run on the cluster. Spark also provides simplicity by providing 80 high-level operators that make it easy to build parallel applications in most popular languages like Java, Scala, Python, R, and SQL.

In addition to multiple programming APIs, Apache Spark allows you to combine frameworks into a single environment. For example, You can do SQL processing, stream processing, machine learning, and graph processing in a single program, which makes Apache Spark not only powerful but widely adopted in the industry. Figure 4.9 shows the different components of Apache Spark framework.

FIGURE 4.9   Apache Spark Framework overview

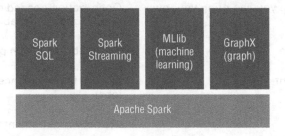

Architecture of Spark

Apache Spark's architecture, shown in Figure 4.10, has the following major components:

- Driver program
- Cluster manager
- Worker nodes

- Executors
- Tasks

FIGURE 4.10 Apache Spark architecture

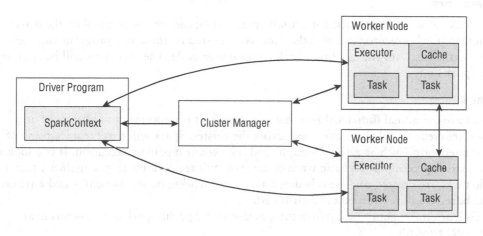

Driver Program

All Spark applications consist of a driver program that runs the `main()` function of your program and is typically on one of the nodes of the cluster. The driver "drives" the spark application and is basically the brains of the application, maintaining all relevant and crucial information about the program. It has three major responsibilities:

- Maintain all the information about the application.
- Respond to user's inputs.
- Analyze, distribute, and schedule the work across the executors.

Cluster Manager

A cluster manager is typically a service that is used to acquire resources on the cluster on behalf of the application. Apache Spark supports a number of different cluster managers:

- *Standalone* – Apache Spark distribution supports a simple cluster manager that is included with Spark, which makes it easy to set up a cluster.
- *Apache Mesos* – Apache Mesos is a general-purpose cluster manager, which is very popular in the open-source world and allows effective resource sharing between applications running on a cluster of computers. Apache Mesos can also run Hadoop MapReduce applications.
- *Hadoop YARN* – Hadoop YARN is the default resource manager for Hadoop clusters and supports running of Spark.
- *Kubernetes* – Kubernetes is an open-source system for automating, scaling, and managing the deployment of containerized applications.

Worker Nodes

A cluster typically contains many worker nodes that run one or more executors, which process the work assigned by the driver program.

Executors

The executors are responsible for actually performing the jobs as assigned by the driver program. Each executor executes the code as requested by the driver program and then reports the status of the execution back to the driver node. The executors will be running the Spark code.

Tasks

Tasks are the actual individual running of the code. It is important to understand how tasks are created and then scheduled across the cluster. Spark will first create a graph of your execution (such as an RDD graph) and then create a plan of execution. If you look at your driver program for a basic word count, you will see multiple stages against which multiple tasks are created and are scheduled across the worker nodes. Typically, tasks are created based on how your data is distributed.

To learn more about the architecture, please visit Apache Spark documentation at bit.ly/2tNHCmD.

Spark Programming Model

As you can see from the previous section, Spark has a master-slave architecture, with multiple worker nodes and executors running the code in parallel to optimize the processing. Spark introduces the concept of *Resilient Distributed Datasets (RDDs)*, which is basically a pointer/abstraction of the data distributed and cached in memory across the Spark cluster nodes. The concept of RDDs has two major attributes:

- *Resilient* – An RDD is an abstraction of your data distributed across the cluster and is resilient in nature, which means that it provides a fault-tolerant distribution and can be rebuilt if a failure happens.

- *Distributed* – The data that an RDD represents is distributed across the cluster.

  You can create an RDD in two ways:

- Parallelize an existing collection in your driver program.

- Reference a dataset in an external storage system such as S3, HDFS, or HBase.
  RDDs support two major types of operations:

- *Transformations* – Creation of a new dataset from an existing one, such as map, flatmap(), filter(), sample(), union(), distinct(), or groupByKey(). All transformations in Spark are lazy in nature, which means that Spark will not compute the results immediately when you call a transformation but rather wait until an action is called.

- *Actions* – Actions result in the computation of the transformations and the return of the dataset back to the driver program. Examples of transformations include reduce(), collect(), count(), first(), take(), saveAsTextFile(), and saveAsObjectFile().

Shuffle in Spark

Certain operations in Spark trigger an event known as a *shuffle*. A shuffle is one of the most complex and costly operations because it involves copying the data across the executors and machines, typically over a network. The operation involves disk I/O, data serialization, and network I/O, and hence special care needs to be taken whenever an operation requires a shuffle. The following operations cause a shuffle in Spark:

- Repartition
- Coalesce()
- All ByKey operations, such as GroupByKey(), ReduceByKey() (except Counts)
- Cogroup()
- Join()

DataFrames and Datasets API in Spark

A dataset is a distributed collection of data (added in Spark 1.6) that provides the benefits of RDDs with the added advantage of Spark SQL's optimized execution engine. Spark 2.0 combines the DataFrame and Dataset API into one Dataset API. The entry point to Spark SQL is SparkSession from Spark 2.0. Each item is of the type ROW. For example, a DataFrame that contains two columns, column A and column B, with integers looks like DataFrame(ROW(A=25,B=30),ROW(A=3,B=9)).

The DataFrame concept in Spark is inspired by dataframes in Python and R; however, it is a better implementation than that of R and Python from a performance standpoint.

Spark uses the RDD API as the fundamental data structure. All the computations are done in RDDs as the fundamental building block in Spark. Starting in Spark 2.0, the Dataset takes on two distinct APIs characteristics:

- A strongly typed API
- An untyped API

Since Python and R have no compile-time type safety, we only have untyped APIs (DataFrames) and no Dataset APIs in R and Python.

RDDs provide strong compile-time type safety (*type safety* is the extent to which a programming language prevents type errors) and provide object-oriented operations. RDDs can use high-level expressions like lambda functions (anonymous function not related to AWS Lambda) and map function. The disadvantage of an RDD is in its performance due to massive overhead from garbage collection (creation and destruction of JVM objects) and serializing individual objects.

The *DataFrame* API gives a relational and structured view of the data, allowing Spark to manage the schema and pass data between nodes without using the Java serializer. Spark DataFrame uses the Catalyst optimizer to optimize the query execution plan and executing queries. Spark DataFrame also uses a Tungsten execution backend to improve Spark execution by optimizing Spark jobs for CPU and memory efficiency.

Spark DataFrame can use SQL expressions like group, filter, and join on the data as well. The disadvantage of the DataFrame API is that it does not provide a strong compile-time type safety.

The Dataset API provides the best of both RDDs and DataFrames API. It uses strong compile-time type safety, object-oriented operations from the RDDs with the addition of Catalyst optimizer.

Spark SQL

Spark SQL is a module for structured data processing. You can process data on disk or in memory and use a metastore like Hive metastore. In Amazon EMR, you have the option to use a catalog like the Lake Formation catalog. Spark SQL is compatible with Hive, Avro, Parquet, ORC, JSON, JDBC, and other data sources. You can connect via JDBC and ODBC connectors.

To learn more about Spark SQL, please refer to the Apache Spark documentation on Spark SQL at `bit.ly/SparkSQLDoc`.

The exam may ask you about scenarios in which you have to choose from among Spark SQL, Apache Hive, Apache Pig, and Athena.

Spark Streaming

We've already discussed the importance of ingesting streaming data, and Spark offers options for scalable, high-throughput, and fault-tolerant stream processing of live data streams using *Spark streaming*. Spark offers built-in support for a number of data sources including Kafka, Flume, Kinesis, Twitter, and S3/HDFS and then allows you to build complex processing algorithms with functions like `map`, `reduce`, `join`, and window operations. Once the data has been processed it can be pushed out to a variety of filesystems, databases, dashboards, or other streaming applications.

Discretized Streams

Spark streaming provides a high-level abstraction called discretized stream (DStream), where live data coming from the sources is divided into small batches (mini-batches). A DStream is represented by a continuous series of RDDs, which basically contain data from a certain interval. Figure 4.11 shows the relationship between a discretized stream and an RDD.

FIGURE 4.11   Apache Spark DStreams Overview

Spark streaming allows you to run various different transformations on DStreams like `map()`, `flatMap()`, and `filter()`.

Spark streaming provides two categories of built-in streaming sources:

- *Basic sources* are sources that are directly available in StreamingContext API. Examples include file systems and socket connections.

- *Advanced sources* contain sources like Kafka, Flume, and Kinesis, which are available through extra utility classes.

Spark streaming also provides windowed computations, which means that you can apply transformations over a sliding window of data. The common window operations include the following:

- `window(windowLength, slideInterval)`
- `countByWindow(windowLength, slideInterval)`
- `reduceByWindow(func, windowLength, slideInterval)`
- `reduceByKeyAndWindow(func, windowLength, slideInterval, [numTasks])`
- `reduceByKeyAndWindow`
- `countByValueAndWindow`

Structured Streaming

Apache Spark also offers *structured streaming* as a stream processing framework built directly on top of the Spark SQL engine. Structured streaming makes use of existing APIs such as DataFrame, Dataset, and SQL, thus allowing you to benefit from well-known APIs without having to relearn a new way to process the streaming data. In fact, the entire promise is that in structured streaming, you treat the table as an unbounded table, where you would write the computation the same way as you would on a static dataset, and the structured streaming engine would incrementally run your query on the new piece of data as it arrives in the stream.

The benefit of using structured streaming is that you will not have to change your query's code when doing batch or stream processing, and depending on the target upon which you run your query—for example, a static table or a streaming unbounded table—the Spark engine would automatically decide how to best run the query.

If you would like to learn more about Spark streaming, I highly recommend *Spark: The Definitive Guide* by Matei Zaharia and Bill Chambers (`amzn.to/SparkDefinitiveGuide`).

Spark Machine Learning (Spark MLLib)

MLLib is Spark's primary offer for machine learning on the Spark platform. Spark ML is a dataframe-based API (RDD-based API now in maintenance mode since Spark 2.0) that provides new features, such as Tungsten API and the Catalyst optimizer.

SparkML is a plug-in for Spark that is included with every installation since Spark 0.8.0. It offers a scalable, distributed machine learning algorithm library—accessible via Spark's APIs—for use on top of Spark and all of Spark's other modules (Spark SQL, Spark Streaming, and GraphX). It provides machine learning at the speed of your Spark clusters and can save time compared with similar jobs run on MapReduce.

The following types of machine learning algorithms are included:

- *Classification*: Logistic regression, decision tree classifier, random forest classifier, gradient boosting trees, linear support vector machine, Naïve Bayes
- *Regression*: Generalized linear regression (GLM), decision tree regression, random forest regression, gradient-boosted regression, survival regression, isotonic regression
- *Collaborative filtering*: Alternating least squares (ALS)

- *Clustering*: K-means, latent Dirichlet allocation (LDA), Gaussain mixture model (GMM)
- *Decomposition*: Singular value decomposition (SVD), principal component analysis

Spark GraphX/Graph Frames

Graph computation for graph problems is becoming more and more common. Graphs are a natural way to describe relationships and a lot of the problems that we tend to solve with self-joins in relational databases.

Lots of applications are using graph algorithms, which are not only easier to implement compared to traditional set processing but better suited for such relationship analysis. For example, search engines use PageRank algorithms to rank search results, telecommunications and social media platforms use social network analysis to better understand behavior and provide accurate recommendations, banks use graph analysis to understand money laundering, and security agencies use graphs to crack down on terror networks.

GraphX is an important component in Spark used for these purposes. GraphX engine extends Spark RDD interface and introduces a new Graph extension, which is basically a directed multigraph with properties attached to each vertex (node of the graph), and edge (connectivity between the nodes/vertex). Figure 4.12 shows an undirected graph showing seven vertices and nine edges.

FIGURE 4.12 An undirected graph with seven vertices/nodes and nine edges

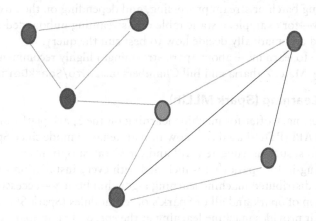

GraphFrames is currently available as a Spark external package that you will need to load when you start your Spark application. While GraphX has remained popular since its inception, the DataFrame API has become more popular over time, and hence Graph-Frames, a DataFrame-based API was introduced in Spark. GraphFrames offers much better user experience, albeit at the expense of a very minimal performance impact.

Hive on Spark

While Spark SQL is the standard for running SQL on Spark, a number of organizations have been using Apache Hive and have their code base in HiveQL but would like to migrate the scripts from Hadoop to the Spark platform to get better performance. Hive on Spark provides the options for those organizations to run Hive programs on Apache Spark and a clear migration path without undergoing lots of maintenance and migration overhead.

When to Use Apache Spark

It is important from an exam perspective to understand when Apache Spark would be better suited than other platforms. Apache Spark is recommended for the reasons listed in Table 4.8.

TABLE 4.8   Apache Spark Benefits

Tenant	Description
Performance	Apache Spark provides better performance than MapReduce.
Deployment	Apache Spark can be deployed via Apache Mesos, Apache Hadoop via YARN, or Apache Spark's standalone cluster manager.
Application types	Apache Spark supports batch, interactive and streaming applications.
Data sources	Supports file, object, relational and non-relational sources
Connectors	Provides standard JDBC/ODBC connectors
API	Provides API in Java, Scala, Python, R and allows use of SQL
Resource handling	Requires fine-tuned resource handling. Memory-intensive jobs require lots of resources.
Streaming	Apache Spark provides streaming via DStreams and Structured Streaming; however, it adopts a mini-batch approach rather than pure streaming. The latency cannot be in milliseconds, and you need to cater for out-of-order stream processing.

Benefits of Running Spark on Amazon EMR

You can run Apache Spark as a standalone application or as a part of your existing Hadoop installation. You also have various options for running Apache Spark as a part of various distributions available with various cloud providers, and one of the options is to run it with Amazon EMR. Table 4.9 lists some of the reasons running it as part of Amazon EMR might benefit you.

TABLE 4.9   Running Apache Spark on Amazon EMR

Tenant	Description
Storage options	Running Apache Spark on Amazon EMR gives you the benefit of using the entire platform, e.g., using EMR-DynamoDB connector to connect to Amazon DynamoDB, connecting to Amazon RDS using JDBC, or using the Elasticsearch connector to connect to Elasticsearch, or using Spark-Redshift connector to connect to Amazon Redshift, or connecting to streaming sources like Amazon Kinesis and Apache Kafka (or MSK) or connect to Amazon S3.
Data catalog	Running Apache Spark on Amazon EMR allows you to benefit from AWS Glue Catalog/Lake Formation catalog (if enabled).
Failover/ recovery	Amazon EMR recovers the failed nodes for you.
Logging	Amazon EMR aggregates the cluster logs and writes them to S3, which allows you to easily debug and determine the problems.
Cost	Amazon EMR allows you to reduce the cost by running a transient cluster or running a small initial cluster and adding the processing capacity by using task instances.
API	Provides API in Java, Scala, Python, R and allows use of SQL.
Amazon EMRFS	Amazon EMR integration with S3 allows you to create RDDs and Data Frames from data in Amazon S3.
Spark metrics and Cloud-Watch	You can monitor metrics of your Spark cluster with Amazon CloudWatch, set alarms on CPU/memory metrics, and receive notification via email, SNS, or an HTTP API call when a threshold is reached/breached, allowing you to take manual or configure automated responses.
Variety of Spark versions	Amazon EMR allows you to work with a variety of Spark releases, allowing you to run the release that your organization has internally agreed with based on compliance standards.

Apache HBase on Amazon EMR

HBase is a distributed column-oriented store, which is built on top of HDFS and used when you need real-time read/write random access to extremely large datasets, which is typically not possible with MapReduce and Apache Spark.

HBase is built with the intent of linear scalability and is one of the most popular NoSQL databases. It does not support SQL out of the box; however, you can run SQL on HBase with projects like Apache Phoenix.

HBase was modeled after Google's Bigtable by Chat Walters and Jim Keller and released as a part of Hadoop 0.15 in October 2007, which eventually spun into a separate sub-project in May 2010.

While HBase is used across industries for a range of use cases, the most popular of them being Facebook's messaging infrastructure being run over HBase and Twitter's use of HBase across its entire Hadoop cluster.

HBase Architecture

HBase follows a master-slave architecture typically with four major components:

- Master
- Region server
- ZooKeeper cluster
- Storage (/HDFS/S3)

Setting Up HBase with Amazon EMR

You can set up HBase in both the Quick Options and Advanced mode (see Figure 4.13).

FIGURE 4.13   Setting up HBase using the Quick Options creation mode

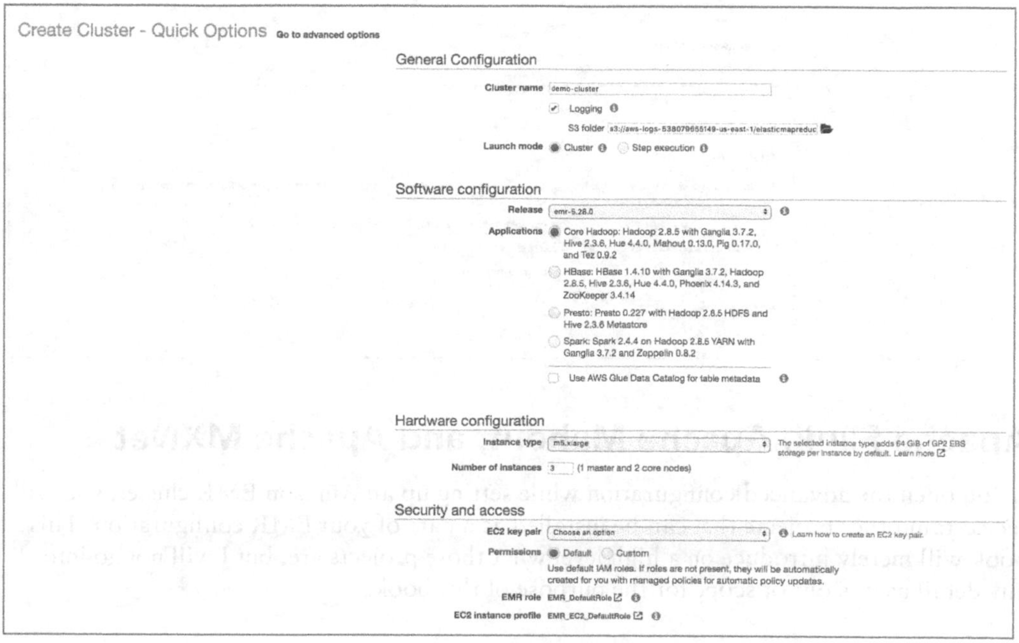

In the advanced options, when you choose HBase in the software configuration options, you can choose the storage layer for your data in HBase, which can be either with HDFS or S3. The HDFS option uses the default location, whereas for the S3, you can choose your destination bucket (see Figure 4.14).

FIGURE 4.14 Setting up HBase using Advanced Options

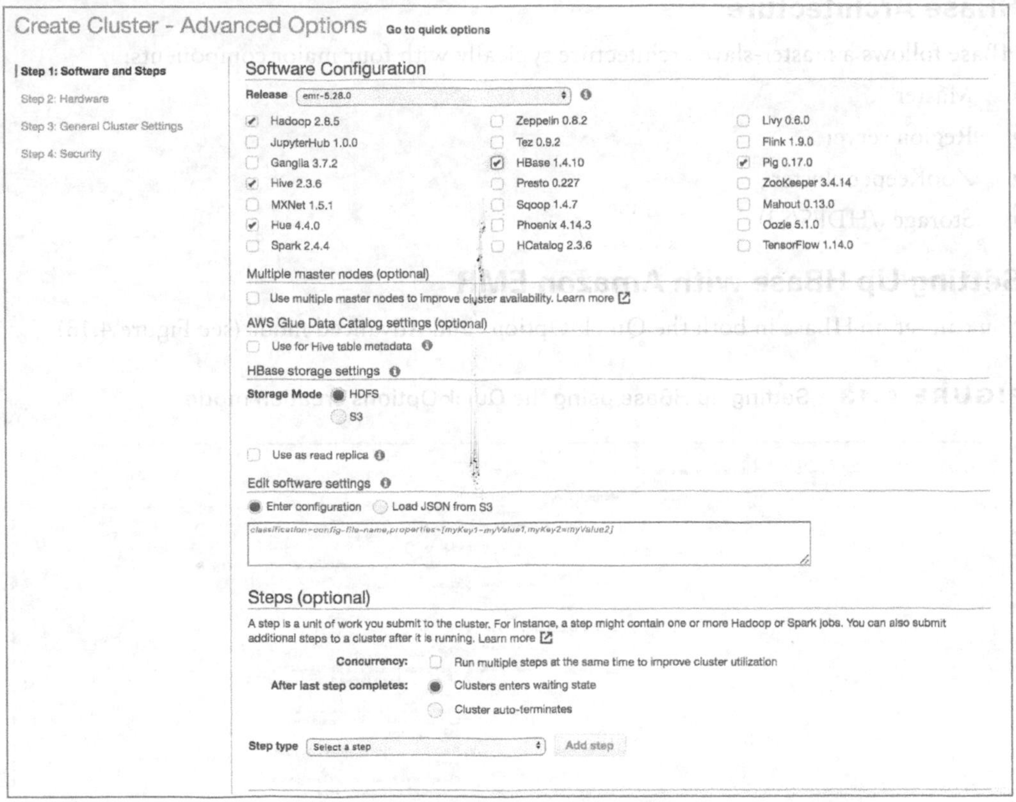

Apache Flink, Apache Mahout, and Apache MXNet

If you open the advanced configuration while setting up an Amazon EMR cluster, you will see certain other projects that can be installed as a part of your EMR configuration. This book will merely introduce on a high level what those projects are, but I will not go into any detail as it is out of scope for the purpose of this book.

Apache MXNet

Apache MXNet is an open-source deep learning framework currently in an incubation state. It is suitable for a number of use cases, such as computer vision, language processing, forecasting, and recommendation engines. MXNet was built for enterprise developers and is very widely used at Amazon.com. It is popular because of the following key factors:

- *Native distributed training supported*: Apache MXNet supports distributed training on multiple CPU/GPU machines to take advantage of the scale of computation offered by cloud platforms.

- *Flexible programming model*: Apache MXNet supports both imperative and symbolic programming to maximize efficiency and productivity.

- *Portable from the cloud to the client*: Apache MXNet runs on a variety of devices from CPU to GPUs and on clusters, servers, desktops or mobile phones.

- *Multilingual*: You can program Apache MXNet in a variety of programming languages, from Python, R, Scala, Julia, C++, Matlab, or JavaScript.

- *Performance optimized*: Apache MXNet has an optimized C++ backend engine that parallelizes computation and I/O regardless of the source language.

Amazon EMR allows you to configure Apache MXNet on an EMR cluster.

Apache Mahout

A mahout is person who rides, controls, and cares for a working elephant. The project got its name in relation to Hadoop (an elephant) and mahout (riding the elephant).

Apache Mahout is an open-source ML library that is primarily used for some of the major ML cases like classification, dimensionality reduction, recommendation engines, and clustering.

Understanding and learning about Apache Mahout is out of the scope of this book, but for the purpose of the exam, it is an analytics library that is available with EMR.

Apache Flink

Apache Flink is a distributed stream processing engine for stateful computations over bounded (definite start and end) and unbounded (definitive start but no end) data streams. Flink has been designed to run in a clustered environment and perform computations at low latency and large volumes.

Apache Flink is popular due to a variety of reasons, but the top reasons are as follows:

- *Event time and processing time semantics*: A lot of stream processing engines work with processing time, but using event time allows you to process out-of-order events where ordering is important. Processing time is generally used for very low-latency applications where an event needs to be processed the moment it arrives.

- *Exactly-once semantics*: Apache Flink provides you with exactly-once processing semantics.

- *Low-latency/high-volume*: Apache Flink provides you with millisecond processing latencies despite processing millions of events per second.

- *Wide connector ecosystem*: Apache Flink provides you with connectors to most commonly used storage and processing systems, like Apache Kafka, Apache Cassandra, Elasticsearch, Amazon Kinesis, and distributed storage systems like Amazon S3 (and HDFS).

- *Variety of deployment options*: Apache Flink provides the ability to deploy your applications with YARN, Apache Mesos, and Kubernetes.

- *Highly available*: Apache Flink gives you the option to run your streaming applications in a 24x7 environment.

To learn more about Apache Flink, please visit flink.apache.org/
flink-architecture.html.

Figure 4.15 shows the overview of Apache Flink, which can be configured as a project on Amazon EMR.

FIGURE 4.15   Apache Flink overview

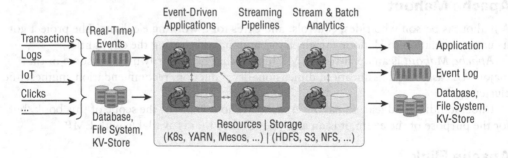

Choosing the Right Analytics Tool

As you can see, Amazon EMR offers a variety of options on the AWS cloud, and often it is hard to understand which option to choose when. Table 4.10 lists some of the criteria that come under discussion.

TABLE 4.10 Choosing the right analytics tool

Criteria	Amazon Athena	Amazon EMR		
		Presto	Spark	Hive	Mahout, TensorFlow, MXNet

Criteria	Amazon Athena	Presto	Spark	Hive	Mahout, TensorFlow, MXNet
Use cases	Ad hoc interactive queries	Interactive queries	General purpose, interactive querying, ML with SparkML	Batch	Machine learning/deep learning
Scalability	Automatic	Configurable	Configurable	Configurable	Configurable
Latency	Seconds	Seconds	Seconds	Minutes	Minutes to hours
Serverless	Yes	No	No	No	No
Storage	Amazon S3, custom sources	Amazon S3, HDFS	Amazon S3, HDFS		Amazon S3, HDFS
File formats	CSV, TSV, JSON, Parquet, ORC	Framework dependent	Framework dependent		Framework dependent
UDF support	Yes	Yes (scalar)		No	No
Federated query	Yes	Yes	No	No	No

Amazon Elasticsearch Service

Operational analytics is sub-category within analytics that typically focuses on measuring the real-time operations of a business, whether through logs generated by the core systems or through any other means. Elasticsearch is an open-source project that allows you to search huge volumes of data at scale with ultra-low latency. Amazon Elasticsearch Service is a managed Elasticsearch offering from Amazon Web Services (AWS).

When to Use Elasticsearch

Operational analytics includes collecting, identifying, and analyzing data to resolve issues to improve application and infrastructure performance.

Operational analytics typically involves the following use-cases:

- *Application monitoring*: Application monitoring involves storing, analyzing, and correlating application and infrastructure log data with the intent to find and fix issues faster and improve overall application performance. You can configure automated alerts if your application is not performing as per expectations, which can then lead to manual or automatic intervention to address and resolve the underlying issues. An example of an application monitoring tool is for an online travel booking company to use a service like Amazon Elasticsearch to analyze logs from its travel applications to understand the latency, availability, and overall performance issues that the customers may be facing and streamline the overall booking process to improve customer satisfaction and increase revenue.

- *Root-cause analysis*: Enables IT operations teams to collect logging information from your IT assets like your servers, routers, switches, and VMS to get a complete insight into your IT infrastructure to reduce MTTD (mean time to detect) and MTTR (mean time to resolve) by quickly resolving issues

- *Security information and event management (SIEM)*: Your security team can benefit from a centralized view of information from disparate applications and systems from across the network for real-time threat detection and incident management.

- *Search*: Providing a fast, scalable and personalized search experience can benefit your applications, websites, and data lakes as it can help users find the data they need. For example, a company can provide its catalog of products to the users, allowing them to search based on product category, price range, and positive reviews, thus improving access to information and reducing overall latency.

Companies that are looking at operational analytics understand that machine generated data is growing 10x faster than business data, and while the data is available, getting value from the data without the right tools becomes quite challenging. For example, many questions (What products were purchased or not? Which are the most-used vs. least-used features? Who are the most active users on our system? Are any users breaking the system? Are we getting an unusually high number of failed logins?) require machine generated data, which is growing at a rapid pace and difficult to analyze because of the following key reasons:

- Data variety and volumes of such data is very high.
- Analytic needs of users are evolving from batch reporting to real-time and predictive analytics.
- Customers want to reduce operational overhead and focus on getting the right answers.
- Customers are looking to enrich their applications by incorporating voice, image recognition, and IoT use cases in the applications.

This requires a different way to provide analytics to the customers, and we cannot rely on batch-based data warehouse solutions. Customers are looking to do the following:

- Ingest a high-volume of machine-generated data in near real time at a cost-effective price point.
- Index this data arriving in real time to start searching based on the key questions.
- Search, correlate, analyze, and visualize this data for insights.

The growing need for such a solution has led to the tremendous growth of Elasticsearch, which has constantly been ranked the top open-source software project built on top of Apache Lucene because of the following key reasons:

- Elasticsearch is open source.
- Elasticsearch provides a simple ingestion mechanism.
- Elasticsearch provides dynamic visualization with Kibana.
- Elasticsearch is distributed and provides very high overall performance.

Setting up an Elasticsearch cluster and maintaining, monitoring, and keeping backups can be quite problematic. Amazon Web Services offers *Amazon Elasticsearch Service*, which simplifies the entire process of deployment, management, and scaling of an Elasticsearch cluster. As Elasticsearch is tightly integrated with other AWS services, it makes it easy to ingest data from other services within AWS.

Elasticsearch Core Concepts (the ELK Stack)

ELK is an acronym used to describe the three most popular open-source projects, Elasticsearch, Logstash, and Kibana, which are often collectively referred to as Elasticsearch.

E = Elasticsearch

Elasticsearch is an open-source RESTful, distributed search and analytics engine built on top of Lucene.

It offers much more than what Lucene offers:

- Elasticsearch is a distributed document store.
- It supports various languages and is highly performant.

- Every field in Elasticsearch can be indexed and made searchable.
- Elasticsearch provides real-time data analytics options (operational analytics).
- It is scalable in nature, which means you can use it to index terabytes to petabytes of data.

The core concepts in Elasticsearch are as follows:

- *Node*: A node is a single instance of Elasticsearch.
- *Cluster*: A collection of nodes form an Elasticsearch cluster, which provides indexing and search capabilities across the nodes.
- *Index*: An index in Elasticsearch is a collection of different types of documents and their properties. You can improve the performance of an index using "shards," described later in this list. In Elasticsearch, all data in every field is indexed by default.
- *Document:* A document in Elasticsearch is a collection of fields in the JSON document. Every document belongs to the type and resides in an index. Every document is associated with a unique identifier called the UID.
- *Shard:* Indexes in Elasticsearch can be split into shards to improve performance and increase parallelism. Each shard is an instance of a Lucene index, and you can think of it as a self-contained search engine that indexes and handles the search queries for the subset of the data for a particular elastic search index.

If you are coming from an RDBMS world, the correlation between terminologies shown in Table 4.11 might help you understand the concepts more easily.

TABLE 4.11   Comparison of Elasticsearch with an RDBMS

Elasticsearch Terminology	Relevant RDBMS Terminology
Cluster	Database
Shard	Shard
Index	Table
Field	Column
Document	Row

L = Logstash

Logstash is an open-source data ingestion tool that allows you to collect data from a variety of sources, transform it, and then send it to your destination. It comes with pre-built filters and support for over 200 different plug-ins. Logstash allows users to ingest data regardless of the data source or type. It was originally created in 2013 by Jordan

Sissel, when he found the need to aggregate and manage a growing number of log files. Logstash has the following most notable features, which make it a very powerful data pipe-lining tool:

- It is a very scalable, mature, and robust solution with the capability to handle really large amounts of data at very high volumes.

- Logstash can ingest data from a huge number of sources, with the option of enriching the data and correlating with other logging sources.

- Logstash has an extensible ecosystem of plug-ins and provides the ability to write custom plug-ins as well.

- Logstash is built to be highly available.

K = Kibana

Kibana is an open-source data visualization tool for reviewing logs and events. It provides interactive charts, pre-built aggregations and filters, and geospatial support, which makes it ideal for visualizing data stored in Elasticsearch. The key features of Kibana, which makes it a very important component in the ELK stack, are as follows:

- Exploratory data analysis using visualization capabilities

- Uses a variety of charting components

- Applies ML for outlier and trend detections.

Amazon Elasticsearch Service

Amazon provides Elasticsearch Service for operational analytics, and using the service provides you the following key benefits:

- *Deployment and manageability* – Amazon Elasticsearch Service simplifies the deployment and management of Elasticsearch on the platform. You can deploy an Elasticsearch cluster within minutes.

- *Highly scalable and available* – Amazon Elasticsearch Service lets you store up to 3 PB of data in a single cluster. Scaling a cluster can be done using the API or AWS Console. You can deploy the service in a Multi-AZ environment and replicate the data between three availability zones within the same AWS region.

- *Highly secure* – Amazon Elasticsearch service provides you with various security features to make your Elasticsearch installation secure:

  - Network isolation within an Amazon VPC

  - Encryption of data at rest

  - Encryption of data in motion

  - Manage authentication and access control with Amazon Cognito and AWS IAM

  - HIPAA eligible; PCI, DSS, SOC, ISO, and FedRamp compliant

- *Cost-effective* – Amazon Elasticsearch Service makes using Elasticsearch affordable as you can use a variety of options depending on your requirements to effectively manage the cost:
  - Use on-demand pricing for short-term needs.
  - Use reserved-instance pricing to benefit from up to 70 percent reduced cost compared to on-demand pricing.
  - Reduce operational cost as the service is fully managed by AWS.

Figure 4.16 shows the working of an Amazon Elasticsearch service.

FIGURE 4.16   Working of Amazon Elasticsearch service

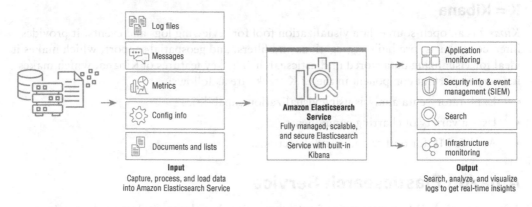

Amazon Redshift

Amazon Redshift is a fully managed, petabyte-scale data warehousing service on the AWS cloud offered by Amazon. Its low-cost and high scalability allows you to get started on your data warehousing use cases at a minimal cost and scale as the demand for your data grows.

What Is Data Warehousing?

Traditional databases are designed for *online transaction process (OLTP)* workloads, where operations are processed in a series, and one operation in a series relies on the previous operation to have completed successfully. The word *transactional* indicates that processing is divided into individual but indivisible operations called *transactions*. For example, you withdraw $200 from your account. This action results in multiple individual processes, all required to happen successfully for the transaction to complete:

- Checking the balance in the account to see if the account has the amount of money you intend to withdraw
- Locking the particular row when the transaction is about to happen

- Debiting $200 from your account
- Dispensing cash from the ATM
- Marking the transaction as complete and releasing the lock on the row

We work the transactional databases knowing or unknowingly on a daily basis, but analytics is a different ball game, and these databases that are optimal to process transactions are unable to provide support for decision-making. For example, suppose you are a CMO (chief marketing officer) looking to understand the marketing spend on various channels and understanding the most optimal channel for advertising spend. This query is much more complex and requires you to go through a relatively large dataset and perform the desired aggregations before responding back with a result.

A *data warehouse* is basically a conceptual approach to solving problems, and while some vendors may claim that their database software that was originally designed for transactional systems can be used for data warehousing, in most cases database software that supports data warehousing applications works differently due to the way the applications are built for decision support. Some of the core differences are mentioned in the following list:

- Typical transactional database applications use normalized data and enforce referential integrity constraints. Data warehouses, however, work with denormalized data, which leads to duplication of data but often provides superior performance. The lack of referential integrity also means that the database software does not use CPU cycles to check the existence of records, thus leading to faster inserts.
- Typical transactional (OLTP) databases are categorized by a large number of short online transactions (INSERT, UPDATE, DELETE) that serve as a persistence layer for applications. Data warehouse applications typically have lower volumes of transactions, and queries are often complex and involve aggregations against large historical datasets for data-driven decision-making.
- Typical transactional databases focus on a single domain, such as, for example, a (CRM) customer relationship management scenario where you are managing data about customers and their relationship with the business, whereas in a data warehouse environment, a CRM is one of the many sources coming into your data warehouse with others like transactions, blogs, and social media.

What Is Redshift?

Amazon offers multiple services for transactional databases, like Amazon Relational Database Service (RDS). However, *Amazon Redshift* is the recommended choice when it comes to building a data warehouse on the AWS platform. Amazon Redshift is a fully managed, petabyte-scale data warehouse service in the cloud; you can start from a small data warehouse environment with a few hundred gigabytes of data and scale to multiple petabytes or more.

Amazon Redshift has the following key features and benefits:

- *Fast* – Amazon Redshift is optimized for data warehousing. It uses a variety of innovations to obtain very high query performance on datasets ranging in size from a hundred gigabytes to a petabyte or more. It uses columnar storage, data compression, and zone maps to reduce the amount of I/O needed to perform queries. Amazon Redshift has a massively parallel processing (MPP) architecture, parallelizing and distributing SQL operations to take advantage of all available resources. The underlying hardware is designed for high-performance data processing using local attached storage to maximize throughput between the CPUs and disk drives and a 10 GB mesh network to maximize throughput between nodes.

- *Scalable* – With the AWS Management Console or a simple API call, you can easily change the number or type of nodes in your data warehouse when your performance or capacity needs to change. Amazon Redshift enables you to start with as little as a single 160 GB DC2.Large node and scale up all the way to 8.2 petabytes with 128 RA3.16xLarge nodes.

- *Cost-effective* – Amazon Redshift has no up-front costs. You pay only for the resources you provision. You can choose On-Demand pricing with no up-front costs or long-term commitments or obtain significantly discounted rates with Reserved Instance pricing. For more details, see the Amazon Redshift Pricing page at aws.amazon.com/redshift/pricing/.

- *Simple* – You can get started in minutes with Amazon Redshift. With the AWS Management Console or simple API calls, you can create a cluster and specify its size, underlying node type, and security profile. Amazon Redshift provisions your nodes, configures the connections between them, and secures the cluster. Your data warehouse should be up and running in minutes.

- *Fully managed* – Amazon Redshift handles all the work needed to manage, monitor, and scale your data warehouse, from monitoring cluster health and taking backups to applying patches and upgrades. You can easily add or remove nodes from your cluster when your performance and capacity needs change. By handling all these time-consuming, labor-intensive tasks, Amazon Redshift helps you to focus on your data and business instead.

- *Fault tolerant* - Amazon Redshift has multiple features that enhance the reliability of your data warehouse cluster. All data written to a node in your cluster is automatically replicated to other nodes within the cluster, and all data is continuously backed up to Amazon S3. Amazon Redshift continuously monitors the health of the cluster and automatically re-replicates data from failed drives and replaces nodes as necessary.

- *Automated backups* – The Amazon Redshift automated snapshot feature continuously backs up new data on the cluster to Amazon S3. Snapshots are continuous, incremental, and automatic. Amazon Redshift stores your snapshots for a user-defined period, which can be from one to 35 days. You can take your own snapshots at any time; they leverage all existing system snapshots and are retained until you explicitly delete them.

- *Fast restores* – You can use any system or user snapshot to restore your cluster using the AWS Management Console or Amazon Redshift APIs. Your cluster is available as soon as the system metadata has been restored, and you can start running queries while user data is spooled down in the background.

- *Security* – Amazon Redshift offers a number of security options, including encryption, network isolation, and compliance with various audit requirements.

  - *Encryption* – You can set up Amazon Redshift to use SSL to secure data in transit and use hardware-accelerated AES-256 encryption for data at rest. If you enable encryption of data at rest, all data written to disk is encrypted with the backups. By default, Amazon Redshift takes care of key management, but you can manage your keys using your own hardware security modules (HSMs).

  - *Network isolation* - Amazon Redshift enables you to configure firewall rules to control network access to your data warehouse cluster. You can also run Amazon Redshift inside Amazon Virtual Private Cloud (Amazon VPC) to isolate your data warehouse cluster in your own virtual network and connect it to your existing IT infrastructure using industry-standard encrypted IPsec VPN.

  - *Audit and compliance* – Amazon Redshift integrates with AWS CloudTrail to enable you to audit all Redshift API calls. Amazon Redshift also logs all SQL operations, including connection attempts, queries, and changes to your database. You can access these logs using SQL queries against system tables or have them downloaded to a secure location on Amazon S3. Amazon Redshift is compliant with SOC1, SOC2, SOC3, and PCI DSS Level 1 requirements. For more details, see `aws .amazon.com/compliance`.

    We'll look into these in more detail in Chapter 6, "Data Security."

- *SQL compatible* – Amazon Redshift is a SQL data warehouse and uses industry-standard ODBC and JDBC connections and PostgreSQL drivers. Many popular software vendors are certifying Amazon Redshift with their offerings to enable you to continue to use the tools you use today. For more information, see `aws.amazon.com/ redshift/partners`.

Redshift Architecture

Redshift has a similar architecture to Hadoop, which you saw earlier. It has a master-slave MPP (massively parallel processing), shared-nothing architecture. Redshift has two major node types, leader and compute:

- *Leader node*: You don't have to define a leader node because it is automatically provisioned with every Redshift cluster and the specifications are similar to the compute nodes. A leader node is the SQL endpoint for your cluster, storing metadata, coordinating parallel SQL processing on the compute nodes, and using machine learning to optimize the query plan. Your SQL editors and BI tools generally connect to your Redshift cluster using the JDBC/ODBC bridge to the leader node endpoint. A leader node will use machine learning to generate efficient query plans, by routing short queries to available queues as needed, caching the results, caching compilation code, and so on. The utilization of ML helps Redshift spot optimization opportunities across a wide variety of use cases.

- *Compute node*: A compute node is the workhorse for your Redshift cluster and sits behind the leader node, executing queries for the user. Since Redshift has a shared-nothing MPP architecture, compute nodes work together to perform the desired task. A compute node is partitioned into multiple slices, the number of which varies between 2 and 16 and depends on the node type you configure in your Redshift cluster. A slice is an essential component in the Redshift compute node architecture, and each slice is allocated a portion of the compute node's memory and disk space, thus acting as a virtual compute node. Each slice acting as a virtual compute node processes a portion of the work assigned to the compute node by the leader node. It is therefore essential to have an appropriate data distribution for the compute node, which is done using various mechanisms that we will discuss later. Each slice acts as a symmetric multiprocessing (SMP) unit and works with other slices to complete operations.

Redshift supports various instance types, and the choice of an instance type is directly dependent on the workload that you are planning to run on your data warehouse. Table 4.12 indicates the type of instances available with Redshift and the corresponding disk type, size, memory, number of CPUs, and number of slices.

TABLE 4.12   Redshift instance types

Instance Type	Disk Types	Size	Memory	# CPUs	# Slices
ra3 4xlarge	RMS	Scales up to 16 TB	96 GB	12	4
ra3 16xlarge	RMS	Scales up to 64 TB	384 GB	48	16
dc2 large	SSD	160 GB	16 GB	2	2
dc2 8xlarge	SSD	2.56 TB	244 GB	32	16
ds2 xlarge	Magnetic	2 TB	32 GB	4	2
ds2 8xlarge	Magnetic	16 TB	244 GB	36	16

Redshift Spectrum/Lakehouse Nodes

The data lake is an important part of the overall analytics architecture, and as discussed earlier, Redshift offers lake house (also referred to as Redshift Spectrum), which is configured with nodes that allow you to query against the data lake. Redshift lake house nodes are free of cost; you don't pay for them, but rather pay for using them to scan your data on S3 when you request data from your data lake.

Amazon Redshift lake house is one of the first solutions that gives you one foot in the data warehouse and the other in the data lake, and hence termed as a lake house. Redshift provides the lake house capability so that you can extend your queries to Amazon

S3 without moving the data to the data warehouse. You can query file formats such as Avro, CSV, JSON, ORC, Parquet and others directly within Amzon S3. The core benefit of Redshift lake house being storing the hot data highly structured data in Amazon Redshift while keeping your exabytes of structured, unstructured and semi-structured data in Amazon S3, and provide the ability to seamlessly query the data.

It is important to note that Redshift Spectrum is not an AWS service, but rather a feature within Amazon Redshift. This is important from exam perspective, as if you get questions asking you to use Redshift Spectrum directly, you need to be aware that it is not possible without using Redshift. Furthermore, the external data in Amazon S3 will be queried in place rather than moving it to Amazon Redshift, and spectrum queries are executed by an Amazon owned-and-maintained fleet of nodes.

Figure 4.17 shows the important components of Amazon Redshift architecture.

FIGURE 4.17   Amazon Redshift architecture

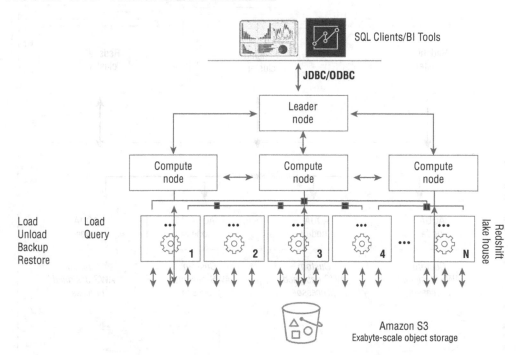

Redshift architecture is evolving as I am writing this book. Amazon recently announced RA3 managed storage for Redshift, which means you can now pay separately for storage and compute. The RA3 instances are backed with large high-speed SSD-backed cache, and automatically scale up to 64 TB per instance. At the time of this writing you can scale the cluster up to 8.2 PB of cluster storage, which AWS believes should fit most use cases in data warehousing. If you have use cases that require more than 8.2 PB of storage, AWS would love to hear back from you.

Redshift AQUA

At the time of this writing, Amazon announced the releasing of another interesting feature for Amazon Redshift, called Advanced Query Accelerator (AQUA) for Amazon Redshift. The feature will probably be available by the time you are reading this book.

AQUA is a new distributed hardware-accelerated caching layer that provides superior performance for analytics for large data sizes. It excels for scan and aggregation-heavy workloads, where additional speed helps you interact with the data and transforms the way you analyze your data. The key objective of AQUA was to improve the performance and scalability of queries by using customized hardware and push-down optimization on a caching layer. The architecture for Redshift AQUA is depicted in Figure 4.18.

FIGURE 4.18   Amazon Redshift AQUA architecture

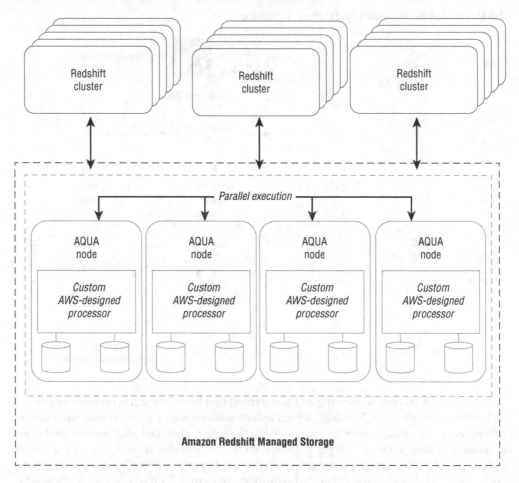

In order to meet the performance requirements with AQUA, a totally custom node was built leveraging the AWS Nitro chip to do hardware accelerated compression, encryption, decompression, and decryption.

Amazon has gone on to build a bespoke instance that has a unique architecture that connects the data drives and the hardware accelerated components and then designed and implemented a custom streaming multi-core hardware accelerated processor specifically for analytics. The node was built from the ground up, starting from AWS custom chips to hardware to a physical interface box, device drivers, operations, and execution layer all the way up to how this connects to your Redshift cluster.

AWS is therefore able to take advantage of speed and benefits from the fastest scanning and aggregating hardware built. This is leveraged by Redshift by adding logic to the Redshift cluster when accessing a data table, which uses the cache that holds the hot data in AQUA. Redshift carves out all of the scanning and aggregation operations and runs them in a scale-out distributed hardware accelerated layer where data has been cached. This combination of Redshift and the additional custom hardware aggregation and scanning layer gives Redshift the ability to provide 10x faster performance over traditional cloud-based data warehouses. Amazon believes that this will truly revolutionize the way growing amounts of data is processed.

Redshift also offers materialized views that tie nicely with AQUA considering that a materialized view can handle joins across multiples tables, essentially performing aggregations and taking a complex query that runs big joins to incrementally update and produce a table.

When you execute a query on a view, you are basically scanning and aggregating the data, which is where AQUA shines. These two work together seamlessly, and therefore Redshift can incrementally do your complicated joins and hardware accelerated scans and aggregations that happen on the resulting data.

Redshift Scalability

Scalability is generally categorized into two major areas:

- Storage scalability
- Compute scalability

Most of the data warehouse environments need to scale up for either storage or compute reasons, and Redshift allows you to scale both independently of each other. The key features in Redshift that provide scalability are as follows:

- Resizing of a Redshift cluster
- Concurrency scaling
- Managed storage for RA3 nodes

Resizing of a Redshift Cluster

You may need to scale your cluster up and down depending on your compute and storage requirements, and you may have the following scenarios:

- Resizing the cluster based on the same node types (Elastic Resize)
- Resizing the cluster to a different node type (Classic Resize)

Elastic Resize

Redshift provides an Elastic Resize option, where an existing cluster is modified to add or remove nodes in a multi-stage process. It is important to understand that the node types added to the cluster can only be the same type as in the original cluster. For example, if your original cluster had DC2 nodes, you can only add DC2 nodes to your cluster with the Elastic Resize option.

STAGE 1

The cluster is temporarily made unavailable while the cluster resize process migrates the cluster metadata. This is a shorter stage and completes relatively quickly, where session connections are held and new queries are held in a queue.

STAGE 2

The session is connected and reinstated. Elastic Resize redistributes the data to the node slices in the background (redistribution is important as there are different numbers of slices due to a cluster configuration change). The cluster is available for read and write operations.

Classic Resize

The other option to resize a cluster is to use Classic Resize. With Classic Resize, a Redshift cluster can be reconfigured to a different node count and instance type.

- Depending on data size, it may take an hour or more to complete.
- Involves streaming all data from the original Redshift cluster to a newly created Redshift cluster with the new configuration. During the resize, the original Redshift cluster is in read-only mode.

This is the approach that you will use when you are switching instance types.

Concurrency Scaling

The concurrency scaling feature in Redshift was made generally available during mid-2019 with the intent of reducing the time needed to service customer requests for temporary spikes in compute needs. A cluster resize is not an ideal option when customers are running low-latency queries. Concurrency scaling adds transient clusters to your cluster to handle concurrent requests with consistency and fast performance in a matter of seconds.

The Redshift cluster rapidly and automatically scales up in a few seconds with additional compute nodes when bursts of user activity occur to provide increased concurrency and avoid queries waiting in queues. The cluster scales back down when the workload pressure subsides.

Amazon Redshift allows you the option to pick the workloads that should use concurrency scaling. For example, you may use concurrency scaling for your BI dashboards that are critical for your C-level reporting but avoid using up your credits or paying extra cost by restricting use for analyst groups who are not running high-priority queries.

Amazon Redshift offers concurrency scaling free for up to 97 percent of the customers. You can earn 1 hour for free for every 24 hours of your main Redshift cluster running. The earned credits expire at the end of the month, and any extra use is charged on a per-second basis.

Redshift Managed Storage

Separation of storage and compute has become a highly debated topic in analytics discussions across the enterprises. While Redshift provides the option to use Amazon Redshift Spectrum to process data in your data lake, it went a step further by announcing Amazon Redshift managed storage at re:Invent 2019. Amazon Redshift managed storage separates the storage and compute quite literally in that you pay for them separately. The RA3 instances have large high-speed SSD-based caches and automatically scale up to 64 TB/instance.

When using Redshift managed storage, data blocks from Redshift compute nodes are automatically swapped from node to S3 (and vice versa) depending on data temperature. The data is stored in Redshift block format and is automatically managed by Redshift.

Amazon Redshift Cluster Policies and Workload Management

Redshift allows you to configure parameter groups, which act as a safeguard for certain querying behaviors on Amazon Redshift like query time-outs, logging, and so on. Parameter groups can be used like profiles. You can manage parameter groups using the AWS Console, AWS SDK for Java, and Amazon Redshift CLI and API.

Table 4.13, referenced from Amazon Redshift documentation, gives you an overview of the parameters and their default values.

TABLE 4.13 Redshift parameter options

Parameter Name	Value	More Information
auto_analyze	true	auto_analyze in the *Amazon Redshift Database Developer Guide*
datestyle	ISO, MDY	datestyle in the *Amazon Redshift Database Developer Guide*
enable_user_activity_logging	false	Database Audit Logging in *Amazon Redshift Cluster Management Guide*
extra_float_digits	0	extra_float_digits in the *Amazon Redshift Database Developer Guide*

TABLE 4.13   Redshift parameter options *(continued)*

Parameter Name	Value	More Information
max_concurrency_scaling_clusters	1	max_concurrency_scaling_clusters in the *Amazon Redshift Database Developer Guide*
query_group	default	query_group in the *Amazon Redshift Database Developer Guide*
require_ssl	false	Configure Security Options for Connections in *Amazon Redshift Cluster Management Guide*
search_path	$user, public	search_path in the *Amazon Redshift Database Developer Guide*
statement_timeout	0	statement_timeout in the *Amazon Redshift Database Developer Guide*
wlm_json_configuration	[{"auto_wlm":true}]	Configuring Workload Management in *Amazon Redshift Cluster Management Guide*
use_fips_ssl	false	Enable FIPS-compliant SSL mode only if your system is required to be FIPS-compliant.

Table source: (amzn.to/36QJ6uZ)

The nice thing about parameter groups is that they are a standalone artifact and can be used across multiple Redshift clusters. You can have different parameter groups to apply for different times of the day depending on the expected workload, such as the "nightly batch" parameter group for the batch ETL jobs overnight and "analytics" parameter group for analytics jobs during the day.

Amazon Redshift also supports workload management (WLM), which allows you to optimize query performance by allocating cluster resources to specific queues. If you do not have a full understanding of your expected workload, or you are running a greenfield project, you can use Auto WLM (Automatic WLM) with query priorities to let Amazon Redshift manage concurrency and memory allocation. Auto WLM determines the amount of resources that are needed by the queries and then adjusts concurrency level (number of parallel running queries). You can define the level of importance for a workload by its priority, which then gives preferential treatment to the workload.

Figure 4.19 shows workload management setup in Amazon Redshift where the user has set up two queues. Queue 1 has been assigned 45 percent of memory, whereas Queue 2 has been assigned 35 percent.

FIGURE 4.19   Amazon Redshift workload management

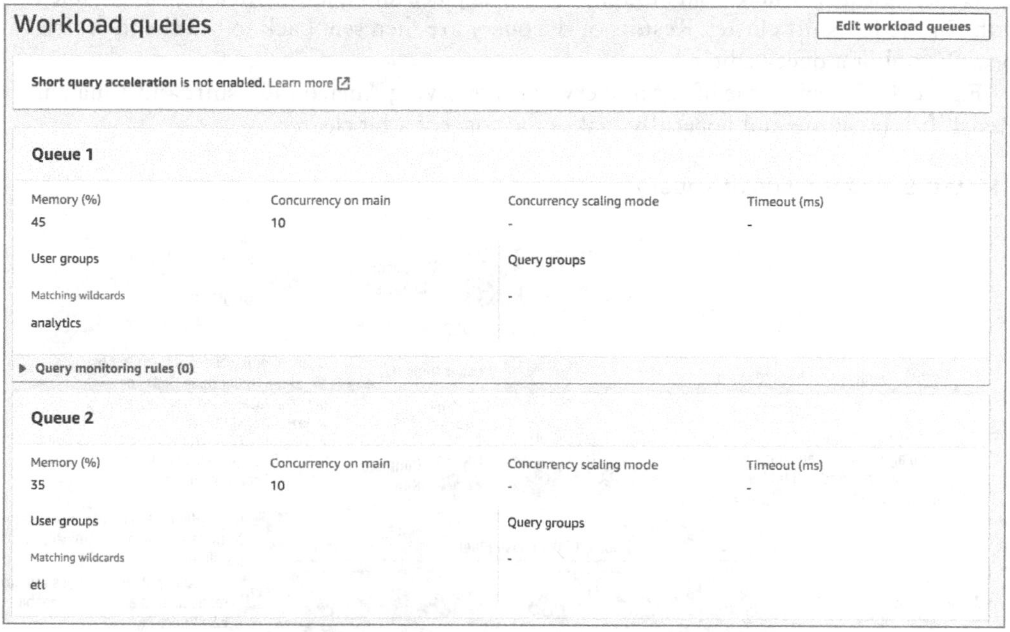

Workload queues				Edit workload queues

Short query acceleration is not enabled. Learn more ↗

Queue 1

Memory (%)	Concurrency on main	Concurrency scaling mode	Timeout (ms)
45	10	-	-

User groups		Query groups	

Matching wildcards   -

analytics

▶ Query monitoring rules (0)

Queue 2

Memory (%)	Concurrency on main	Concurrency scaling mode	Timeout (ms)
35	10	-	-

User groups		Query groups	

Matching wildcards   -

etl

Amazon Redshift Lakehouse

Redshift Lakehouse is not an AWS service but a feature of Amazon Redshift that allows users to query data residing in your data lake (S3), making it transparent for the users whether the data is housed in Redshift or is fetched from the data lake. Users query the tables as they would query any other tables on Redshift, and it therefore allows querying potentially exabytes of data in the data lake through Redshift.

Amazon Redshift Lakehouse allows data to be queried in place, without the need to load the data to your Redshift cluster. This is powered behind the scenes by a fleet of Amazon Redshift Lakehouse nodes. There is a soft limit/allowance of 10 Lakehouse nodes per Redshift cluster slice, which means that a cluster with 16 slices will be able to leverage 160 Lakehouse nodes.

When a user queries an external table (a table with metadata on Redshift but data on Redshift Lakehouse), Amazon Redshift uses ML to optimize and compile the query at the leader node and identifies the components of the plan that can be run locally and components where data needs to be fetched from Redshift Lakehouse. The plan is sent to all the compute nodes, who work with the data catalog to obtain the partition information used for partition pruning. As mentioned earlier, each slice has an allowance of 10 Redshift Lakehouse nodes, and each compute node uses this allowance to issue parallel requests to the Redshift Lakehouse layer. Amazon Redshift Lakehouse nodes will scan your S3 data and project, filter, join, and aggregate based on the need and then send the results back to Amazon Redshift, where final aggregation takes place and a join with a Redshift table is done in the Redshift cluster. Results of the query are then sent back to the client, which can be a BI tool or a query editor.

Figure 4.20 depicts the life of a query when querying Amazon Redshift and Amazon Redshift Lakehouse and hopefully makes the concept a bit clearer.

FIGURE 4.20   Life of a query

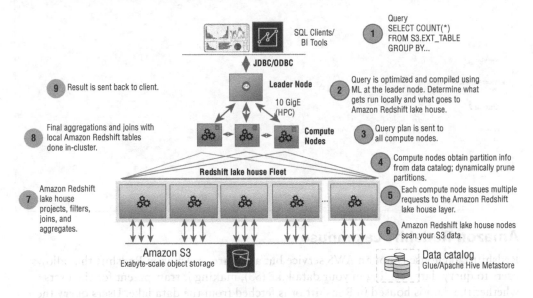

Amazon Redshift Lakehouse seamlessly integrates with your existing SQL and BI applications and supports the following key capabilities, which make it a very useful tool in your analytics arsenal:

- Support for American National Standards Institute (ANSI) SQL

- Support for a variety of file formats on your data lake, including Parquet, ORC, JSON

- Ability to read compressed and encrypted files

- Ability to push down optimization to your data lake without loading any data to Redshift

- Support for complex joins, nested queries, and window functions often used in analytical queries

- Support for partitioned data on S3, including dynamic partition pruning

- Ability to leverage the Glue Data Catalog and Amazon EMR Hive Metastore

- Ability to use Redshift's cost-based optimizer

- Parallelization of queries against your data in the data lake to provide better performance
- Sharing of data across multiple Redshift clusters

Using Amazon Redshift Lakehouse is quite simple. The three-step process is as follows:

1. Set up an external schema. This can be using the AWS Glue Data Catalog or an Apache Hive Metastore.

```
CREATE EXTERNAL SCHEMA <schema_name>
```

2. Register the external tables from the following sources:

- Amazon Athena
- Hive Metastore
- Amazon Redshift CREATE EXTERNAL TABLE syntax.

```
CREATE EXTERNAL TABLE <table_name>
[PARTITIONED BY <column_name, data_type, ...>]
STORED AS file_format
LOCATION s3_location
[TABLE PROPERTIES property_name=property_value, ...];
```

3. Start querying your tables using:

```
<schema_name>.<table_name>
```

Data Modeling in Redshift

Redshift is a fully ACID- and ANSI-compliant data warehouse *(ACID stands for atomicity, consistency, isolation, durability)*. Redshift doesn't have the concept of indexes but provides the concept of distribution keys and sort keys to give you the same performance benefits as you would building an index. Performance in an MPP database is always dependent on how well the data is distributed across the cluster, and Redshift is no exception, where the choice of distribution key, sort key, and compression can significantly impact performance of the cluster.

Redshift is a relational database, which means you need to know the structure of the data before you write it to Redshift. Data inside Redshift is organized in databases (the recommendation is to have one database per Redshift cluster). A database can have one or more schemas (namespaces), which contain tables and other database objects (such as stored procedures). Tables are composed of a tabular structure in the form of rows and columns.

Redshift only supports scalar data types, which means you cannot use List or Map. While Redshift is built for relational data, it does support semi-structured data in the form of JSON or AVRO, and using Redshift Lakehouse, you can work with a variety of file formats on the Redshift data lake using a SerDes (Serializer/Deserializer).

There are five major design considerations to achieve optimal performance in Redshift. Thankfully, Amazon has now automated most of these features, which means either the system performs the job automatically or it provides you with recommendations to achieve them using the Redshift Advisor in the Redshift console:

Sort Keys   Ensure that sort keys exist to facilitate filter in the WHERE clause. Sort keys are important because Amazon Redshift stores the data on the disk in a sorted manner. The Redshift query optimizer uses sort orders to determine the optimal query plan for your data. For example, if you are frequently querying the most recent data, or data based on a time range, you can choose the time stamp column as your sort key. When you run a query with a time stamp as a filter, Redshift can skip entire blocks that would fall outside the range of your filter and thus provide you with optimal performance. You can use Redshift Advisor, which can recommend picking up appropriate sort keys.

Compression   You can use compression in Redshift to reduce query I/O and thus improve overall performance. In Redshift, different columns can have different compression types, as Redshift has a columnar architecture. This allows you to identify the best possible compression type and most optimal performance. You can apply compression manually or use the COPY command, which will analyze the dataset and apply compression automatically. Using COPY command to apply automatic compression is highly recommended in Redshift.

Distribution Style   You can ensure distribution keys are used to distribute the data across the cluster uniformly and to facilitate most common join types, thus reducing data movement during query execution. When you load data to a Redshift table, Redshift will distribute the table's rows to the compute nodes and slices according to the distribution style you choose when you created the table. We'll look into the distribution styles later in the chapter.

Table Maintenance (Vacuum, Analyze)   Redshift does not delete the data when you delete a particular data item from a table; it only marks it as deleted. This means that as more data gets deleted, your cluster has space that is occupied by deleted rows, which is where a Vacuum operation can help you recoup the space. Furthermore, data stored on Redshift is stored in sorted order, which means that when new rows come in, they will be stored in an unsorted fashion unless they are arriving in the incremental order of sort key, which is generally not possible for data other than transactional data. A Vacuum sort is required to re-sort the data on disk, to provide better sorted-ness of data. Redshift now runs both VACUUM SORT and VACUUM DELETE automatically to improve your overall query performance.

In addition to VACUUM, ANALYZE helps you update table statistics, which helps the optimizer to provide an optimal cost assessment for different query plans. The table statistics increase sort key effectiveness, thus improving overall performance for the queries.

Workload Management   Redshift uses ML algorithms to profile queries and then places them in an appropriate queue where they will be allocated appropriate resources. This is also done automatically, but the user has the option to manually override the AutoWLM settings or configure queues manually.

Popular Data Models in Redshift

While there are a number of ways to implement data warehouses, the most common of them are listed here:

STAR Schema (Most Commonly Used)   In a STAR schema, the data is separated into a large fact table that then references lots of smaller dimension (dim) tables. A fact table refers to specific events, events that do not change once submitted. For example, credit card transactions are facts, but the details of a transaction, like the product sold, the store details, and the category, are all dimensions. The dimensions that make up the facts often have attributes that are more efficiently stored in separate tables.

Snowflake / Denormalized Tables   The snowflake model is similar to the STAR schema; however, the schema is represented by a normalized central fact table that is connected to multiple dimensions. Snowflaking is actually the method of normalizing dimension tables in a STAR schema. When it is completely normalized along all dimension tables, the resultant model looks like a snowflake, where you have a fact at the center and all dimensions attached to it.

The other option that people often used in data warehousing is going to the opposite end of the spectrum by creating aggregated tables.

Data Types in Redshift

Amazon Redshift offers a variety of different data types, listed in Table 4.14. You can use these during the construction of your Data Definition Language (DDL) queries and when you are creating your tables.

TABLE 4.14   Redshift data types

Category	Data Type	Description
Numeric	SMALLINT	Signed 2-byte integer
	INTEGER	Signed 4-byte integer
	BIGINT	Signed 8-byte integer
	DECIMAL	Exact numeric of selectable precision
	REAL	Single precision floating-point number
	DOUBLE PRECISION	Double precision floating-point number
Text	CHAR	Fixed-length character string
	VARCHAR	Variable-length character string with user-defined limit

TABLE 4.14 Redshift data types *(continued)*

Category	Data Type	Description
DATETIME	DATE	Calendar date (year, month, day)
	TIMESTAMP	Date and time (without time zone)
	TIMESTAMPTZ	Date and time (with time zone)
LOGICAL	BOOLEAN	Logical Boolean (true/false)
GEOSPA-TIAL	GEOMETRY	Geospatial data (supports multiple geometric shapes such as point, multipoint, polygon, and more)

Choosing the correct data types is important for performance reasons, and hence it is important to make the columns only as wide as needed. For example: you should avoid BIGINT for country identifier, CHAR(MAX) for country names, and CHAR for dates. You should use TIMESTAMP or DATE instead of CHAR and use CHAR instead of VARCHAR when you know the length of your character strings and domain. This is an important performance optimization tip and can potentially be asked during the exam.

Another important performance optimization technique is to materialize frequently computed values into pre-aggregated columns or make use of materialized views. Materialized views offer an automatic way to pre-compute the aggregations and result in a much simpler code.

For semi-structured data like JSON, you should model the attributes from your application domain that you know are useful, in the form of explicit columns. The explicitly stored columns can be used in filters and joins, but the remaining columns that are part of JSON record but have not been explicitly extracted cannot be used in joins and filters. Amazon Redshift provides various JOSN functions that can be used for working with JSON columns:

- IS_VALID_JSON
- IS_VALID_JSON_ARRAY
- JSON_ARRAY_LENGTH
- JSON_EXTRACT_ARRAY_ELEMENT_TEXT
- JSON_EXTRACT_PATH_TEXT

While modeling your data, you should always remember Redshift's columnar nature and how it impacts your queries. As discussed earlier, Redshift can automatically configure column compression settings and use a number of built-in compression algorithms.

Data Distribution Styles in Redshift

Redshift is a distributed database, which means that it can scale horizontally by adding more nodes when the data size grows. Redshift has a single leader node with one or more compute nodes that actually contain the data. Data distribution style impacts the performance of the queries that you run on Redshift. Redshift offers four distribution styles:

KEY   You can choose KEY distribution when you have a column with high cardinality, which can offer an even distribution of the data across the cluster. When you choose the KEY distribution, the column chosen for the distribution is hashed and the same hash value is placed on the same slice. A generally accepted principle is that FACT tables are distributed across the cluster using the row identifier in the FACT table.

ALL   In data warehouse applications, quite often you would need to copy the entire table and place it on all the nodes in the cluster. This is especially true for dimension tables, which are generally smaller in size. This would generally provide superior performance for a FACT-DIMENSION join. Whenever you need such a distribution, you can choose ALL distribution, which results in the full copy of the table on the first slice of every node.

EVEN   There is often a case where you are unable to identify what is the right distribution key for a table because you have a number of different use cases where a join happens using different keys. In this scenario, an EVEN distribution helps you place the data evenly across all the nodes in a round-robin fashion.

AUTO   This is the default option with Redshift, where Redshift starts with an ALL distribution and then switches to EVEN when the table grows larger. Auto-distribution is recommended when you are unsure about the type of distribution style and let the optimizer choose the distribution style for your table.

Exam Tip: You will see questions in the exam that provide you with a scenario and then ask about the right distribution choice. It is important for you to understand the distribution styles and the right choice in different scenarios.

Sort Keys in Redshift

Redshift stores the data in a sorted order on the disk. Sort keys help you provide similar performance benefits as indexes. Redshift uses the concept of zone maps, where Redshift keeps an in-memory listing of the minimum and maximum values of data of each data block and uses it to prune the blocks that cannot contain the data for a given query. This minimizes unnecessary I/O, resulting in superior performance for your queries. Redshift supports two types of sort keys:

Compound Sort Key (Default)   The compound sort key is a key composed of one or more columns. The order of the columns in the sort key is crucial as they define how the actual data gets stored on the disk. As a best practice, you should order the columns in the lowest to highest cardinality. These are effective when a majority of the queries on a table filter or join are on a specific subset of columns.

Interleaved Sort Key   Each column in the sort key is sorted with equal weighting. This is useful when multiple queries use different access paths and different columns for filters and joins. This should be used with caution and edge cases only.

Here are some things to consider when using sort keys in Redshift:

- Most customers will use a compound sort key. Interleaved sort key may seem like the panacea to all your problems, but the performance improvement gained by implementing an interleaved sort key may have to be offset by increased load and vacuum times.

- A sort key should actually contain columns that are most often used in the WHERE clause.

- Column ordering is important when choosing a sort key.

- It is recommended to use four columns or fewer in a compound sort key. Using any more columns will result in marginal performance improvement but increased ingestion overhead.

- If your table is frequently joined, then use the DIST key as the first column in your sort key.

- Using CAST() functions in the predicate clause on a SORT key will result in a full table scan and the sort key will not be utilized during querying.

- You can alter the sort key, but Amazon Redshift will need to reorder the data in the underlying table.

Temporary Tables in Redshift

Redshift also supports Temporary tables. You can create temporary tables as follows:

```
CREATE TEMPORARY TABLE <TableName> {Table Definition}

CREATE TEMPORARY TABLE <TableName> as {Select Query}

SELECT .... INTO #MYTEMPTAB FROM {TableName}
```

Temporary tables are stored like all other tables in Redshift but have the lifetime of a session and are dropped when your session terminates. By default, there is no columnar compression, and the tables are evenly distributed across the cluster. You can use TEMP tables to substitute for permanent tables, and they can often offer better performance as they exhibit faster I/O (as they are not mirrored to other nodes). You can COPY and UNLOAD temporary tables.

It is often recommended to include the column encodings when you are using the CREATE statement in a temporary table and include the distribution style required for your use case. If you are planning to use them as a part of an ETL process, please do ensure that you compute statistics for those tables.

Materialized Views in Redshift

Materialized views contain a precomputed result set based on a SQL query over one or more base tables. When you create a materialized view, Redshift runs the associated SQL query and persists the result set. A materialized view's precomputed result set can be refreshed anytime via the REFRESH command, and Redshift determines the best way to update data in the materialized view (incremental or full refresh).

The key benefits of materialized views include optimization of complex, long-running, resource-intensive queries on large tables, such as SELECT statements with multiple-table joins and aggregations on tables that contain millions of rows.

When a materialized view is queried, Redshift returns precomputed results without having to access the base tables, which is especially useful for predictable and repeated queries such as ETL or BI pipelines that perform repeated stages of computations over very large datasets.

Some key considerations of materialized views are listed here:

- Queries referencing MVs will run on the primary cluster (as opposed to concurrency scaling clusters).

- MVs can reference all Redshift objects except other MVs, standard views (although standard views can reference MVs), external tables, system tables or views, or temporary tables.

- Certain SQL operations require full-refreshes (such as outer joins, math functions such as RAND, window functions, and so on).

- Data changes in base tables reflected in MV when the REFRESH command is invoked. At the time of this writing, Amazon has not released automatic refreshing of MVs, although it is a part of the road map and expected to be released soon.

- Columns can be added to base tables without affecting MV, but you have to re-create MV if you are dropping or renaming columns, renaming MV, or changing MV's SQL definition.

- Some user-initiated operations on base tables force an MV to be fully recomputed next time REFRESH is run (for example, manually invoked vacuum, classic resize, alter distkey, alter sortkey, and truncate).

Data Modeling for Data Lakes

As discussed in the section on Redshift Lakehouse, you can have tables in Redshift that would point to data files in your data lake. However, the tables that point to data in your data lake and the tables that persist data in Redshift have certain different considerations.

The filetypes, sizes, and compression have a huge impact on the performance of your tables that point to data in your data lake. The best practices are as follows:

- The number of files in the data lake should be a multiple of your Redshift slice count (general best practice). Redshift Lakehouse can automatically split Parquet, ORC, text-format, and Bz2 files for optimal processing.
- File sizes should be in the range 64 to 512 MB.
- Files should be of uniform size (especially for files that can't be automatically split by Redshift Lakehouse such as Avro and Gzip) to avoid execution skew; Lakehouse queries only run as fast as the slowest node in the cluster.
- Use data lake file formats that are optimized for read by Redshift Lakehouse (and Athena!).
- ORC and Parquet apply columnar encoding, similar to how data is stored inside Redshift.
- Redshift Lakehouse can also work with Avro, CSV, and JSON data, but these files are *much* larger on S3 than ORC/Parquet.
- Lakehouse will perform "partition pruning" based on the structure of data on S3:
  - This is actually based on Hive metastore pruning rather than being Redshift Lake-house-specific–it also works in EMR, Glue, and so on.
  - Uses Glue Data Catalog partition columns.
- Partitions should be based on the following items:
  - Frequently filtered columns (either through join or WHERE clause)
  - Business units
  - Business groups (user cohorts, application names, business units)
  - Date and time
- Consider how your users query data:
  - Do they look month by month, or current month and year versus previous year for the same month? (And so on.)
  - Do they understand the columns you have created?
- Date-based partition columns have a type:
  - Full dates included in a single value may be formatted or not (*yyyy-mm-dd* or *yyyymmdd*).
  - Formatted dates can only be strings.
  - Either type of date needs to consider ordering. (date=dd-mm-yyyy cannot be used in order by clause, but date=yyyy-mm-dd can!)

Data Loading and Unloading

Now that you understand Redshift architecture and its modeling techniques, it's time to look at the different ways in which you can load data into Amazon Redshift. While Redshift provides many options to load data into the cluster, they can broadly be categorized into two major categories:

- Loading operations using a single transaction
- Loading options using multiple transactions involving the leader node for each transaction

Theoretically speaking, you should limit the number of transactions Redshift takes to load your data because the number of transactions is inversely proportional to better loading performance, which is often a key performance indicator (KPI) in data warehouse environments. If your loading operations involve a leader node for every single row, that operation is only suitable for smaller amounts of data. For the majority of the operations, it is recommended to use those where compute nodes are engaged in parallel.

The following data loading operations traverse the leader node for each single transaction:

- INSERT
- INSERT (multi-value)
- UPDATE
- DELETE

The following data loading operations traverse a leader node once using a single transaction and then engage compute nodes in parallel:

- COPY
- UNLOAD
- CTAS
- CREATE TABLE (LIKE . . .)
- INSERT INTO (SELECT . . .)
- Loading data from S3, Dynamo DB, EMR, and SSH commands

Redshift COPY Command

COPY will outperform single row inserts for most use cases because it engages compute nodes in parallel. The general syntax of the COPY command is as follows:

```
COPY <TABLE> from <location>
credentials "aws_access_key_id=<access_key>;
aws_secret_access_key=<secret_key>"
iam_role "arn"
region;
```

While using COPY, you can use a number of options:

- Kind of data being loaded – CSV, JSON, AVRO
- Compression options
- Encryption options
- Transformation options
- Data formats through DATEFORMAT, TIMEFORMAT
- ACCEPTINVCHAR to replaced invalid characters with the question mark (?)
- COMPUPDATE PRESET/ON ensures optimal column encodings are determined for an empty table and existing encodings are overwritten if necessary.
- An optional manifest file can instruct the COPY command to load only required input files for a data load and how to respond in case input files are missing.
- You can use the COPY command to handle errors and can choose to either ignore errors or fail upon encountering errors.

You should use multiple input files to parallelize the loading process. It is often recommended to have a multiple of the slice count.

Best Practices for Data Loading

We've looked at some of the options for loading data into Redshift. The following best practices will provide optimal performance during the COPY operation.

- Use the COPY command to load data whenever possible.
- Use a single COPY command per table.
  - Writes are serial per table.
  - Commits are serial per cluster.
- Use multi-row inserts if COPY is not possible.
  - Bulk insert operations (INSERT INTO. . .SELECT and CREATE TABLE AS) provide high performance data insertion.
- Use staging tables to perform an upsort.
- Load your data in sort key order to reduce the potential need of (auto-)VACUUM.
- Use time-series tables when appropriate.
  - Organize your data as a sequence of time-series tables, where each table is identical but contains data for different time ranges.
  - Unify partitioned time-series tables with a late-binding view.
- Split your data into multiple files.
  - Ideally an even multiple of slice count
- Compress your data files.
- Be sure to remember column encoding and distribution keys on temporary tables.

- Redshift automatically performs vacuum and analyzes in the background during periods of low workloads, but Redshift users are still empowered to explicitly invoke VACUUM and then ANALYZE as part of their workflow after adding, deleting, or modifying a large number of rows (> 5%).
  - Explicitly invoking VACUUM and then ANALYZE ensures that a table is sorted, defragmented, and analyzed immediately and with priority for the benefit of the next step in a workflow
- Disable column encoding analysis (COMPUPDATE) and statistics update (STATUPDATE) from COPY if loading a small amount of data relative to overall table size.
- Enforce primary, unique, or foreign key constraints outside of Amazon Redshift.
- Wrap workflow/statements in an explicit transaction.
- Consider using DROP TABLE or TRUNCATE instead of DELETE.
- When moving all rows from a table (e.g., source table to staging table, or vice versa), use the faster ALTER TABLE APPEND (which moves rather than copies data) instead of INSERT INTO SELECT.
- Staging tables:
  - Use a *temporary* or *permanent* table with the BACKUP NO option.
  - Mirror compression settings from a production table by using CREATE TABLE LIKE or using ANALYZE COMPRESSION to add the column-level compression into the DDL; also, turn off automatic compression analysis in the COPY command (i.e., COMPUPDATE OFF).
  - If applicable, use DISTSTYLE KEY on both the staging table and production table (on the same key column) to speed up an INSERT INTO SELECT statement.

Loading Data from Other AWS Services

You can load data to Redshift from other AWS services, including but not limited to the following:

Kinesis Data Firehose   Kinesis Firehose can automatically load data to Redshift. It micro-batches streaming data to S3 and then uses the COPY command to load the data to Redshift using a manifest file. You can specify the batch size and the number of seconds before a load occurs. Kinesis Firehose can do multi-AZ buffering of data prior to a load and manages all compression and encryption.

Amazon EMR   You can load data from Amazon EMR (essentially HDFS). However, the cluster needs to be started with Redshift compatibility bootstrap action.

```
COPY <table> from 'emr://emr_cluster_id/hdfs_file_path' iam_role "arn"
```

DynamoDB   You can load from DynamoDB using the COPY command. However, a COPY command will count against your provisioned read capacity.

```
COPY <redshift_tablename>
from 'dynamodb://<dynamodb_table_name>' iam_role "arn" readratio
'<integer>';
```

SSH Endpoint   You can load data to Amazon Redshift from any endpoint connected via SSH. This option is useful for SFTP, NAS, or on-premises remote hosts. It requires an SSH manifest file containing the information COPY will use to open SSH connections and execute the remote commands.

```
COPY <redshift_tablename>
from 's3://'ssh_manifest_file' iam_role "arn"
SSH [| optional-parameters];
```

AWS Lambda   You can use AWS Lambda to load to Amazon Redshift using *aws-lambda-redshift-loader*. The connector is available on GitHub at github. com/awslabs/aws-lambda-redshift-loader. You should consider an AWS Lambda session limit if you are planning to load data to Amazon Redshift from AWS Lambda.

Federated Query   You can use Federated Query to query and analyze data across operational databases, data warehouses, and data lakes. This feature allows you to integrate queries on live data in Amazon RDS for PostgreSQL and Amazon Aurora PostgreSQL with queries across your Amazon Redshift and Amazon S3 environments. Redshift's intelligent optimizer pushes down and distributes portions of computation directly into remote operational databases to reduce data moved over the network.

You can therefore incorporate live data as part of your business intelligence (BI) and reporting applications. This option makes it easy to ingest data into Redshift by querying operational databases directly, applying transformations on the fly, and loading data into target tables without complex ETL pipelines.

Unloading Data from Amazon Redshift

Building a complete information architecture often means that you will need to unload data from Redshift on occasion. Sometimes this could be due to the fact that you want to unload data marts that were built inside Redshift but now host cold data, and at other times it could be due to other applications that would be consuming data available on your Redshift cluster.

You have three common ways to unload data from Redshift:

- AWS Glue
- AWS Data Pipeline
- UNLOAD statement

You can use the UNLOAD command to extract data from Redshift. UNLOAD is basically a reverse of the COPY statement. The UNLOAD statement outputs data from

Amazon Redshift to S3 in CSV or Parquet format. The key semantics of an UNLOAD are as follows:

- Runs from a SELECT statement. Since the output is generally large and performance is a concern, the statement runs on all the compute nodes in parallel. If you would like an ordered output, you have to define ORDER BY in the SELECT statement, in addition to setting PARALLEL=OFF.

- Encryption and compression are handled automatically.

- The number of files generated is larger than the slice count, generally more than one file per slice.

- You can create a manifest file as a part of the output operation. This is especially useful if you would like to move the data to another cluster.

- You can control the maximum file size written to S3 and the overwrite semantics as to whether you would like to control the output or not.

Query Optimization in Redshift

Redshift is an ACID- and ANSI SQL–compliant cloud data warehouse and uses similar syntax to PostgreSQL while supporting stored procedures and custom UDFs with SQL SELECT or Python. A typical Redshift query passes through three major phases:

1. Planning – A user-submitted query is parsed and optimized to create a query plan.

2. Compilation – Redshift checks its compile cache to see if it can find a query-plan match. If it can find a query-plan match, it reuses the existing compiled objects; otherwise it converts it to sub-tasks that are then individually compiled into C++.

3. Execution – The compiled code is executed by the compute node slices in parallel and the results are then aggregated by the leader node to be sent back to the requestor.

A query plan is a basic tool that can help you understand and analyze a complex query. It gives you an insight into how the query will actually be run on the cluster. When the query plan is compiled, the execution engine translates the query plan into steps, segments, and streams (see Figure 4.21):

Step   A step is an individual operation that is required during the execution of a query.

Segment   A segment is a compilation of several steps that need to be done by a single process. This is the smallest compilation unit executable by the individual slice of a compute node. The compute node slices will execute the segments in parallel.

Stream   A stream is a collection of segments to be parceled out over the available compute node slices. You can have multiple segments in a stream, and the segments are then run in parallel.

FIGURE 4.21 Relationship between streams, segments, and steps

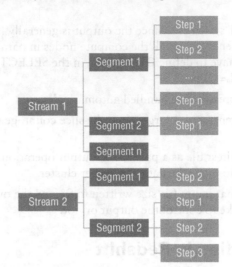

Explain Plans in Redshift

You can generate explain plans using the EXPLAIN statement, which allows you to generate a pre-formatted output with one row per step and a single column indicating the step. If you use Redshift Query Editor, you can generate a visual explain plan. Explain plans are read from the bottom up, and they provide information like the following:

- Execution order of steps for local and Lakehouse portions
- Estimated number of rows to be returned by a step
- Amount of data to be sent across slices per step (Network I/O is expensive and should be optimized as much as possible.)
- Relative cost of a step

You can look at historic trends of explain plans generated for queries that were previously run on the system using STL_EXPLAIN table. One of the key components in understanding explain plans is understanding the terminology being used during the explain plan generation. As discussed earlier, Redshift is an MPP database, where many compute nodes work together to produce efficient results, which means that the network becomes a really important component during data processing, especially join processing. During a particular step in a join, you may need to work on data that is not stored locally and hence data from a different slice on the same node, or in the worst-case scenario, a different node may need to be fetched. Since network transmission is by far the most expensive operation a query will do, it is important to understand how data is moving across the nodes. Table 4.15 describes the terminology that you will see in explain plans.

TABLE 4.15   Network transmission in query processing

Transmission Type	Description
DS_DIST_NONE	This is the ideal situation, which indicates that the data for the join is co-located on the same slice; this is the most efficient option as no network transfer will occur.
DS_DIST_ALL_NONE	Indicates that the join is occurring with a table that has DISTSTYLE ALL and also does not incur network transfer
DS_DIST_ALL_INNER	Indicates that the 'inner' join table is being sent to a single node because the join table uses DISTSTYLE ALL; this join is executed on a single node and will likely be very slow.
DS_DIST_ INNER (|OUTER)	Indicates which table is being redistributed when using an outer join (inner or outer table); if one of the tables is much smaller or infrequently updated, consider changing it to DISTSTYLE ALL.
DS_BCAST_INNER	Indicates that the 'inner' join table is being broadcast to all nodes
DS_BCAST_BOTH	Indicates that both tables in the join are being broadcast to all nodes. This is the worst possible option.

Best Practices for Writing Queries

Following are some of the best practices for writing queries to consume the data from Redshift. It is important that you build up your own set of best practices and use these as a guideline:

- The team should work on coding standards, including syntax styles for SQL. For example, you may prefer ANSI over equijoin, but you should choose one or the other.

- An ideal query only fetches the columns it needs and the rows that are of interest. This is managed using a projection list and filters.

- Make use of sort keys, compression, distribution styles, automated table maintenance (vacuum, analyze), and workload management.

- Sort key columns being used in filters should not use functions. If application of functions (e.g., casting into a different format) is a necessity, ensure that you materialize that into a separate column.

- Make sure statistics are up to date.

- You can use SVL_QUERY_SUMMARY to evaluate the effectiveness of sort keys.

- For Lakehouse queries, ensure that you are using columnar encoding (Parquet or ORC).

Redshift Workload Management

Workload management (WLM) is a feature that helps manage workloads and avoid short, fast-running queries getting stuck in queues behind long-running queries. These three WLM methods are complementary to each other:

Queues (Basic WLM)   WLM always assigns every query executed in Redshift to a specific queue on the basis of user group, query group, or WLM rules (for example, [return_row_count > 1000000]).

Short-Query Acceleration (SQA)   Redshift uses machine learning to determine what constitutes a "short" running query in your cluster. "Short" running queries are then automatically identified and run immediately in short-query queue if queuing occurs.

Concurrency Scaling   Redshift uses machine learning to predict queuing in your cluster, and when queuing occurs, transient Amazon Redshift clusters are added to your cluster where queries are routed for execution. Concurrency scaling was discussed earlier in the chapter, along with the semantics of how it gets triggered.

Auto WLM is enabled by default when the default parameter group is used and must be explicitly enabled when a custom parameter group is used. Auto WLM can be enabled in a customer parameter group through the Amazon Redshift console by choosing Switch WLM Mode and then choosing Auto WLM. With this choice, one queue is used to manage queries, and memory and concurrency on main fields are both set to auto. When Auto WLM is not enabled, manual WLM requires you to specify values for query concurrency and memory allocation.

WLM queues can be defined with a specific priority (relative importance), and queries will inherit a queue's priority. Administrators can use priorities to prioritize different workloads (such as ETL, ingestion, audit, and BI). Amazon Redshift uses priority when letting queries into the system to determine the amount of resources allocated to query, which provides predictable performance for high-priority workloads. However, this comes at the cost of other, lower-priority workloads. It is important to realize that *lower-priority queries are not starved, but they might run longer because they are waiting behind more important queries or running with fewer resources.* You can enable *concurrency scaling* to maintain predictable performance for lower-priority workloads.

WLM: Query Monitoring Rules

We have all seen users in production environments who would run expensive joins on data causing the system to fetch occasionally billions of rows and consume all resources (Cartesian product). Redshift provides query monitoring rules (QMRs), which, as their name implies, are intended to provide rules to monitor queries, especially runaway queries.

Query monitoring rules can be defined for a WLM queue via the Redshift console, which can result in one of the following four actions for queries, which are offending the rules:

- LOG – Log info about the query. This information is available in the STL_WLM_RULE_ACTION table.

- ABORT – Log the action of the query and terminate it.

- HOP – Log the action and move the query to another appropriate queue if it exists; otherwise, terminate the query.
- PRIORITY – Change the query priority.

Security in Redshift

Redshift host's your company's most valuable resource, data, and hence security becomes a day zero job. Access to Amazon Redshift is controlled at four levels:

Cluster Management – AWS IAM (Identity and Access Management) is used to control the AWS user's ability to create, configure, and delete Amazon Redshift clusters. Once users have the ability to access a Redshift cluster via IAM, they will connect via JDBC/ODBC or the query editor in the Redshift console.

Cluster Connectivity – Security groups are used to allow other AWS instances to connect to the Redshift cluster.

Database Access – Access to database objects such as tables and views is controlled by user accounts within the Amazon Redshift database.

Temporary DB Credentials and Single Sign-on – Leverage IAM credentials for logging onto the DB or to sign on using federated Single Sign-On (SSO) through a SAML 2.0–compliant identity provider.

Redshift Cluster VPCs

Compute nodes reside in a private, Amazon-managed, internal VPC that is only accessible by the Redshift leader node. The *leader node* resides in both the private/internal VPC for compute nodes and the customer's VPC to allow access to the Redshift cluster and to handle data distribution among the compute nodes. High-bandwidth connections, close proximity, and custom communication protocols provide private, very high-speed network communication between the leader node and compute nodes. *Compute nodes* interact with other AWS services such as S3, EMR, and DynamoDB for ingestion, backup, and so on.

Figure 4.22 indicates Redshift VPCs and their interaction with other Amazon Web Services.

Redshift Network Topology and Security Groups

Cluster subnet groups indicate which subnets within a VPC a Redshift cluster can run; however, most customers configure Redshift with multiple subnets so that Redshift can choose the subnet. An Amazon Redshift cluster exists in only one subnet/AZ at a time.

Amazon Redshift clusters are locked down by default, which means no users can connect to the cluster. To grant users access to the cluster, a security group must be associated with the cluster that opens up the appropriate ports and accepts incoming connections from the white-listed IP addresses, CIDR block ranges, or security groups.

FIGURE 4.22   Redshift cluster VPCs

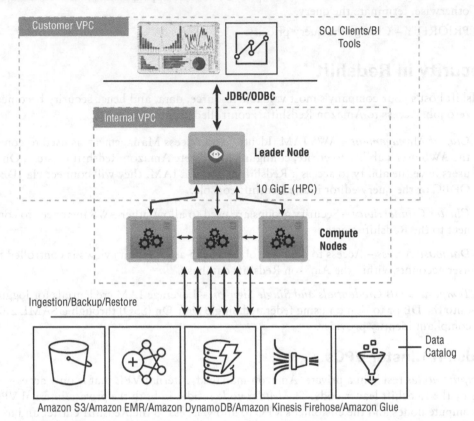

AWS recommends the use of security groups to authorize other VPC security groups or CIDR blocks to connect to your Redshift instance. You should use VPC security groups for other AWS Services and EC2 connectivity, or Cross Account Access (recommended approach) while CIDR blocks should be used for connections from on-premises/other side of customer gateway.

It is generally a good practice to have separate cluster security groups per application. Since S3 is an important component in the overall architecture, Redshift's route to S3 can be via an Internet gateway, an Egress-only NAT gateway, a NAT gateway, or a private S3 endpoint and enhanced VPC routing.

Redshift offers enhanced VPC routing (EVR) that will require all COPY, UNLOAD, backup, and Redshift Lakehouse operations to flow through a customer VPC endpoint instead of directly over the Internet. EVR will also ensure that the traffic appears in VPC flow logs, thus making it auditable, and you can apply VPC endpoint policies.

Data Security in Redshift

Redshift uses the concepts of schemas, users, and user groups like most other databases:

Schemas   Collection of database tables and other database objects (similar to namespace)

Users   Named user accounts that can connect to a database

Groups   Collections of users that can be collectively assigned privileges for easier security maintenance

You can control the database security by controlling which users have access to specific database objects, which depends on privileges that you grant to user accounts or groups. By default, the creator of the object is the owner, and hence privileges are only granted to them. A user account is granted privileges either explicitly or implicitly by being a member of the group that has been assigned the appropriate privileges.

A master user is created at the cluster provisioning time and acts as a superuser by having access to all databases created within the cluster. The master user (also known as superuser) can create other superuser and user accounts.

Often in the exam, you can get questions about securing access to specific rows or columns. In Redshift, you can achieve this in three ways:

- Use materialized views, which contain the rows/columns permitted to given users and give privileges to the users on specific views.

- You can use a column indicating allowed users and ensure that the column is honored in your queries. This will not work if you have not locked down your data and users are not limited to access the data for their own queries.

- You can also use Redshift's Lake Formation integration for fine-grained column-level policies defined within Lake Formation.

Encryption of Data in Motion

All Redshift cluster communications are secure by default. Redshift will always use hardware-accelerated SSL to communicate with other AWS services. You can require connectivity to be made to Redshift only via SSL by setting the `require_ssl` parameter to true.

When you load data into Redshift, Redshift supports encryption in three major ways:

- Client-side encrypted data with symmetric encryption. A symmetric key is included in the COPY command.
- Server-side encryption via S3 using KMS (SSE-KMS)
- Encrypted with S3 SSE (SSE)

Data is transferred encrypted into each compute node performing a data load, and decryption is performed on-node using your symmetric key. Data can also be unloaded using KMS encryption keys or a symmetric key.

Encryption of Data at Rest

Data for a Redshift cluster can be stored in S3 or Redshift local drives or as a backup on your S3. Redshift can encrypt data using AWS with 256-bit keys. Key management can be performed within Redshift, by AWS KMS or using your HSM. Rotation of keys can be handled via API.

Redshift data blocks on S3 are encrypted using the cluster's encryption key. Redshift uses hardware-based crypto modules to keep the load down to less than 20 percent on the CPU.

KMS-based encryption is the recommended setup for encrypting data at rest in Redshift, which supports key rotation and bring-your-own-key. You can use envelope encryption using a robust key hierarchy. Redshift supports a four-tier hierarchy of encryption keys (see Figure 4.23):

FIGURE 4.23 Four-tier hierarchy—encryption keys in Redshift

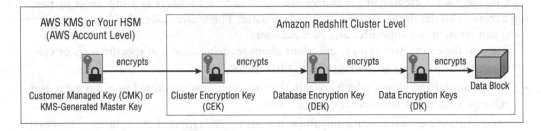

- Master key
- Cluster encryption key
- Database encryption key
- Data encryption keys

Single Sign-On (SSO) with Redshift

You can use Single Sign-On to leverage user identities that already exist in the organization outside of AWS.

You configure your SAML 2.0-compliant identity provider (IdP) to permit your federated users access to an IAM role. With that IAM role, you can generate temporary database credentials and log on to Amazon Redshift databases. You can also attach IAM policies to the IAM role, which can grant or restrict access to specific resources such as Amazon Redshift clusters, databases, database usernames, and user group names.

Audit Logging in Redshift

Redshift provides three options for audit logging database-level activities such as which users are logged in to the system and their related activities:

- Audit logs: Audit logs are stored in three files—connection log, user log, and user activity log—and must be explicitly enabled. They are stored on S3 indefinitely unless you have a lifecycle rule in place to archive or delete files automatically. Since the logs are on S3, audit logs are not impacted by a cluster restart, and you can access the logs independently of Redshift cluster access. This means if your auditor needs access to the audit logs for Redshift, you can provide them direct access to the logs without giving them access to your Redshift cluster.

- System (STL) tables: There are multiple system tables in Redshift, like SVL_STATEMENTTEXT and SVL_CONNECTION_LOG, that contain auditing information. The superuser has full control on these tables, and they are automatically available on every node in the Redshift cluster. By default, logging history is stored from two to five days, depending on log usage and disk space availability. It is good practice to keep a backup of these tables and, if required, offload them to S3 for auditors to have access.

- CloudTrail logs: CloudTrail logs are used for auditing service-level activities, which include the success/failure of a request and the originator of the request, including the date/time when it was made. They are stored on S3 indefinitely.

Kinesis Data Analytics

You learned in Chapter 3, "Data Storage." about the importance of capturing streaming data; however, capturing data without analyzing and acting on the information is like having a goldmine of information and not benefitting from it. Amazon Kinesis Data Analytics provides an option to analyze streaming data, gain actionable insights, and respond to your business and customer needs in real time. The core objective of Amazon Kinesis Data Analytics was to reduce the complexity normally associated with building, managing, and integrating streaming applications with other AWS services.

Analysts love SQL as it is their language of choice for interacting with data. Kinesis Data Analytics allows SQL users to easily query streaming data or build entire streaming applications using templates and an interactive SQL editor. Kinesis Data Analytics for Java allows Java developers to build sophisticated streaming applications using open-source Java libraries (Apache Flink framework) and AWS integrations to transform and analyze data in real time.

Amazon Kinesis Data Analytics takes care of scalability required for streaming applications with increasing scale and volume of the data on a pay-as-you-go model, with no minimum costs.

Figure 4.24 shows the working of Kinesis Data Analytics. It can work with data captured using popular streaming applications like Amazon Kinesis Data Streams, Amazon MSK, and other popular sources. It can then be used to analyze the streaming data, and output can be sent to analytics tools to create alerts and respond in real time.

FIGURE 4.24   Working of Kinesis Data Analytics

Capture streaming data with Amazon MSK, Amazon Kinesis Data Streams, and other data sources.

Amazon Kinesis Data Analytics
Query and analyze streaming data.

Output
Amazon Kinesis Data Analytics can send processed data to analytics tools so you can create alerts and respond in real-time.

The most common real-time streaming use cases include fraud detection and mobile and web-application notifications where the response time has to be in milliseconds. Messaging between micro-services is also one of the core streaming use cases.

We also see log ingestion, IoT device maintenance, and change-data-capture as the second type of streaming cases, where the response time is generally in seconds.

A new type of requirement that is cropping up is real-time data warehousing where customers are looking to ingest data into data lakes and data warehouses in near real time, and the typical expected response time is single-digit minutes.

How Does It Work?

An application is the primary resource in Kinesis Data Analytics that you can create in your account using the AWS Console or the Kinesis Data Analytics API. Streaming applications are built to read and process the data in real time, and Kinesis Data Analytics is no different as it allows you to write SQL to process incoming streaming data and process output. Kinesis Data Analytics versions the application when it is created and updated by the developer along with maintenance of a time stamp indicating the creation and updating of the application.

Each Kinesis Data Analytics application consists of the following elements:

Input   Every Kinesis data stream has a source that can be a Kinesis data stream or a Kinesis Data Firehose stream, which can be mapped to an in-application input stream in the input configuration. The in-application stream is like a continuously updating table upon which you can call the SELECT and INSERT SQL operations.

Application Code   In a SQL application, application code is basically a series of SQL statements that process input from the input streams and produce output. You can write SQL statements against in-application streams and reference tables and optionally perform joins between these two.

An in-application stream is essentially an unbounded stream of data that is being processed through your application code. While it may be reasonable to operate on a record-level basis, it is often seen that data is processed in terms of a certain amount of time, such as the last 5 minutes, or a certain number of records, such as the last 50 transactions.

An example could be a financial institution looking at the last 24 hours of cash withdrawal data to see if a user has already withdrawn funds from their account as per their daily limit.

Another example could be a telecommunications company offering unlimited minutes if your average spend within a particular day is one dollar on a pay-as-you-go subscription.

Amazon Kinesis Data Analytics offers the ability to process data using windowed SQL queries, where data in the stream can be bound by time or the number of records. The windowed queries can be either time-based windows or row-based windows. For a time-based window, the window size can be defined in terms of time (for example, the last 24 hours). A time-based window, however, needs a time stamp column in your data, which is increasing over time. For a row-size window, you can specify the window size in terms of the number of rows.

There are three window types supported in Amazon Kinesis Data Analytics:

Staggered windows: A staggered windowing method is useful when you are analyzing data that may arrive at inconsistent times. They are useful for addressing tumbling window issues around records not falling in a particular time-restricted window. The window is opened when the first event matching the partition arrives rather than at a fixed time interval, and it closes based on the age of the window measured against the time when the first record was encountered and window was opened. To learn more about staggered windows please visit AWS documentation at docs.aws.amazon.com/ kinesisanalytics/latest/dev/stagger-window-concepts.html.

Tumbling windows: A tumbling windowing method is useful when you are analyzing data in time windows that are not overlapping. Each record is processed only once during the time window when it occurs. To learn more about tumbling windows please visit AWS documentation at docs.aws.amazon .com/kinesisanalytics/latest/dev/tumbling-window-concepts.html.

Sliding windows: A sliding windowing technique is useful when you are analyzing data based on certain internal variables that moves based on either the latest time or the latest record. For example, if you are calculating an average of the past 5 minutes, the result might be different every time you run the query, depending on the time when the query is run. To learn more about sliding windows, please visit AWS documentation at docs.aws.amazon.com/kinesisanalytics/latest/dev/sliding-window-concepts.html.

Output   In application code, query results go to in-application streams. You can also create multiple in-application streams to hold intermediate results (acting as temp tables) or configure an application to persist data in-application output streams.

Figure 4.25 shows the creation of a Kinesis application and choosing the runtime environment.

FIGURE 4.25   Working of Kinesis Data Analytics

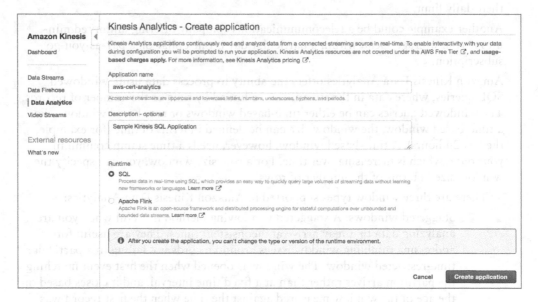

What Is Kinesis Data Analytics for Java?

Kinesis Data Analytics for Java is essentially managed Apache Flink, which is a distributed engine and a framework for stateful processing of data streams. Apache Flink was discussed a bit earlier in the book, but people who have used Apache Flink and managed a Flink cluster would realize that it can quickly become quite challenging to run and manage an Apache Flink cluster. Amazon gives you an option to run your Apache Flink applications with Amazon Kinesis. The process of running such an application is quite simple and can be summarized in three steps:

- Build your application in your IDE of choice using Apache Flink.
- Upload your application code to Amazon Kinesis.
- Run your application in a fully managed, highly scalable, and elastic service without the need to manage underlying infrastructure.

When you run your Apache Flink application with Amazon Kinesis, you can monitor, scale, and back up your application from within Amazon Web Services:

Monitoring Your Application   You can monitor your application using CloudWatch metrics and logs and the Apache Link job graph in the AWS Management Console.

Scaling Your Application   You can scale the resources of your application such as assigned KPUs (Kinesis process unit; 1 KPU = 1 vCPU + 4 GB RAM). They can either be provisioned in advance or automatically scaled as required. You can also scale the number of instances of a task.

Backing Up Your Applications   Amazon Kinesis backs up the application state automatically (by default). You can restore your application to a previous point in time using snapshots taken by Amazon Kinesis.

Comparing Batch Processing Services

The AWS platform offers a depth and breadth of services for data processing. We looked at AWS Glue in the previous chapter and Amazon EMR in this chapter. It is important to know which service to choose based on the specific requirement. Table 4.16 highlights some of the key differences between the two services.

TABLE 4.16   Comparing batch services

Comparison Criteria	AWS Glue	Amazon EMR
Summary description	AWS Glue is a fully managed serverless ETL service offering managed Apache Spark and the Python shell.	Amazon EMR is a fully managed Hadoop environment offering a number of different projects, including Hadoop, Spark, HBase
Scale	Automatic scaling	Autoscaling/EMR managed scaling
Compute	Serverless	EMR software on EC2 instances
Supported projects	Apache Spark, Python Shell	Apache Hive, Apache Spark, Apache Pig, Apache Mahout, Apache Presto, Apache Hadoop, Apache Livy, Tensorflow, MXNet + others
Pricing	DPU (data processing unit)	EC2 instance cost + EMR software (per node)

TABLE 4.16   Comparing batch services *(continued)*

Comparison Criteria	AWS Glue	Amazon EMR
Ideal use case	Serverless ETL, low admin overhead, often good for new workloads	Fully managed environment, often good replacement for on-premises Hadoop migrations
Spin-up time	Seconds (Glue 2.0)	Minutes
Cluster type	Transient	Long running + transient

Comparing Orchestration Options on AWS

We looked at data ingestion in an earlier chapter and data processing and analysis in this chapter. None of these tasks live independently of each other, and they are often tied in the form of a pipeline to automate the processes from end to end. This end-to-end automation process is referred to as data orchestration. AWS offers a number of options for data orchestration, including AWS Glue workflows and AWS Data Pipeline, mentioned in an earlier chapter, and AWS Step Functions, discussed in this section. I'll then compare the various options available to use on AWS, including a very popular option in the open-source domain called Apache Airflow.

AWS Step Functions

AWS Step Functions offers fully managed state machines on AWS. It allows you to coordinate multiple AWS services into serverless workflows so that you can build and update your apps quickly and easily. You can stitch together multiple services like Amazon DynamoDB, AWS Glue, Amazon EMR, and Amazon Sagemaker into a resilient workflow with built-in error handling and retrying support. AWS Step Functions also provide you with visual monitoring and an auditable history of your execution process.

If you would like to learn more about AWS Step Functions, I highly recommend the following workshop, which should take you a maximum of three hours to complete: step-functions-workshop.go-aws.com/.

Comparing Different ETL Orchestration Options

Table 4.17 provides a comparison of various ETL orchestration options on AWS Platform.

TABLE 4.17 Comparing orchestration options

	AWS Glue Workflow	AWS Data Pipeline	AWS Step Functions	Apache Airflow
Service Description	Workflow orchestration provided with AWS Glue	Managed workflow orchestration service	Managed stateless workflow orchestration service	Open-source workflow orchestration service
Scalability	Automatic scale-out execution	Autoscaling configurable	Automatic Scaling configurable	Scale through worker nodes
Installation	Serverless	EC2 instance based	Serverless	Installed on EC2 instances
Supported Engine	Spark	Shell	N/A	Airflow
Support Programming Environment	Scala and Python	UI based	Python, Go, Node.JS, C#, Java	Python
Pricing	Per second	Per activity	Per step in a workflow	Per EC2 instance compute
Usage	Greenfield customers with less complex ETL	Data movement including on-premises to on-cloud data integration	Large volume, short-duration workflows	Comprehensive workflow support, requires monitoring and maintenance

Table 4.17 provides you with an overview of the different orchestration options on the AWS Platform for your data and analytics pipeline and provides insights on when to choose which particular option.

Summary

This chapter was one of the most important chapters as it covered lots of different AWS services. From a data and analytics pipeline perspective, data processing and data analysis take the majority of your time. As you can see, you have a number of options available for the data processing and analysis, and some of them overlap in functionality as well. For example, we covered Amazon EMR in this chapter and covered AWS Glue in Chapter 2, "Data Collection." Both of these services offered Apache Spark, one of the most popular data processing frameworks available. Similarly, we covered data orchestration services, and there are a number of orchestration services on the AWS platform. Being a solution architect means you should be able to guide your customers and users to the right technology based on the use case.

Once you are done, please take some rest before we start with the next chapter, "Data Visualization."

Exam Essentials

Understand data processing and data analysis.   Data processing and data analysis are the topics of more than one third of all exam questions, which makes this chapter super important. The main reason for covering these two major domains in one chapter was that I feel that a lot of technologies used for data processing are used for data analysis as well.

Become familiar with the pertinent Amazon service offerings.   From a services perspective, we've looked at Amazon Athena, Apache Presto, Amazon EMR, Apache Hive, Amazon Elasticsearch, Amazon Redshift, and Kinesis Data Analytics. There was a lot of content covered in this chapter, but while this is quite important, it will not suffice on its own. It is highly recommended that you look at the blogs, documentation, and workshops suggested in the references section of this chapter.

Exercises

For assistance in completing the following exercises, refer to the user guides of the associated services.

EXERCISE 4.1

Creating an EMR Cluster

Please follow these steps to create an EMR cluster.

1.   Go to Service ➢ Analytics ➢ EMR.

2.   Select Create Cluster.

3.   You have two options to create a cluster: Quick Create or Advanced Options (provides more control and choice). Select Quick Create.

4.   Give your cluster a name, e.g., wiley-demo-chapter4.

5.   You can check the Logging option. This will log all cluster logs to Amazon S3.

6. Choose the launch mode.

   You have two models of launching a cluster:

   - Cluster – You create a long-running cluster with a set of applications chosen from the list of apps in the next step.

   - Step Execution – With this option, EMR will create a cluster, execute the added steps, and terminate when the steps have completed.

7. For the purpose of this exercise, we will choose the Cluster mode of operation.

8. Choose a software configuration. Select EMR Release. At the time of this writing, the latest release was emr-5.28.0.

   You can select from a list of applications to be configured on the cluster that is being spun up:

   - Core Hadoop: Hadoop 2.8.5 with Ganglia 3.7.2, Hive 2.3.6, Hue 4.4.0, Mahout 0.13.0, Pig 0.17.0, and Tez 0.9.2

   - HBase: HBase 1.4.10 with Ganglia 3.7.2, Hadoop 2.8.5, Hive 2.3.6, Hue 4.4.0, Phoenix 4.14.3, and ZooKeeper 3.4.14

   - Presto: Presto 0.227 with Hadoop 2.8.5 HDFS and Hive 2.3.6 Metastore

   - Spark: Spark 2.4.4 on Hadoop 2.8.5 YARN with Ganglia 3.7.2 and Zeppelin 0.8.2

9. For the sake of this exercise, we'll choose Core Hadoop.

   You also have the option to choose AWS Glue Data Catalog for Table Metadata. This will provide an option of using an external Hive metastore that you can use with these applications.

10. Hardware configuration:

    You have to choose the hardware configuration for your cluster, which includes the following settings:

    - Type of an instance

    - Number of instances (One of the instances will be a master node, and the remaining will act as core nodes.)

11. Security & Access configuration:

    - You can choose an EC2 key pair. If you don't select an EC2 key pair, you won't be able to SSH into your master node.

    - You can choose from two levels of permissions:

      - Default Permission – This will use default IAM roles. If roles are not present, they will be automatically created for you with managed policies for automatic policy updates.

        1. EMR role – EMR_DefaultRole

        2. EC2 instance profile – EMR_EC2_DefaultRole

EXERCISE 4.1 *(continued)*

- Custom Permission – You can select custom roles to tailor permissions for your cluster.

  1. Select an EMR role.

  2. Select an EC2 instance profile.

12. Select the Create Cluster option. It will take around 5–7 minutes to spin up a cluster.

EXERCISE 4.2

Getting Started - Configuring and Testing and Elasticsearch domain

Please complete the following tutorial to use Amazon Elasticsearch Service to create and configure a test domain:

amzn.to/39lh9gt

EXERCISE 4.3

Getting Started - Hosting an Elasticsearch index

In the following lab, you will use Amazon Elasticsearch Service to create a domain and host two indexes in Amazon Elasticsearch. You will then use various tools within the AWS platform like ElastiCache, Logstash. and Kibana and get an understanding of a real-world example.

search-sa-log-solutions.s3-us-east-2.amazonaws.com/logstash/html/
Lab_Guide_ABD326.html
bit.ly/ElasticSearchLab

EXERCISE 4.4

Building a Log Analytics Solution

In this lab, you will build a log analytics solution using Kinesis Agent, Kinesis Firehose, Kinesis Analytics, Amazon Elasticsearch, and Kibana. The exercise should take 60 minutes to complete.

aws.amazon.com/getting-started/projects/build-log-analytics-solution

---

Review Questions

1. You are working as an Enterprise Architect for a large fashion retailer based out of Madrid, Spain. The team is looking to build ETL and have large datasets that need to be transformed. Data is arriving from a number of sources and hence de-duplication is also an important factor. Which of the following is the simplest way to process data on AWS?

    A. Load data into Amazon Redshift, and build transformations using SQL. Build custom de-duplication script.

    B. Using AWS Glue to transform the data using built-in FindMatches ML Transform

    C. Load data into Amazon EMR, build Spark SQL scripts, and use custom de-duplication script.

    D. Use Amazon Athena for transformation and de-duplication.

2. Which of the following is a distributed data processing option on Apache Hadoop and was the main processing engine until Hadoop 2.0?

    A. Map Reduce

    B. YARN

    C. Hive

    D. Zoo Keeper

3. You are working as a consultant for a telecommunications company. The data scientists have requested direct access to the data to dive deep into the structure of the data and build models. They have good knowledge of SQL. Which of the following tools will you choose to provide them direct access to the data and reduce the infrastructure and maintenance overhead, while ensuring that access to data on Amazon S3 can be provided?
    Which of the following would you recommend to them? (Choose One.)

    A. Amazon S3 Select

    B. Amazon Athena

    C. Amazon Redshift

    D. Apache Presto on Amazon EMR

4. Which of the following file formats are supported by Amazon Athena? (Choose Three.)

    A. Apache Parquet

    B. CSV

    C. DAT

    D. Apache ORC

    E. Apache AVRO

    F. TIFF

5. You are working for a large utilities company which has deployed smart meters across its customer base. They are getting near real-time usage data from their customers and ingesting it into Amazon S3 via Amazon Kinesis. They were previously running some large scale transformations using PySpark on their on-premises Hadoop cluster. They have the Pyspark application available and expect no change other than input and output parameters while running the job. They are looking to reuse their code as much as possible, while looking at the possibility to tune the environment specific to their workload.

   Which of the following is the right data processing choice for their workload that meets the customers' requirements at the lowest cost? (Choose One.)

   A. Run the data processing on AWS Glue using the PySpark code.

   B. Run the data processing on Amazon EMR using Cluster mode.

   C. Run the data processing on Amazon EMR using Step execution mode using on-demand instances.

   D. Run the data processing on Amazon EMR using Step execution mode to utilize Spot instances.

6. You are looking to run large scale data processing jobs on Amazon EMR running in a step-execution mode. The data processing jobs can be run at any time with input data available on Amazon S3. Which of the following options will ensure that the data remains available, provides a consistent view, and is encrypted for protection during and after the cluster is terminated after the completion of steps? (Choose One.)

   A. Use HDFS.

   B. Use EMRFS.

   C. Use Local disk on the EMR EC2 instances.

   D. Use EBS volumes.

7. You are working for a large ecommerce retailer who would like to search the web-logs for specific error codes and their reference numbers. You have the ability to choose any tool from the AWS stack. Which of the following tools would you highly recommend for this use-case? (Choose One.)

   A. Amazon Redshift

   B. Apache Hive on Amazon EMR

   C. Apache Presto on Amazon EMR

   D. Amazon Elastic Search

8. Your customer is all in on AWS and most of the data has high velocity using Amazon S3, Amazon Kinesis Data Streams, Amazon Kinesis Data Fireshose, and Amazon DynamoDB. They are looking to analyze this streaming data and are contemplating choosing a service from the AWS stack. Which of the following services will you recommend to analyze this data? (Choose One.)

   A. Amazon Redshift

   B. Apache Hive on Amazon EMR

    C. Apache Pig on Amazon EMR

    D. Amazon Elastic Search

9. You are looking to build a Datawarehouse solution with the ability to flexibly transfer your data between data lake and Datawarehouse. Which of the following is the most cost effective way to meet your requirements? (Choose One.)

    A. Use S3 as your Datalake and Amazon EMR as your Datawarehouse.

    B. Use HDFS as your Datalake and Amazon Redshift as your Datawarehouse.

    C. Use S3 as your Datalake and Amazon Redshift as your Datawarehouse.

    D. Use HDFS as your Datalake and Amazon EMR as your Datawarehouse.

10. Which of the following statements are true about Redshift Leader nodes? (Choose Two.)

    A. Redshift cluster can have a single leader node.

    B. Redshift cluster can have more than one leader node.

    C. Redshift Leader node should have more memory than the compute nodes.

    D. Redshift Leader node has the exact same specifications as the compute nodes.

    E. You can choose your own Leader node sizing and it is priced separately.

    F. Redshift leader node is chosen automatically and is free to the users.

References

Recommended Workshops

Data Ingestion and Processing workshop: dataprocessing.wildrydes.com

Incremental Data Processing on Amazon EMR (Apache Hudi): incremental-data-processing-on-amazonemr.workshop.aws/en

Serverless Data Lake workshop: incremental-data-processing-on-amazonemr.workshop.aws/en

Data Engineering 2.0: aws-dataengineering-day.workshop.aws/en

Amazon Athena workshop: athena-in-action.workshop.aws

Amazon EMR with Service Catalog: s3.amazonaws.com/kenwalshtestad/cfn/public/sc/bootcamp/emrloft.html

Realtime Analytics and Serverless DataLake Demos: demostore.cloud

Streaming Analytics workshop: streaming-analytics.workshop.aws/en

Amazon Athena Blogs

"Query and Visualize AWS Cost and Usage Data Using Amazon Athena and Amazon QuickSight" – aws.amazon.com/blogs/big-data/
query-and-visualize-aws-cost-and-usage-data-using-amazon-athena-and-
amazon-quicksight

"Predict Billboard Top 10 Hits Using RStudio, H2O and Amazon Athena" – aws
.amazon.com/blogs/big-data/
predict-billboard-top-10-hits-using-rstudio-h2o-and-amazon-athena

"Visualize AWS CloudTrail Logs Using AWS Glue and Amazon QuickSight" – aws
.amazon.com/blogs/big-data/
streamline-aws-cloudtrail-log-visualization-using-aws-glue-and-amazon-
quicksight

"Using Amazon Redshift Spectrum, Amazon Athena, and AWS Glue with Node.js in Production" – aws.amazon.com/blogs/big-data/
using-amazon-redshift-spectrum-amazon-athena-and-aws-glue-with-node-js-
in-production

"Genomic Analysis with Hail on Amazon EMR and Amazon Athena" – aws.amazon
.com/blogs/big-data/
genomic-analysis-with-hail-on-amazon-emr-and-amazon-athena

"How Realtor.com Monitors Amazon Athena Usage with AWS CloudTrail and Amazon QuickSight" – aws.amazon.com/blogs/
big-data/analyzing-amazon-athena-usage-by-teams-within-a-real-es-
tate-company

"Create real-time clickstream sessions and run analytics with Amazon Kinesis Data Analytics, AWS Glue, and Amazon Athena" – aws.amazon.com/blogs/big-data/
create-real-time-clickstream-sessions-and-run-analytics-with-amazon-
kinesis-data-analytics-aws-glue-and-amazon-athena

"Visualize over 200 years of global climate data using Amazon Athena and Amazon QuickSight" – aws.amazon.com/blogs/big-data/
visualize-over-200-years-of-global-climate-data-using-amazon-athena-and-
amazon-quicksight

"Easily query AWS service logs using Amazon Athena" – aws.amazon.com/blogs/
big-data/easily-query-aws-service-logs-using-amazon-athena

"Trigger cross-region replication of pre-existing objects using Amazon S3 inventory, Amazon EMR, and Amazon Athena" – aws.amazon.com/blogs/big-data/
trigger-cross-region-replication-of-pre-existing-objects-using-amazon-
s3-inventory-amazon-emr-and-amazon-athena

"Detect fraudulent calls using Amazon QuickSight ML insights" – aws.amazon
.com/blogs/big-data/
detect-fraudulent-calls-using-amazon-quicksight-ml-insights

"Extract Salesforce.com data using AWS Glue and analyzing with Amazon Athena" – aws.amazon.com/blogs/big-data/
extracting-salesforce-com-data-using-aws-glue-and-analyzing-with-
amazon-athena

"Separate queries and managing costs using Amazon Athena workgroups" – aws
.amazon.com/blogs/big-data/
separating-queries-and-managing-costs-using-amazon-athena-workgroups

"Query your data created on-premises using Amazon Athena and AWS Storage Gateway" – aws.amazon.com/blogs/big-data/query-your-data-created-on-premises-using-amazon-athena-and-aws-storage-gateway

"Analyzing AWS WAF logs with Amazon ES, Amazon Athena, and Amazon QuickSight" – aws.amazon.com/blogs/big-data/analyzing-aws-waf-logs-with-amazon-es-amazon-athena-and-amazon-quicksight

"Perform biomedical informatics without a database using MIMIC-III data and Amazon Athena" – aws.amazon.com/blogs/big-data/perform-biomedical-informatics-without-a-database-using-mimic-iii-data-and-amazon-athena

"Access and manage data from multiple accounts from a central AWS Lake Formation account" – aws.amazon.com/blogs/big-data/access-and-manage-data-from-multiple-accounts-from-a-central-aws-lake-formation-account

"Simplify ETL data pipelines using Amazon Athena's federated queries and user-defined functions" – aws.amazon.com/blogs/big-data/simplify-etl-data-pipelines-using-amazon-athenas-federated-queries-and-user-defined-functions

"Query any data source with Amazon Athena's new federated query" – aws.amazon.com/blogs/big-data/query-any-data-source-with-amazon-athenas-new-federated-query

"Prepare data for model-training and invoke machine learning models with Amazon Athena" – aws.amazon.com/blogs/big-data/prepare-data-for-model-training-and-invoke-machine-learning-models-with-amazon-athena

"Connect Amazon Athena to your Apache Hive Metastore and use user-defined functions" – aws.amazon.com/blogs/big-data/connect-amazon-athena-to-your-apache-hive-metastore-and-use-user-defined-functions

"Extract, Transform and Load data into S3 data lake using CTAS and INSERT INTO statements in Amazon Athena" – aws.amazon.com/blogs/big-data/extract-transform-and-load-data-into-s3-data-lake-using-ctas-and-insert-into-statements-in-amazon-athena

"Collect and distribute high-resolution crypto market data with ECS, S3, Athena, Lambda, and AWS Data Exchange" – aws.amazon.com/blogs/big-data/collect-and-distribute-high-resolution-crypto-market-data-with-ecs-s3-athena-lambda-and-aws-data-exchange

"Cross-account AWS Glue Data Catalog access with Amazon Athena" – aws.amazon.com/blogs/big-data/cross-account-aws-glue-data-catalog-access-with-amazon-athena

"How Siemens built a fully managed scheduling mechanism for updates on Amazon S3 data lakes" – aws.amazon.com/blogs/big-data/how-siemens-built-a-fully-managed-scheduling-mechanism-for-consistent-updates-on-amazon-s3-data-lakes

"A public data lake for analysis of COVID-19 data" – aws.amazon.com/blogs/
big-data/a-public-data-lake-for-analysis-of-covid-19-data

"Build a cloud-native network performance analytics solution on AWS for wireless
service providers" – aws.amazon.com/blogs/big-data/
build-a-cloud-native-network-performance-analytics-solution-on-aws-for-
wireless-service-providers

"Query, visualize, and forecast TruFactor web session intelligence with AWS Data
Exchange" – aws.amazon.com/blogs/big-data/
query-visualize-and-forecast-trufactor-web-session-intelligence-with-
aws-data-exchange

"Build an AWS Well-Architected environment with the Analytics Lens" –aws.amazon
.com/blogs/big-data/
build-an-aws-well-architected-environment-with-the-analytics-lens

"Analyzing Google Analytics data with Amazon AppFlow and Amazon Athena" – aws
.amazon.com/blogs/big-data/
analyzing-google-analytics-data-with-amazon-appflow-and-amazon-athena

"Enforce column-level authorization with Amazon QuickSight and AWS Lake
Formation" – aws.amazon.com/blogs/big-data/enforce-column-level-
authorization-with-amazon-quicksight-and-aws-lake-formation

Amazon Redshift Blogs

"Restrict Amazon Redshift Spectrum external table access to Amazon Redshift IAM users
and groups using role chaining" – aws.amazon.com/blogs/big-data/
restrict-amazon-redshift-spectrum-external-table-access-to-amazon-
redshift-iam-users-and-groups-using-role-chaining

"Best practices for Amazon Redshift Federated Query" – aws.amazon.com/
blogs/big-data/
amazon-redshift-federated-query-best-practices-and-performance-
considerations

"Speed up your ELT and BI queries with Amazon Redshift materialized views" – aws.
amazon.com/blogs/big-data/
speed-up-your-elt-and-bi-queries-with-amazon-redshift-materialized-views

"Accelerate Amazon Redshift Federated Query adoption with AWS CloudFormation" – aws.amazon.com/blogs/big-data/
accelerate-amazon-redshift-federated-query-adoption-with-aws-
cloudformation

"Build a Simplified ETL and Live Data Query Solution using Redshift Federated
Query" – aws.amazon.com/blogs/big-data/
build-a-simplified-etl-and-live-data-query-solution-using-redshift-
federated-query

"Improved speed and scalability in Amazon Redshift" – aws.amazon.com/blogs/
big-data/improved-speed-and-scalability-in-amazon-redshift

"Lower your costs with the new pause and resume actions on Amazon Redshift" – aws
.amazon.com/blogs/big-data/
lower-your-costs-with-the-new-pause-and-resume-actions-on-amazon-
redshift

"Integrate Power BI with Amazon Redshift for insights and analytics" – `aws.amazon` `.com/blogs/big-data/` `integrate-power-bi-with-amazon-redshift-for-insights-and-analytics`

"Analyze your Amazon S3 spend using AWS Glue and Amazon Redshift" – `aws` `.amazon.com/blogs/big-data/` `analyze-your-amazon-s3-spend-using-aws-glue-and-amazon-redshift`

"ETL and ELT design patterns for lake house architecture using Amazon Redshift: Part 1" – `aws.amazon.com/blogs/big-data/` `etl-and-elt-design-patterns-for-lake-house-architecture-using-amazon-` `redshift-part-1`

"ETL and ELT design patterns for lake house architecture using Amazon Redshift: Part 2" – `aws.amazon.com/blogs/` `big-data/etl-and-elt-design-patterns-for-lake-house-architecture-using-` `amazon-redshift-part-2`

"Orchestrate Amazon Redshift-Based ETL workflows with AWS Step Functions and AWS Glue" – `aws.amazon.com/blogs/big-data/` `orchestrate-amazon-redshift-based-etl-workflows-with-aws-step-functions-` `and-aws-glue`

"Automate Amazon Redshift cluster creation using AWS CloudFormation" – `aws` `.amazon.com/blogs/big-data/` `automate-amazon-redshift-cluster-creation-using-aws-cloudformation`

"Bringing your stored procedures to Amazon Redshift" – `aws.amazon.com/blogs/` `big-data/bringing-your-stored-procedures-to-amazon-redshift`

"Orchestrate an ETL process using AWS Step Functions for Amazon Redshift" – `aws` `.amazon.com/blogs/big-data/` `orchestrating-an-etl-process-using-aws-step-functions-for-amazon-` `redshift/`

Amazon EMR Blogs

"Simplifying and modernizing home search at Compass with Amazon ES" – `aws.amazon` `.com/blogs/big-data/` `simplifying-and-modernizing-home-search-at-compass-with-amazon-es`

"Introducing Amazon EMR Managed Scaling – Automatically Resize Clusters to Lower Cost" – `aws.amazon.com/blogs/big-data/` `introducing-amazon-emr-managed-scaling-automatically-resize-clusters-to-` `lower-cost`

"Run Spark applications with Docker using Amazon EMR 6.0.0 (Beta)" –`aws.amazon` `.com/blogs/` `big-data/run-spark-applications-with-docker-using-amazon-emr-6-0-0-beta`

"Migrate and deploy your Apache Hive metastore on Amazon EMR" – `aws.amazon` `.com/blogs/big-data/` `migrate-and-deploy-your-apache-hive-metastore-on-amazon-emr`

Amazon Elasticsearch Blog

"Building a visual search application with Amazon SageMaker and Amazon ES" – `aws` `.amazon.com/blogs/machine-learning/building-a-visual-search-application-` `with-amazon-sagemaker-and-amazon-es`

Amazon Redshift References and Further Reading

Redshift Architecture – docs.aws.amazon.com/redshift/latest/dg/c_high_level_system_architecture.html

Redshift Lakehouse – docs.aws.amazon.com/redshift/latest/dg/c-using-spectrum.html

Nodes & Slices – docs.aws.amazon.com/redshift/latest/mgmt/working-with-clusters.html#rs-about-clusters-and-nodes

VPC – docs.aws.amazon.com/redshift/latest/mgmt/getting-started-cluster-in-vpc.html

Cluster Subnet Groups – docs.aws.amazon.com/redshift/latest/mgmt/working-with-cluster-subnet-groups.html

Cluster Security Groups – docs.aws.amazon.com/redshift/latest/mgmt/working-with-security-groups.html

Cluster Parameter Groups – docs.aws.amazon.com/redshift/latest/mgmt/working-with-parameter-groups.html

Loading data to Redshift using COPY Command – https://docs.aws.amazon.com/redshift/latest/dg/t_Loading_tables_with_the_COPY_command.html

Loading data to Redshift from S3 – https://docs.aws.amazon.com/redshift/latest/dg/t_Loading-data-from-S3.html

Loading data to Redshift from Amazon EMR – https://docs.aws.amazon.com/redshift/latest/dg/loading-data-from-emr.html

Loading data to Amazon Redshift from Amazon Kinesis Data Firehose – aws.amazon.com/kinesis/data-firehose/firehose-to-redshift

Amazon Redshift Data Loading Best Practices –docs.aws.amazon.com/redshift/latest/dg/c_loading-data-best-practices.html

Table Tuning Tutorial –docs.aws.amazon.com/redshift/latest/dg/tutorial-tuning-tables.html

Micro-batch Loading – aws.amazon.com/blogs/big-data/best-practices-for-micro-batch-loading-on-amazon-redshift

Security Overview – docs.aws.amazon.com/redshift/latest/dg/c_security-overview.html

Cluster Access – docs.aws.amazon.com/redshift/latest/mgmt/iam-redshift-user-mgmt.html

Managed Users and Privileges – docs.aws.amazon.com/redshift/latest/dg/r_Database_objects.html

Chapter

5

Data Visualization

THE AWS CERTIFIED ANALYTICS SPECIALTY EXAM OBJECTIVES COVERED IN THIS CHAPTER MAY INCLUDE, BUT ARE NOT LIMITED TO, THE FOLLOWING:

✓ **Domain 4: Analysis and Visualization**

- 4.1 Determine the operational characteristics of an analysis and visualization solution

- 4.2 Select the appropriate data analysis solution for a given scenario

- 4.3 Select the appropriate data visualization solution for a given scenario

Introduction

We have now seen how you can ingest, store, process, and analyze your data on your analytics platform. However, the objective of doing most of this work is to prepare data for consumption by multiple stakeholders. One of the most common ways to consume this data is using a data visualization tool, and the solution that you choose needs to meet certain requirements. In the age when we have abundant data coming from multiple sources, data visualization becomes a challenge, and there is no single way to optimally visualize your data across the broad spectrum of use cases. The Amazon Web Services platform offers a number of ways by which you can visualize the data, including EMR and SageMaker notebooks, Kibana dashboards, and a purpose-built tool called Amazon QuickSight. In this chapter, we'll look at the different ways and means by which you can visualize your data, the pros and cons of each approach, and the scenario under which each visualization approach is recommended.

The AWS Data Analytics Specialty Certification exam will test you on various scenarios and will expect you to choose the best solution based on cost, performance, and security perspective. Your scenario might have options around a dynamic or static nature of a presentation, and the solution that you choose must represent the use case. You will also come across cases where you are provided with certain performance parameters for the solution and you will be required to choose the most optimal solution, which can be either an on-demand aggregation of data or a need to pre-aggregate the data for the user requirements.

You will also be tested on the appropriate delivery mechanisms (web, mobile, email, and so on) and a potential refresh schedule of the visualizations. Other areas where a candidate is tested include the ability of the candidate to select the right visualization for an interactive analysis.

Data Consumers

A data platform has multiple consumers, each needing a slightly different way to consume the data.

Data consumers on your analytical platform can be categorized into the following categories:

Data Experts   Data experts make up a category of consumers who are subject matter experts and have deep domain knowledge around the data. They are responsible for building new key performance indicators (KPIs) to measure business performance using a variety of techniques, including their dependence on advanced data visualizations to create and communicate the KPIs to other stakeholders.

Business Users   Business users are typically the prime users of visualization tools as they use the KPIs that have been developed by the data experts to steer the business. They typically operate at an aggregated level of data and often perform slice-and-dice analysis, including building and using dashboards and depending on standardized reports that might have been created by other members in the team or were created on a self-service basis.

Data Scientists   Data scientists look at the datasets that have arrived from source systems or the ones that have been prepared by data engineers to find evidence for the ideas that could be implemented and build new data products. They are interested in exploring the datasets to understand the correlation between features and the spread of the data to build machine learning models. These data scientists often access raw data and need the ability to work with datasets in as raw a form as possible.

Downstream Systems   Your data platform may act as an information hub that feeds internal and external systems, where your main role is to centralize the data flow for other systems and provide ad hoc or scheduled feeds to other systems.

Operational Applications   Your operational applications may depend directly on your data platform to enable smart applications and services. In most cases the applications will depend on granular data with ultra-low latency. An example could be your call-center application trying to understand a consumer's past transactions or complaints to provide a better experience.

Data visualization is therefore a critical component and helps various consumers meet their needs. Figure 5.1 shows the various consumers in a data and analytics platform and the services from which they typically consume the data.

FIGURE 5.1   Data and analytics consumption patterns

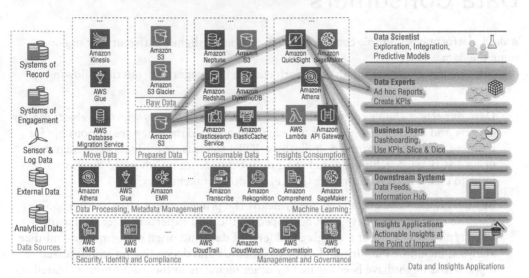

Data and Insights Applications

Data Visualization Options

AWS platform provides various options to visualize the data. The options include using EMR notebooks, Kibana, and Amazon QuickSight. As seen in the preceding section, different consumers prefer different sorts of data visualizations, and hence the needs differ. For example, a data scientist using EMR notebooks or Amazon SageMaker for feature engineering is trying to understand the patterns in the data in an ad hoc fashion. They might prefer staying in the environment where they are doing the majority of the work to generate appropriate visualizations to better explore and understand the data.

On the other hand, we have a business analyst who would like to explore the data that has been made available with Amazon Athena and build dashboards for the campaigns that have recently been launched. This particular user is perhaps better suited working with Amazon QuickSight instead of making use of the Python libraries to generate the charts.

You can also use open-source libraries like D3.JS, Graphviz, Plotly, and Highcharts for web-based visualizations.

Let's look at all the options provided by AWS and understand the intricacies of using the right visualization tool for the right requirement.

Amazon QuickSight

Business intelligence (BI) refers to a combination of processes, technologies, architectural patterns, and best practices that are used to convert data from data sources into information that is meaningful to the business and aids in measuring and driving key performance indicators (KPIs). BI is usually performed by a set of software tools and services provided by various consulting vendors to convert raw data into actionable information.

There is an abundance of enterprise BI tools in the market, from legacy BI providers to upcoming BI startups; however, there is a clear shift toward self-service BI. The shift is happening due to the expensive traditional BI setups in terms of scale, time, and cost. A traditional BI setup requires experienced data engineers to prepare the dataset and build up complex backend infrastructure, which can then be used to build reports, which can often mean unnecessary complexity in the build process when all that is required is quick access to the data to understand patterns and make decisions based on the data. The time for traditional BI implementations ranges from six to nine months, often delivering results in a waterfall model, where the typical challenges of customer requirements changing due to changing business needs results in unsatisfied customers and stakeholders. This has resulted in a market shift toward the self-service BI movement, and Amazon QuickSight is one of the most popular cloud-powered BI services offering to bridge this gap between traditional BI and the growing need for self-service BI.

Amazon QuickSight has been architected to deliver superior low-latency performance. The following key areas differentiate Amazon QuickSight from other solutions:

- *Short Learning Curve:* Amazon QuickSight was built with the intention to empower all roles within the organization to benefit from the vast amounts of data being generated from various sources. With basic IT knowledge, you can load the data by pointing to a data source and start building data visualizations and generating actionable insights within minutes.

- *Support for a Variety of Data Sources:* Amazon QuickSight's popularity stems from the fact that it supports a number of sources, including various AWS native services like Amazon S3, Amazon Redshift, Amazon RDS, Amazon DynamoDB, and Amazon Kinesis in addition to various non-native services. This is a key requirement for self-service BI, as business users often like to point to a source, load the data, and start exploring it without looking into the complexity of the underlying integrations.

- *In-Memory Data Backend:* Amazon QuickSight is powered by the SPICE (Super-Fast. Parallel, In-Memory Calculation) engine, which allows you to perform calculations on data that is memory resident, which in turn allows you to perform better due to fewer trips to fetch the data back from the source.

- *Simplicity to Create and Share Analytics:* Amazon QuickSight is built for nontechnical users, allowing them to interact on the data directly to build reports and dashboards and share it with other users. Amazon QuickSight's ability to allow users of all technical expertise to handle data directly is a powerful construct that has led to its widespread adoption among a wide variety of organizations.
- *Scalability and Cost:* Amazon QuickSight's serverless nature allows you to work with datasets of various sizes at a fraction of the cost of various on-premises BI solutions.

Getting Started

Amazon QuickSight is available in the Analytics section of your AWS services. If you are the first Amazon QuickSight user on your AWS account, you will be eligible for free use of Amazon QuickSight with one gigabyte of SPICE capacity. When you open Amazon QuickSight, you will see a screen similar to Figure 5.2.

As Figure 5.2 indicates, you can start by managing your datasets (top right), which includes viewing existing datasets, setting permissions, duplicating datasets, sharing datasets, or creating analysis on a particular dataset. We'll look at data preparation with Amazon QuickSight in a bit more detail later in this chapter. You can also start by creating a new analysis, using the New Analysis option on the top left of the screen, which will take you to a new analysis screen, allowing you to choose a dataset on which the analysis can be based.

FIGURE 5.2 Amazon QuickSight overview

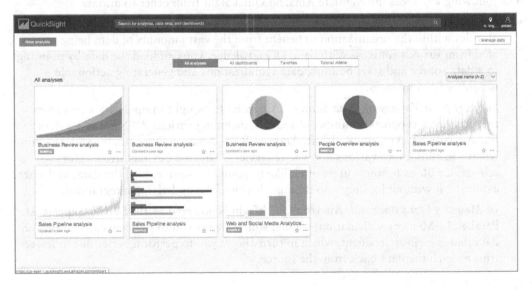

Let's build an analysis on Sales Pipeline data available as a sample dataset in your Amazon QuickSight console.

1. Log in to Amazon QuickSight and click the New Analysis button.

2. This will load your existing datasets. For the purpose of this quick demo, we will use the Sales Pipeline dataset that is available with Amazon QuickSight.

3. Click the Sales Pipeline dataset.

4. You will see the status as the Sales Pipeline dataset loads; it should contain 20,994 rows. You can set permissions, edit, share, or delete the dataset. We are going to simply select the Create Analysis button.

5. This will open the QuickSight screen with a new sheet. You will see a list of visual types on the bottom left. At the moment, we will be looking at the stage at which different opportunities lie. Let's drop the opportunity stage on the empty pane. Amazon QuickSight's auto-graphing ability will render a bar chart (see Figure 5.3) to display the number of records per opportunity stage.

As you saw in the preceding example, Amazon QuickSight used AutoGraph to choose a visual type based on the dataset it saw. Amazon QuickSight uses a rule-based engine behind the scenes to select the most appropriate visual based on the data cardinality and offers a set of visuals based on the usage patterns that some other users might be interested in. The user can, however, customize the visuals based on the specific business requirements.

FIGURE 5.3   Frequency per opportunity stage

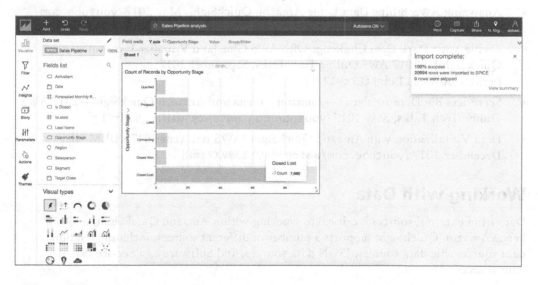

I hope this has given you a basic understanding of the service itself. I would highly recommend viewing some of the following demos that demonstrate Amazon QuickSight and give you a basic understanding of different features and functions:

- Data Visualization with Amazon QuickSight (AWS re:Invent 2017 - DEM74), December 2017 (youtube.com/watch?v=Ul3J8VX7zmM)

- Sharing Your Analysis and Insights Using Amazon QuickSight, May 2017 (youtube .com/watch?v=xusKVM5NiCE)

- Customizing Your Visuals in Amazon QuickSight, May 2017 (youtube.com/ watch?v=UKxkPi5mJno)

- Using SQL to Import Data into Amazon QuickSight, May 2017 (youtube.com/ watch?v=x9RUtTzqpr0)

- Accessing Amazon Redshift Data from Amazon QuickSight, May 2017 (youtube .com/watch?v=CRcRS3qos-A)

- Deep Dive on Amazon QuickSight—January 2017 AWS Online Tech Talks, January 2017 (youtube.com/watch?v=gy1AcdJMsMk)

- Building Visualizations and Dashboards with Amazon QuickSight (AWS re:Invent 2017 - ABD206), December 2017 (youtube.com/watch?v=dprtSTSbCEE)

- Serverless Analytics—Amazon Redshift Spectrum, AWS Glue, and Amazon QuickSight, October 2017 (youtube.com/watch?v=fORJ6y572gs)

- Visualizing Amazon S3 Storage Management with Amazon QuickSight—2017 AWS Online Tech Talks, August 2017 (youtube.com/watch?v=4vmL05KVqTA)

- Deploying Business Analytics at Enterprise Scale with Amazon QuickSight (AWS re:Invent 2017 - ABD311), December 2017 (youtube.com/watch?v=G4Dgzlo3gQI)

- Analyzing AWS Billing Data Using Amazon QuickSight, May 2017 (youtube.com/ watch?v=2JnfuAA-TiU)

- Tackle Your Dark Data Challenge with AWS Glue (and Visualize It in Amazon QuickSight)—2017 AWS Online Tech Talks, September 2017 (youtu.be/Q0m2TligKtE?t=1226)

- Serverless Big Data Analytics—Amazon Athena and Amazon QuickSight—2017 AWS Online Tech Talks, May 2017 (youtube.com/watch?v=m1HTL_SJHrE)

- Data Visualization with Amazon QuickSight (AWS re:Invent 2017 - DEM74), December 2017 (youtube.com/watch?v=Ul3J8VX7zmM)

Working with Data

Data from external sources is critical to working within Amazon QuickSight, and hence Amazon QuickSight supports a number of different sources, including relational data sources, file data sources, JSON data sources, and Software as a Service (SaaS) data sources.

There are some key concepts that you need to be aware of before working with data in Amazon QuickSight. Amazon QuickSight offers the ability to tap into data sources and then create datasets from the configured sources:

- A *data source* is the origin of the data, such as a data file, a database, or an SaaS-based source.

- A *dataset* is the data that you have loaded into SPICE after extracting relevant columns from the source doing filtering and other aggregations.

At the time of this writing, Amazon QuickSight supports the creation of datasets from the data sources listed in the sections listed below.

File Data Sources/JSON Data Sources

Amazon QuickSight supports loading data from the common file formats CSV, TSV, CLF (Common Log Format), ELF (Extended Log Format), XLSX (Microsoft Excel files), and JSON data files. Amazon QuickSight provides native support for JSON data and automatically performs schema and type inference on JSON files and embedded JSON objects.

Relational Data Sources

Amazon QuickSight supports the following relational data sources:

- Amazon Athena
- Amazon RDS
- Amazon Redshift (auto-discovered)
- Amazon Redshift (manual connect)
- MySQL
- PostgreSQL
- Microsoft SQL Server
- Amazon Aurora
- MariaDB
- Apache Presto
- Apache Spark
- Teradata
- Snowflake
- Amazon S3 Analytics
- Amazon S3
- AWS IoT Analytics

Software as a Service (SaaS) Data Sources

Amazon QuickSight supports the following SaaS data sources:

- Salesforce (connecting to a Salesforce domain)
- GitHub
- Twitter
- Jira
- ServiceNow
- Adobe Analytics

When loading data from Amazon S3, Amazon QuickSight seamlessly handles zip and gzip compression. If you have used a different compression algorithm, you have to un-compress the files locally before loading them onto Amazon QuickSight. Figure 5.4 shows the data connectivity options with Amazon QuickSight.

As you can see, Amazon QuickSight offers support for a number of different data sources, each of which provide different read performance. Amazon QuickSight can, however, provide uniform performance with SPICE, an engine that powers Amazon Quick-Sight. SPICE is an in-memory calculation engine, which stores the data in a columnar format, making it ideally suitable for analytical queries. You can bring a portion of the dataset or the complete dataset into memory, and you can create additional calculated columns as you need them. Data loaded into the SPICE engine is stored across multiple Availability Zones with backups in Amazon S3, which makes it a highly durable engine.

In a traditional BI environment, organizations build replicas of their data or data marts, which are precalculated and pre-aggregated to provide an acceptable performance for their users. The challenge, however, with those approaches is that you are limited by the pre-aggregations and calculations that have been done on the dataset, and this limits your

FIGURE 5.4 Amazon QuickSight supported data sources

ability to find responses to new questions as you interact and better understand the data. Amazon QuickSight loads this dataset in memory, which provides you with the ability to perform calculations and slice and dice the data as per your requirements on a huge scale.

While the exam does not test you on the specific limits for Amazon QuickSight, it is good to know from an architectural perspective the key limits that may help you decide between one architecture and another. Table 5.1 lists the key limits in SPICE at the time of this writing.

Amazon QuickSight allows you to create new data sources, edit an existing data source, and delete a data source as well. If you would like Amazon QuickSight to be able to access data from your database, you need to make it accessible and hence configure it appropriately. Please follow the network and database configuration requirements (amzn .to/2PV8NnJ) for your databases to be accessible by Amazon QuickSight. As you can see from the list of data sources, Amazon QuickSight also offers the ability to analyze data from SaaS applications by using SaaS connectors to connect to the data sources using OAuth, thus removing the need for an intermediate data store as is often required for these sources. The key requirement is that Amazon QuickSight should be able to access the applications Domain Name System (DNS) name over the network. If Amazon QuickSight can't access the SaaS application, it will generate an unknown host error.

TABLE 5.1   Key SPICE limits

SPICE Key Area	Description/Limit
No. of columns per dataset	1000
No. of Unicode characters per column name	127
No. of Unicode characters per column value	2047
No. of files in Amazon S3 Manifest	1000
No. of rows per dataset (Standard edition)	25 million (25,000,000) rows per dataset
No. of rows per dataset (Enterprise edition)	100 million (100,000,000) rows per dataset.
Maximum size of dataset (Standard edition)	25 GB
Maximum size of the dataset (Enterprise edition)	200 GB
Query timeout to a database	2 minutes
Query projection list	1000 columns

You can edit an existing database data source and update the connection information (such as server name or updated user credentials). You can also edit an existing Amazon Athena data source and update the data source name, but you can't edit Amazon S3 or Salesforce data sources.

You can delete a data source based on your needs. Deletion of a query-based database data source will make all associated datasets unusable. If you are deleting an Amazon S3, Salesforce, or SPICE-based database data source, you are essentially just deleting the data source, but you can continue to use the associated datasets. The data for the data sources is stored in SPICE. However, you can no longer refresh those datasets, as the associated data sources may no longer exist.

Amazon QuickSight allows you to create datasets from existing data sources or new data sources, in addition to providing the option to edit a dataset where you can select a subset of the fields, add calculated fields, or augment your data from SageMaker. You can also rename the column headers and apply filters to your datasets. Figure 5.5 shows the various options available to you for editing an existing dataset.

Amazon QuickSight also offers the possibility to duplicate the dataset to create an entirely new copy of the data and refresh the dataset from the source. You can also change or replace the dataset, share a dataset with other Amazon QuickSight users in the same AWS account, verify the permissions on the dataset, or revoke access to the dataset from other users.

You can also restrict access to the dataset using row-level security; however, this feature is only available in the Enterprise edition of the product.

Finally, just like a data source, you can delete a dataset, which will render all dependent objects including analysis to stop working. It is highly recommended to replace the dataset for any dependent analysis or dashboard before you delete the underlying dataset.

FIGURE 5.5 Editing a dataset – Amazon QuickSight

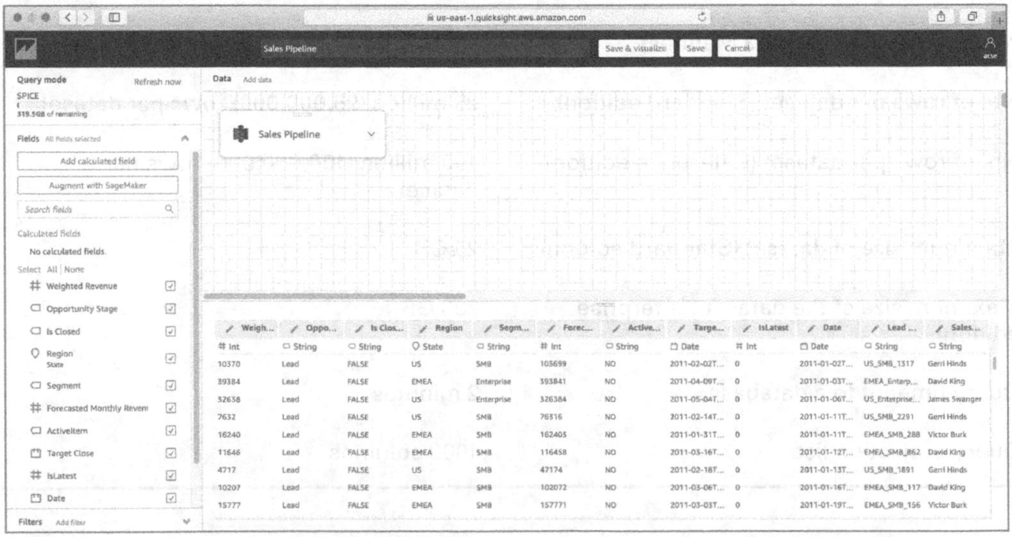

Data Preparation

We had looked in earlier chapters on the options to prepare and transform data using a variety of tools. Data Analysts and business users have the ability to prepare the data within Amazon QuickSight so that the dataset can be reused across multiple analysis.

Data preparation within Amazon QuickSight includes the following:

- Adding new fields calculated based on data from other fields
- Applying data filters based on business needs to the original data fields or the calculated fields
- Changing field names and data types
- Joining tables to merge data between different datasets if the source data is a SQL database
- Working with data from more than a single table using SQL queries to enable you to work across multiple datasets

Once you have prepared the dataset using any number of the above options, you can save it for reuse later across multiple analysis, including creating a copy of the dataset.

Amazon QuickSight uses the AND condition while applying all top-level filters. For example, if you have a filter of age=35 and salary>=35000, you will get the results that meet the criteria for both of these filters. You can view the filters applied on the dataset in the filters pane.

Data visualization often requires data visualized over the map of a state, a province, or a country. Amazon QuickSight also provides the option to flag geographic fields in your data so that Amazon QuickSight can display them on a map. Amazon QuickSight can automatically chart latitude and longitude coordinates, and it also recognizes geographical components such as country, state, county, city, and zip code. The Data Preparation page on the Amazon QuickSight application allows you to label the geographical data with the correct data type.

Amazon SageMaker Integration

While visualization is typically focused on events that have happened in the past, you can author dashboards that are powered with machine learning and you can augment them with Amazon SageMaker machine learning (ML) models.

Applying inference on data stored in SPICE from any data source supported by Amazon QuickSight makes it a very powerful combination as it allows you to combine hindsight and foresight at the same time. Examples of cases where you need integration with machine learning capabilities includes predicting likelihood of customer churn or employee attrition, scoring sales leads, and assessing credit risks. You can use any kind of machine learning model from Amazon SageMaker as long as the data is in tabular format. To learn more about setting up Amazon QuickSight and Amazon SageMaker integration, please refer to amzn.to/2TBEXqB.

Data Analysis

Creating, acquiring, and preparing datasets were all typically done for the purpose of analyzing data. You can use various analysis options with Amazon QuickSight to analyze the data using visuals and stories. An analysis within Amazon QuickSight is a container of related visualizations and stories, all built with the objective of satisfying a particular business goal or providing the ability to measure one or a set of key performance indicators for the business. You can create up to 20 visuals in a single analysis.

Amazon QuickSight allows you to create, save, rename, and delete an analysis in addition to using multiple sheets in an analysis to organize the content. A sheet is a set of visuals that are viewed together in a single page. You can add to your analysis more sheets that can work independently or together in the analysis. At this point I would like readers to open the Amazon QuickSight application and explore the features around analysis creation and management. If you have not used Amazon QuickSight before, I highly recommend you look at the videos that I shared in the section "Getting Started" earlier in the chapter. During AWS re:Invent 2017, Luis Wang (then principal product manager with AWS) was presenting with Randy Carnevale (then working as director of data science at Transfix) on the topic of building visualization and dashboards with Amazon QuickSight. His talk can be accessed at (bit.ly/3cGZdi7); he starts the demo at around 20 minutes into the talk, and the demo lasts for about 20 minutes. Although Amazon QuickSight has added lots of new features over the past three years, the demo should give you a good starting point with Amazon QuickSight.

You might often need to export the data powering an analysis for various reasons, including regulatory compliance. Amazon QuickSight provides you the option to explore data from an analysis or dashboard to a comma-separated value (CSV) file.

You can add datasets to analysis, replace, or edit existing datasets or to modify dataset fields in an analysis.

Setting Up Parameters in Amazon QuickSight

Business users require simple ways to interact with dashboards and connect them with one another. For example, you might want to visualize a dashboard with sales for the southeast of England rather than all areas, and you would want to pick a value from a list that then filters and updates the dashboard for that specific region. This is often achieved by using parameters in Amazon QuickSight.

Parameters are therefore named variables that can be used to contain or transfer a value to be used by an action or an object. Parameters help nontechnical users navigate the dashboard and visuals within a dashboard while also allowing them to connect dashboards or provide drill-down features.

Parameters are made available to the viewers of the dashboard via parameter control. Amazon QuickSight allows you to set up cascading controls, so that a selection in one control filters the options that are being displayed in another control. A control can appear in one of the following three ways:

- List of options
- A slider
- Text entry area

Controls are not the only way to pass the values to the dashboard. You can also pass values to the parameters with a dashboard URL, which means you can create custom URLs depending on the different job profiles or areas under management.

Parameters need to be connected to your analysis via calculated fields, filters, dashboard and analysis URLs, or actions. When you are using parameters in a URL, you can use the parameter name and value in Amazon QuickSight to set a default value for the parameter in a dashboard or analysis.

Amazon QuickSight can use *custom actions* to launch URLs or filter visuals by selecting a data point in a visual or choosing an action name from the context menu. When you use a URL action with a parameter, you can pass or send parameters dynamically to the URL. The parameters on both the sending and the receiving end must match in name and data type. All parameters are compatible with URL actions.

Using Themes in Amazon QuickSight

I have been fortunate enough to work with a number of corporations during my career and have come across various organizations in which it was mandated to prepare corporate reports on a standard theme. Having to reapply the settings repeatedly can become a challenge and often leads to reports where the settings are not standardized across multiple reports or dashboards. Amazon QuickSight offers themes as a collection of settings that you can apply to multiple analyses and dashboards, thus allowing you the ability to standardize the outputs within your organization. Amazon Quick-Sight includes some prebuilt themes, but it also allows you to add your own themes by using the theme editor. You can share themes with permissions levels set to user or owner. Anyone who has access to the theme can apply it to analyses and dashboards or use Save As to make their own copy of it. As a theme owner you can edit and share your theme with other users.

At any given point in time a single theme can be applied to an analysis, and application of a theme is instantaneous for everyone using the analysis and dashboard.

Sharing Amazon QuickSight Analysis

You can share analysis with other users by sending a shareable link, which helps in sharing the work that you have done across the organization. At the time of this writing, an analysis can only be shared with users within the same account, and hence if you have a multi-account strategy, you will not be able to share the analysis to users in other accounts.

For various compliance reasons, you might need to know the users who have access to your analysis. This can be achieved with Amazon QuickSight using the Manage Analysis Access option. You can also optionally revoke access to an analysis if you feel that a particular user or group should no longer have the privilege to view the analysis that you have created.

Storyboarding within Amazon QuickSight

Storyboarding is an important way to understand the operation of a business. You can also preserve multiple iterations of an analysis using a story. An example could be looking at the same charts for revenue numbers. You can use customer acquisition and churn numbers and average revenue per user but across various quarters over the past two years to understand how the business has performed over time. You can also use a scene, which is just a captured iteration of an analysis. A scene preserves visuals that are in the analysis at the time of creation, including filters and sort orders. Data that powers the visuals is not part of the scene. When you are playing the story, visuals will reflect the current data in the dataset. Every analysis comes with a default storyboard called Storyboard 1. You can add scenes to the storyboard by choosing the Capture option on the application bar.

Data Visualization

A visual is a graphic representation of your dataset. An analysis can contain a number of different visuals from various datasets. Visuals can be created, edited, and modified, including things like visual types, changing behind-the-scenes visual data, and applying filters on the data. You can have up to 20 datasets per analysis, and up to 20 visuals in a single analysis.

You can create visuals in three different ways:

- **AutoGraph** – AutoGraph is an Amazon QuickSight feature that lets you solicit help from Amazon QuickSight to determine the most appropriate visual type.

- **Choosing Visual Type** – You can optionally choose a visual type and choose the fields to populate the visual.

- **Amazon QuickSight Suggested Visuals** – If you are unsure what queries your data can help you answer, you can choose the Suggested on the tool bar and choose one of the Amazon QuickSight suggested options.

The key elements to visualize data are "dimensions" against which you "measure" your KPIs. Dimensions in Amazon QuickSight have blue icons, and measures have green icons. Examples of dimensions are products, items, orders, channels, order dates, and so on, whereas examples of measures are numeric values that can be used to measure, compare, or aggregate against KPIs. You will typically use a combination of dimensions and measures while building a visual. For example, customer acquisition numbers (a measure) by acquisition date (a dimension) can produce a visual that generates the number of customers being acquired during various times of a year, quarter, month, or day.

You can learn more about creating a visual by following AWS documentation at `amzn .to/2WjS4hI`. You can duplicate visuals, rename visuals, delete visuals, export the underlying data to CSV files, change the layout of a visual, view the underlying data and apply different kinds of formatting (such as title, legends, labels, styling, and conditional formatting). Once you have created a visual, you can always add or modify the fields used in the visual from the Fields List pane or by dropping the fields directly on the visual.

Amazon QuickSight also supports drill-downs in all visuals (except pivot tables), which can be achieved by building a hierarchy of fields. For example, you can associate country, state, and city fields with the x-axis on the bar chart and then drill down to see data at each of the levels. The exam will ask you about the possibility of Amazon QuickSight's drill-down feature. However, I would highly recommend that you learn more about adding drill-downs by visiting the following AWS documentation page (since the details are out of scope for this certification preparation title): amzn.to/38L6sSU.

Amazon QuickSight also gives you the ability to use custom actions for your visuals. You can create a *Filter action* and a *URL action*. A Filter action can help you filter one or more visuals when you choose a data point or a menu item. For example, you can choose a department in a visual, and the action filters the data according to the selection. You can show the highest sales performers from that particular department, revenue numbers, or any other metrics of importance. Filter actions can be used across multiple datasets. The URL action can be used for things like creating a link to another URL from your visual or creating an email directly from the visual. Users viewing the dashboards can use the URL action to send data points to other URLs (dashboards, analysis, and websites) by selecting a data point (left-click) or selecting the action from the data point context (right-click) menu. It is highly recommended that you practice the addition of custom actions to your visuals before the exam to give you more clarity about the purpose of creating custom actions and the possibilities within Amazon QuickSight.

Finally, Amazon QuickSight offers a variety of visual types that you can use in your analysis, including bar charts, combo charts, donut charts, gauge charts, geospatial charts (maps), heat maps, KPIs, line charts, pivot tables, scatter plots, tree maps, and word clouds.

One of the most common questions on the exam concerns choosing an appropriate visualization type for the scenario in question. The following table is a quick overview of the type of visualizations available in Amazon QuickSight and the most suitable use case for each.

TABLE 5.2   Amazon QuickSight visualization types

Visualization Type	Description	Suitable Use Case
AutoGraph	AutoGraph is Amazon QuickSight's way of assisting you in choosing the right visual for you.	Any
Bar chart	Amazon QuickSight offers a variety of bar charts, in both horizontal and vertical orientation, including single-measure, multi-measure, clustered, stacked, and stacked 100 percent.	Compare groups, track and measure changes over time.
Line charts	Amazon QuickSight offers a variety of line charts, including simple line charts, area charts, and stacked area line charts.	Compare changes in value for one or more measures or dimensions over time.

TABLE 5.2   Amazon QuickSight visualization types *(continued)*

Visualization Type	Description	Suitable Use Case
Combo charts	Amazon QuickSight supports both clustered and stacked bar combo charts. Combo charts (often referred to as line and column charts) are useful for comparing categories over time, which is essentially a strength of line and bar charts.	Compare groups, track and measure changes over time.
Donut charts	Donut charts, shaped like a donut, represent a value in a dimension and are quite popular aesthetically.	Compare values for items in a dimension such as percentage of a total amount.
Gauge charts	Gauge charts are like an analog gauge in an automobile. They are often used to compare measures and are a good representation for attainment of various KPIs in dashboards with green, yellow, and red showing the various ranges.	Compare values for items in a measure.
Geospatial charts/ Maps	Geospatial charts represent data values over a map allowing zoom capabilities.	Geographical datasets such as sales across various states in the US
Heat maps	Heat maps are graphical representations of data that utilize color-coded systems. They can be used to show a measure at the intersection of two dimensions with color coding to provide additional visual representation of the ranges.	Color-coded systems, identify trends, outliers
Histograms	Amazon QuickSight supports histograms, which look similar to bar charts but are quite different as each bar represents a bin/bucket rather than an individual value.	Understand the distribution of your data. Often used by data scientists and ML engineers
KPIs	One of the most common items in a dashboard is a KPI measurement, which is actually a comparison between two values, often an achieved value vs. the target value. Amazon QuickSight offers KPI as a visualization option, which provides a value and an attainment progress bar.	Dashboards, KPI measurements
Pie charts	The pie chart is another chart type used to compare values for a given dimension and is a good way to show a percentage of a total amount.	Composition understanding, Number of observations per category, etc.

Visualization Type	Description	Suitable Use Case
Pivot charts	Pivot charts are similar to heat maps as both measure values at the intersection of dimensions. However, pivot charts are better at analyzing the data on the visual, unlike heat maps, which are for trends and outliers.	Analyzing data on a visual
Scatter plot	Scatter plots are one of the most common visuals that are used to visualize two or three measures for a dimension. While the bubble appears at the intersection of the two measures for a particular dimension, the size of the bubble is often represented by a third dimension.	Patterns in data, understanding unexpected data gaps or outliers. Often used by data scientists or ML engineers
Tree maps	Tree maps are used to visualize one or two measures for a dimension. The rectangle size represents the value of the selected measure that the item represents compared to the whole for the dimension. You can use rectangle color to represent another measure for the item.	Best used to study high-level summary of similarities and anomalies within one category as well as multiple categories
Word clouds	A word cloud is a good way to do text analytics and determine how a word is used in relation to other words in the dataset.	Best for phrase or word frequency. Used to text analytics like tweet text and Facebook posts to identify the patterns in the data

Machine Learning Insights

As the volume of data grows, the challenges to make sense of that data and act upon it increase as well. Amazon QuickSight allows the customers to retrospectively inspect their data in addition to using some of the ML capabilities built over the years at Amazon.com. The capabilities include ML-powered anomaly detection, which helps the customers uncover hidden insights by continuously analyzing billions of data points; auto-narrative using natural language processing, which helps the customers tell the story of their dashboard in a plain-language narrative; and ML-powered forecasting and what-if analysis in dashboards.

At the time of this writing, ML-powered sentiment analysis and ML-powered entity extraction were on the roadmap but were not released yet. I am hoping that by the time this book is released, you will have the ability to experiment with these capabilities with Amazon QuickSight.

Anomaly detection is basically detection of outliers, which can help you identify top drivers that contribute a significant change to your business metrics, such as, for example, higher than expected customer sales, or a significant customer churn or an increase or a dip in the number of downloads of your mobile app. Amazon QuickSight uses the Random

Cut Forest algorithm on millions of metrics and billions of data points to highlight the deep insights often impossible to find using manual analysis.

Figure 5.6 shows anomaly detection being run on Sales Pipeline data, which is available with Amazon QuickSight as demo data.

Forecasting is an important operational research technique used for management planning and decision-making and can be instrumental in turning a company into a profitable venture or a loss-making entity. Having the right amount of inventory can reduce your overall inventory cost or can be the difference between unsatisfied customers and increased revenue. Amazon QuickSight uses nontechnical users to forecast key business metrics using built-in ML Random Cut Forest algorithm, which automatically handles complex real-world scenarios like detecting seasonality and trends, excluding outliers, and automatically imputing missing values.

Support for auto-narratives in Amazon QuickSight can help build rich dashboards with embedded narratives that explain the story of your data in plain language, thus making it simple to understand and actionable. This will help you build the same understanding of the graph across the enterprise and can be thought of as having a personal data analyst telling the story to your users.

Building Dashboards

A dashboard is a read-only snapshot of analysis that is built to share and report key information across and outside of your Amazon QuickSight account. A dashboard is a point-in-time representation of analysis at the time of publishing that includes things like

FIGURE 5.6   Anomaly detection in Amazon QuickSight

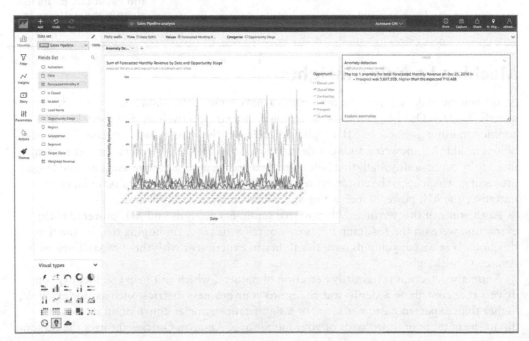

filters applied to the data, parameters that have been set, controls, and sort order. When you create a dashboard, the data that powers the analysis is not captured, which means that a dashboard will always reflect the current data in the analysis.

Dashboard owners can edit and share the dashboard in addition to the ability to edit and share the analysis (see Figure 5.7). A shared dashboard can be embedded in your website or application, which we will look into in slightly more detail in the next section.

FIGURE 5.7 Sharing dashboards in Amazon QuickSight

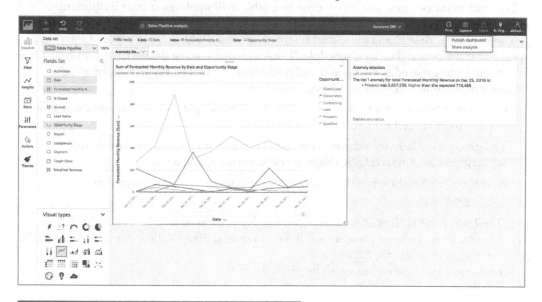

Sharing an analysis as a dashboard is as simple as selecting the Share option and publishing it as a dashboard. This will allow you to either publish it as a new dashboard or replace an existing dashboard, and provide advanced options around dashboard controls, visual options, and data point options. For example, for dashboard options you can select expanding on-sheet controls, enabling ad hoc filtering, and enabling on-hover tooltips to provide better usability.

For visual options, you can enable visual menus and CSV downloads of your underlying data.

For data point options, you can choose to enable drill up/down if your dashboard doesn't offer drillable field hierarchies, enable on-click tooltips, and enable sorting options.

You can copy, delete, and share dashboards and send dashboards in report forms via email either on-demand or on a schedule. The feature of sharing dashboards is only available in the Enterprise edition of Amazon QuickSight. To receive reports via email, the group members must meet the following conditions:

- Group members should be part of an Amazon QuickSight subscription and you should already have shared the dashboards with them.

- The group members should have completed the sign-up process to activate the subscription as Amazon QuickSight readers, authors, and admins.

- Amazon QuickSight limits the scheduled emails to groups with fewer than 5,000 members.

In the Enterprise edition of Amazon QuickSight, you can subscribe to dashboards in report form. To learn more about subscribing to reports, please follow Amazon QuickSight documentation at amzn.to/2U8WR2T.

Dashboards and analyses can also be printed.

Embedding QuickSight Objects into Other Applications

While you can provide users within your account access to Amazon QuickSight, you might need to embed the dashboards in your web properties or mobile applications. This might help you focus on your core product and leave the heavy lifting of scalability and faster response times to Amazon QuickSight. Users can receive a personalized dashboard without performing a user-facing authentication, and the dashboard viewers can be any Amazon QuickSight users such as readers, authors, or admins who may have been authenticated into your account:

- Active Directory (AD) users or group members
- Invited non-federated users
- IAM users and IAM role-based sessions authenticated using federated single sign-on using SAML, OpenID Connect, or IAM Federation

Embedding a dashboard involves five major steps:

1. Create a dashboard in Amazon QuickSight. Publish the dashboard and share it with the groups and users who should be able to view it. Add domains in allow lists, including the domain of the web application where you will embed the dashboard.

2. In your AWS account, set up permissions for viewers of the embedded dashboard. Users who will view the application with an embedded dashboard should be able to authenticate using IAM, AWS Managed Microsoft AD, SAML, or Web Identity.

3. Create or choose an IAM role which grants permissions for the user to become a reader in Amazon QuickSight and the ability to retrieve the dashboard(s) in that need to be embedded.

4. On your application server, authenticate the user and get the embedded dashboard URL by using one of the AWS SDKs.

5. Embed the dashboard on your application. You can use the Amazon QuickSight Embedding SDK to simplify the embedding process. The Amazon QuickSight embedding SDK is available at the following locations:

   - npmjs.com/package/amazon-quicksight-embedding-sdk
   - github.com/awslabs/amazon-quicksight-embedding-sdk

There are various steps involved on the application side where the dashboard needs to be embedded.

1. Download and include Amazon QuickSight Embedding SDK.

   a. Use the Amazon QuickSight Embedding SDK in your browser.

   b. Install and use Amazon QuickSight Embedding SDK in Node.js.

3. Configure the dashboard to embed.

4. Embed the dashboard by calling QuickSightEmbedding .embedDashboard(options).

5. Set up load callback (optional).

6. Set up error callback (optional).

7. Update the parameter values (optional).

To learn more about creating embedded dashboards, please visit the following page on the Amazon Documentation site: amzn.to/2Qflnyg. Jose Kunnackal, the principal product manager at Amazon Web Services, also wrote a wonderful blog about embedding dashboards at the time of the release of the product. You can follow his blog at go .aws/2U7Yzlf.

From an exam perspective, you need to know the possibility of embedding dashboards with Amazon QuickSight and the security aspects that you need to consider in terms of how users can get access to the dashboards via their web and mobile applications.

Administration

At the time of this writing, Amazon offers two editions of Amazon QuickSight, a Standard edition and an Enterprise edition. The differences are primarily in the use of AWS by individual users or an enterprise. Table 5.3 gives a comparison of the two editions.

TABLE 5.3   Differences between Amazon QuickSight Standard and Enterprise edition

	Standard Edition	Enterprise Edition
Regional Availability	All regions	All regions
User Management	Identity Federation. IAM users. Enable QuickSight-only account with email address.	Identity Federation Enable AD integration Bulk Add/Remove user accounts
Permissions	All Users can manage subscription, SPICE capacity. All users can add/modify/delete user accounts. IAM users or AWS root account can manage resources.	Add users or groups to IAM role rather than IAM users. Microsoft AD users can manage subscriptions and SPICE capacity. Additional AWS permissions needed to manage Microsoft AD groups, manage access to resources

Amazon QuickSight supports a number of browsers, including Apple Safari (7 or later), Google Chrome (up to three previous versions), Microsoft Edge (Latest version), Microsoft Internet Explorer (11 or later), and Mozilla Firefox (Last three versions).

Security

Amazon QuickSight provides a secure platform that enables you to distribute insights across the enterprise with thousands of users in a secure and reliable way.

Security issues around authorization, authentication, and data protection at rest and in motion, including logging and monitoring of access, is of utmost importance.

As discussed earlier, if you have administrative privileges in Amazon QuickSight, you can create and delete user accounts. You can create user accounts based on IAM credentials, or you can create Amazon QuickSight–only user accounts using the email address of the user. You can't create Amazon QuickSight user accounts using non-IAM AWS credentials.

QuickSight allows you to either leverage a built-in user directory deployed into your AWS account and invite users to join via email or invite existing IAM users. Another option is with Enterprise edition, you can connect to your Active Directory servers and manage QuickSight access to existing users and groups; this can simplify user management and provide stronger security.

Hosted content created in Amazon QuickSight is shared with secure links, which prevents versions of reports and dashboards from staying in circulation. We'll look more into security later in the next chapter, "Data Security," and how specifically different pieces are secured across the enterprise.

Other Visualization Options

While Amazon QuickSight is the preferred option for data visualization, there are third-party options or other options within the AWS platform that might be a more suitable fit for your BI requirements. The more common BI tools that you see in the data pipeline in addition to Amazon QuickSight include but are not limited to the following:

MicroStrategy   MicroStrategy is a powerful mobile and BI solution that enables organizations to analyze large amounts of data and distribute actionable insights across the enterprise. MicroStrategy allows various persons within the organization to conduct ad hoc analysis and build reports and dashboards, which can be delivered via web clients or mobile devices. MicroStrategy is an advanced technology partner for AWS and is certified with a number of AWS services including Amazon Redshift and Amazon RDS. To learn more about MicroStrategy on AWS, please visit the AWS marketplace page at go.aws/2vtbSo4.

Business Objects   Business Objects is another popular business intelligence tool, which was acquired by SAP AG in 2007. It contains applications that enable users to discover data, perform analysis, and create reports and dashboards. Business objects includes applications like these:

> **Web Intelligence:** A web browser tool that allows users to perform analysis and product reports and distribute them across the enterprise

> **Crystal Reports:** A data and analytics tool aimed at individual users or small to mid-sized businesses

> **SAP BO Dashboards:** A data visualization tool that allows you to create dashboards from reports

> **Query as Web Service:** A tool that allows users to create and publish web services that can be consumed in Crystal Reports and BO as well as other software applications

> **SAP Lumira:** A self-service data discovery and visualization tool that allows users to explore and analyze data

Large-scale organizations have been using SAP Business Objects Universe, which is actually multiple layers of metadata that act as an interface between backend data and the front-end application layer.

Tableau   Tableau is a lightweight self-service BI tool offering features similar to those in Amazon QuickSight, with a drag-and-drop interface and the ability to analyze large-scale datasets and tap into multiple data sources. Tableau provides direct connectivity to various Amazon Analytics offerings, including Amazon Redshift, Amazon Athena, Amazon Aurora, and Amazon EMR.

Tableau offers a number of products, including data management, server, desktop, web and Tableau Mobile edition products.

You can follow the following white paper to learn about best practices on deploying Tableau on AWS: `tabsoft.co/2WiYxJW`.

TIBCO Spotfire   TIBCO Spotfire is another self-service data analytics tool that enables organizations to analyze large datasets, utilizing in-memory processing to provide better performance and faster response times. TIBCO Spotfire works with Amazon Redshift and Amazon RDS and provides a wide variety of visualization options.

Some of the key capabilities of TIBCO Spotfire include smart visual analytics that provide ML-powered recommendations and analytics driven using natural language and the ability to create powerful dashboards. TIBCO Spotfire also provides intelligent data wrangling, built-in predictive analytics, real-time streaming analytics, and location analytics. It is available on the AWS platform in the Business Intelligence and Advanced Analytics section on the AWS marketplace: `go.aws/3dfSKLo`.

To learn more about TIBCO Spotfire. you can visit `bit.ly/2WjhBI1`.

TIBCO Jaspersoft   TIBCO Jaspersoft is also a self-service BI tool with reporting and analytics capability. It provides a drag-and-drop capability similar to Amazon Quick-Sight. It works with Amazon Redshift, Amazon EMR, and Amazon RDS and is available on the marketplace at `go.aws/3d7RDwX`.

Qlik   Qlik is another platform built to deliver self-service analytics with the core objective of bringing analytics to every user within the organization. Qlik offers two products on Amazon Web Services: Qlik Core (`go.aws/2UbYWv7`) and Qlik Sense Enterprise (`go.aws/39XW0J5`). Qlik Core is a cloud development platform developed for "non-BI" applications that generate insights based on data across a variety of data sources. Qlik Sense Enterprise is an enterprise-level platform for building cool business applications and driving insights that can be shared across the enterprise with a larger feature set. You can deploy both of these on the AWS platform in a Bring Your Own License (BYOL) mode.

Kibana on Amazon Elasticsearch   As discussed in Chapter 4, "Data Processing and Analysis," Amazon offers ELK (Elasticsearch, Logstash, and Kibana) on the AWS platform. Kibana in the earlier days was built to provide a graphical user interface for the log analytics. However, with the latest features, Kibana provides an interface with data analysis and exploration, visualization with ever-growing types of charting capabilities, and anomaly detection using machine learning.

On the Amazon Elasticsearch service, you can find the link to the Kibana dashboard on the main domain dashboard. Figure 5.8 shows the Kibana dashboard on Amazon Elasticsearch.

FIGURE 5.8   The Kibana dashboard on Amazon Elasticsearch

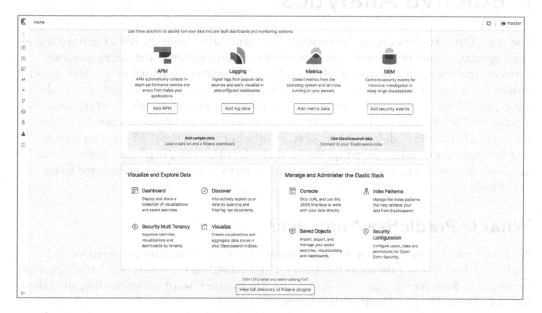

Kibana provides a number of different visualization options. Figure 5.9 shows the Kibana dashboard with sample e-commerce data displaying various chart controls and some cool graphic options.

FIGURE 5.9   Kibana dashboard with sample e-commerce data

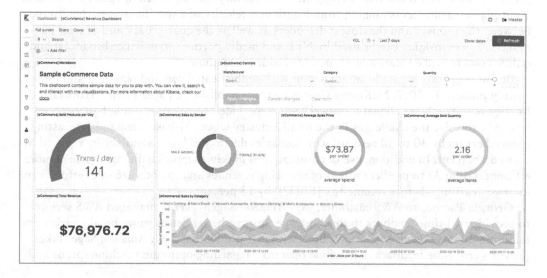

Predictive Analytics

The AWS Data Analytics Specialty certification exam differs from the AWS Certified Big Data Specialty exam in various ways. One of the most important is the clear separation between analytics and advanced analytics (also called machine learning or artificial intelligence). AWS has announced the machine learning specialty to cover the predictive analytics topics, including but not limited to an understanding of machine learning and the services offered by AWS around machine learning at the framework and infrastructure level, the service level, and the high-level AI services. For the purpose of the AWS Data Analytics certification exam, you might get questions that refer to building machine learning products, but the core focus would be on the analytics services that we have discussed so far in the book.

What Is Predictive Analytics?

We have looked at various technologies around data acquisition, data preparation, and analysis, where most of the focus has been on understanding the events that have happened in the past. However, as organizations mature, they strive toward understanding what the future holds and how to position themselves.

Examples include retailers trying to forecast the demand of products and ensuring that appropriate inventory levels are maintained, or large media companies recommending content to users that will be relevant and potentially liked by the users, thus increasing revenue and customer satisfaction.

Another example is how we worked with the NFL on NextGen Stats (NSG) to use data to reveal insights about the game dynamics to both the fans and players. One example of predictive analytics is the NGS's completion probability metric, which integrates more than 10 in-play measurements ranging from length and velocity of a specific pass to the distance between the receiver and the closest defenders as well as the quarterback and nearest pass rushers. These insights can be used by NFL and media partners to enhance broadcast and online content and educate and excite fans inside the stadium.

Business operations are being improved with sophisticated demand planning and forecasting models. In 2017, McKinsey Global Institute published a paper titled "Artificial Intelligence: The Next Digital Frontier?" which provided some eye-opening figures about how AI can solve the challenges in the retail industry where AI-based demand forecasting reduced errors by 30 to 50 percent, with lost sales due to product unavailability reduced by up to 65 percent. In addition, use of automation is making supply chain management more efficient. Using AI to predict sources of servicing revenues and to optimize sales efforts can increase (earnings before income tax [EBIT/]) by 13 percent.

Georgia-Pacific, an AWS customer, uses Amazon SageMaker (a managed AWS service) to provide real-time feedback to machine operators to better detect paper breaks earlier and maintain quality. Using ML models built with raw production data, Amazon SageMaker provides real-time feedback to machine operators regarding optimum machine speeds and other adjustable variables, enabling less-experienced operators to detect breaks earlier and maintain quality. For one converting line, the company eliminated 40 percent of parent-roll tears during the converting process.

The AWS ML Stack

We'll not be diving deeper into the AWS ML stack, but it is good to highlight the various services offered by AWS and their core business purpose.

The AWS ML Stack has three layers, which offer a broad range of machine learning capabilities for different personas, from users who are expert ML practitioners to users who want to operate at a higher level of abstraction.

Figure 5.10 shows the different layers of the AWS ML Stack.

At Amazon, we think about machine learning at three different levels for our customers.

At the bottom layer is frameworks, interfaces, and infrastructure for ML practitioners. For example, Amazon Web Services offers all three frameworks—that is, TensorFlow, PyTorch, and MXNet, which are most popular among ML practitioners and predominantly being used.

TensorFlow is a comprehensive end-to-end open-source platform for machine learning and has the most resonance along with the largest community. It was developed by the Google brain team in 2012 and written in C++, Python, and CUDA. TensorFlow offers C++ and Python APIs, which makes it relevant to a wider audience. In addition to that, it has a faster compilation time and supports both CPUs and GPUs.

Despite the popularity and widespread use of TensorFlow, most ML practitioners use more than one framework, and hence AWS supports other frameworks like MXNet and PyTorch as well. PyTorch is a scientific computing library aimed at becoming the standard for deep learning research by providing flexibility and speed and also replacing NumPy to enable and utilize the power of GPUs.

MXNet is another open-source deep learning framework that is becoming quite popular among developers as it supports multiple languages, including C++, Python, Julia, Perl, and R. MXNet models offer portability by bringing the ability to scale to machines and devices with a smaller footprint but also having the ability to scale to multiple GPUs and multiple machines.

In addition to the frameworks supported, AWS supports various Deep Learning AMIs, including BASE AMI and CONDA AMI, which support the most popular deep learning frameworks and can help you get started quickly. The AMIs can help you expedite your development and model training as they include the latest NIVIDIA GPU acceleration through pre-configured CUDA and CuDNN drivers as well as Intel MKL (Math Kernel Library), in addition to popular Python packages and the Anaconda platform. To learn more about the deep-learning AMIs, please visit go.aws/2J1u0bR.

FIGURE 5.10 AWS Machine Learning Stack

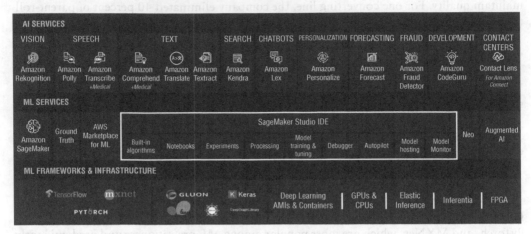

While AWS provides support for a number of frameworks that you can natively use on the platform, the fact of the matter is that we don't have too many expert ML practitioners. AWS therefore provides various ML services like the following:

Amazon SageMaker   A fully managed service that provides every developer and data scientist with the ability to build, train, and deploy machine learning models.

Amazon SageMaker Ground Truth   Amazon SageMaker Ground Truth helps you build more accurate models by providing easy access to labelers through Amazon Mechanical Turk and provides built-in workflows and interfaces for common labeling tasks. You can also use your own labelers or choose from vendors recommended on the Amazon Marketplace.

Amazon SageMaker Studio   Amazon SageMaker Studio provides a single, web-based visual interface where you can perform all ML development tasks by giving you the ability to build, train, and deploy models while giving you full access, control, and visibility into each step. Using SageMaker Studio, you can upload data, create new notebooks, train and tune models, move back and forth between various modeling steps to adjust experiments, compare results, and deploy models to production from a single IDE, thus bringing you more productivity. You can perform all ML development activities, including notebooks, experiment management, automatic model creation, debugging and profiling, and model drift detection within the unified SageMaker Studio visual interfaces.

Amazon SageMaker Neo   Amazon SageMaker Neo enables developers to train machine learning models once and run them anywhere in the cloud and at the edge. It optimizes models to run up to twice as fast, with less than a tenth of the memory footprint and no loss in accuracy.

You start with a machine learning model built using MXNet, TensorFlow, PyTorch, or XGBoost trained using Amazon SageMaker, and you can choose your target hardware platform from Intel, NVIDIA, or ARM. With a single click, SageMaker Neo will then compile the trained model into an executable. The compiler uses a neural network to discover and apply all of the specific performance optimizations that will make your model run most efficiently on the target hardware platform. The model can then be deployed to start making predictions in the cloud or at the edge. Local compute and ML inference capabilities can be brought to the edge with AWS IoT Greengrass.

The top layer of the stack consists of AI services that focus around simplicity and providing built-in machine learning models that you can use to build your applications without worrying about developing, training, and deploying the underlying models. Their focus is on the key services that we touch upon in our daily lives, like vision (Amazon Rekognition), speech (Amazon Polly and Amazon Transcribe), text (Amazon Comprehend, Amazon Translate and Amazon Textract), search (Amazon Kendra), chatbots (Amazon Lex), personalization (Amazon Personalize), forecasting (Amazon Forecast), fraud (Amazon Fraud detector), development (Amazon CodeGuru), and contact centers (Contact Lens).

I hope this gives you a good overview of the various AI/ML services about the AWS platform. You can learn more about these topics on the AWS documentation and blogs page. I highly recommend watching our AWS re:Invent videos to keep you updated on the new releases and learn more about these services.

Summary

This chapter marks the end of our discussion of visualization, where we have looked at the various options for visualization on the AWS platform, including native options like Amazon QuickSight and Kibana and third-party partner options like Tableau, Qlik, Spotfire, and others.

We also touched upon AI/ML services, which are not covered directly by the exam but may appear in the text and are also useful to know from the completeness perspective of an analytics pipeline.

Exam Essentials

The Data Analysis and Visualization section makes up 18 percent of the exam questions. While there is no hard segregation between how much of the exam is focused on data analysis and how much is focused on visualization, it is fair to say that visualization is an important component, since it is explicitly mentioned in exam objectives. The AWS Data Analytics Specialty certification exam intends to test you on the characteristics of the visualization solution for a given scenario. You will often find more than one way to visualize for a given scenario, and in most cases, there could be multiple plausible solutions; however, there would be one of the solutions that meets the given requirements, which could be cost, scale, performance, flexibility, simplicity, and reliability.

You will often get questions on visualization, which might be solved by open-source third-party libraries like D3.js, High charts, and other charting libraries, and you need to understand the viability of the solution in the context of the question.

You might also get queries around suitability of visualization types given a current problem, and unless you have experience with the technology, you will find it challenging to answer those questions. It is recommended that you practice using some of the workshops that are provided at the end of the chapter and go through the recommended blogs, which often cover practical aspects of the visualization solutions.

Exercises

It is highly recommended that you have practical experience with Amazon QuickSight before you take the exam. For assistance in completing the following exercises, refer to the user guides of the associated services.

1. "Analyze Salesforce data with Amazon QuickSight" - aws.amazon.com/blogs/big-data/analyzing-salesforce-data-with-amazon-quicksight

2. "Analyze Top-N DynamoDB Objects using Amazon Athena and Amazon QuickSight" - aws.amazon.com/blogs/big-data/analysis-of-top-n-dynamodb-objects-using-amazon-athena-and-amazon-quicksight

3. "Visualize Amazon S3 Analytics data with Amazon QuickSight" - aws.amazon.com/blogs/big-data/visualize-amazon-s3-analytics-data-with-amazon-quicksight

4. "Harmonize, Search, and Analyze Loosely Coupled Datasets on AWS" - aws.amazon.com/blogs/big-data/harmonize-search-and-analyze-loosely-coupled-data sets-on-aws

5. "Embed Amazon Quicksight dashboards into your applications" – https://embed-workshop.learnquicksight.online/1.introduction.html

Review Questions

1. Which of the following business analytics services is provided by AWS?

   A. Micros Strategy

   B. Business Objects

   C. Tableau

   D. QuickSight

2. You are looking to understand the correlation between the price vs. quantity sold of various products within your merchandise? Which is the best charting technique to display this?

   A. Combo charts

   B. Donut charts

   C. Heat maps

   D. Scatter plots

3. True or false? Amazon QuickSight Standard edition allows you to provide access to users in your Microsoft Active Directory groups.

   A. True

   B. False

4. You have recently been hired by a large e-commerce organization that is looking to forecast its annual sales in order to optimize the inventory storage. Which of the following services will provide the organization with the simplest forecasting option allowing native integration with data from S3, Redshift, and Athena?

   A. D3.js

   B. MicroStrategy

   C. Kibana

   D. Amazon QuickSight

5. A large manufacturing organization has started capturing data from sensors across the assembly lines. It is looking to perform operational analytics and build real-time dashboards based on specific index patterns and looking at ultra-low latency. The data is available in Elasticsearch. Which of the following visualization techniques is best suited for such an organization?

   A. Tableau

   B. EMR Notebooks

   C. Kibana

   D. Amazon QuickSight

References

aws.amazon.com/blogs/awsmarketplace/
using-aws-marketplace-for-machine-learning-workloads
http://mck.co/2JdHmoJ

Additional Reading Material

Data Visualization with Amazon QuickSight (AWS re:Invent 2017 - DEM74) – youtube
.com/watch?v=Ul3J8VX7zmM

Sharing Your Analysis and Insights Using Amazon QuickSight – youtube.com/
watch?v=xusKVM5NiCE

Customizing Your Visuals in Amazon QuickSight – youtube.com/
watch?v=UKxkPi5mJno

Using SQL to Import Data into Amazon QuickSight – youtube.com/
watch?v=x9RUtTzqpr0

Accessing Amazon Redshift Data from Amazon QuickSight – youtube.com/
watch?v=CRcRS3qos-A

Deep Dive on Amazon QuickSight—January 2017 AWS Online Tech Talks – youtube
.com/watch?v=gy1AcdJMsMk

Building Visualizations and Dashboards with Amazon QuickSight (AWS re:Invent 2017
- ABD206) – youtube.com/watch?v=dprtSTSbCEE

Serverless Analytics—Amazon Redshift Spectrum, AWS Glue, and Amazon
QuickSight – youtube.com/watch?v=f0RJ6y572gs

Visualizing Amazon S3 Storage Management with Amazon QuickSight—2017 AWS
Online Tech Talks – youtube.com/watch?v=4vmL05KVqTA

Deploying Business Analytics at Enterprise Scale with Amazon QuickSight (AWS
re:Invent 2017 - ABD311) – youtube.com/watch?v=G4Dgzlo3gQI

Analyzing AWS Billing Data Using Amazon QuickSight – youtube.com/
watch?v=2JnfuAA-TiU

Tackle Your Dark Data Challenge with AWS Glue (and Visualize It in Amazon QuickSight)—2017 AWS Online Tech Talks – youtu.be/Q0m2TligKtE?t=1226

Serverless Big Data Analytics—Amazon Athena and Amazon QuickSight—2017 AWS

Online Tech Talks – youtube.com/watch?v=m1HTL_SJHrE

Data Visualization with Amazon QuickSight (AWS re:Invent 2017 - DEM74) – youtube.com/watch?v=Ul3J8VX7zmM

Embedding analytics into applications with Amazon Quicksight – youtube.com/watch?v=8m3iJayTpxI

Five data lake considerations with Amazon Redshift, Amazon S3, and AWS Glue – youtube.com/watch?v=U74vOMzUBoI

Blog posts and reference reading material:

Data visualization: aws.amazon.com/data-visualization

"10 visualizations to try in Amazon QuickSight": aws.amazon.com/blogs/big-data/10-visualizations-to-try-in-amazon-quicksight-with-sample-data

"Visualizing Sensor Data in Amazon QuickSight": aws.amazon.com/blogs/compute/visualizing-sensor-data-in-amazon-quicksight

"Analyze and visualize nested JSON data with Amazon Athena and Amazon QuickSight": aws.amazon.com/blogs/big-data/analyze-and-visualize-nested-json-data-with-amazon-athena-and-amazon-quicksight

Workshops:

Amazon QuickSight Workshop - COVID-19 Data Analysis – d3akduqkn9yexq.cloudfront.net

Build Advanced Analytics and Dashboards with Amazon QuickSight – d3h1oz7s9b419c.cloudfront.net/en/introduction.html

Embed Amazon QuickSight in a Web App from beginning to end – embed-workshop.learnquicksight.online/1.introduction.html

Chapter

6

Data Security

THE AWS DATA ANALYTICS SPECIALTY
CERTIFICATION EXAM OBJECTIVES
COVERED IN THIS CHAPTER MAY
INCLUDE, BUT ARE NOT LIMITED TO, THE
FOLLOWING:

✓ **Domain 6: Data Security**

- 6.1 Determine encryption requirements and/or implementation technologies

- 6.2 Choose the appropriate technology to enforce data governance

- 6.3 Identify how to ensure data integrity

- 6.4 Evaluate regulatory requirements

Introduction

Security is a day one job at AWS, and it is our top priority. We have covered the entire analytics pipeline from data ingestion, to processing, to analysis, and finally to visualization. However, during the exam you will get a number of questions concerning authorization, authentication, compliance, and encryption, which in essence translates to securely accessing and working with your data and analytics services. Around 18 percent of the questions on the exam will be related to security, thus giving it the same weight as data collection, data analysis, and visualization.

   During this chapter we will discuss the AWS shared responsibility model, before looking into the authentication and authorization aspects within Amazon Web Services and how they apply to various data and analytics services that are covered during the exam. We look at security of Amazon S3, Amazon DynamoDB, Amazon Redshift, Amazon Elasticsearch, Amazon EMR, AWS Glue, and Amazon Kinesis. Let's get started.

> The AWS Data Analytics Specialty Certification exam will test you on various security scenarios around authentication and authorization. It is important to remember that while you will get choices around creating an AWS user or an AWS role to meet a certain security requirement, the general best practices of security—i.e., limiting access to the permissions needed to perform an operation, and creating a role vs. a user—apply to most of the scenarios.

Shared Responsibility Model

A typical data platform built on the AWS cloud involves five to six different layers, including the global AWS infrastructure like AWS Regions such as us-east-1 (North Virginia), Availability Zones, and edge locations. This is the hardware and the global infrastructure that AWS manages for its customers. On top of the global infrastructure, we have various software components, such as compute, storage, databases, and networking, that connect these hardware components together. These layers essentially form the basis of the cloud that AWS operates, and hence AWS is responsible for these components. You will hear the term *security of the cloud,* which refers to these components. The lower layer labelled as "AWS" in Figure 6.1 refers to the components that are under AWS responsibility. Essentially this includes the physical security of the data centers and controlling who gets access to them as well as ensuring that people who have a direct need can get physical access, ensuring that storage is commissioned and decommissioned as per the needs, ensuring that all access to the underlying hosts running the EC2 instances have access to logging and auditing mechanisms in place, setting up intrusion detection mechanisms for the network infrastructure (which includes routers, switches, load balancers, firewalls, cabling, and so on), and ensuring isolation of instances across the platform.

As a customer, you will be responsible for the AWS cloud services that customers choose to operate. The selection of the services will determine the kind of configuration that is required by the customer. For example, if a customer chooses to run an Amazon EC2 (Elastic Compute Cloud) instance, that customer will be using the infrastructure provided by AWS and will hence be responsible for all security configurations and management tasks. This could include security patches, application software components, and the configuration of the security groups, to name a few. However, for abstracted services such as the analytics services S3 and DynamoDB, AWS operates the infrastructure, the operating system, and platforms; customers can access the provided endpoints to these services to store and retrieve data. Customers, however, are responsible for managing the data using the services and options available to them in these services. The upper layer labelled as "Customer" in Figure 6.1 are the components that fall under customer responsibility, and these are often referred to collectively as *security in the cloud.*

FIGURE 6.1 AWS shared responsibility model

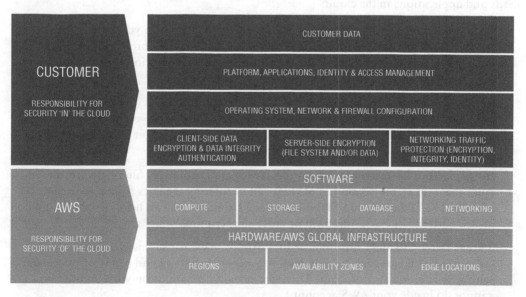

Customers are responsible for EC2 instance operating systems, which can include things like patching them with the latest updates and ongoing maintenance, whereas from an application perspective, customers manage the password and access to them via roles and users. Customers will be responsible for security groups and setting up operating system and host firewalls, including intrusion detection and prevention mechanisms. While you can benefit from a number of AWS services, you will still be responsible for setting this up.

Security Services on AWS

AWS delivers a platform that is scalable, highly available, dependable, and most important, secure and that enables the customer to build a wide variety of applications. Because of the wide range of applications being built on the AWS platform, customers require confidentiality, integrity, and availability of the data and services on the platform. You can look at AWS's compliance resources (https://amzn.to/32E0rGa) to learn about essentials and best practices, guides and workbooks and resources around privacy.

To automate your often manually performed security tasks, AWS provides a variety of services that allow you to focus on scaling and innovating your business, all on a pay-per-use model. AWS as a platform must cater to the needs of the most security-sensitive organizations running their top-secret workloads on the platform, which means that customers who don't need that level of rigor can still benefit from the same level of security for the traditional workloads being run on the platform.

AWS protects your data in the cloud and offers five different ways to secure your workloads and applications in the cloud:

Data Protection   AWS provides various services that can help you protect your data, accounts, and workloads from unauthorized access. The data protection services provide encryption, key management, and automatic threat detection that continuously monitors and protects your accounts and workloads.

Identity and Access Management   AWS provides identity services that help you manage identities, resources, and permissions at scale. With AWS, you have identity services for your workforce and customer-facing applications to get started quickly and manage access to your workloads and applications.

Infrastructure Protection   AWS protects web applications by filtering traffic based on rules that you create. Examples of rules can be filtering requests from a particular IP address, HTTP header, HTTP body, or URI string, which can help you block common attack patterns like SQL injection or cross-site scripting.

Threat Detection and Continuous Monitoring   AWS is responsible for the infrastructure and hence continuously monitors network activity and behavior of accounts within your cloud environment. There are certain limitations on what you can and cannot do inside your AWS account.

Compliance and Data Privacy   AWS provides you with a full view of your compliance status in an automated way using AWS best practices and industry standards followed by your organization.

Table 6.1 lists the AWS security, identity, and compliance services that you can use while building your data and analytics applications on the AWS cloud.

TABLE 6.1   AWS security, identity, and compliance services

Service Category	Service Name	Description
Identity and Access management	AWS Identity and Access Management	Manage access to AWS services and resources such as compute, storage, analytics, databases, s3 buckets.
	AWS Single Sign-On	Provides ability to centrally manage access to multiple AWS accounts and business applications
	Amazon Cognito	Set up identity management for your web and mobile apps easily and quickly. Scales to millions of users and supports social identity providers such as Facebook, Google, and Amazon
	AWS Directory	AWS Directory service for Microsoft Active Directory
	AWS Resource Access Manager	Share resources with any AWS account or within your AWS organization. You can share AWS Transit gateways, Subnets, AWS License Manager configurations, and Amazon Route 53 Resolver rules resources.
Detective Controls	AWS Security Hub	Comprehensive view of high-priority security alerts and security posture across your AWS accounts
	Amazon GuardDuty	Amazon GuardDuty is a threat detection service that continuously monitors for malicious activity and unauthorized behavior to protect your AWS accounts and workloads.
	Amazon Inspector	An automated security assessment service that helps improve security and compliance of applications deployed on AWS by automatically assessing applications for exposure, vulnerabilities, and deviations from best practices.
	Amazon Detective	Analyze, investigate, and identify the root cause of potential security issues or suspicious activities by automatically collecting log data and use ML, statistics, and graph theory to build a linked set of data to enable more efficient security investigations.

TABLE 6.1 AWS security, identity and compliance services *(continued)*

Service Category	Service Name	Description
Infrastructure Protection	AWS Shield	AWS Shield is a distributed denial of service protection service that protects applications running from AWS via always-on detection and automatic inline mitigation to minimize application downtime and latency.
	AWS Web Application Firewall (WAF)	AWS Web Application Firewall is used to protect your web applications or APIs against common web exploits and thus improve overall availability of your web application.
	AWS Firewall Manager	AWS Firewall Manager is a security management service that allows you to centrally configure and manage firewall rules across your accounts and applications in AWS Organizations.
Data Protection	Amazon Macie	Amazon Macie is an ML powered security service that can help discover, classify and protect sensitive data like PII information or intellectual property in AWS; it provides customers with dashboards and alerts to give visibility into how this data is being accessed or moved.
	AWS Key Management Service	AWS KMS makes creation, management, and control of cryptographic keys simpler and can be integrated with CloudTrail to provide logs for your regulatory and compliance needs.
	AWS CloudHSM	AWS CloudHSM is a cloud-based hardware security module (HSM) that enables you to easily generate and use your own encryption keys on the AWS Cloud.
	AWS Certificate Manager	AWS Certificate Manager is a service that lets you provision, manage, and deploy public and private SSL/TSL certificates for use with AWS services and your internal connected resources.
	AWS Secrets Manager	AWS Secrets Manager is used to rotate, manage, and retrieve secrets like database credentials, API keys, etc.; it offers built-in integration with Amazon Redshift, Amazon DocumentDB, and Amazon RDS.

Service Category	Service Name	Description
Compliance	AWS Artifact	AWS Artifact is your go-to, self-service portal for compliance-related information that matters to you, offered at no cost in an on-demand manner.

Now that you have seen a list of services that can be used to set and improve the security posture of your applications in the cloud, let's look at the AWS services and the security model that they offer.

AWS IAM Overview

Before we start with the analytics services, we need to look at the core service that offers identity and access management in AWS, called AWS IAM. The AWS platform offers a number of resources, and IAM is used to securely control access to those AWS resources. IAM is used for authentication (who can sign into the AWS platform) and authorization (what services this user can access). It is important to understand the key terminology before we start discussing IAM features.

IAM User

An IAM user is an entity in AWS that can represent either a person or an application that interacts with AWS. A user in AWS consists of a name and credentials. There is a special type of user in most AWS accounts. When you first create an AWS account, you would typically use a sign-in identity that has complete access to all AWS services and resources. This AWS identity is called the *root account*.

It is highly recommended not to use root user for everyday tasks, but rather use the root user to create your first IAM user, and then securely lock away the credentials to use them for only a few account and service management tasks. To create an admin for daily use, please follow the AWS Documentation at amzn.to/3d37CeU.

An IAM user can access AWS in a number of different ways, as described in Table 6.2.

TABLE 6.2   AWS security credentials for accessing an AWS account

Credentials Type	Typical Usage
Email address and password	These are typically associated with your root AWS account.
IAM username and password	These are typically used for accessing the AWS Management Console.
Access keys	These are typically used with CLI and programmatic requests like APIs and SDKs.
Key pairs	These are used for only specific AWS services like Amazon EC2. You will need to use key pairs if you want to ssh into the master node for Amazon EMR.

To learn more about AWS IAM users, please visit the AWS Documentation at amzn .to/2Sn5eYL.

IAM Groups

While the IAM user is a powerful concept, managing permissions for individual users is cumbersome and can become a management nightmare. This is where IAM groups can be useful. An IAM group is basically a collection of IAM users, and you can use it to specify permissions for multiple users, which can make it easy to manage permissions for those users.

Managing groups is quite a simple process. You can create a group called *Administrators* and provide permissions that are needed to administer the platform. This is the single place where you provide the permissions, and they can be as fine-grained as possible. Any user that is assigned to the group will automatically inherit permissions that are assigned to that group. If you need to make a new admin user, you can simply add them to the Administrators group. If a user leaves your specific organization or moves to a different role where they no longer need those admin permissions, you can remove them from the group.

A group cannot be identified as a Principal in a permission policy; rather, it is simply a way to attach policies to multiple users at one time. A group has the following characteristics:

- A group may contain many users, and a user can belong to multiple groups.

- A group cannot contain another group.

- You can have a maximum of 300 groups in an AWS account.
- You can have up to 5000 users in an AWS account, and 5000 users in an IAM group.

To learn more about IAM groups, please visit `amzn.to/2KUwt8N`.

IAM Roles

An IAM role is an IAM identity that you can create in your account with specific permissions. An IAM role is similar to an IAM user from the perspective that it is an AWS identity with permissions policies that define what the identity is allowed to do on the AWS platform. A role is different from the user in the sense that it is not uniquely associated with one person (like a user) and can be assumed by anyone who may need it. Furthermore, unlike a user, a role does not have long-term credentials like passwords and access keys. Instead, assuming the role will result in provision of temporary security credentials for the role session.

When to use roles:

- You can use roles to delegate access to AWS resources when users do not have access to them.
- Roles can be used to grant access to resources in a different AWS account.
- Roles are also pretty common when you want to provide access to certain AWS resources from a mobile application but you do not want to embed AWS keys within the app.
- Roles can be used to give access to users who have identities outside of AWS, such as, for example, users from your corporate directory.
- Roles can also be used to grant access to third-party auditors who might want to audit your account.

> The AWS Data Analytics Specialty Certification exam will test you on various security scenarios around usage of IAM roles. Take particular note of the cases involving accessing AWS resources from mobile apps, providing access to auditors, and users defined outside of AWS. The appropriate usage of roles in these scenarios will help you ace the security section in the exam.

There are various types of roles, as shown in Table 6.3, and it is important to get the terminology clear as you will frequently see these terms appearing through the remainder of this chapter.

Now that you have a basic understanding of the terminology, let's look into the security around various AWS services.

TABLE 6.3   Types of roles/terminology in AWS

Role Type	Role Description
Role	A role is an IAM identity that you can create in your account and that has specific permissions. Roles can be used by an IAM user in the same or different account or a web service offered by AWS such as Amazon EC2, or they can be used by an external user authenticated by an external identity provider (IdP) service compatible with SAML 2.0, OpenID Connect, or a custom-built identity broker.
AWS service role	An AWS service role is a role that a service assumes to perform tasks and actions in your account on your behalf. The service role therefore needs the permissions necessary to operate on your behalf. Service roles are only used within your account and cannot be used to grant access to services in a different account. There are two types of AWS Service roles: **AWS service role for an EC2 instance:** This is a special type of service role that an application running inside your EC2 instance can assume and perform actions on your behalf. This role is assigned to the EC2 instance when it is launched. Applications running on the EC2 instance can retrieve temporary security credentials and perform actions that the role allows. **AWS service-linked role:** This is another special type of service role that is linked directly to an AWS service. Service-linked roles are predefined by the service and include all permissions that the service needs to call other AWS services on your behalf.
Role chaining	Role chaining indicates the process of assuming a second role through the AWS CLI or API. Say Roger has the permissions to assume the role of a *developer* or *sysadmin*. Also, *developer* can assume the role of *sysadmin*. Roger assumes the role of a *developer* using his long-term credentials in the AssumeRole API operation. This operation will return short-term credentials for the *developer* role. Roger can then engage in a role chaining, by using the short-term credentials from the *developer* role to assume the role of a *sysadmin*.
Delegation	Delegation is the process of granting permissions to someone to access the resources that you control; however, this requires a trust relationship between the two accounts. To learn more about delegation, please visit the AWS Documentation page at amzn.to/2ylSACu.
Federation	Federation is the process of creating a trust relationship between an external identity provider and AWS. Users can sign in to a web identity provider such as Amazon, Facebook, Google, or an IdP compatible with OpenID Connect (OIDC). Users can also sign into a SAML (Security Assertion Markup Language) 2.0 compatible enterprise identity system such as Microsoft AD. When you use OIDC and SAML 2.0 to create a trust relationship between these external identity providers and AWS, the user is assigned an IAM role and receives temporary credentials that allow the user to access your AWS resources. Federation is a very important concept from an exam perspective.

Role Type	Role Description
Federated user	Once you have established federation, you can use the existing identities from your AWS Directory Service, enterprise user directory, or a web identity provider to access your AWS resources. These users are called federated users and AWS will assign a role to a federated user when access is made through an identity provider.
Trust policy	A trust policy, as the name indicates, is a policy document where you define the trust relationships for principals that are allowed and trusted to assume a particular role. The trust policy is a resource-based policy and is attached to a role in IAM. The principals that you specify in trust policy include users, roles, accounts, and services.
Permission Policy	A permission policy is a document where you define the actions and resources a role can use.
Principal	A principal is an entity in AWS that can perform actions and access resources. The Following can act as principals: • AWS account root user • IAM user • Role
Role for cross-account access	Let us say you have your AWS resources (e.g., S3 buckets) in Account-A, and your principal is an IAM user in Account-B. If you would like to assign permissions to resources from Account-A to principals in Account-B, you should use roles to grant the cross-account access. Although you can use resource-based policies to grant principals from other accounts access to the resources, roles are often a better implementation mechanism for setting up cross-account access.

Amazon EMR Security

We looked at Amazon EMR as a service in Chapter 4, "Data Processing and Analysis" data processing section.

When you spin up an EMR cluster, irrespective of whether it is a transient or a long-running cluster, it is spun up inside a VPC. Amazon VPC enables you to provision your resources within a private area within AWS where you can configure a private network and control aspects such as private IP address ranges, subnets, routing tables, and network gateways. The EC2 instances for Amazon EMR run inside that VPC, and the instances can be inside a private subnet or a public subnet. For a public subnet, you must create an Internet gateway and attach it to the subnet.

Once you have set up and configured a subnet where you would like to launch an Amazon EMR cluster, you can launch the cluster in the subnet by specifying the subnet identifier when creating the cluster. When the cluster is launched, Amazon EMR adds the security groups based on whether the cluster is launching in a private subnet or a public subnet.

Public Subnet

Figure 6.2 shows Amazon EMR inside a public subnet connecting to your on-premises data center via a VPN connection and to other AWS services via an Internet gateway. When you use a public subnet, you can use an Internet gateway to connect your EMR clusters to public endpoints of services like Amazon S3 and Amazon DynamoDB. Some services like Amazon S3 provide the ability to create a VPC endpoint, which means that you can access those services via the endpoint rather than via the Internet gateway over a public Internet, thus providing better security and performance.

FIGURE 6.2   Amazon EMR inside a public subnet

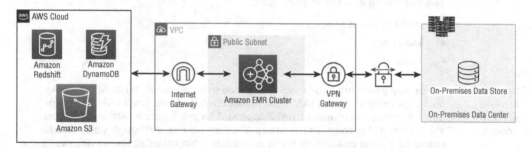

Similar to other EC2 instances, the EC2 instances running EMR software have all inbound and outbound traffic controlled via security groups. Two types of security groups are used for Amazon EMR: Amazon-EMR managed security groups and additional security groups.

Amazon-EMR Managed Security Groups

As the name indicates, these security groups are managed by Amazon EMR service for the sole purpose of having rules required by the cluster to communicate internally and with other AWS services. You can allow users and other applications to access a cluster from outside the cluster, and you can edit the rules in managed security groups or create additional security groups. It is generally recommended to define your custom access rules for configuring additional security, as editing a managed security group can have unintended consequences. It is quite common for people to edit managed security groups to protect their environment and spend many man hours only to realize that they had unintentionally blocked the ports required for the inter-cluster traffic as well.

One of the default managed security groups for the master node is called ElasticMapReduce-master, which is pre-configured with a role that allows inbound SSH traffic (port 22) from all sources (IPv4 0.0.0.0/0). As a best practice, you should restrict incoming traffic to only trusted sources and hence specify a custom security group to do that.

Amazon EMR provides different managed security groups for the master and the task instances. An additional managed security group for service access will be created when you create a cluster in a private subnet. Amazon EMR will use the default managed security groups, creating them if required.

The default managed security groups are described in Table 6.4.

TABLE 6.4 Managed security groups – Amazon EMR

Security Group Name	Security Group Description
ElasticMapReduce-master	Default security group for master instance in the public subnet
ElasticMapReduce-slave	Default security group for the core and task instances in the public subnet
ElasticMapReduce-Master-Private	Default security group for the master instance in the private subnet
ElasticMapReduce-Slave-Private	Default security group for the core and task instances in the private subnet
ElasticMapReduce-ServiceAccess	Default security group for service access in private subnets. It has no inbound rules and only allows outbound traffic over HTTPS (8443). These rules allow cluster manager to communicate with master node and with the core and task nodes.

Additional Security Groups (Optional)

Additional security groups are optional and are defined when you need to define custom access rules that you provide and manage. Amazon EMR does not add/remove rules from additional security groups.

Private Subnet

Private subnets differ from public subnets in the following manner:

- AWS services that provide a VPC endpoint can be accessed using the endpoint; however, services that do not provide an endpoint must use a NAT instance or an Internet gateway. For example, if you are using EMRFS features, you will need to have an

Amazon S3 VPC endpoint, and if you are using DynamoDB, you will need to provide a route from your private subnet to DynamoDB.

You should provide a route to the Amazon EMR service logs bucket and Amazon Linux repository in S3.

For debugging, provide a route from your private subnet to an Amazon SQS endpoint.

A sample architecture diagram for Amazon EMR running inside a private subnet is depicted in Figure 6.3.

FIGURE 6.3 Amazon EMR inside a private subnet

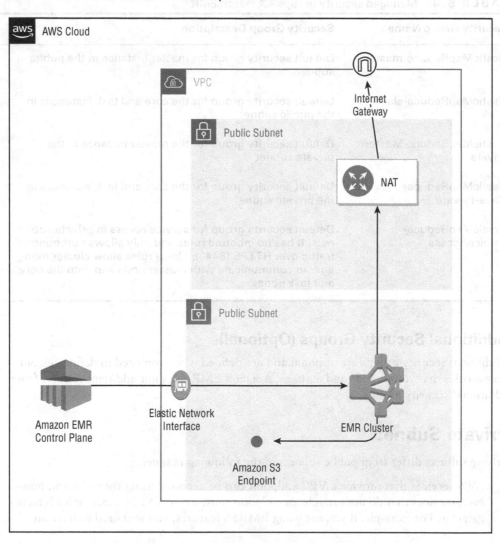

As you open the EMR console, and even before creating an EMR cluster, the three key security-related things that you see are Security Configurations, VPC Subnets, and Block Public Access (see Figure 6.4).

FIGURE 6.4 Security options within Amazon EMR Console

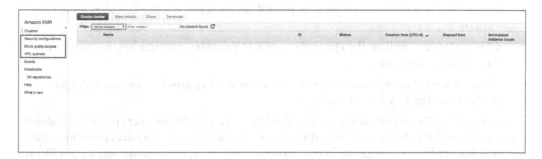

Let's look at those before we look at other security options inside an Amazon EMR cluster.

Security Configurations

Amazon EMR allows you to create a security configuration that can be applied across multiple clusters. The configuration settings can be categorized into four major categories:

- Encryption
- Authentication
- IAM Roles for EMRFS
- AWS Lake Formation Integration

Let's look at each one of those in more detail.

Encryption

Data encryption is required to ensure that data is only visible to the authenticated and authorized user. EMR can work with data on S3 via EMRFS and on data stored in HDFS, also known as *data at rest*. EMR also needs to transmit the data over the wire, also known as *data in transit*. To protect your data from prying eyes, you will need to encrypt data at rest and in transit. Amazon EMR's security configuration options provide three options for data encryption: S3 encryption, local disk encryption, and data-in-transit encryption.

S3 Encryption: Enable At-Rest Encryption for Data in Amazon S3

Amazon S3's encryption modes work with EMR File System (EMRFS) objects read and written from Amazon S3. You can define server-side encryption (SSE) or client-side encryption in this configuration option. The available options are as follows:

- SSE-S3

- SSE-KMS (You will need to provide your KMS customer master key to encrypt the data on the server side.)

- CSE-KMS (You will need to provide your KMS customer master key to encrypt the data on the client side.)

- CSE-Custom (You will have to provide the custom key provider location [An S3 bucket] and the Key Provider class.)

Amazon EMR's configuration option also allows you to choose encryption overrides for specific buckets. You can specify different encryption modes and encryption materials for each bucket by specifying the bucket name and the encryption mode you would like to apply for this bucket.

Local Disk Encryption

Amazon EMR has three types of local storage that are encrypted using various mechanisms and work together to provide optimal security for your data at rest.

HDFS ENCRYPTION

HDFS is used not only for intermittent storage, but also when data is read and written from instance store volumes and EBS volumes attached to instances. There are a number of Hadoop encryption options that are activated when you enable local disk encryption:

Secure Hadoop RPC (Remote Procedure Calls)   This option controls the `hadoop` `.rpc.protection` setting in `core-site.xml` to activate data protection and is used to encrypt data between Hadoop services and clients.

Data Encryption on HDFS Block Data Transfer   This option allows us to configure data encryption on a data node. The setting `dfs.encrypt.data.transfer` is set to "`true`" in the `hdfs-site.xml` and is configured to use AES-256 encryption.

Transparent Data Encryption on Amazon EMR   While the settings in this configuration do not activate Transparent Data Encryption in Amazon, you can configure it manually. Transparent encryption is implemented through the use of HDFS encryption zones, which are HDFS paths that you define. Each encryption zone has its own key, which is stored in the key server specified using the "hdfs-site" configuration classification. Amazon EMR uses KMS by default, but you can use a different key management service as long as it implements the KeyProvider API operation.

INSTANCE STORE ENCRYPTION

Since Amazon EMR uses EC2 instances to install and configure the Hadoop software, you can end up in one of the two types of encryption, depending on the instance store volume type (see Table 6.5).

TABLE 6.5   Encryption options – EMR

Instance Store Volume Type	Encryption Options
NVMe-based SSDs	NVMe (Non-volatile memory express) encryption
Other instance store volumes	Amazon EMR uses LUKS (Linux Unified Key Setup) to encrypt instance store volume when local disk encryption is enabled.

EBS VOLUME ENCRYPTION

Amazon Web Services has regions where encryption of EBS volumes is enabled by default in the account. If your account falls into such a region, your EBS volumes will be encrypted even if you have not explicitly enabled local disk encryption. When you specify local disk encryption in the security settings, Amazon EMR settings will take precedence over the Amazon EC2 encryption-by-default settings for cluster EC instances.

Figure 6.5 shows some of the encryption options available to you from the security configurations screen.

FIGURE 6.5   Security Configurations Amazon EMR- Encryption options

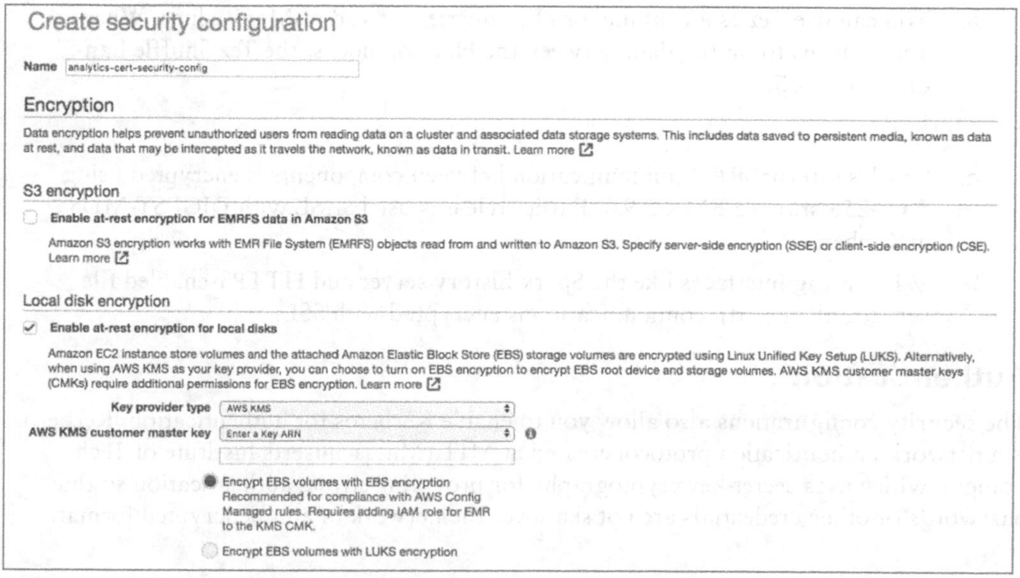

Data-In-Transit Encryption

EMR offers several mechanisms for encrypting data in-transit, which may vary by EMR release. From a security configurations page, you can enable the following application-specific encryption features:

1. Hadoop

   a. Encrypted Shuffle – Shuffle is an important concept with MapReduce and requires data to be transmitted across various nodes. MapReduce encrypted shuffle (bit .ly/2L5CGPm) allows encryption of MapReduce shuffle using HTTPS.

   b. Secure RPC calls in Hadoop – We've already looked at this earlier in the chapter. For more details, please visit Apache Hadoop documentation at bit.ly/3beq4jq.

   c. Data Encryption on Block data transfer – We covered this in the previous section. For more details, please visit bit.ly/3cb88Yk.

2. Hbase

   a. If you are setting up a kerberized EMR (supported from EMR release 5.10.0 onward), communication within the cluster is encrypted. This is defined by the hbase.rpc.protection property and is set to privacy for a kerberized EMR cluster. For information about Amazon EMR and Kerberos, please visit: amzn .to/3bgj85m.

3. Presto

   a. We discussed Presto architecture in an earlier chapter. Any internal communication between Presto nodes uses SSL/TLS (Secure Sockets Layer/Transport Layer Security)—Amazon EMR versions 5.6.0 and later only.

4. Tez

   a. You can use Tez as a runtime for Hive queries instead of MapReduce. When Tez requires to shuffle data between the Hadoop nodes, the Tez Shuffle handler uses TLS.

5. Spark

   a. Spark's internal RPC communication between components is encrypted using AES-256 starting EMR 5.9.0. Earlier releases used SASL with DIGEST-MD5 as Cipher.

   b. When using interfaces like the Spark history server and HTTPS-enabled file servers, all the http communication is encrypted with SSL.

Authentication

The security configurations also allow you to enable Kerberos for authentication. Kerberos is a network-authentication protocol created at MIT (Massachusetts Institute of Technology), which uses secret-key cryptography for providing strong authentication so that passwords or other credentials are not sent over the network in an unencrypted format.

When you enable Kerberos authentication, Amazon EMR configures Kerberos for the applications, components, and subsystems that it installs on the cluster so that they are authenticated with each other.

Amazon EMR provides the options to set up a cluster dedicated to a Key Distribution Center (KDC) or for setting up an external KDC. You can configure ticket lifetime in the console in both cases, which by default is set to 24 hours. You can also set up a cross-realm trust, which means that you allow principals (typically users) from a different Kerberos configuration to authenticate to application components on an EMR cluster. There are certain considerations for setting up cross-realm trust that are provided in more detail in the documentation (`amzn.to/2SNZTtw`).

IAM Roles for EMRFS

EMRFS is the recommended permanent store for EMR clusters. When you request the data stored in Amazon S3 using the *s3://mybucket/mydata* format, Amazon EMR will use EMRFS to fulfill your request. By default, Amazon EMR uses the permission policies that you had defined in the service role that was attached to the cluster when it was created. This means that you use the same role regardless of the user or group who is accessing that data, and regardless of the location on Amazon S3.

In some cases, Amazon EMR is a shared cluster where multiple users accessing the cluster require different levels of access to the underlying data. You can achieve that fine-grained access using IAM roles for EMRFS.

In the security configurations, you can specify role mappings in the IAM roles for the EMRFS section, where each role mapping corresponds to an identifier, which is used to determine the access to Amazon S3 via EMRFS. The identifiers can be users, groups, or Amazon S3 prefixes that indicate the location of a dataset.

How IAM Roles for EMRFS Work

When you have set up role mappings and use EMRFS to make a request to Amazon S3, if the request matches the basis for access (user, group, S3 location), EMRFS makes the cluster EC2 instance assume the corresponding role for the specific request. This essentially allows you to pick from a number of IAM roles that the EC2 instances can assume when making a request.

When a request is made via EMRFS, EMRFS evaluates the role mappings in the top-down order, which means that not only is ordering important, but the policies attached to the role should limit permissions on Amazon S3. If no match is found, EMRFS falls back to the original service role that you defined at the cluster creation time.

There are scenarios where you need application-level isolation between users of the application vs. host-level isolation between users on the host. IAM roles for EMRFS provide application-level isolation, and hence any user with access to the cluster can bypass the isolation to assume any of the roles.

AWS Lake Formation Integration

You can also configure your Amazon EMR with AWS Lake Formation to provide fine-grained column-level access to databases and tables in AWS Glue Data Catalog. Amazon Lake Formation also allows you to enable federated single sign-on to EMR and Apache Zeppelin notebooks from your SAML-compliant enterprise identity system. At the time of this writing, the feature was in beta, and we hope that the feature will be in GA by the time you are reading this book.

The following requirements must be met before enabling Amazon EMR and Lake Formation integration:

1. Corporate identities should be managed in a SAML-based identity provider such as Active Directory Federation Services (ADFS).

2. Your metadata store should be AWS Glue Data Catalog.

3. You will have to use Apache Zeppelin or EMR notebooks to access your data managed by AWS Glue and AWS Lake Formation.

4. You should have permissions defined in AWS Lake Formation.

Amazon EMR and AWS Lake Formation support the following applications:

- Apache Spark
- Apache Zeppelin
- Amazon EMR notebooks

At the time of this writing, other applications were not supported.

To learn more about AWS Lake Formation integration, please visit amzn.to/3cqaySV.

Block Public Access

Amazon EMR is typically used as your main processing engine for the data on your data lake. It is therefore a critical resource and needs to be protected as such to ensure that access is limited to only relevant users. One of the most critical aspects of security is to block public access to your resources, which is why Amazon EMR provides this feature directly on the console.

EMR console allows you to switch the setting between On and Off, while also providing the ability to set up port exceptions for clusters with specific ports, which will continue to allow inbound traffic from all public IP addresses.

When you switch the setting to On, any EMR cluster whose security settings allow all inbound traffic from all public addresses (IPv4 0.0.0.0/0 or IPv6::/0) is prevented from being launched. This setting applies to all clusters launched in the current region.

VPC Subnets

You can use this option to configure private subnets for your cluster by adding Amazon S3 endpoints to access Amazon S3 or by adding a NAT instance to access public AWS service endpoints. We discussed the details of working with private subnets in the earlier section.

Security Options during Cluster Creation

You can choose to create an EMR cluster using quick options mode or advanced options mode.

Quick Options Mode

The purpose of Quick Options mode is to quickly launch an EMR cluster, and hence it provides limited options (see Figure 6.6). TIt allows you to choose an EC2 key pair, which is needed to connect to the master instance via SSH.

FIGURE 6.6   EMR security configuration – Quick Options mode

The Quick Options mode allows you to choose from two permission modes:

Default   When you choose the default permission mode, EMR will choose the default options for the EMR role and EC2 instance profile.

The EMR role is used by EMR to call other services on your behalf, and by default EMR chooses EMR_DefaultRole as your default EMR role.

The EC2 instance profile is the role that is used by the EC2 instance running the EMR software and is used to provide access to other AWS services like S3 and DynamoDB from the EC2 instances. The default role for EC2 instance profile is EMR_EC2_DefaultRole.

Custom   The custom mode allows you to choose custom roles for EMR role and EC2 instance profile.

Advanced Options Mode

The Advanced Options mode provides you with a lot more security options than the quick options. Let's look at some of them:

EC2 Key Pair   This option allows you to choose the EC2 key pair that you can then use to log into your master node. You can connect to your cluster nodes similarly to how you connect to your EC2 instances. You also have the option to create a cluster without a key pair, an option that is quite common for transient clusters.

Cluster Visible to All IAM Users in Account   This option allows you to make the cluster visible to other IAM users in the account. Deselecting this option means that only the creator of the cluster can see the cluster in the account.

Permissions   This option allows you to choose the roles that are required by EMR to call other AWS services and offers options between default and custom permissions.

Default permissions provide default roles for the EMR role and EC2 instance profile role. The new role that we see here, which was not available in the quick options, is Auto Scaling role. This role allows autoscaling to add or remove EC2 instances when an autoscaling rule is triggered. The default role for this is EMR_AutoScaling_DefaultRole, which has a default policy called AmazonElasticMapReduceforAutoScalingRole, which basically allows you to describe cloud watch alarms, and list and modify instance groups.

Custom permissions provide you with the option to choose customized roles.

Security Configuration   We discussed security configurations earlier, and the options available in security configurations. The default is None. However, you can choose the security configuration that you would like to apply to this EMR cluster.

EC2 Security Groups   We've discussed the role of subnets and security groups earlier in this chapter. As a reminder, a security group is basically a firewall for your cluster nodes (master, core, task) and helps you control the traffic coming into the cluster and leaving the cluster. You can choose EMR managed security groups and additional security groups in this section of security options.

Figure 6.7 demonstrates the security options available during advanced cluster setup.

EMR Security Summary

We have looked at various EMR security options, including running EMR in private/public subnets, accessing other services from EMR, security configurations, blocking public access to the service, and the clusters managed by the service. This should not only prepare you for running a secure EMR cluster, it should also help you navigate the security-related questions around EMR in the exam. Finally, I would highly recommend you practice with these security options and review the following blogs before you attempt the exam.

- "Best Practices for Securing Amazon EMR" – aws.amazon.com/blogs/big-data/best-practices-for-securing-amazon-emr

- "Securing your cluster with Block Public access configuration" – aws.amazon.com/blogs/big-data/secure-your-amazon-emr-cluster-from-unintentional-network-exposure-with-block-public-access-configuration

- "Implement perimeter security in Amazon EMR using Apache Knox" – aws.amazon.com/blogs/big-data/implement-perimeter-security-in-emr-using-apache-knox

FIGURE 6.7   Security options in Amazon EMR – advanced cluster setup

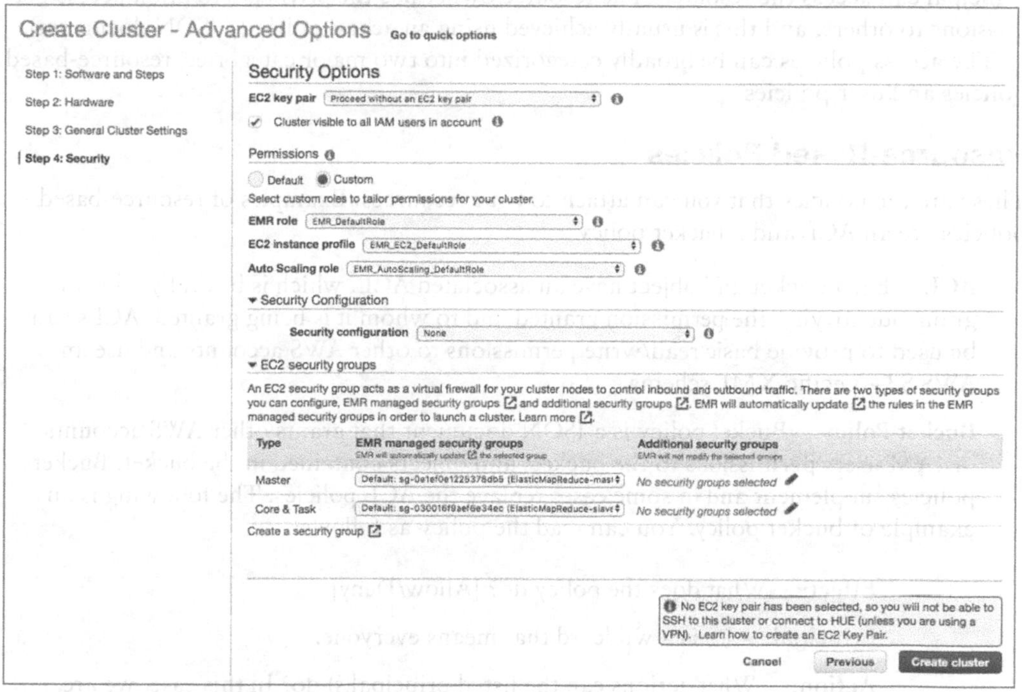

Amazon S3 Security

We've looked at Amazon S3 in Chapter 3, "Data Storage" and we discussed that Amazon S3 forms the basis of your data lake in your modern data architecture. We have already looked at options of securing Amazon S3 data when it is accessed from Amazon EMR, and we will continue to look at this when we discuss other services later in this chapter.

Since S3 is primarily a storage solution, we need to look at multiple aspects of security, including protection of data in terms of encryption, managing access to the resources, logging the access to different buckets and files, and finally, best practices around securing your data on Amazon S3.

Managing Access to Data in Amazon S3

The key resources that we would like to protect are buckets, objects, and other sub-resources like lifecycle configurations, website configurations, and versioning configuration. Managing access refers to granting others (AWS accounts and users) permission to perform a resource operation by writing an access policy. By default, other than the resource owner (the AWS account who creates the resources), who has full access to the resource, no other principal can access the resource. The resource owner has the privileges to grant access permissions to others, and this is usually achieved using an access policy (a JSON document).

The access policies can be broadly categorized into two major categories, resource-based policies and user policies.

Resource-Based Policies

These are the policies that you can attach to your resources. Examples of resource-based policies are an ACL and a bucket policy.

ACL Each bucket and object have an associated ACL, which is basically a list of grants identifying the permission granted and to whom it is being granted. ACLs can be used to provide basic read/write permissions to other AWS accounts and use an AWS S3–specific XML schema.

Bucket Policy Bucket policy is a JSON document that grants other AWS accounts or IAM users permissions to the buckets and objects contained in the bucket. Bucket policies supplement and in some cases replace the ACL policies. The following is an example of bucket policy. You can read the policy as follows:

Effect: What does the policy do? [Allow/Deny]

Principal: (*) is a wildcard that means everyone.

Action: What actions can the listed principal(s) do? In this case, we are providing read permission on objects.

Resource: Since a bucket policy is an example of a resource-based policy, you can see that we are providing the name of the resource that gets impacted by the policy.

```
{
    "Version":"2012-10-17",
    "Statement": [
        {
            "Effect":"Allow",
            "Principal": "*",
            "Action":["s3:GetObject"],
            "Resource":["arn:aws:s3:::analyticscertbucket/*"]
        }
    ]
}
```

User Policies

The policies that are attached to IAM users, groups, and roles in your account are called *user policies*.

The following is an example of a user policy:

```
{
    "Version": "2012-10-17",
    "Statement": [
        {
            "Sid": "FirstStatement",
            "Effect": "Allow",
            "Action": [
                "s3:PutObject",
                "s3:GetObject",
                "s3:ListBucket",
                "s3:DeleteObject",
                "s3:GetBucketLocation"
            ],
            "Resource": [
                "arn:aws:s3::: analyticscertbucket /*",
                "arn:aws:s3::: analyticscertbucket "
            ]
        },
        {
            "Sid": "SecondStatement",
            "Effect": "Allow",
            "Action": "s3:ListAllMyBuckets",
            "Resource": "*"
        }
    ]
}
```

To protect resources in Amazon S3, you can use either a resource-based policy or a user policy or a combination of both. When Amazon S3 receives a request, it will evaluate all access policies to determine if the requester has the necessary permissions and based on that authorize or deny the request. At runtime, Amazon S3 will convert all relevant policies (user policies, bucket polices, ACLs) into a set of policies for evaluation, which are then evaluated based on the context in which the request was made.

Requests made to Amazon S3 can be authenticated and unauthenticated. You can have an unauthenticated request in the following scenarios:

- Bucket has a public bucket policy.
- Bucket ACL grants WRITE or FULL_CONTROL to All Users group.
- Bucket ACL grants WRITE or FULL_CONTROL anonymous user specifically.

All unauthenticated requests are made by the anonymous user with a specific canonical user ID. This user will become the owner of all objects that are uploaded via an unauthenticated request.

AWS does not encourage use of bucket policies that allow anonymous public writes to your bucket, and it provides the Amazon S3 Block Public Access option to enforce this behavior.

Choosing between Various Resource-Based Policies

Resource-based policies include bucket policies, bucket ACLs, and object ACLs. You might be wondering when to use various ACL policies. AWS Documentation is pretty comprehensive in providing various technical scenarios and example walk-throughs. You can dig deeper into the differences at the following link: amzn.to/2Tm70i0. The exam does not cover these differences.

Blocking Public Access

Blocking public access is an account-level setting and is a very handy feature within Amazon S3 that provides settings for access points, buckets, and accounts to help manage the public access to your Amazon S3 resources. To keep your account and resources secure, Amazon S3 blocks all public access by default; however, with the tools available at your disposal, like bucket policies, access point policies, and object permissions, you may inadvertently craft policies in a way that allow public access to certain important resources. S3 Block Public Access is a savior in these situations and allows you to override the policy and permission settings so you can limit public access to these resources.

In fact, this is the first check that is applied when a request is made for a resource within Amazon S3. Amazon S3 Block Public Access offers four settings:

- Blocking public access for buckets and objects granted through new access control lists (ACLs)
- Blocking public access for buckets and objects granted through any access control lists (ACLs)
- Blocking public access to buckets and objects granted through new public bucket or access point polices
- Blocking public and cross-account access to buckets and objects through any public bucket or access point policies

Figure 6.8 shows the settings on the AWS Console.

FIGURE 6.8   S3 Block Public Access settings

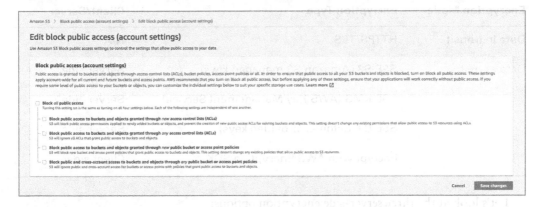

These settings apply account-wide for all current and future buckets and access points. While it is highly recommended to switch on public access, it is important to check if your existing applications will continue to work with this setting switched on.

To learn more about blocking public access to S3, please visit amzn.to/2WMb8W4.

Data Protection in Amazon S3

Earlier in Chapter 3, "Data Storage," we looked at the reliability of Amazon S3 and the fact that it provides 11 nines of durability with a design that is built to sustain concurrent loss of data in multiple facilities in addition to default object versioning. While a standard GET request will always fetch the latest version of an object, you can retrieve older versions by specifying the version number.

S3 provides encryption for data at rest and in motion. This is achieved using S3 client-side encryption and server-side encryption and applying encryption to data in transit.

Client-Side Encryption

You can encrypt your data on the client side before you send it to Amazon S3. This can be achieved using a master key store on AWS using AWS Key Management Service (AWS KMS) or a master key store within your application. Amazon's SDKs for Java, PHP, .NET, Go, Ruby, and C++ support client-side encryption.

Server-Side Encryption

As the name indicates, server-side encryption is encryption of data at its destination, in this case Amazon S3; it essentially protects data at rest. Server-side encryption encrypts object data but not object metadata. Amazon S3 automatically encrypts your data when it is stored on the disks in AWS data centers and automatically decrypts the data when it is being accessed. The entire process is transparent to the user, and users have three mutually exclusive options for server-side encryption, with the key difference being how the keys are managed between various options (see Table 6.6).

TABLE 6.6 S3 data encryption options

Encryption Mode	Encryption Type	Client/Server
Data in transit	HTTPS/TLS	N/A
Data at rest	SSE-S3 (Amazon S3 managed keys)	Server side
	SSE-KMS (AWS Key Management Service)	Server side
	SSE-C (customer-provided keys)	Server side
	Encrypt with AWS Encryption SDK	Client side

Let's look at the three server-side encryption options:

Server-Side Encryption with Amazon S3 Managed Keys (SSE-S3)   When SSE-S3 is selected, each object is encrypted with a unique key, and each key is encrypted with the master key, which is regularly rotated as an additional safeguard mechanism.

Server-side Encryption with Customer Master Keys (CMKs) Store in AWS Key Management Service (SSE-KMS).   SSE-KMS is similar to SSE-S3, with the additional benefit of an audit trail showing when a CMK (customer master key) was used and by whom. There is an additional cost element as well. In an exam scenario, where you need to identify the usage of CMK and an appropriate audit trail, make sure to choose SSE-KMS as your preferred encryption option.

Server-Side Encryption with Customer-Provided Keys (SSE-C).   While SSE-S3 and SSE-KMS both have key stores managed by AWS, SSE-C means that the customer manages the encryption keys and Amazon S3 manages the encryption process when data is written to disk and decryption when the objects are accessed. This feature allows the customer to use their own encryption keys. Customers provide the encryption keys as a part of the request, which are then used to manage the encryption and decryption of the data to/from the disk.

Figure 6.9 shows Amazon S3 encryption options available to you when you upload a new object via the console.

Logging and Monitoring with Amazon S3

We have looked at managing access to resources in Amazon S3 and protecting data using a variety of encryption options. We have not yet looked at how you can log and monitor requests to Amazon S3. Monitoring is an essential part of maintaining reliability, availability, and performance of Amazon S3. Logging is essential from an auditing purpose to keep track of who accessed your data and when.

FIGURE 6.9   S3 encryption options

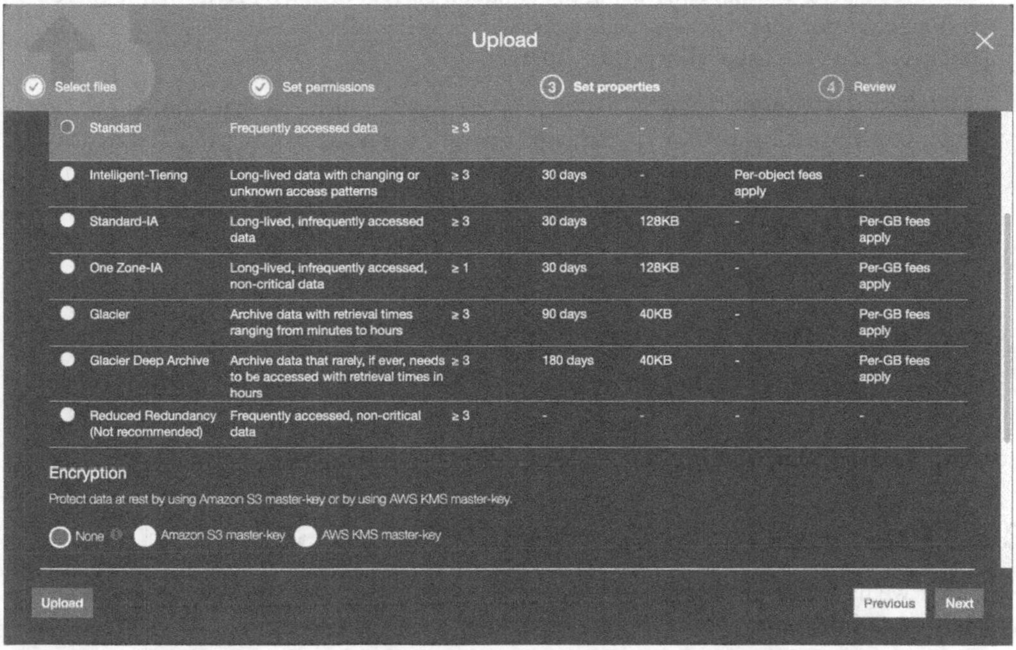

Amazon S3 provides a number of tools for monitoring your Amazon S3 resources for potential incidents. The key tools are as follows:

Amazon CloudWatch Alarms   Amazon CloudWatch allows you to monitor metrics over a time period that you specify. Exceeding a metric threshold can result in notification to Amazon SNS or an autoscaling policy.

AWS CloudTrail Logs   Auditing is an essential component of a system for various compliance reasons. AWS CloudTrail enables governance, compliance, operational auditing, and risk auditing of your AWS account and provides event history of your AWS account activity, including actions through the AWS Management Console, AWS SDKs, command-line tools, and other AWS services. This history simplifies security analysis, resource change tracking, and trouble shooting. You can use the information from AWS CloudTrail to determine the request that was made to Amazon S3, the IP address from which the request was made, who made the request, when it was made, and additional details. Understanding the usage of this service is also important from an exam perspective as you will see certain auditing questions.

AWS S3 Access Logs   Server access logging is another useful feature that allows you to track the requests that are made to an Amazon S3 bucket. Server access logs are useful for security auditing and helping customers understand Amazon S3 billing where data scans play an important part. You can enable server access logging on the AWS console or programmatically using the Amazon S3 API or AWS SDKs. While there is no charge for server access logging as such, any log files that are delivered to your bucket accrue the usual charges for storage.

AWS Trusted Advisor   AWS Trusted Advisor is an application that draws upon best practices learned from AWS's aggregated operational history of serving hundreds of thousands of AWS customers. Trusted Advisor inspects your AWS environment and makes recommendations for saving money, improving system performance, or closing security gaps. AWS Trusted Advisor has the following S3-related checks, which are helpful from a security context:

Logging configuration of Amazon S3 buckets

Security checks for Amazon S3 buckets that have open access permissions

Fault tolerance checks for buckets that don't have versioning enabled or have versioning suspended

Best Practices for Security on Amazon S3

Now that we have looked at some of the best practices for security on Amazon S3, let's look at some of the best practices for security to protect your data:

- Enable account-level Block Public Access.
- Leverage access points to scope application permissions.
- Send secure traffic with VPC endpoints and access points.
- Use bucket policy to enforce TLS.
- Encrypt everything: SSE-KMS &SSE-S3.
- Enable object lock, versioning, MFA delete to protect data.
- Monitor using AWS tools, such as AWS CloudTrail and AWSConfig.

Amazon Athena Security

We've looked at Amazon Athena in Chapter 4, "Data Processing and Analysis" and how it is a great tool built on Apache Presto to enable ad hoc data analysis. Since Amazon Athena will be used by data analysts and data scientists, it becomes very important to understand how it secures the data.

Managing Access to Amazon Athena

Amazon Athena allows users to perform a variety of operations and uses IAM to manage access to the underlying resources and the operations. Essentially when people log in to Amazon Athena, they will be running SQL queries, which require the following permissions:

- Access to Amazon Athena API actions, including actions for Athena workgroups
- Access to the underlying storage, primarily S3, where the data is located
- Access to the metadata layer in AWS Glue Catalog

To perform Athena API actions, work with data in S3, and access/create metadata in AWS Glue Data Catalog, your IAM principals have identity-based policies attached to them. The policies consist of statements that define actions that are allowed or denied. Instead of the user trying to identify what actions will be needed for Athena to work, Amazon Athena provides two managed policies, which are easy to set up and are updated automatically with the required actions as the service evolves and new features are released. The policies are as follows:

AmazonAthenaFullAccess   This policy grants full access to Amazon Athena and includes permissions to AWS Glue, Amazon S3, Amazon SNS, and Amazon CloudWatch. You should attach it to principals who require such an access. To view the latest contents of the policy, please visit AWS Documentation at `amzn.to/2zZx7zP`. While you can always create custom policies using this policy as a reference and fine-tune the permissions required by the users of Amazon Athena, it is recommended to use AmazonAthenaFullAccess as a starting point and then allow or deny specific permissions based on your needs.

AWSQuickSightAthenaAccess   This policy grants access to actions that Amazon QuickSight needs to integrate it with Athena and hence is the right policy for principals who would use Amazon QuickSight to display and visualize the data from Amazon Athena. This policy primarily offers actions for Amazon Athena, AWS Glue, and Amazon S3. To look at the latest contents of this policy, please visit AWS Documentation at `amzn.to/2zUvao9`.

Athena also provides JDBC and ODBC drivers to allow other applications to connect and read data from Amazon Athena. To access Athena using JDBC/ODBC, you need to provide the JDBC/ODBC credentials to your application. You need to ensure that the IAM permissions policy includes the actions listed in the AWSQuickSightAthenaAccess managed policy.

Amazon Athena also needs access to Amazon S3, which is provided using the managed policies. If your Athena users need to create tables and work with underlying data, they must have access to the S3 location of the data, along with appropriate permissions.

If you are using the AWS Glue Data Catalog for Amazon Athena, you can define resource-level policies for the databases and tables being used in Athena. Athena only provides fine-grained controls at the database and table level, but not at the individual partition level. Furthermore, if your AWS Glue Data Catalog is in a different account (cross-account access), Athena does not support the option at the time of this writing.

Access to Athena Workgroups

The Amazon Athena workgroup is a resource type that can be used to separate query execution and query history between users, teams, and applications running under the same AWS account. Because workgroups are a resource, you can use resource-based policies to control access to them.

For example, if you have a team called "adhoc-analysts" that typically does an ad hoc data analysis and another team called "automated-reporting" that typically runs automated reports, you can create two workgroups, one for each team. Since workgroups are IAM resources, they have an associated ARN, which can be used in the IAM policy associated with the users. You can create a single IAM user representing the team of ad hoc users and add the individual to an IAM group. The group contains a policy that enforces what actions these users can perform. You can also use an IAM policy to set up permissions for your analyst user and grant the user only the permissions required for working in the ad-hoc-users workgroup. The blog post at go.aws/3bTW3pB provides a great walk-through of setting up workgroups and restricting access based on the workload.

Federated Data Access with Athena

If you manage user credentials outside of AWS in Microsoft Active Directory, you can still provide federated access to Amazon Athena. The authentication can be done with a JDBC or ODBC driver with SAML 2.0 support to access ADFS 3.0 (Active Directory Federation Services) and enable a client application to call Athena API actions. There are certain prerequisites for this scenario:

1. Configure ADFS 3.0 as your identity provider inside your organization.
2. Install and configure the latest version of JDBC clients on your client applications. Your drivers should support federated access and must be compatible with SAML 2.0.

The architecture diagram in Figure 6.10 indicates a typical architecture for a federated setup.

Data Protection in Amazon Athena

Athena is a data processing and analysis engine and hence works with data from sources and can transform and create new and updated versions from it. Amazon Athena does not modify the source data.

Athena uses the schema-on-read paradigm when reading data from sources, which means that schema is applied at runtime to the data stored in your source engine. Athena allows you to modify the data catalog using Data Definition Language (DDL) statements.

FIGURE 6.10   Federated access for Amazon Athena

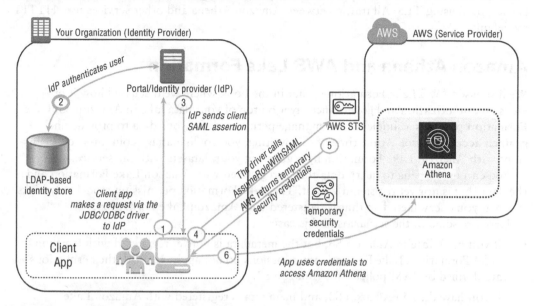

The key artifacts produced within Amazon Athena are query results and query history. Query results are stored in Amazon S3 in the default location as specified in the workgroup definition, and you have full control over the buckets where the query results are saved and queries are stored.

Athena stores your query history and query results for 45 days, which can be viewed using AWS Console, Amazon Athena APIs, and the AWS CLI. For compliance reasons, if is recommended to save the query results and queries in addition to restricting access to them using Athena workgroups.

Data Encryption in Amazon Athena

Amazon Athena allows you to work with encrypted data and encrypted query results and metadata in the AWS Glue Data Catalog. Amazon Athena supports SSE-S3, SSE-KSM, and CSE-KMS (client-side encryption with AWS KMS) as encryption options, but does not support SSE-C (SSE with customer-provided keys) or client-side encryption using a client-side master key and asymmetric keys.

Athena workgroups that we discussed in the previous section allow you to enforce encryption of query results. If you are connecting using the JDBC or ODBC driver, you must configure the appropriate driver for the encryption type and S3 staging location.

Since Amazon Athena uses data from a variety of sources, but primarily S3, it uses Transport Layer Security (TLS) for data in transit between data sources and Amazon Athena. TLS is also used between applications consuming data from Amazon Athena, and hence all data in transit is encrypted. Even if you are using JDBC or an ODBC driver, data is encrypted using TLS. All traffic between Amazon Athena and other services uses HTTPs by default.

Amazon Athena and AWS Lake Formation

We discussed AWS Lake Formation earlier in the book where we discussed how it provides an authorization and governance layer on top of your data lake in Amazon S3. Lake Formation provides a simple way to manage permissions for your data to provide fine-grained access control. At the time of this writing, you could manage column-level permissions with Amazon Lake Formation by registering your datasets with the service.

You can use Athena to query data that is registered with Amazon Lake Formation and the data that is not yet registered with it. The Lake Formation permission model only kicks in when you query metadata that is registered with Amazon Lake Formation.

Here are some of the scenarios in this case:

- If you have data in Amazon S3, but the metadata is not yet registered with Amazon Lake Formation, Lake Formation permissions do not apply. Instead, the permissions are defined by IAM policies for Amazon S3.

- If you have data in Amazon S3, and metadata is registered with Amazon Lake Formation, Lake Formation permissions will apply and you can enable fine-grained access control (FGAC).

- If you have Amazon Athena results in an AWS bucket, you cannot register it with AWS Lake Formation.

- If you have Athena query history, you cannot use lake formation permissions to control access to this data and instead will have to use Athena workgroups to control access to query history.

This completes our section on Amazon Athena security. We have touched upon some of the key concepts but have by no means looked at the end-to-end security options within Amazon Athena. It is highly recommended that you look at the AWS Documentation and Amazon Athena workgroups and other security features listed in the additional reading and references section at the end of this chapter before you attempt the exam.

Amazon Redshift Security

Security has always been a day one thing at Amazon, and Amazon Redshift is no exception. Each service offered by AWS offers a comprehensive suite of security features that helps you protect your data.

Amazon Redshift offers the following features to help you protect your data warehouse environment, which typically hosts your most critical data, often prepared to serve the business users:

- End-to-end encryption for data protection, including encryption of data at rest and encryption of data in motion

- Integration with IAM and SAML identity provider for federation (SSO)

- Network isolation of your cluster using Amazon VPC
- Security of your data using a database security model with users, groups, and privileges.
- Audit logging and notifications for compliance and monitoring purposes
- Security compliance certifications including SOC 1/2/3, PCI-DSS, FedRAMP, and HIPAA

Levels of Security within Amazon Redshift

Amazon Redshift resources are secured at four levels within AWS: cluster management, cluster connectivity, database access, and temporary DB credentials and Single Sign-On.

Cluster Management

IAM is used to control an AWS user's ability to create, configure, and delete Amazon Redshift clusters. An Amazon Redshift cluster can be created from the AWS Management Console, AWS Command Line Interface (CLI), or the Amazon Redshift application programming interface (API). Once users have access to Amazon Redshift service, they can choose to connect via the JDBC/ODBC driver or Query Editor in the Redshift console. We looked at Redshift resources in Chapter 4, "Data Processing and Analysis," like Redshift cluster, Redshift cluster snapshots, parameter groups, and event subscriptions. The primary IAM resource is the Redshift cluster, whereas snapshots, parameter groups and event subscriptions are sub-resources. An account administrator will attach permission policies to IAM identities to allow users to perform operations like create/delete a cluster, create a snapshot, and so on.

Cluster Connectivity

Amazon Redshift uses security groups that allow AWS instances to connect to a Redshift cluster. With regard to network configuration, Amazon Redshift's compute nodes are placed in a private/internal VPC that is only accessible by the leader node. The *leader node* resides in both the private/internal VPC for compute nodes and the customer's VPC to allow customer access to Redshift cluster and to handle data distribution among the compute nodes. This is what makes it possible for client applications such as QuickSight to communicate with the Redshift cluster and the leader node to communicate with the compute nodes. High-bandwidth connections, close proximity, and custom communication protocols provide private, very high-speed network communication between the leader node and compute nodes. *Compute nodes* interact with other AWS services such as S3, EMR, and DynamoDB for ingestion, backup, and so on. Most customers configure Redshift with multiple subnets to choose from, whereas an Amazon Redshift cluster exists in only one subnet/AZ at a time.

Amazon Redshift clusters are locked down by default, which means no users can connect to the cluster. To grant users with access to the cluster, a security group must be associated with the cluster to open up the appropriate ports and accept incoming connections from the whitelisted IP addresses, CIDR block ranges, or security groups.

Enhanced VPC Routing (EVR) is an optional feature that forces all Redshift COPY, UNLOAD, and backup operations to flow through a customer's designated VPC endpoint instead of going over the Internet.

It is possible to enable Enhanced VPC Routing for Redshift Lakehouse traffic as well.

Database Access

Redshift is a relational database and hence supports concepts like schemas, users, groups, tables, and views.

- *Schemas* are collections of database tables and other database objects (similar to namespaces).

- *Users* are named user accounts that can connect to a database.

- *Groups* are collections of users that can be collectively assigned privileges for easier security maintenance.

Access to these databases objects is controlled by user accounts within the Amazon Redshift database, providing an additional layer of security. Users can only access resources in the database that their user accounts have been granted permissions to access. You can create Amazon Redshift user accounts and manage permissions using CREATE USER, CREATE GROUP, GRANT or REVOKE SQL statements.

By default, when you create an object, you are the owner and you have the privileges to the object. A user account can receive privileges to a database object in the following ways:

- Explicit privileges assignment using GRANT statement

- Implicit privileges by being a member of a group having the appropriate privileges

When you create a Redshift cluster, you are required to specify a master user and password. This master user has superuser privileges and has access to all databases created within the cluster and can create other superusers and accounts.

You can achieve row-/column-level security in a Redshift database in three ways:

- Create (materialized) views that contain the rows/columns permitted to given users and give privileges on those views to the given users.

- Emulate row- or column-level security by having a column indicating allowed users and honoring the column in your queries—obviously this only works if the data is locked down and users can only access the data via your queries.

- Redshift Lakehouse supports fine-grained column-level policies through Redshift's Lake Formation integration.

Temporary DB Credentials and Single Sign-On

Amazon Redshift allows you to sign in to a database using the IAM credentials or using a federated SSO (Single Sign-On) through a SAML 2.0–compliant identity provider. You can configure your SAML 2.0–compliant IdP to permit you federated access to an IAM role, and using the role you can generate temporary database credentials to log on to an Amazon Redshift database.

To set up SSO with Redshift, you need the following:

- Redshift JDBC/ODBC drivers
- A SAML 2.0 compliant IdP such as these:
  - PingFederate
  - Okta
  - Microsoft ADFS
  - Azure AD

These are the steps:

1. Setting up IdP(s) and federation
2. Creating IAM roles for access to the Amazon Redshift cluster
3. Setting up database access (CREATE GROUP, GRANT, and so on)
4. Connecting to Amazon Redshift using the JDBC/ODBC SQL client

Data Protection in Amazon Redshift

Redshift as a service stores the most critical element of your enterprise: your enterprise data crafted to serve the business users who will make decisions based on the data available in data marts, and hence it needs to be protected at all costs. Redshift provides options to protect your data in transit and in motion. Let's look at the options provided by Redshift for data protection.

Encryption of Data in Transit

All Redshift cluster communications are secured by default. Redshift always uses hardware-accelerated SSL to communicate with other AWS services (such as Amazon S3, Amazon DynamoDB, and Amazon EMR for data loads).

Encryption of Data at Rest

In Amazon Redshift, you can enable database encryption to protect data at rest. When you enable encryption, the data blocks and system metadata are encrypted for the cluster and its snapshots. You can enable encryption when you launch a cluster, or you can modify an unencrypted database to start using KMS encryption. When you modify encryption of a database to KMS encryption, Amazon Redshift automatically migrates your data to a new encrypted cluster.

KMS-based encryption is recommended since it supports key rotation and bring your own key.

Amazon Redshift uses the following hierarchy (shown in Figure 6.11) of encryption keys to encrypt the data in Redshift database:

- *Tier 1:* Master key — This can be a customer-managed key (CMK) or KMS-generated master key and is used to encrypt the cluster encryption key.

- *Tier 2:* Cluster encryption key is used to encrypt the database encryption key.
- *Tier 3:* Database encryption key is used to encrypt the data encryption key.
- *Tier 4:* Data encryption key is used to encrypt the actual data block.

FIGURE 6.11   Key hierarchy in Amazon Redshift

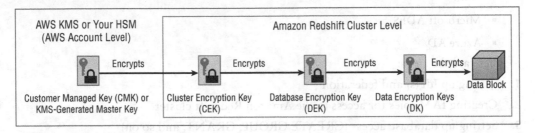

You can configure encryption in Amazon Redshift in the AWS Console (amzn
.to/2WSY1Cm) or the Amazon Redshift API and AWS CLI (amzn.to/3bVYsQD).

Redshift Auditing

By now you are well aware of the importance of auditing for various services. Redshift
provides two options for audit logging database-level activities such as which users logged
in and when: audit logs and system tables. The logs are stored in Amazon S3 buckets and
hence provide convenient access to users who are responsible for monitoring activities in
the database.

Audit Logs

Amazon Redshift logs information in the following log files:

- *Connection log* – This log file logs all connection attempts, connections, and discon-
  nections. This log is primarily for security purposes.
- *User log* – This log file logs information about changes to database user definitions.
  This log is primarily for security purposes.
- *User activity log* – This log provides every query that is submitted to the database.
  The user activity log is primarily for debugging purposes as it helps you understand all
  the queries sent to the database, which includes queries from the users and the data-
  base itself.

System Tables

Amazon Redshift audit logs are also available as system tables listed here: amzn
.to/2Xpi3n6. The main security-related system tables are as follows:

- *SVL_STATEMENT_TEXT* – This is a system view based on the system tables containing the statements that are running on the system. This view is made available to

all users; however, superusers can see all data, whereas a regular user can only see their own data.

- *STL_CONNECTION_LOG* – This is a system table based on the connection log data file and only available to superusers.

Redshift Logging

Logging is an important part of any system to understand the requests made to the system and an audit trail of the principal making the request and the time when the request was made. Amazon Redshift integrates with CloudTrail for audit logging service-level activities to provide such information.

Cloud trail logs are stored indefinitely in S3, unless S3 lifecycle rules are in place to archive or delete files automatically. CloudTrail captures the last 90 days of management events by default without charge (available using CloudTrail APIs or via the console).

You can maintain a history longer than 90 days; however, additional CloudTrail charges and S3 charges will be applicable. Access to log files does not require access to the Redshift database, which means that if you have auditors who are looking at security-related incidents, you can simply provide them access to log files without providing access to the Redshift database.

Amazon Elasticsearch Security

In Chapter 4, we looked at Amazon Elasticsearch and how it is a useful engine for operational analytics. Amazon Elasticsearch provides a number of ways to control access to your domains: authentication for Kibana, protecting your domain by encrypting the data at rest as well as in motion, providing super fine-grained access control, and enhanced logging and monitoring.

Amazon Elasticsearch service has three main layers of security:

- *Network* – This is the first layer that determines if a request can reach an Amazon Elasticsearch domain at all. We'll look at this in more detail in the next section.

- *Domain Access Policy* – Once the request reaches the Amazon Elasticsearch domain or a domain endpoint, you can use a resource-based access policy to accept or deny the request to a specific URI. The access policy therefore rejects requests at the end of a domain before they reach Elasticsearch itself.

- *Fine-Grained Access Control (FGAC)* – Once the request has passed the network and domain access policy check, FGAC checks the user credentials and authenticates or denies a request. Once FGAC authenticates the request, all the roles mapped to that user and a complete set of permissions are fetched to determine how to best handle the request.

Elasticsearch Network Configuration

You can launch an Amazon ES domain in your virtual private cloud (VPC) or make it publicly accessible. You are provided these options when you create an Elasticsearch domain in Amazon Elasticsearch.

VPC Access

When you place an Amazon ES domain within a VPC, you can enable secure communications between Amazon ES and other services without the need for an Internet gateway, a NAT device, or a VPN connection. Setting up your ES domain within a VPC means all traffic will remain within the AWS cloud and hence have an additional layer of security over ES domains that are publicly accessible (see Figure 6.12).

FIGURE 6.12   Amazon Elasticsearch network configuration

You can choose an ES domain to be configured in multiple Availability Zones, which means that Amazon ES will place an endpoint in one, two, or three subnets within your VPC. Furthermore, Amazon ES will place an elastic network interface (ENI) in the VPC for each of your data nodes. The ENI will be assigned a private IP address from the IPV4 address range of your subnet, and a public DNS hostname (domain endpoint) will be assigned to it. To access the service, you should use the public DNS service resolution.

Some limitations of VPC access are as follows:

- You must choose between launching your domain inside a VPC or using a public endpoint.

- You can't switch from an ES domain in a VPC to a public endpoint or vice versa. If you need to switch once an ES domain has been created, you will have to follow the ES migration process, typically using snapshots, which offer a convenient means to migrating your data.
- You can't switch an ES domain's VPC once it is created.
- You can't apply IP-based policies to ES domains inside a VPC since the security groups already enforce IP-based access policies.

Accessing Amazon Elasticsearch and Kibana

The key resource within Amazon Elasticsearch is an ES domain. Amazon Elasticsearch offers a number of ways to control and manage access to an ES domain. Amazon ES supports three types of policies:

- Resource based policies
- Identity-based policies
- IP-based policies

Resource-Based Policies

The key resource within Amazon ES is an ES domain. You also have a domain's sub-resources, like Elasticsearch indices and APIs. You can add resource-based policies, sometimes called domain access policies, when you create a domain. The policy specifies which actions a principal can perform on the domain's sub-resources. The following policy grants analytics-user full access (es:*) to analytics-cert-domain.

```
{
  "Version": "2012-10-17",
  "Statement": [
    {
      "Effect": "Allow",
      "Principal": {
        "AWS": [
          "arn:aws:iam::987654321098:user/analytics-user"
        ]
      },
      "Action": [
        "es:*"
      ],
      "Resource": "arn:aws:es:us-west-1:123451234501:domain/analytics-cert-
domain/*"
    }
  ]
}
```

Key points to note here are as follows:

1. The principal who will be granted access is identified with the ARN
    `arn:aws:iam::987654321098:user/analytics-user`.

2. The actions that the user is allowed to perform is an `es:wild-card`, which means all
    Elasticsearch actions.

    The resource part is critical as it mentions the following:

    a. The privileges that the user has been granted will apply to only the analytics-
    cert-domain.

    b. The trailing wildcard `/*` in the resource indicates that this policy is applicable to
    the sub-resources (such as indices) within a domain and note the domain itself.

3. You can further limit the analytics user to specific actions such as `es:ESHttpGet`,
    `es:ESHttpDelete`, `es:ESHttpPost`, `es:ESHttpPut`, and `es:ESHttpHead`.

Note: If your resource-based access policy contains IAM users or roles, you must send a
signed request using AWS Signature Version 4 (Sigv4 in short).

Identity-Based Policies

You can attach an identity-based policy to users or roles using the AWS IAM service.
Identity-based policies specify who can access a service, what actions they can perform,
and the resources on which the actions can be performed.

Identity-based policies are attached to principals (users/roles), and hence the JSON itself
doesn't need to specify the principal it is attached to. The following is an example of a
policy that is typically assigned to administrators and provides full access to Amazon ES
and all the data stored in the domains:

```
{
  "Version": "2012-10-17",
  "Statement": [
    {
      "Action": [
        "es:*"
      ],
      "Effect": "Allow",
      "Resource": "*"
    }
  ]
}
```

IP-Based Policies

You can also restrict access to your ES domain to a particular IP address or a CIDR block.
IP-based policies are actually resource-based policies with an anonymous principal and a
special Condition element with a source IP mentioned.

The primary objective of creating an IP-based policy is to allow an unsigned request to an Amazon ES domain, which lets you use clients like curl and Kibana or access the domain through a proxy server.

The following is an example of an IP-based policy that allows all HTTP requests from a specific IPrange for the analytics-cert-domain:

```
{
  "Version": "2012-10-17",
  "Statement": [
    {
      "Effect": "Allow",
      "Principal": {
        "AWS": "*"
      },
      "Action": [
        "es:ESHttp*"
      ],
      "Condition": {
        "IpAddress": {
          "aws:SourceIp": [
            "192.168.10.0/24"
          ]
        }
      },
      "Resource": "arn:aws:es:us-west-1:123451234512:domain/analytics-cert-domain/*"
    }
  ]
}
```

From an exam perspective, you need to know the types of policies that can be used to restrict access to an ES domain using resource-based, user-based, and an IP-based policy.

Making and Signing Amazon Elasticsearch Requests

All requests to Amazon ES must be signed. If your access policies specify an IAM user or a role, the requests to ES APIs must be signed using AWS SigV4. You can sign a request yourself or use an AWS SDK like *Boto 3* to sign the request for you. Signing a request using an SDK is always a recommended approach as it not only simplifies the process of signing a request but also saves you a considerable amount of time to do so.

Fine-Grained Access Control

You saw earlier that fine-grained access control (FGAC) provides the third layer of security for an Amazon Elasticsearch domain. FGAC provides the ability to use roles to define granular permissions for the indices, documents, and fields. You can have a number of teams sharing an Amazon ES domain without being able to see or modify other team's indices, dashboards, or visualizations, enabling greater efficiency and centralizing management.

Your access policies can conflict with fine-grained access control, especially if you are using internal user databases and HTTP basic authentication. You can't sign a request with a username/password and also an IAM credential. Hence, if you are enabling FGAC, it is recommended to use a domain access policy that doesn't require signed requests.

How Does Fine-Grained Access Control Work?

Figure 6.13 illustrates a sample flow of when FGAC comes into play when a user sends a request to a domain within a VPC with IAM credentials.

Figure 6.14 represents the second most common configuration, which is a public Elasticsearch domain with fine-grained access control enabled, using an access policy that doesn't use IAM principals and a master user in the internal user database.

You can enable fine-grained access control using AWS Console or CLI or via the configuration API. You can't enable fine-grained access on existing domains and can't disable it once you configure a domain with fine-grained access control.

Authentication for Kibana

Fine-grained access control has a plug-in for Kibana. You can use it to manage users, roles, mappings, action groups, and tenants.

If you choose to use IAM for user management, you must enable Amazon Cognito authentication for Kibana and sign in using credentials from your user pool to access Kibana. One of the assumed roles from the Amazon Cognito identity pool must match the IAM role that you specified for the master user.

If you choose to use the internal user database, you can sign in to Kibana with your master username and password. You must access Kibana over HTTPS.

During the exam, you may be asked about Kibana and Amazon Cognito and if it can be enabled. If you would like to learn more about configuring Cognito authentication using AWS Console, AWS CLI, or AWS SDK, you may want to visit the following AWS Documentation page to learn more: amzn.to/2zrGwjB.

Data Protection in Amazon Elasticsearch

The two key types of encryption are encryption of the data and elements inside an Elasticsearch domain which is often referred to as encryption of data at rest and encryption of data in motion.

FIGURE 6.13 Fine-grained access control within a VPC sample workflow
(Source: amzn.to/3bZQwh2)

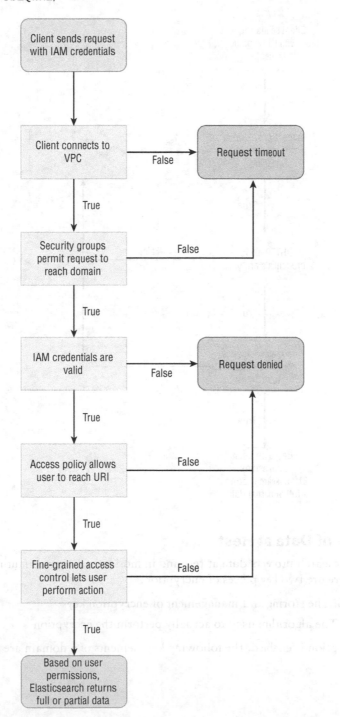

FIGURE 6.14 Fine grained access control with a public domain sample workflow
(Source: amzn.to/3bZQwh2)

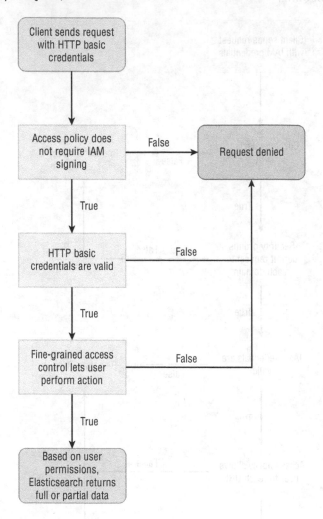

Encryption of Data at Rest

Amazon Elasticsearch protects data at rest and in motion to prevent unauthorized access to your data. There are two key pieces of encryption:

- **AWS KMS:** The storing and management of encryption keys
- **AWS-256:** The algorithm used to actually perform the encryption

When encryption is enabled, the following key elements of a domain are encrypted.

- Indexes
- Elasticsearch logs
- Swap files
- All other data in the application directory
- Automated snapshots

When you enable encryption at rest, the following items will not be encrypted (you can, however, use alternate mechanisms to encrypt them):

- *Manual Snapshots* – At the time of this writing, you can't encrypt manual snapshots using KMS master keys. You can use S3 server-side encryption to encrypt the bucket containing the snapshots.
- *Slow Logs and Error Logs* – You can encrypt these logs in the CloudWatch Logs group using the AWS KMS master key.

Amazon Elasticsearch does not support asymmetric customer master keys.

Encryption of Data in Motion

An Amazon Elasticsearch domain resides within its own PVC, irrespective of whether you choose VPC access or not. By default, the traffic within a VPC is unencrypted. If you enable node-to-node encryption, Amazon Elasticsearch uses TLS encryption for all communications within the VPC.

When you send data to Elasticsearch over an HTTPS connection, data is sent in an encrypted fashion to Amazon Elasticsearch. Node-to-node encryption means that the data will remain encrypted whenever it is in motion.

If you are sending the data to Amazon Elasticsearch over a standard HTTP connection, Amazon ES will encrypt it before it reaches the cluster. Since using HTTPS is a best practice, you can require your traffic to arrive over HTTPS. This setting can be enabled in the console, AWS CLI, or the configuration API.

Amazon Kinesis Security

We discussed Amazon Kinesis in Chapter 2, "Data Collection" earlier in the book. Security is an important concern for streaming data processing, and hence Amazon Kinesis offers comprehensive security options.

Managing Access to Amazon Kinesis

You control logical access to Amazon Kinesis resources and management functions by creating users under your AWS account using AWS IAM and controlling which Amazon Kinesis operations these users have permission to perform. To facilitate running your producer or consumer applications on an Amazon EC2 instance, you can configure that instance with an IAM role. That way, AWS credentials that reflect the permissions associated with the IAM role are made available to applications on the instance, which means you don't have to use your long-term AWS security credentials. Roles have the added benefit of providing temporary credentials that expire within a short time, which adds an additional measure of protection.

Data Protection in Amazon Kinesis

The Amazon Kinesis API is only accessible via an SSL-encrypted endpoint (kinesis .us-east-1.amazonaws.com) to help ensure secure transmission of your data to AWS. You must connect to that endpoint to access Amazon Kinesis, but you can then use the API to direct Amazon Kinesis to create a stream in any AWS Region.

Amazon Kinesis synchronously replicates data across three facilities in an AWS Region, providing high availability and data durability.

In Amazon Kinesis, data records contain a sequence number, a partition key, and a data blob, which is an uninterrupted, immutable sequence of bytes. The Amazon Kinesis service does not inspect, interpret, or change the data in the blob in any way. Data records are accessible for only 24 hours from the time they are added to an Amazon Kinesis stream, and then they are automatically discarded.

AWS Key Management Service is seamlessly integrated with several AWS services, such as Amazon Kinesis Firehose. This integration means that you can easily use AWS KMS master keys to encrypt the data you store with these services. You can use a default master key that is created for you automatically and is usable only within the integrated service, or you can select a custom master key that you either created in KMS or imported from your own key management infrastructure and have permission to use.

Amazon Kinesis Best Practices

The Amazon Kinesis security model follows the general approach of policy-based access, and access to the Amazon Kinesis service and actions are controlled via IAM policy. Here is a list of best practices:

1. Create an IAM entity for admin actions. For example, CreateStream, DeleteStream, AddTagsToStream, and RemoveTagsFromStream.

2. Create an IAM entity for re-sharding of a stream. For example, MergeShards and SplitShard.

3. Create an IAM entity for producers to write. For example, DescribeStream, PutRecord, and PutRecords.

4. Use temporary security credentials (IAM roles) instead of long-term access keys wherever appropriate.

5. If data encryption is required in flight, perform client-side encryption before sending to Amazon Kinesis.

6. Allow producers/consumers based on their expected user agent and source IP addresses.

7. Enforce use of aws:SecureTransport condition key for every API call made to AWS.

For more information about actions and condition context keys for Amazon Kinesis, see docs.aws.amazon.com/IAM/latest/UserGuide/list_amazonkinesis.html.

Amazon QuickSight Security

Amazon QuickSight is a business intelligence tool that we have discussed in depth during the Chapter 5, "Data Visualization." In the following sections, we will look at the security aspects of Amazon QuickSight, ranging from managing access to Amazon QuickSight, data protection, logging and monitoring, and some best practices around securing data.

Managing Data Access with Amazon QuickSight

We looked at the two editions of Amazon QuickSight in Chapter 5, the Standard edition and Enterprise edition. There are slight nuances as some of the features apply to both editions, while some are applicable only to the Enterprise edition.

Amazon QuickSight Enterprise edition can integrate with your existing directories using Active Directive or SSO using SAML. If you are embedding dashboards within client applications, you can use AWS IAM to further enhance security.

Amazon QuickSight Standard Edition allows you to manage users within the service. You can, however, still integrate existing users with AWS IAM.

Table 6.7 gives a quick summary of the options available for security.

TABLE 6.7 Security options in Amazon QuickSight

Security Option	Usage	Applicable Editions
IAM (Identity and Access Management)	You can use • Identity-based policies • Access control lists Resource-based policies are not supported.	Both
AWS Active Directory	Supports the following: • AWS Directory Service • AWS Directory service with AD Connector • On-premises Active Directory with SSO and AD Connector • SSO using AWS Single Sign-On service	Enterprise edition only

TABLE 6.7   Security options in Amazon QuickSight *(continued)*

Security Option	Usage	Applicable Editions
SAML-based Single Sign-On (SSO)	Invite users with valid email address.	Both
Multi-Factor Authentication (MFA)	You can use MFA with AWS QuickSight using AWS Directory Service for Microsoft Active Directory.	Both

Data Protection

Amazon QuickSight supports the following encryption features:

- Encryption at rest (Enterprise edition only)
- Encryption in transit
- Key management

Encryption at Rest

Amazon QuickSight encrypts the following data and metadata using block-level encryption with AWS-managed keys:

- All user data (usernames, email addresses, passwords)
- Data source connection data
- Uploaded file names, data source names, dataset names
- Statistics that power ML insights

In the Standard edition, data is securely stored in SPICE but not encrypted.

Encryption in Motion

All data transfers from data sources to SPICE and from SPICE to the user interface are encrypted. By default, all transfers are encrypted using SSL, but for some databases you can choose whether you want an encrypted transfer or not. The connectivity of users accessing Amazon QuickSight from the Internet is encrypted using SSL.

Key Management

All keys used by Amazon QuickSight are managed by AWS. Database service certificates are not managed by AWS.

Logging and Monitoring

Amazon QuickSight is integrated with AWS CloudTrail, which means all calls to the AWS Console and AWS QuickSight API are recorded.

Amazon CloudWatch is not natively supported at the time of this writing.

Security Best Practices

The following are security best practices for Amazon QuickSight:

- Access to Amazon QuickSight should be using HTTPS or WebSockets secure (`wss://`).

- Access to data sources outside of AWS means that you will need to allow Amazon QuickSight's IP address range to be able to connect to those sources.

- Always use SSL to connect to your databases.

- Wherever possible, try to use enhanced security features provided by the Amazon QuickSight Enterprise edition.

- (Enterprise edition users only) Use VPC connectivity wherever possible to secure your communication to AWS data sources. Use DirectConnect to connect to your on-premises resources for a secure private connection.

Amazon DynamoDB Security

We looked at DynamoDB in Chapter 3, "Data Storage." Let's look at the Amazon DynamoDB security model in the next section.

Access Management in DynamoDB

You can use IAM to grant access to Amazon DynamoDB resources and API actions. To do this, first write an IAM policy, which is a document that explicitly lists the permissions you want to grant. Then attach that policy to an IAM user, group, or role. For example, an IAM user named Joe could create an Amazon DynamoDB table and then write an IAM policy to allow read-only access to this table. Joe could then apply that policy to selected IAM users, groups, or roles in his AWS account. These recipients would then have read-only access to Joe's table. In addition to controlling access at the resource level using IAM, you can control access at the database level using fine-grained access controls. You can create permissions that allow or deny access to specific items (rows) and attributes (columns) in your database.

If you are writing an application targeted at a large number of users, you can optionally use web identity federation for authentication and authorization. Web identity federation removes the need for creating individual IAM users; instead, users can sign in to an identity provider and then obtain temporary security credentials from AWS Security Token Service (AWS STS).

Fine-Grained Access Control

Fine-grained access control is the ability to determine who can access individual data items and attributes in Amazon DynamoDB tables and indexes, and the actions that can be performed on them. To implement fine-grained access control, write an AWS IAM policy that specifies conditions for accessing security credentials and the associated permissions. Then apply the policy to IAM users, groups, or roles. Your IAM policy can restrict access to individual items in a table, access to the attributes in those items, or both at the same time. You can configure fine-grained control by adding condition elements in your IAM policies.

Here are some possible use cases for fine-grained access control:

- An app that displays flight data for nearby airports, based on the user's location. Airline names, arrival and departure times, and flight numbers are all displayed; however, attributes such as pilot names or the number of passengers are restricted.

- A social networking app for games, where all users' saved game data is stored in a single table, but no user can access data items that they do not own.

- An app for targeted advertising that stores data about ad impressions and click tracking. The app can only write data items for the current user and can only retrieve targeted ad recommendations for that user.

IAM Policy with Fine-Grained Access Control

Consider a mobile gaming app that lets players select from and play a variety of different games. The app uses a DynamoDB table named GameScores to keep track of high scores and other user data. Each item in the table is uniquely identified by a user ID and the name of the game that the user played. The GameScores table has a primary key consisting of a partition key (UserId) and sort key (GameTitle). Users only have access to game data associated with their user ID. A user who wants to play a game must belong to an IAM role named GameRole, which has a security policy attached to it.

In addition to granting permissions for specific DynamoDB actions (Action element) on the GameScores table (Resource element), the Condition element uses the following condition keys specific to DynamoDB that limit the permissions as follows:

- dynamodb:LeadingKeys: This condition key allows users to access only the items where the partition key/value matches their user ID. This ID, ${www.amazon.com:user_id}, is a substitution variable. For more information about substitution variables, see "Using Web Identity Federation" (docs.aws.amazon.com/amazondynamodb/latest/developerguide/WIF.html).

- `dynamodb:Attributes`: This condition key limits access to the specified attributes so that only the actions listed in the permissions policy can return values for these attributes. In addition, the `StringEqualsIfExists` clause ensures that the app must always provide a list of specific attributes to act upon and that the app can't request all attributes.

When an IAM policy is evaluated, the result is always either true (access is allowed) or false (access is denied). If any part of the Condition element is false, the entire policy evaluates to false and access is denied.

If you use `dynamodb:Attributes`, you must specify the names of all of the primary key and index key attributes for the table and any secondary indexes that are listed in the policy. Otherwise, DynamoDB can't use these key attributes to perform the requested action.

See the following section in DynamoDB documentation to enable fine-grained access control: (`https://docs.aws.amazon.com/amazondynamodb/latest/developerguide/specifying-conditions.html`).

Identity Federation

Web identity federation supports the following identity providers:

- Login with Amazon
- Facebook
- Google

Figure 6.15 illustrates how web identity federation works.

FIGURE 6.15 Web identity federation with Amazon DynamoDB

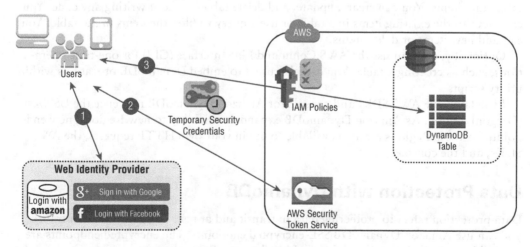

1. The app calls a third-party identity provider to authenticate the user and the app. The identity provider returns a web identity token to the app.

2. The app calls AWS STS and passes the web identity token as input. AWS STS authorizes the app and gives it temporary AWS access credentials. The app is allowed to assume an IAM role and access AWS resources in accordance with the role's security policy.

3. The app calls Amazon DynamoDB to access a table (for example). Because it has assumed a role, the app is subject to the security policy associated with that role. The policy document prevents the app from accessing data that does not belong to the user.

How to Access Amazon DynamoDB

Amazon DynamoDB is a web service that uses HTTP and HTTPS as a transport and JavaScript Object Notation (JSON) as a message serialization format. There are three primary ways to access Amazon DynamoDB:

- Amazon DynamoDB API
- AWS Software Development Kits (SDKs)
- AWS Management Console

Applications access Amazon DynamoDB using the DynamoDB API or using AWS SDKs. Instead of making the requests to the DynamoDB API directly from your application, AWS recommends that you use AWS SDKs. The SDKs contain libraries that can take care of request authentication, serialization, and connection management. To further simplify application development, the SDKs also provide Java and .NET APIs.

Amazon DynamoDB also provides a management console that enables you to work with tables and items. You can create, update, and delete tables without writing any code. You can view all the existing items in a table or use a query to filter the items in the table. You can add new items or delete items.

Optionally, you can use the AWS Command Line Interface (CLI) for one-time operations, such as creating a table. You can also use it to embed DynamoDB operations within utility scripts.

By default, the AWS SDKs and console for Amazon DynamoDB reference the US West (Oregon) Region. As Amazon DynamoDB expands availability to new Regions, new endpoints for these Regions are also available to use in your own HTTP requests, the AWS SDKs, and the console.

Data Protection with DynamoDB

Data protection refers to protecting data in transit and at rest. To protect data in transit, you can use Amazon DynamoDB SSL-encrypted endpoints. The encrypted endpoints are accessible from the Internet and from within Amazon EC2 instances.

Additionally, Amazon DynamoDB requires each request to the service to contain a valid HMAC-SHA256 signature, or the request is rejected. The AWS SDKs automatically sign your requests; however, if you want to write your own requests, you must provide the signature in the header of your request to Amazon DynamoDB. To calculate the signature, you must request temporary security credentials from the AWS Security Token Service. Use the temporary security credentials to sign your requests to Amazon DynamoDB.

For protecting data at rest, encrypt your data before uploading it to Amazon DynamoDB. This client-side encryption can also protect your data while in transit.

You can use SDK libraries to encrypt and sign your Amazon DynamoDB data.

For more information, see `java.awsblog.com/post/TxI32GE4IG2SNS/Client-side-Encryption-for-Amazon-DynamoDB`.

Amazon DynamoDB point-in-time recovery (PITR) provides automatic backups of your DynamoDB table data. Point-in-time recovery helps protect your Amazon DynamoDB tables from accidental write or delete operations. With point-in-time recovery, you don't have to worry about creating, maintaining, or scheduling on-demand backups. Point-in-time operations don't affect performance or API latencies.

Monitoring and Logging with DynamoDB

AWS provides several options to monitor your Amazon DynamoDB databases. Amazon DynamoDB and Amazon CloudWatch are integrated, so you can gather and analyze performance metrics. You can monitor these metrics using the CloudWatch console, the AWS Command Line Interface, or programmatically using the CloudWatch API. CloudWatch also allows you to set alarms when you reach a specified threshold for a metric.

Amazon DynamoDB is integrated with CloudTrail, a service that captures API calls made by or on behalf of DynamoDB in your AWS account and delivers the log files to an Amazon S3 bucket that you specify. CloudTrail captures API calls made from the Amazon DynamoDB console or from the DynamoDB API. Using the information collected by CloudTrail, you can determine what request was made to DynamoDB, the source IP address from which the request was made, who made the request, and when it was made. You can store your log files in your bucket for as long as you want, but you can also define Amazon S3 lifecycle rules to archive or delete log files automatically. By default, your log files are encrypted by using Amazon S3 server-side encryption.

You can have CloudTrail publish Amazon SNS notifications when new log files are delivered if you want to take quick action upon log file delivery. You can also aggregate Amazon DynamoDB log files from multiple AWS Regions and multiple AWS accounts into a single Amazon S3 bucket. You can also use the AWS Management Console to monitor the performance of your tables. Using CloudWatch metrics in the console, you can monitor table throughput and other performance metrics.

Summary

In this chapter, we have looked at the security aspects of different analytics services and how you can access the services, protect the data at rest and in motion, and enable federated access. For most services, I have laid out some best practices. Security is one of the most important topics in the exam and your performance in this area can make or break your results. Even more important, when you run your applications in production, security is a topic that needs to be addressed on day one and hence it is important to get things right.

While we have discussed a number of different services and options, please go through the workshops listed later .

Exam Essentials

Security is the most important component when it comes to the AWS platform, and hence data security accounts for 18 percent of all exam questions. You need to be aware of data protection mechanisms offered by various services covered under the analytics umbrella, setting up identity and access management, configuring logging of activities and monitoring the usage of the service, and ensuring that you are aware of the resiliency mechanisms.

Security is a very critical component of the AWS platform, analytics services, and the AWS Data Analytics Specialty certification exam.

Exercises/Workshops

The following are essential workshops that you need to run on your own to prepare yourself better for the security aspects of the exam as well as your general knowledge of AWS security.

- Securing Serverless Workloads - github.com/aws-samples/aws-serverless-security-workshop/blob/master/README.md

- AWS Identity: Using Amazon Cognito for serverless consumer apps - serverless-idm.awssecworkshops.com

- AWS Security Workshops - awssecworkshops.com

- Adding Security into DevOps - devops.awssecworkshops.com

- Scaling threat detection and response in AWS - scaling-threat-detection.awssecworkshops.com

- Getting Hands on with Amazon GuardDuty - `hands-on-guardduty` `.awssecworkshops.com`
- IAM deep dive - `identity-round-robin.awssecworkshops.com`
- Security Automation - `louay-workshops.com.au/` `security-automation-workshop.html`
- Identity Round Robin - `https://identity-round-robin` `.awssecworkshops.com/`

Review Questions

1. You are a data architect working for a large multinational organization that allows various suppliers to access inventory details available as files in your S3 bucket. The supplier has an AWS account. How can you provide access to the vendor to this bucket?

   A. Create a new IAM group and grant the relevant access to the supplier on that bucket.

   B. Create a cross-account role for the supplier account and grant that role access to the S3 bucket.

   C. Create a new IAM user and grant the relevant access to the supplier on that bucket.

   D. Create an S3 bucket policy that allows the supplier to read from the bucket from their AWS account.

2. You are a data engineer who has been responsible for building a data warehouse using Redshift. You have set up the analysts with Redshift client applications running on an EC2 instance to access Redshift. The analysts have complained about the inability to access the Redshift cluster. Which of the following will you do to ensure proper access to the Redshift cluster?

   A. Use the AWS CLI instead of the Redshift client tools.

   B. Modify the NACL on the subnet.

   C. Modify the VPC security groups.

   D. Attach the proper IAM role to the Redshift cluster for proper access to the EC2 instance.

3. You are working for a mid-sized tractor manufacturing company, which is providing access to the latest sales analytics stored on Redshift to its sales advisors' mobile devices. Applications on those mobile devices will need access to Amazon Redshift where data marts are housed for large-scale analytics. Which of the following is the simplest and most secure way to provide access to your Redshift data store from your mobile application?

   A. Create a user in Redshift and provide the credentials to the mobile application.

   B. Allow a web identity federated user to assume a role that allows access to the Redshift tables and data marts by providing temporary credentials using STS.

   C. Create an IAM user and generate encryption keys for that user. Provide the user access to Redshift and hard-code the user credentials in the mobile application.

   D. Create a Redshift read-only access policy in IAM and use the policy within your mobile application.

4. True or false? Amazon Kinesis Firehose does not offer server-side encryption.

   A. True

   B. False

5. Which of the following can be used to restrict user access to Athena operations, including Athena Workgroups?

    A. Athena Workgroups

    B. Athena Federated Query

    C. AWS Glue Catalog

    D. IAM (Identity and Access Management)

References and Further Reading

"Using AWS Marketplace for ML Workloads" – aws.amazon.com/blogs/awsmarketplace/using-aws-marketplace-for-machine-learning-workloads

"Setting up trust between ADFS and AWS using Active Directory Credentials to connect to Amazon Athena with ODBC driver" – aws.amazon.com/blogs/big-data/setting-up-trust-between-adfs-and-aws-and-using-active-directory-credentials-to-connect-to-amazon-athena-with-odbc-driver

"How to rotate Amazon Redshift Credentials in AWS Secrets Manager" – aws.amazon.com/blogs/security/how-to-rotate-amazon-documentdb-and-amazon-redshift-credentials-in-aws-secrets-manager

"Enabling Serverless security analytics using AWS WAF full logs, Amazon Athena, and Amazon QuickSight" – aws.amazon.com/blogs/security/enabling-serverless-security-analytics-using-aws-waf-full-logs/

"Amazon QuickSight now supports audit logging with AWS CloudTrail" – aws.amazon.com/blogs/security/amazon-quicksight-now-supports-logging-with-aws-cloudtrail

Appendix

Answers to Review Questions

Chapter 1: History of Analytics and Big Data

1. C. A is incorrect as Amazon S3 is great for storing massive amounts of data but is not suitable for real-time data ingestion and visualization.

    B is incorrect as Amazon Redshift is a good tool for large-scale data inserts and scans. However, real-time querying is not a great use case for Amazon Redshift due to potential concurrency limits.

    C is correct as Elasticsearch is the right technology for operational analytics.

    D is incorrect as Amazon DynamoDB is a technology that can provide sub-second latency for your applications, and it is recommended when you have well-known access paths. Typical dashboard applications run a scan of the data, which is not a key-based access, and hence DynamoDB is not a great choice.

2. B. A is incorrect because, while you can load the gzipped data, gzip is not a splittable file, and hence you will not benefit from the system parallelism.

    B is correct as it is a best practice to split the data into multiple files. Please read AWS documentation.

    `https://docs.aws.amazon.com/redshift/latest/dg/t_splitting-data-files
.html`

    Also, because you have multiple slices, it is better to have the number of your files as a multiple of Redshift slice count.

    C is incorrect as dividing into a large number of smaller files would result in slow S3 listing operation and ineffective utilization of the S3 reads. Each block read will read a considerably small amount of data, resulting is unnecessary reads.

    D is a plausible option. However, B is better due to the number of files being a multiple of Redshift slice count. If we did not have B as an option, D would have been correct.

3. C. A is incorrect, as while the solution will help build a dashboard, the sub-second latency requirement would not be met. Amazon S3 and Athena are good for ad hoc reporting. However, when the data is queried frequently, the latency is higher, and furthermore, the cost involved in frequent data scans would make this an invalid architecture.

    B is incorrect as Redshift is great for building data marts and data warehouses, but a sub-second latency is not possible considering you will have to connect using JDBC from QuickSight.

    C is correct as Amazon Elasticsearch is the right approach. Elasticsearch is a great tool for near real-time operations (`aws.amazon.com/elasticsearch-service/
what-is-elasticsearch`). Using Kibana would help you create a dashboard with lower TCO.

    D is incorrect as Hive cannot be used to query the logs in a sub-second latency. Hive is a better tool for batch operations.

4. B. A is incorrect. Migrating 50 TB of data using CLI interface for Amazon S3 on an Internet connection will be time consuming. Since the requirement is to perform this migration quickly, this solution will not work.

B is correct as the data migration with Snowball will be a better option. Once the data is in S3, crawling with Glue to build a catalog and analyzing using Athena would be preferable because the customer wanted to manage as few servers as possible, and both Athena and Glue are serverless.

C is incorrect as the data migration with Snowball will work but using Hive on EMR running Spark to build a catalog is more expensive and requires more resources and additional scripting, which can be avoided if we select option B.

D is incorrect because of the data migration with CLI interface for Amazon S3 (which is expensive) and more complex (cataloging with Glue).

5. C. A is incorrect as the solution will be expensive. Since only 30 TB of data is needed, loading the data into HDFS and paying the associated storage cost on the Hadoop cluster is unnecessary and is less likely to generate any benefits for the customer from a cost perspective.

B is incorrect due to the reasons mentioned in the explanation for option A. While Redshift is a good solution for cloud data warehousing, maintaining all the hot and cold data on Redshift is not a good approach and is an anti-pattern considering the earlier discussion on data lakes. The solution will work but will be more expensive to maintain. While Redshift offers cost advantages and is 10x cheaper than traditional datawarehouse solutions, the customer can get better cost savings from other architectures.

C is correct and a good solution to set up a multi-temperature warehouse. This solution will not only reduce the cost in the short term, it will also be a good architecture for the long term when the data grows. The data growth would mean that the customers could start using more of S3 and use Redshift Spectrum when the join between hot and cold data is required.

D is incorrect. Elasticsearch is not a good tool for building a data warehouse where multiple access paths to access the data need to be created. 30 TB data on ES would be very expensive, and with each index, the requirement for the storage would increase manifold. Amazon Redshift is a better architecture choice for building a data warehouse.

6. D. A is incorrect because CSV is a row format. Using Athena to query CSV would mean reading lots of unnecessary attributes of data, which would result in lower performance and higher data scanning cost.

B is incorrect as loading the data into a VARCHAR column and then querying using JSON extraction functions would be more expensive and the join performance would be very poor.

C is incorrect as attributes' extraction will perform better, but data stored on Redshift is more expensive than on S3. Furthermore, in the long run this solution will not be cost effective.

D is correct, as this uses a serverless option to convert the data into a columnar format like Parquet and allows for a more robust solution that would be future proof even with growing data sizes.

7. C. A is incorrect as the number and types of columns should not be the first thing to look at. While there are certain cases where the column type may impact a query join, that should be looked at after the basics, which includes looking at predicates and sort keys, which limit the amount of data being scanned in a query.

B is incorrect. Redshift primary key constraints are informational only.

C is correct as sort keys act as an index and are responsible for limiting the data scanned from the disk.

D is incorrect. Redshift is an MPP database, and if it's designed properly, the number of rows in a table should not impact the query performance directly.

E is incorrect. The data is in the database, and partitioning is not an option in Redshift.

8. C. A is incorrect. AWS can capture the initial dump but the changes from databases that do not have incremental keys cannot be captured by AWS Glue. See the following web page: aws.amazon.com/blogs/database/how-to-extract-transform-and-load-data-for-analytic-processing-using-aws-glue-part-2/

B is incorrect as AWS DMS can't be used for capturing CSVs.

C is correct as the initial dump can be done with Glue and incremental captures can be done with DMS for databases and AWS Glue for CSV files.

D is incorrect as DMS cannot capture changes or the initial dump from CSV files.

9. A. Amazon QuickSight does not allow you to make changes to the data in the reports.

10. A. Amazon QuickSight allows you to create auto-narratives. See the following web page: https://docs.aws.amazon.com/quicksight/latest/user/narratives-creating.html

Chapter 2: Data Collection

1. D. Option A does not provide any support analyzing data in real time. Option B is incorrect and vague. Option C involves Kinesis Firehose which helps in aggregating the data rather than real-time data analysis. Option D is correct as it involves Kineiss Analytics and KCL.

2. A. Amazon Kinesis is the service that is used to ingest real-time streaming data. Data Pipeline is primarily for batch, Amazon SQS is for message-based communication, and Amazon EMR has multiple engines that are primarily batch in nature. You can use Spark streaming, but that is not explicitly mentioned in the options.

3. B, C, D. Explanation: A is incorrect as AWS Glue built-in classifiers cannot be used for any data type. B, C, D are correct – Refer to: `https://docs.aws.amazon.com/glue/latest/dg/populate-data-catalog.html`.

4. A. IoT Rules Engine gives you the ability to transform the data being received from IoT devices.

5. D. AWS Database Migration Service helps you migrate databases to AWS quickly and securely. The source database remains fully operational during the migration, minimizing downtime to applications that rely on the database. The AWS Database Migration Service can migrate your data to and from most widely used commercial and open-source databases.

   `https://aws.amazon.com/dms`

6. D. AWS Glue is the recommended option as it is serverless in nature and offers a pay-as-you-go model with no fixed costs.

7. A. Explanation: Using the queue length will help you scale the servers based on the demand, and also help to scale it back down when the demand is low. Refer to the following link: `https://amzn.to/3bWbDma`.

8. B. Explanation: AWS Schema conversion tool is the right choice to convert schema from Oracle to Amazon Aurora.

9. A. Explanation: AWS Snowmobile is the recommended option for large petabyte scale data transfer.

10. A,B. Explanation: Since this is large amounts of data, a Data Pipeline will not be a viable option considering you need it to be simple and fast. A data pipeline will require you to build a custom pipeline.

    Similarly, AWS Snowball is also not a fast option as the turn around time can be quite high. However, if you have Direct Connect and the ability to do Import/Export, that will be the fastest way to bring the data to Amazon S3 and copy it to Amazon Redshift.

Chapter 3: Data Storage

1. B. A is incorrect as Amazon DyamoDB is not suitable for storing Audio/Video and PDF files.

   C is incorrect as storing metadata in DynamoDB might be suitable for faster access however it is not an ideal fit for BI applications.

   D is incorrect as HDFS is not an ideal fit for storing metadata.

   B is correct as Redshift is a great tool for analysis.

   Author note: If you got the answer wrong, do not worry as you should be able to get a better handle on this after the Chapter 4.

2. B. A is incorrect as the question expects little to no coding, however Spark streaming will require effort to batch the data into Amazon S3.

C is incorrect as Amazon Kinesis Data Streams is not a good fit to flush the data to Amazon S3.

D is incorrect as Redshift is not a good fit for streaming use cases.

E is incorrect as Amazon EMR itself provides streaming options like Flink and Spark Streaming but both require additional effort.

B is correct as Amazon Kinesis Data Firehose provides native connectivity to Amazon S3.

3. A. The nature of the request states that it is infrequent access and hence option A is the best. All other options are either more expensive or do not fit the requirements due to access and reliability needs of the request.

4. B. DAX is a DynamoDB compatible service.

See link: `https://aws.amazon.com/dynamodb/dax`

5. B. A is incorrect as access has to be based on subscriber Id.

6. B, D. A is incorrect as Amazon DocumentDB is not Cassandra-compatible and is in fact MongoDB-compatible.

C is incorrect as Amazon DocumentDB can scale up to 64 TB.

7. A. Amazon DocumentDB cluster can only be deployed inside a VPC.

8. D. All of the use cases are graph use cases.

Chapter 4: Data Processing and Analysis

1. B. AWS Glue is the simplest way to achieve data transformation using mostly point-and-click interface, and making use of a built-in de-duplication option using FindMatches ML Transform.

2. A. Option A is correct as Map Reduce was the default processing engine one Hadoop until Hadoop 2.0 arrived.

Option B is incorrect as YARN is a resource manager for applications on Hadoop.

Option C is incorrect as Hive is a SQL layer which makes use of processing engines like Map Reduce, Spark, Tez, etc.

Option D is incorrect as ZooKeeper is a distributed configuration and synchronization service which acts as a naming registry for large distributed systems.

3. B. Amazon Athena is an interactive query service that makes it easy to analyze data in Amazon S3 using standard SQL. Athena is serverless, so there is no infrastructure to manage, and you pay only for the queries that you run.

`https://aws.amazon.com/athena`

4. A, B, D. Amazon Athena supports a wide variety of data formats like CSV, TSV, JSON, or Textfiles and also supports open source columnar formats such as Apache ORC and Apache Parquet. Athena also supports compressed data in Snappy, Zlib, LZO, and GZIP formats. By compressing, partitioning, and using columnar formats you can improve performance and reduce your costs.

   https://aws.amazon.com/athena/faqs

5. D. A – incorrect as Glue provides limited options for custom configurations.

   B – incorrect as EMR using Cluster mode is more expensive.

   C – incorrect as EMR using Step-mode is cheaper than cluster mode but more expensive with on-demand instances.

   D – Correct

6. B. The EMR File System (EMRFS) is an implementation of HDFS that all Amazon EMR clusters use for reading and writing regular files from Amazon EMR directly to Amazon S3. EMRFS provides the convenience of storing persistent data in Amazon S3 for use with Hadoop while also providing features like consistent view and data encryption.

   https://docs.aws.amazon.com/emr/latest/ManagementGuide/emr-fs.html

7. D. Elasticsearch provides a fast, personalized search experience for your applications, websites, and data lake catalogs, allowing your users to quickly find relevant data. You get access to all of Elasticsearch's search APIs, supporting natural language search, auto-completion, faceted search, and location-aware search. You can also use it to store, analyze, and correlate application and infrastructure log data to find and fix issues faster and improve application performance.

   https://aws.amazon.com/elasticsearch-service

8. D. You can load streaming data into your Amazon Elasticsearch Service domain from many different sources. Some sources, like Amazon Kinesis Data Firehose and Amazon CloudWatch Logs, have built-in support for Amazon ES. Others, like Amazon S3, Amazon Kinesis Data Streams, and Amazon DynamoDB, use AWS Lambda functions as event handlers. The Lambda functions respond to new data by processing it and streaming it to your domain.

   https://docs.aws.amazon.com/elasticsearch-service/latest/developerguide/es-aws-integrations.html

9. C. Please refer to the following documentation.

   https://aws.amazon.com/redshift

10. A, D, F. Please read the section, "Redshift Architecture," Chapter 4, "Data Processing and Analysis."

    https://docs.aws.amazon.com/redshift/latest/mgmt/overview.html

Chapter 5: Data Visualization

1. D. Amazon QuickSight is the native tool provided by AWS. All others are partner products that can work with AWS tools but are not available directly as native AWS services.

2. D. A correlation is basically visualizing two to three measures against each other. Combo charts are good for trends and categories, whereas donut charts compare values for items in a dimension, such as percentages to a total amount. Heat maps show a measure for the intersection of two dimensions. A scatter plot, however, is a visualization technique that is often used to understand correlation between different variables, such as salary of an employee vs. the employee's grade. Both of these are measures that, when plotted against one another, indicate their relevance to each other.

3. B. Please see the following documentation page: docs.aws.amazon.com/quicksight/latest/user/aws-directory-service.html.

4. D. The question is looking for the simplest way to provide integration with S3, Redshift, and Athena. While D3.js, MicroStrategy, and Kibana can be used to visualize data from multiple sources, only Amazon QuickSight provides native integration to S3, Redshift, and Athena with forecasting capabilities.

5. C. Amazon QuickSight, EMR Notebooks, and Tableau can be used for reporting, and Tableau and QuickSight specifically can be used for building dashboards. However, real-time reporting at ultra-low latency with data from Elasticsearch is best provided using Kibana as part of the ELK stack.

Chapter 6: Data Security

1. D. Sharing resources with other accounts is done using cross-account access. Option A is incorrect as the supplier already has an account in place. The answer is vague as it does not specify where to create an IAM group and is missing the details. Option B is incorrect as there is no such thing as a cross-account role. Option C is incorrect. Please see details captured here: https://aws.amazon.com/premiumsupport/knowledge-center/cross-account-access-s3

2. C. By default, Amazon Redshift is locked down for access. In order for you to provide access to the cluster, you need to configure the security groups for the cluster with proper access paths.

3. B. Whenever you come across such a question, it is important to understand that an IAM role is generally the preferred way vs. creating an IAM user. Furthermore, using STS (AWS Security Token Service), which offers web identity federation, can help your federation application from identity providers like Facebook, Amazon, and Google. This not only allows fine-grained access control but also provides a much tighter control.

4. B. See the following link for more information: aws.amazon.com/about-aws/whats-new/ 2019/11/amazon-kinesis-data-firehose-adds-support-for-customer- provided-keys-for-server-side-encryption.

5. D. See the following link for more information: docs.aws.amazon.com/athena/ latest/ug/security-iam-athena.html.

Index

Online Test Bank

Register to gain one year of FREE access to the online interactive test bank to help you study for your AWS Certified Data Analytics certification exam—included with your purchase of this book! All of the chapter review questions and the practice tests in this book are included in the online test bank so you can practice in a timed and graded setting.

Register and Access the Online Test Bank

To register your book and get access to the online test bank, follow these steps:

1. Go to bit.ly/SybexTest (this address is case sensitive)!
2. Select your book from the list.
3. Complete the required registration information, including answering the security verification to prove book ownership. You will be emailed a pin code.
4. Follow the directions in the email or go to www.wiley.com/go/sybextestprep.
5. Find your book on that page and click the "Register or Login" link with it. Then enter the pin code you received and click the "Activate PIN" button.
6. On the Create an Account or Login page, enter your username and password, and click Login or, if you don't have an account already, create a new account.
7. At this point, you should be in the test bank site with your new test bank listed at the top of the page. If you do not see it there, please refresh the page or log out and log back in.